EVELYN BARING:
THE LAST PROCONSUL

EVELYN BARING

THE LAST PROCONSUL

Charles Douglas-Home

COLLINS
St James's Place, London
1978

William Collins Sons & Co Ltd
London · Glasgow · Sydney · Auckland
Toronto · Johannesburg

FOR DAVID
grandson, godson

First published 1978
© Charles Douglas-Home 1978
ISBN 0 00 216457 4
Set in Linotype Baskerville
Typeset and Printed in N. Ireland by
W & G Baird Ltd, bound by
W & J Mackay, Chatham, England

Contents

Maps

Illustrations

Acknowledgments

I would like to acknowledge with gratitude the help I have received from Mr J. R. Ede (Keeper) and the staff of the Public Record Office; Miss Joan Lancaster and staff of the India Office Library; Mr Cheeseman, Chief Archivist of the Foreign and Commonwealth Office, and his staff; Mr E. Burke, National Archives of Rhodesia; Mr Matsibula, Keeper, National Archives of Swaziland; Mr T. R. Sareen, Archivist for the National Archives of India; the staff of the Colonial Records Project, Rhodes House, Oxford; Mr J. Lonsdale and staff of the Intelligence Department at *The Times*; and the Editor's permission to quote from *The Times* Archives.

At the back of the book I have listed many of the hundreds of correspondents who wrote or talked to me about some aspect of Evelyn Baring's life, but I would like to single out a few who clearly set aside much of their time to help me: Emma, Lady Northampton; Mrs Iris Portal; Mr D. Y. Fell, Secretary of the ICSA; Mr J. Johnston, late ICS; Lt Colonel W. B. R. Neave-Hill, Army Historical Branch; Sir John Whyatt; Sir Arthur Young; Mrs Joan Woods; Mr John Gwynne who read the manuscript and contributed much sound advice.

My travels through Africa in the steps of Baring were made easier and my researches more fruitful by Miss Eleanor Emery, CMG; Mr Dick Wilson of the Commonwealth Development Corporation; Mr C. Harland, Manager, Usutu Pulp Mill, and Mr Hubbard; Sir Humphrey and Lady Gibbs; Mr and Mrs Evan Campbell; Mr Michael Knipe; Mr Charles Njonjo; Sir Ernest Vasey; Sir Michael Blundell; the Manager and staff of the Nairobi Serena Hotel.

My thanks are due to Lady Mary Howick for her constant help and encouragement and for complete access to the Baring Papers and her own private correspondence.

Finally I owe an enormous debt of gratitude to two secretaries – Cynthia Tutt. without whom I could not have started the book and Ann Niven, who typed the entire manuscript twice, and without whose indomitable efficiency and industry I could never have finished.

7

Introduction

'To my father, there is no monument, no statue, no tribute to his work in Egypt, but I do not think he would have minded this. I do not think he would have given it a thought. I think that in his mind the monument was part of the change that had taken place in the country itself, and perhaps in the minds of the Egyptians themselves, and perhaps still more the memory he left in the minds of the greatest number of them – the Fellahin – the people of the Egyptian soil.'
Evelyn Baring, in a broadcast on his father, BBC 1952.

In the British Empire there were two Evelyn Barings – father and son. The father's life spanned the high period of British imperialism and reached its peak, with the peak of the empire, during the last quarter of the 19th century. It was the last quarter century of that empire itself – fifty years later – which coincided with the son's greatest contribution to it. It is always dangerous to try to draw comparisons between generations. It can be unfair personally, and unsound historically. But in the case of Evelyn Baring, the younger, whose biography this is, there was throughout his life, and in particular throughout his proconsular periods, such a consciousness of his father's own career – not so much a desire to imitate it as an aspiration to those high standards which he believed his father had set on the imperial stage – that no study of his life would be complete without a portrait of the life of Evelyn Baring, the elder.

In fact the two Evelyns did not see much of each other. Evelyn Baring, Lord Cromer, was in his early sixties when young Evelyn was born in 1903, and he died thirteen years later. So one must assume that a great deal of Evelyn's reverence for and knowledge of his father's career came from reading his books and his writings, and particularly from his mother, Katie Thynne, Lord Cromer's second wife, whose only child Evelyn was.

From a very early age, certainly by the time he left Winchester and went to Oxford, young Evelyn was steeped in his father's career. Years later, when he had himself become a colonial governor, there was a picture of Lord Cromer hanging on the walls of the son's office, and the younger Evelyn would often stop his Ministers in front of it and enquire of them what they thought *he* would have done in the circumstances under discussion.

If one wants to look for similarities, they certainly exist both in the public, proconsular lives and in their private personalities, where the strong, rather simple characteristics (not in any way to be confused with either naivety or stupidity) of the elder Evelyn seemed to show up much more clearly in younger Evelyn than in the two sons by Cromer's first marriage.

Take the public similarities first. They both spent most of their lives overseas on imperial service; both as young men had an Indian interlude which may have had a lasting influence; both were knighted and then ennobled for their services; both had periods of stress when their essential humanity and sympathy for the peasant had to be tempered by military necessities; both were troubled by local military commanders and the chain of command from Whitehall – Gordon in Khartoum, Erskine in Kenya; both were natural financiers, an ability derived perhaps from their close kinship with the banking family.

Now for the personal similarities. They were both the sons of elderly fathers – and by a second marriage; their mothers surviving their husbands for many years, determined women with above average musical and literary enthusiasms, probably responsible for inculcating in their sons what Joseph Chamberlain described in the elder as 'the cross-bench mind'; there was a mutual love of nonsense (Cromer was a great friend of Lear); a strong, simple, but unshakeable christianity; a convinced monogamy but an amused compassion for the marital shortcomings of others.

Old Evelyn was born near Cromer in Norfolk in February 1841, the sixth son of a family of seven children by Henry Baring's second wife. (He had six by his first wife.) Henry Baring died in 1848, when Evelyn was only seven years old, but his wife survived him until 1874. Though she was a musical and literary lady, whose commonplace book was as full of Latin, Greek, French and German extracts as it was of English ones, her son had to wait until after he had left school before he was able to develop a taste for liberal subjects. His formal education appears to have been militarily orientated, since he left prepatory school early to go to the Ordnance School at Carshalton, en route for the Woolwich Academy for the Royal Artillery. An early setback was soon overcome by Mrs Baring who, showing the same sort of drive which was to animate her daughter-in-law, reacted to the news that her son had been turned down for Woolwich on account of bad eyesight by driving round personally to the Horse Guards to see Lord Raglan, then Master General of the Ordnance. Evelyn was soon reinstated.

Baring actually stayed in the army until he was thirty eight and had reached the rank of major, but his military career was not nearly as pedestrian as that sounds. He was almost permanently on secondment, either as an ADC, or at the staff college, where he passed out top in 1867, or in the statistical branch of the War Office, or as private secretary to his cousin, Lord Northbrook, then Viceroy of India. It was his first years in India which, according to his biographer, Lord Zetland, 'planted in his heart the seeds of sympathy with the toiling masses of a subject people,' – a sympathy which influenced him so much in Egypt later on. He also learnt something from his vice-regal kinsman, 'One may do a great deal of good in this world if one does not care who gets the credit.'

He was still only a captain when he was invited to be a member of the Commission on Public Debt in Egypt in 1877. There, with the exception of one more interlude in India, he was destined to continue serving in various guises for the next thirty years and to earn the title of 'Maker of Modern Egypt' when he left.

In spite of Baring's relative youth when he reached Egypt he tackled the problems of the Khedive's debt for two years before resigning and returning to Britain intent on seeking a Liberal seat in Parliament. His resignation was based on a belief that the problems were insoluble so long as Britain refused to participate more actively in the domestic and financial affairs of Egypt. His own role had originally been that of representative of the bond holders, but this came increasingly to conflict with his personal view that it was the Egyptian peasant – rather than foreign bond holders – whose interests in the economy had to be protected.

Baring returned for a second spell in India in 1881, as finance member of the Governor General's council. He achieved a successful turn round in the Indian national debt. But in 1883, with further trouble on the Nile, he returned, knighted, to Egypt as Controller General to a country occupied by British troops and with the Khedive deposed by a Tory government under Disraeli, with Lord Salisbury as Foreign Secretary. Baring accepted the reactivated post in spite of his political differences with the Tories. He was once asked if he supported Disraeli, 'No I am not a Tory – very much the reverse. I am a Whig with the same profound mistrust of the present Prime Minister with which you are inspired,' he told his questioner. Indeed at his only brief meeting with Disraeli, according to Lord Zetland, 'The PM made but a solitary reference to the affairs of Egypt and then only to enquire if there were many pelicans on the banks of the Nile!' He stayed in Egypt for 24 years, leaving in May, 1907, a very sick man but with a colossal achievement behind him. It must have been strange returning to the England of Asquith and Lloyd-George, so different from the country of Palmerston which he had left as a young officer years before.

He returned one of the empire's most famous and successful servants, chastened and moulded by the experience of empire, its problems, and fundamentally, its lack of solutions.

'The problem,' he told the House of Lords in 1909, 'really is how European civilisation is to be introduced into eastern countries without undermining the foundations on which the whole fabric of society rests.' And he wrote at about the same time, as though aware of the basic flaw to imperialism-by-consent, 'It is one of the inevitable incidents of the execution of an imperial policy that as a political force the gratitude shown to the foreigner who relieves oppression is of a very ephemeral character. We have learnt this lesson both in India and Egypt.'[1]

With or without gratitude, however, Baring clearly found his own gratification in fighting vigorously for the interests of the Egyptian economy against the customary predations of the Exchequer. His basic conception of his Egyptian policy was the need to relieve the population of taxation. This could only be achieved by increased agricultural production, and that could only be achieved by better irrigation.

As the years went by he came to dominate Egypt from his lovely palace on the banks of the Nile. Lytton Strachey was clearly offended by the man, 'All in monochrome, touched in the cold blues and indecisive greys – eminently unromantic.'[2] It is not a widely corroborated portrait. Zetland described him thus: 'Tall beyond the average, broad shouldered, burly from tip to toe, clear eyed, fresh complexioned, with features carved seemingly with a broad-edged chisel out of matter of granitic strength, he moved solidly and imperturbably about his world.'

He had a reputation for brusqueness – even rudeness. He was often known as 'over-Baring', (and to many others he was just 'The Lord') but behind this manner according to Zetland there lurked a genuine geniality, and particularly with Egyptians, 'whose oriental modes of approaching a subject he thoroughly understood. He would show infinite patience, suffering with complete outward composure the inroads upon his sorely needed time by the redundancies and irrelevancies, the pauses and hesitations, the wide circumnavigation of the real subject eventually to be broached, unavoidable if anything of value was to be obtained from an interview with anyone of eastern birth or upbringing.'

His personality uncannily foreshadows some things said about young Evelyn occupying his own white palace in Nairobi. Cromer played tennis in crises to show his unconcern. His Excellency had a boyish sense of humour, much remarked upon, and a sense of the ridiculous. He was, wrote Zetland, 'Neither staid nor prudish, but particularly impervious to feminine blandishments. His self respect depended on a rigid adherence to the institution of monogamy.'

Outside the family circle the same proconsular difficulties seemed to afflict father and son. Evelyn the older suffered the Sudan emergencies, both when he arrived with Gordon at Khartoum, and again during the Omdurman campaign in 1896. He said later he found himself 'in the somewhat singular position of a civilian . . . whose proper functions were diplomacy and administration but, who, under the stress of circumstances in the land of Paradox, had to be ultimately responsible for the maintenance, and even to some extent, for the movements of an army of some 25,000 men in the field . . .'[3]

His earlier quarrels over the chain of command with Gordon ('He must take instructions from the British representative in Egypt') convinced him he should stand no nonsense from the War Office when Kitchener was sent out, and he insisted that the latter be under his control and not that of the War Office. Eventually, after the Omdurman campaign, he visited the Sudan himself and arranged the condominium.

Meanwhile tragedy had struck him at home when his wife Ethel died in 1898. He had first met her in 1862, while serving as an ADC in the Mediterranean, but it was decided that he was too poor to marry her for another 15 years. She was a Roman Catholic but their children were brought up as Protestants – two sons, Rowland and Windham. Her death must have been a great blow and it in no way detracts from the success of his first marriage that, within four years, he had met and married Lady Katherine Thynne, daughter of the Marquess of Bath, his beloved Katie, the mother of Evelyn, the object of so many adoring but bantering poems and letters from husband and son.

Katie and her two childless sisters, Alice and Beatrice – indeed the whole Thynne menagerie including the family home at Longleat in Wiltshire – attracted old Evelyn's amusement rather than his awe. His private book of poems bears witness to the affectionate fun he poked at his relations' good but scattered brains.

When he returned from Egypt – an ill man and feeling his age – Parliament voted him an almost unprecedented gift of £50,000 in recognition of his distinguished service. For a year or two he led a quiet life, working on his two-volume work on Modern Egypt and refusing a host of offers to take a chair at universities or the leadership of some learned society or other. Finally he began filtering back into public life through the House of Lords, though he was not a natural public speaker. He could be found supporting the free-traders, and vivisection, or opposing women's suffrage, or explaining the background to German policy based on his wide experience of diplomacy over the years. He delved more deeply into his beloved classics, and became something of an essayist. He reviewed books for *The Spectator*. As the *Dictionary of National Biography* puts it, 'The public, which had long labelled him man of action, was a little disconcerted by this fresh foliage budding on the eve of winter; and malice sneered that the new laurels were torn from his old crown. But unheeding he went on his masterful way, fulfilling green old age.'

His final public duty was to chair the commission set up to enquire into the Dardanelles campaign, but he died before it finished its work. In December, 1916, failing, he took to calling its meetings at his home when he was not allowed to go out. There was a short rally in January, when he insisted on seeing the drafts of the final report, but he died finally on January 29th, a month short of his 76th birthday.

In *The Times*, his obituary stated that 'To the oriental, he appeared to walk like a leopard among dogs. It is known', it continued, 'that he greatly valued readiness to accept responsibility and disliked a frequent reference to headquarters. For himself as for others the whole bent of his mind turned to efficiency of the most practical kind. He hated every sort of shadowy concealment of fact or refusal to face things as they were. . . . To the Government which employed him and to which he gave a loyal obedience, he was always a considerable asset, but also at times a disagreeable fact which could not be circumvented.' This was the father's life. Much of it was to be relived by his son.

CHAPTER I
Childhood

Evelyn Baring was born on September 29, 1903, in his grand-mother's house at Manchester Square in London. His father was then 62 and his mother, Katie, was having her first child at the age of 40. Lord Cromer was to spend a further four years in Egypt, and Evelyn, the baby, was bottle fed and taken out to Cairo quite soon after he was born. There he was 'short coated' – relieved of the long drapes which in those days seemed to en-compass most babies. Lord Cromer's muse was soon aroused:

> My Katie think upon the strife,
> Which baby must endure in life!
> With foes he'll have to grapple.
> As Evelyn's not a little Eve
> He never never will deceive
> Some Adam with an apple.
> But still some civil incarnation
> Of Satan will present temptation
> In one form or another
> Then to avoid the tempter's snare
> I offer up this humble prayer
> May he be like his mother.

Young Evelyn did not stay long in Cairo. He returned to England in June, 1904, with his nanny. Katie followed sometime later. Nurse Alice Tree, the nanny, wrote bleak but proper letters to the anxious parents, reporting progress. From a holiday in Nor-folk 'Baby is very well but will not say Papa. He crawls every-where. I remain my lady . . .' etcetera etcetera. Lord Cromer, ailing slightly by then but destined to serve out another three years, composed once again on 'Baby's Departure':

> With Baby we were wont to play
> But here alas he could not stay
> And now that he has gone away
> > We miss him.
>
> He went, and left us in the blues

We lived upon the weekly news,
Meanwhile exchanged parental views,
                    Vicissim.

And now my Katie too is flown
She has the baby all alone
For lengthened absence she'll atone
                    She'll kiss him.

When Katie returned to England she found it hard to keep
a nanny. This was probably because she could not resist interfering but it became rationalised in her desire to make it clear to
Evelyn that he could not expect to be waited on. It was rare for a
mother of her age and standing to look after a child herself but
the burden was hardly crippling. By the time the family moved
into their Wimpole Street house it was shared by the other
servants in the house – of whom there were about six.

However, Katie continued to be obsessed with the fear that he
might come to expect the good things in life. She always kept him
short of money, and though she adored him, seemed to believe
that bad food was positively good for him, so much so that the
family had to remonstrate with her for the lack of care she was
showing. Notwithstanding these privations Evelyn responded with
affection, 'You have the beautifullest face and the ugliest body in
the world' he said to her early on

Young Evelyn was soon introduced to the world at large. Katie
bought him enormous maps, like carpets, so that he crawled from
one continent to another. She also taught him to learn poetry, not
just his father's couplets. He was writing poetry himself quite
young. Lord Cromer had something to say about 'Baby's Education':

Father wants to teach him Greek,
Loving mother thinks that he
Though as yet he cannot speak
Is an infant prodigy.

'Won't he be creation's wonder?'
Asks a fondly doting aunt
Baby with a voice of thunder
Tears her hair and shouts 'I shan't'.

When his conduct I excuse
'Oh' she says 'it might be wuss
'Let him do as he may chose
'For its only Baring fuss'.

It is well he should resemble
Those who are his kith and kin
Will he at the thought I tremble
Be a tidy punctual Thynne?

Until Lord Cromer returned finally from Egypt, Katie divided her time mainly between her mother's house in London, and her sister Alice's. Alice was married to Sir Hugh Shaw Stewart who lived on a beautiful estate called Ardgowan perched on a high promontory at the mouth of the Clyde – a large Georgian house built of that strange grey rust-coloured stone peculiar to Glasgow. So Evelyn's early childhood oscillated between the house of his grandmother and the house of his aunt. Later on, Ardgowan, where he went for every holiday, was probably the house he most regarded as home. But more important than these houses was the imposing nature of the ladies in them; and in the baby's life. They were strong, if rather eccentric women. Apart from the distant, even rather Olympian influence of Lord Cromer, the baby Evelyn's life was dominated by the Thynne sisters, all of whom came to regard little Evelyn as their own.

Katie had married late. Apart from her sisters, the two people closest to her before she met and married Lord Cromer (and perhaps the only other men in her life) were her father and her brother, Alexander, who used to write her long, intimate, almost flirtatious letters from South Africa. She was Lord Bath's favourite of the three daughters. He used to take her alone to Venice for Christmas, leaving his wife, old Lady Bath, behind. Yet Lady Bath was clearly something of a character, in spite of Lord Curzon's alleged remark that she was so stupid she had in a generation ruined one of the cleverest families in England. To judge by her daughters this was clearly not true, though not much could probably have been said for Lord Bath's intellect. Somebody who stayed at Longleat during his time recalled how there was an argument about Shakespeare over dinner and the only copy of his works to be found in the house was a first folio.

Life at Longleat at the turn of the century was an eccentric mixture of grandeur and austerity, though somewhat modernised from the day in 1848 when Evelyn's great-grandmother, Harriet Baring (daughter of Lord Ashburton and therefore great-grandmother twice over) arrived as the bride of Lord Bath to find that her stately home had 43 lavatories but only one stable bucket in which to wash. Even in the 1900s there was no electricity and Lord Bath gave his guests candles at the foot of the stairs. The children lived right at the top.

Lady Bath brought her daughters up very strictly, and Katie imposed on Evelyn a great deal of the eccentric discipline she had imbibed from her mother. The Thynne girls were not allowed to look at themselves in mirrors. Indeed there were no mirrors at Longleat available, since they were all turned back to front except Lady Bath's own which was so festooned in muslin that all she could do in it was to check whether or not her hat had been pinned on straight. Consequently the daughters, though exceptionally striking to look at, perhaps almost beautiful in their bone-structure, were also exceptionally scruffy. Katie used to buy her hats from the bargain basement in Selfridges, and later on she would wear young Evelyn's black lace-up shoes when he grew out of them. Once she arrived to stay at Longleat looking enormous, apparently wearing dozens of petticoats. 'Why so large?' asked her mother. 'I have all my clothes on for the visit to save on the luggage,' she replied.

When Lord Bath died, his widow moved to Beaconsfield, where she tried, with the help of her daughters, to make a garden. But they quarreled so violently about their different ideas that they would rip out each others plants. When Lady Bath died, they found between £5,000 and £10,000 in cash – a massive sum in those days – tucked away in the drawers of her desk. She had always been so lazy that, rather than work out the monthy wages' bill, she cashed a cheque for £50 and tucked away the change. Strangely, Katie and her sisters had an almost obsessive thrift – even parsimony. When sister Alice was married to Sir Hugh Shaw Stewart, she was given a £10,000 dowry by her father. Though she died an extremely rich woman – leaving all her money to Evelyn – she never travelled first class, and used to keep the most meticulous and troubled household accounts until her dying day. She gave all her money to be managed by Evelyn's half-brother, Windham, who turned it into £250,000 before she died.

Katie would presumably have received the same dowry. The younger Thynnes used to look on Uncle Cromer with awe when he visited Longleat. Everybody, even 'my Katie', called him Cromer. He did not crack many jokes, and those he did crack seemed to be mainly in Greek. In fact he clearly had great fun at the expense of his wife and her intelligent, but eccentric sisters. Both he and Katie, indeed all of the sisters, were intolerant and consequently unnerving company for the slow, shy, or thought-to-be-stupid younger generation.

Evelyn's upbringing was basically decided by Katie, and the Thynnes. Even before Lord Cromer died in 1917, totally after that, Evelyn grew up as a Thynne and not a Baring. Lord Cromer early on took an interest in his third son, but he did not interfere. It was customary then to think that the pre-school period was a mother's business. The Baring element was definitely in the descendant all during Evelyn's youth. In fact Evelyn never really discarded an amused, detached, sometimes rather rumbustuous approach to the Baring family which he probably cultivated in reaction to the vehemence of his mother's antipathy for his father's family.

Although Windham, Katie's younger step-son, became a close friend until he died, Lady Cromer never concealed her dislike of his brother Rowland Baring, who succeeded his father as second Lord Cromer, and later became Lord Chamberlain. He was clearly a pompous and rather insensitive man, and there seem to have been bitter squabbles after the old man died when Katie had to move out of their Wimpole Street home.

Katie's upbringing of Evelyn tended to be as eccentric as she herself was, but it blossomed into a most remarkable friendship between mother and son. It sounds as though she tried to be extremely strict, though from an early age Evelyn clearly had licence to abuse his mother affectionately, and indeed treat her with the same kind of loving condescension as Lord Cromer did. Katie and administration did not seem to mix. She is said to have run the Cairo Government House inefficiently, if not chaotically, her reputation being built on the fact that she used to fall asleep during dinner, like her mother before her and her son after her, and refused to talk to many of the Cairenes whom she said were all fools except Sir Edward Grigg.

Katie was much against ostentation. Evelyn was not allowed to mix with people above his financial station (though one could hardly say that his uncle Hugh Shaw Stewart was poor). He was brought up fairly rough, and Katie's readiness to punish him eventually induced the Thynne sisters to exercise a restraining hand on her, at least until she had ascertained the facts. Evelyn got hardened to this, and developed his galumphing, ponderous, if rather solemn approach to grown-ups as a result.

One of Katie's great disappointments was that he was virtually tone deaf as a child, in contrast to her own musicianship. It was routine for her at Ardgowan to play through Bach preludes before breakfast. His tone deafness was not passed on to the next generation and perhaps developed in response to the fiendish way his mother taught him music. The scene in Wimpole Street was recalled by his cousin, Emma Thynne, who was ten years older. From the piano room would come the sound of Katie hammering away on one note, followed by the howling of a wolf – poor Evelyn struggling to get his pitch – followed only too swiftly by the sound of slap, slap, slap. Katie used to say it was the sorrow of her life that Evelyn was no good at music.

In spite of Katie's carelessness with his upbringing she went through the ritual phase of thinking Evelyn was a consumptive, or that he 'had glands' (every child had glands in those days). This meant no winters in London. Lord Cromer was left in the dark book-lined study in Wimpole Street while Katie and Evelyn went off to a little house in Broadstairs called *Ourangi*. It was here that Evelyn's eventual disgust for her milk puddings got the better of his filial respect and he attacked his mother with a plank of wood, eliciting a promise to do better! He used to wear a high collar under his jersey to protect his glands, but since the collar was apparently never, or very seldom, washed it probably involved more dangers than the one which Katie feared. Anyway, glands and consumption were soon forgotten when Evelyn went to school in 1909, to Miss Fanny Frank's kindergarten in York Place. We know little about this academy other than that, in the first term – summer 1909 – Evelyn attended the school 12 times out of 58 (more illnesses?), was never late and brought home a report which said, 'Self Control: very good.'

Whatever he learnt at the kindergarten, it is a fair assumption, with parents like his, that most of his early education would have taken place under their tutelage at home. In 1912 he wrote a poem which they decided was good enough to be kept, and Lord Cromer had it typed out by a secretary. 'The Storm':

> We are tossing away on the billows, lads,
> We are tossing away on the billows;
> The lightning flashes, and the thunder roars,

And we are tossing away on the billows.

A thousand miles from land, lads,
A thousand miles from land;
The waves curl fiercely round the deck, lads,
And fiercely round the deck.
Our sails are tattered and torn, lads,
Our sails are tattered and torn
As we sweep through the storm.

Now hoist the Union Jack, lads,
Now hoist the Union Jack,
For the Frenchman's lying on ahead, lads,
For the Frenchman's lying on ahead.

Now load the guns, lads, quickly,
Now load the guns full quick!
The waves roar and the cannon roars.
Now we've caught her in the broadside, lads,
Now we've caught her in the broad side.

They flee, lads, they flee!
Pursue, lads, pursue!
Onward, lads, onward!
We've caught her in the stern, lads,
We've caught her in the stern.

The waves roar, the lightning flashes,
And she's gone down below, lads,
And she's gone down below.

It was also this year that he finally went away to a boarding preparatory school, and from then on his life can be charted by the
letters he wrote to Katie, many of which she kept until she died
in 1934. Inevitably, this makes for a distorted picture, because
one knows so much more about Evelyn's life when he was not
with Katie – during school and university terms, or later when
he was in India – than when he was with her in the holidays.
But one can tell from the tone of the letters, and the great
regularity with which he wrote them, how deeply affectionate he
was.

His prep school was *The Wick* in Sussex. Fellow pupils were
R. A. Butler and Lord David Cecil. Evelyn was called Clydesdale,
or Bill, because he was such a large bull of a boy. But, whatever

Lord Cromer mused in his poems, it was not all Greek that the boy was learning. Certainly by 1914 his parents had taught him so much about trees that one day, when he was due to attend hospital as an out-patient, he had to wait some time and used it by walking round Kensington Gardens taking notes of all the trees there, their Latin names and countries of origin.

One can imagine the two elderly parents waiting anxiously for word of the boy wonder, now torn so cruelly from them. May, 1913, 'Dear Mother, I am very happy at school though I miss you.' He had made two friends he said and asked for a number of items, 'but please send them altogether otherwise I will be accused of having too many parcels.' He was soon getting into his stride. Two weeks later a letter starts, 'Fat ould woman is yer swanky titled ladyship dotty I mean I am in the lowest form but with prospects of getting up at ½ term.' Katie had reassuring letters from the headmaster, the tone of which, though respectful, suggests that Lady Cromer was perhaps being tiresomely over-solicitous. Certainly Evelyn was of that opinion by early the next year. In dissuading his mother from a visit which he clearly thought was importunate, he wrote, 'You really ought not to come down. Your coming down in such a short term would seem ridiculous, if you don't mind.'

Things were not always easy for the young child of old and ambitious parents. 'Dear Darling Mother, (May, 1914) I am very sorry but again I was bottom but I promise you that I am trying. I was very glad to hear that father was better. *I do hope he will live.*' (underlined twice). Cromer did live, and was rewarded with the next news about his son! 'June 1914 Dear Mother, I am very sorry but I got one with the stick for not doing swat for Andy and also another thing.' Soon the small world of sticks and preps was overshadowed. 'Dear Mother, there is a rumour that Austria has declared war isn't it dreadful yours very loving Evelyn.' The great world had come in on the very loving Evelyn. It never left him.

Thereafter, throughout the war until the old man died, Evelyn's letters to his father were involved with the strategies of Britain, Germany or Russia, the types of ship, aircraft, zeppelin, the Belgians at Antwerp, the fate of little Willie, the calibre of guns, and so on. ('Dear Father glorious news yesterday evening. How long do you think we will be able to keep it up. I see the front we have advanced on is about 16 miles.') Endless questions. Were they ever answered by the great man? Did he write back in kind, and were the statemen's dissertations then read with awe by Evelyn and his fellow prep school boys?

It was not all grand strategy. 'May 31, 1915. Smack! Smack! Smack! he had a hefty mark of valour all blue and black and purple on its little bum. And why has this awful thing happened, well three naughty people called Collins, Gibbs and me talked when they should not.' Nor all horseplay – Feb 1916, 'when solids expand with heat or conduct heat it is called conduction when liquids do it is called convection the great difference is that in conduction the particles merely pass the heat on to each other without moving while in convection the particles do move.' What did Lady Cromer make of that?

Holidays were spent at Ardgowan, often without his parents but under the loving eye of Lady Alice. 'Ardgowan. Dear Father, tell the old'un that I am extremely shocked and pained at not having had a letter from her. Therefore I have no intention of writing to her and that she will cop it'ot when I come down.'

At Ardgowan Lady Alice enlisted a holiday tutor to keep Evelyn up to the mark. A Miss Morison was sent through the good offices of Mr James Beattie, headmaster of Greenock Higher Grade School. She reported, 'He is undoubtedly a remarkably clear boy with not an ounce of slackness in him. . . . It was important to get him to understand the meaning of certain operations he was doing mechanically. . . . Your nephew could complete the square of a quadratic equation without understanding why he had added the square of half the coefficient of X. He just knew it would come right if he did so. But the trouble arises later. Will you pardon me if I have said more than I ought?'

In March, 1916, aged twelve and a half, as part of a school exercise, Evelyn had to write a dialogue between a Britain and a German.

His headmaster, Mr Thring, was so excited about it that he sent it to Lord Cromer and suggested publication. Lord Cromer sent it on to J. St Loe Strachey, Editor of *The Spectator,* to see what he thought of it. Strachey was also impressed. He wrote back:

April 10, 1916. Private and Confidential. My dear Lord Cromer, Evelyn's school examination paper is really quite amazing. My boy and girl were supposed to be a bit precocious, but they never did anything like that at twelve and a half. It really makes one gasp.

In the end Lord Cromer decided against publication, but they were all delighted with Evelyn's performance.

23

It was probably one of Lord Cromer's last great pleasures. Not long after that the old man became ill, and died early the following year, when Evelyn was thirteen and a quarter. For most of the last period of his father's life Evelyn would have been at *The Wick*. The Christmas holidays intervened between Cromer's last bad collapse and his death on January 29, but Evelyn was probably packed off to Ardgowan for the holidays. Certainly when Cromer died, it was Aunt Alice who came down to fetch him. Katie, one imagines, stayed by her husband in London, but whether she was too distracted to keep Evelyn's letters during those last weeks, or he did not write, or he was kept more or less in the dark about it, we cannot tell. A little of the bleak, rather stoical affection one would expect to find in a 13 year old school boy for his old father filters through from those letters which have survived.

'Dear Mother, I am most dreadfully sorry to hear your letter, do you really think father will die? I do so much hope he will not, what does Dr Hale White say. I suppose the only thing to do is to pray that he may recover. When did he begin to get so bad Yours very loving Evelyn.' January 30, 1917. 'Dear Mother, I was so sorry to hear of father's death. I got your telegram in the break today. I am glad he passed peaceably. I saw in the paper it was from a stroke about 10 o'clock. Miss Thring told me Aunt was coming down for me sometime tomorrow and that she was expecting her anytime. Yours' very loving Evelyn.'

His father's death probably affected him more deeply than that. His school report for that term referred to him as being somewhat slow, and went on, 'Rather disappointing of late, as on several occasions he has not taken the stand that he ought to have done.' During the next term, in June, it was decided that he was not up to taking a scholarship to Winchester as his Greek was a bit weak, though in his final report ('As head of school he has been a distinct success' and 2nd in his class) his master was saying he had come on so considerably that 'I almost regret not having taken him to Winchester.' Scholarship or no scholarship it was to Winchester that he went in September, 1917.

CHAPTER II

Winchester at War

When Evelyn arrived at Winchester the war was dominating everything. The shock caused by the deaths of young officers in the trenches was often sharpened by the fact that their friends were still school-boys. That winter fuel was scarce, it was bitterly cold and there never seemed enough food. In the summer the term was extended to enable the boys to help the war effort by working for threepence an hour on the harvest. Most of the younger masters were away. Presiding over the school was Dr Montague John Rendall, Winchester's first lay headmaster – also the first non-Wykehamist to occupy the post. He spent 37 years at Winchester, many of them as an assistant master starting in 1887. Lay man he may have been, but according to Cecil King (an almost exact contemporary of Evelyn's) the boys thought he was a religious humbug.[1]

From his letters home Evelyn showed himself well able to endure the hardship and lack of privacy at school, indeed his nature was probably already enough formed by then to enable him to detach himself from his surroundings, or at least insulate him from their worst effects. One of his contemporaries, Sir Anthony Hornby remembers him as a 'large somewhat ponderous good-natured boy with an undistinguished record. He did not emerge as a leader, much less a ring leader. He was a massive calm-tempered friendly chap who didn't push himself forward or make a noise. At football his weight, persistance and courage were useful.'

Another contemporary recalled that everybody liked him. He worked hard and reached the 6th form but was not academically conspicuous at school; and he played hard but rather clumsily at games. He was a big, though not fat boy, and almost immediately was nicknamed Big Bertha after the heavy guns used in the war. Even at this age, although diffident and unassuming he apparently had a dignity which came partly from his height and also from his expression which was serious but not solemn. He seemed to hold aloof from school life, though not in a priggish or superior way. Like Roger Makins (later Lord Sherfield, who became his best friend for the rest of his life and had a not dissimilar career in the diplomatic service) he gave the impression of being in a sense adult, and of having little time for the things which absorb most schoolboys' interests and emotions. How strange that Evelyn and Roger Makins appeared so serious and so adult to their schoolboy contemporaries, when the one thing that everybody else, who saw them together in later life, remarked upon, was how extraordinarily juvenile and schoolboyish their behaviour could be!

Evelyn went to a house nicknamed Chawkers, after its founder Hawkins. The housemaster for his first two years was G. H. 'Georgie' Blore, a great lover of reading. He admired heroes and wrote a book called *Victorian Worthies,* which consisted of 10-page sketches of a great variety of public men, mostly from the world of arts or letters. His teaching was based on the view that the history of the world had been shaped by the characters of great men. He used to call everybody 'Miserable Man! Miserable Man!' (it was very bad form at Winchester to call anybody a boy). After two years Blore was succeeded by the Reverend Robert Quirk, a prim well-meaning man. The change did not noticeably affect Evelyn.

When he arrived he went into the army class (in preparation for which he had already read Fortescue's 12 volume *History of the British Army*) which taught science, mathematics and French to boys who were destined for one of the military academies – Sandhurst or Woolwich. Presumably at that stage his parents had still mapped out for him a start to his career something similar to Lord Cromer's own. His first two weeks must have been pretty strange, even apart from the war, the enlarged scale of things, towering senior boys and the olympian masters. The first thing to do, during those two weeks when he was relieved of fagging for older boys – 'sweating' to Wykehamists – and was free from being beaten for any misdemeanours, was to learn the strange new vocabularly, which some Wykehamists never forget (though they often *do* forget that the rest of us have never learnt it, a mistake never made by Evelyn). He had to learn 'notions', special words peculiar to Wykehamists. He had to wear stiff collars, until as a blessed relief the shortage of starch got all the boys into soft collars. In 1917, when the nation's crop failed, there were no potatoes for days on end. The boys had lentils with their meat, and once rhubarb leaves boiled as a vegetable.

Typically Evelyn's first letter home to Katie was mostly about food. 'September 20, 1917. Breakfast, porridge without sugar, eggs or kippers, tea, bread and butter (plenty). Dinner, roast beef and veg (two helpings) toast, tea, bread and butter. Later, milk or water and biscuits.' It didn't sound too bad. He was also 'beginning to learn all the things that are good or bad notion'.

About a month later we have a full timetable:

Day's routine:

6.25	get up, cold tap
6.45	biscuits and tea
7–7.45	mug [work]
7.45–8.0	prayers in chantry
8.0	breakfast – porridge (two helpings), meat (two helpings), as much bread and butter + marmalade/jam, as much sugar
9.15–12.45	work
1.0	lunch – always very good
1.30–4.15	ekker [Exercise]
4.15–6.15	work
6.15	prayers
6.30	tea, bread and butter
7–8.45	toye time [prep]
9.0	prayers
9.45	lights out

In his second term he provides a list of the things he can be sent and those he cannot. Potted fish yes, meat no. Sardines and fruit yes, chocolate no, (though a good many do have it sent). There was a sugar ration weekly, with that for puddings being deducted. The boys were also asked not to have more than 12 ounces of bread per week which was weighed out for them in the 'grubbing' (dining) hall. They were down to only one helping of porridge and no bread at lunch. The margarine at tea was rationed.

He was clearly surviving it. March, 1918, 'Fool, dunce, thick idiot, harebrained miserable old hag! ! ! How often have I told you that . . . (some obscure piece of Winchester nomenclature). And to think that such a gudgeon should have given birth to such a marvellously clever son.'

At about this time Evelyn's future came up for discussion. It appears that one of his masters still took the view that he should go on to Woolwich rather than to Oxford, so he continued in the army class for another year or so. It was not until May, 1920, that he told his mother that he had finally decided to try for Oxford. He used to say later that the smattering of science he learnt during his time in the army class was very useful. It gave him a basic understanding of the language of science which he retained for the rest of his life.

Meanwhile he was rowing and fencing, probably a little boxing too, and he joined the cadet corps, whose high moments seemed to be field days against Eton and Marlborough. The object of the exercise was to catch as many boys as possible from the 'enemy' school and rip off their trouser buttons. The boys' rifles only had blank ammunition, but there were always temptations. One senior officer in the Rifle Brigade, finding himself in the, for him, unaccustomed position of directing proceedings from horseback, drew up the ragged school-boy army in front of him and told them, 'I've only one thing to say to you. I'm a bloody bad rider and if any of you fire a pencil up my horse's arse there'll be a hell of a row.'

Almost no letters have been kept from Evelyn during his last year at Winchester. He left in the spring of 1921, without any obvious feeling of regret or nostalgia, and he went up to New College in October. He told his mother that his history tutor was called Ogg, that he looked 'sweet' in a gown, asked her to get him a bicycle and announced he was going to play rugger. Soon the Oxford magic was working, 'I am doing *NO* work.' The authorities had apparently threatened to send him down when he had got drunk for the fifth time. He was also going in for a boxing match, which more or less ended in tears when, after too little training (too much drinking?) he was soundly beaten by a more experienced American.

Evelyn did not cut a very considerable figure at Oxford. He had a fairly small circle of friends – good, enduring ones – who remained close to him for the rest of his life, having penetrated the shy, rather slow personality which all his contemporaries remarked upon, and which many advanced as the reason why he was not either gregarious or much sought after by his fellow undergraduates. His closest friends he probably brought with him from Winchester – Roger Makins, Ralph Ricketts, Francis Portal. At Oxford he picked up Alec Douglas-Home (then Lord Dunglass) and Bill Anstruther Grey (a Tory MP who became Deputy Speaker and then Lord Kilmany) who, together with Roger, and his cousin Neddy Baring, shared digs with him in Brewer Street. Although numerous other contemporaries remem-

WINCHESTER AT WAR

ber him at Oxford these four or five young men formed the solid core of his friends.

He was clearly not thought very brilliant, perhaps because he did not shine in the rarified intellectual environment of undergraduates. He was shy outside his own circle, a lonely character who did not fraternise easily and used to go away and read on his own. When he got a first in History his friends were quite surprised, though his elders, perhaps more familiar with the old block from which he had been chipped, claimed to perceive more promise in the young man. Certainly John Buchan, who had quite a reputation for lion hunting at his house north of Oxford and asked Evelyn to attend his tea parties – which were laced with readings by the great man from his works, and intellectual walks – opined that he was like his father – 'invariably right.' Others would agree; neither brilliant nor original, but always of sound judgment.

If his work was quiet and unassuming, his play seldom seemed so. Roger Makins took him riding, which he attacked with great gusto though repeatedly falling off. There was a certain ponderousness about him, even in his pleasures. He probably drank no more or less than the others, but there was an impression that his hangovers lasted longer, accompanied by the most terrible groans of pain (even then he was apparently very concerned about his health though there is no sign that it deserved that much attention). He once lurched into Alec Dunglass' rooms and announced, 'If I could see you I would hit you'. Amidst all these more tempting preoccupations, the letters to Katie became patchy. Perhaps the telephone was insinuating itself into their relationship although that would not have been consistent with Katie's style or her sense of thrift. However, the old banter was still here, 'May 5, 1922. Woman, if you cannot restrain yourself all correspondence must cease. . . . Have you tidied your hair? Have you washed your neck? Yr v loving Evelyn.' Presumably this was a counterblast to one from Katie expressing maternal concern over some aspect of her son's commissariat.

There seemed to be no sign of any romantic attachment. In his last year Evelyn was induced to go to the 'Commem balls by Ralph Ricketts, who asked him to stand in at the last minute. He agreed, probably reluctantly, and there met K. Tennant (later Lady Elliott of Harwood) who became a lifelong friend and frequent guest at Ardgowan. He then went to three Com-

29

mems in a row, each running until 5.30 a.m., immediately before his OTC camp at Seaford, where he fell off his immense horse into a gorse bush, probably from exhaustion. He wrote to Katie and asked her to send '1. my bathing dress, 2. £1 – it will be difficult to cash a cheque here.'

Most of Evelyn's vacations were spent at Ardgowan. There he was treated like a son, and a favourite one at that. 'Evelyn, though entirely at ease, almost like a son, never took a liberty. He was never late for dinner,' said one Oxford contemporary.

For the first time in his life he was able to ask his Oxford friends to stay, without the fear that he would be boring them or placing an intolerable load on the modest house his mother ran in London. It was the nearest thing to a home he ever had, and the flavour of Ardgowan permeates the memories of all those people whose friendships blossomed there. It was to Ardgowan that Katie and Evelyn came when they returned from Egypt prior to the retirement of Lord Cromer. There the first photographs of Alice's adored nephew appear in her album for 1905. Alice was some years older than Katie and had been married for twenty childless years by the time Evelyn was born. In 1974 the house still bore traces of her regime, in the dark red silk hanging on the sitting room walls, in the last few bars of Monkey Brand soap, bed boards rather than springs under the mattresses, no central heating and no wash basins in the bedrooms. Napoleon's hat still sat in a glass case in the hall, under a huge portrait of the Emperor painted for his mother, and given by that lady in Rome in 1816 to the Shaw Stewart of the day.

The house is peaceful and totally cut off. The sound of waders drifts up on most days from the shoreline at the bottom of the steep banks down to the sea. Inland you can see the moors above Inverkip. Yet it is suffused with that heavy west coast atmosphere which Evelyn later found so enervating once he became ill during the 1930s. Lady Alice's house was often full of guests, and there were always enough servants but – in the true Thynne tradition – there was no ostentation and no luxury. Alice was as thrifty as her younger sister. Right until she died she kept meticulous accounts and Hughie was never allowed to forget any lapse into overspending. He was made to travel to Glasgow by third class. Alice herself drove round in a Baby Austin car which she frequently overturned. To drive with her as a passenger was an alarming experience which few attempted, and pedestrians learned to take to the hills whenever they heard the incessant hooting of her horn.

Between them Alice and Katie presided over the summer house parties where there was always a judicious mixture of the generations. The house in the summer revolved round the grouse shooting, which Katie had tried to resist for Evelyn. She was forced to give up the unequal struggle with the monosyllabic headkeeper, Mr Macalpine, who taught Evelyn to shoot, and who was said to hold every bird in contempt except the grouse. Evelyn became a keen shot, but never a very good one.

The guests normally arrived on Saturdays and stayed a whole week. To judge by the recollections of many of Evelyn's friends who were invited to Ardgowan, there was a settled pattern to the scene. There was grouse for *every* meal. Alice and Katie seemed to be dressed permanently in black with small diamond brooches and little hats or black bandeaux. Of Katie an eyewitness has written, 'In spite of incredible tatty clothes and complete disregard of her appearance she was one of the most aristocratic people I have ever seen.'

After the shooting, the men would stay in the smoking room and so not be seen at all until dinner. After dinner there always seemed to be charades, sardines or kick-the-bucket. Perhaps this explains why, years later, Evelyn's own Government Houses used to resound to after-dinner games, however dignified the company. Sir Hugh, disguised in his wife's shawls, or some other garment, was said to be a brilliant charades actor. Alice and Katie would sit back and watch them, with their needlework or more often than not a pair of Evelyn's grey flannel pyjamas. In conversation they were free – not to say sharp – with their opinions.

As for romance, the atmosphere seems to have been too boisterous and good humoured for serious attachments to be formed – apple pie beds rather than anything more adventurous. It was at Ardgowan that Evelyn first met his future wife, Molly Grey, and there is some evidence that their two mothers mused on the suitability of their marriage. But in spite of his banter, Evelyn was still very much on the leash. He had no career and no money. Even while he was at Oxford he seems to have been in abject financial dependence on his mother. There was one characteristic occasion at Ardgowan when Evelyn was invited to a tennis party and asked his mother for some money to buy white trousers to wear instead of his baggy grey flannels and brown rope shoes. Katie refused. 'He must always remember he is going to be poor,' she said. In one way Evelyn did, because although later when he inherited money he was naturally and easily generous with the big things, he never entirely overcame a certain prudence, almost parsimony, where the cash in his pocket was concerned.

CHAPTER III
Passage to India

It is not clear when Evelyn finally decided to join the Indian Civil Service. When he left army class at Winchester and decided to go to Oxford rather than Woolwich he was clearly putting a military career behind him. There is no mention in his letters of any thoughts about the imperial service. Perhaps it was not mentioned because it was a foregone conclusion between him and his mother that he would follow the path trodden by his father. One would anyway imagine that Katie would have been determined to keep him out of the clutches of the family bank or any of his Baring relations. When he was 21 his half-brother, Cromer, wrote to him saying it was time he realized he was a Baring, or words to that effect, and suggesting that the unspoken rift between them should be healed. Katie probably saw to it that Evelyn either did not reply, or in replying, did not respond to the overture. Some of his school friends have in later life suggested that the inspiration to service in India sprang from a talk on India given at Winchester by Lord Chelmsford, who had been Viceroy. Be that as it may, by the time he was at Oxford there appeared to be no doubt in peoples' minds that it was to the ICS that he would go. Consequently, when he got his first, he left Oxford for a year and then returned for a fourth year as an ICS probationer.

During the interlude in the winter of 1924, he went to the Middle East, on a sort of minor grand tour, giving himself a first introduction to the east, and – more important – enabling him to visit Egypt and drink in the memories of his father's former triumphs on the Nile. We pick him up in Venice on November 1, 1924, writing to 'Darling Ma.' He didn't like the baroque churches, thought St Marks and the Grand Canal 'splendid', and gondoliers 'too expensive'. There was also lunch with the English consul. He was glad to see how badly the women candidates did in the British general election. Clearly he had inherited his father's distaste for women in politics.

And then to Athens. He saw the Parthenon by moonlight. . . . 'the youthful Byron (that's me),' he climbed Mount Hymettus (as cold as England) and obtained an introduction to Princess Demidoff. 'My dear, do you know it was remarked I spoke French

33

not like an Englishman, but with an *"accent bien pur"* – which was ascribed to my Russian blood. I felt pleased at the compliment but annoyed at the idea of being an infernal Russian! – and what is more a Greek lady (a young one too) to whom I was talking on the boat said I must go to Olympia, as I would see my double there which was – no, not the statue of a pig but – THE HERMES OF PRATIXELES!!! [sic] So all those remarks to my old Ma by Irish stewardesses etc are *"pour ainsi dire".'*

He toured the Peloponnese, commenting on the soil, the architecture, the racial origins and habits of the peasants, on the mountains, many of which he climbed. Sunset at Pyrgos, 'my word you would be sentimental if you were here, you old funny . . . I love you, your v loving E.'

But there was a change of tone in Athens, two weeks later, 'Really you try me *very* high. I have just received a most impertinent letter from you saying that I do not write to you enough; And this, ungrateful wretch, when I sent you, sometime ago, an immense letter of 10 pages containing the most magnificent description of my journeys in Greece written in the most romantic and lofty style and in English worthy of the Elizabethan age. Really if I get treatment like this I shall be driven to a course of life that will cause one to write:

> My days are in the yellow leaf
> The flowers and fruits of love are gone
> The worm the canker and the grief
> Are mine alone.
>
> [Byron on his 36th birthday]

(on my 26th, instead of my 36th birthday. Such a thing has never been heard of, remember your place woman!)' He enclosed a bracelet as a Christmas present, which had had 'a glorious history. The man asked 12 lires for it but your son being also a Jew (the man's name was Isaac Moses) and a German one, got him down to tossing a Turkish piastre as to whether it should be 5 or 6 – and he won.'

In Constantinople he treated Katie to a complete description of the mosques of that great city – not all of them, but a good many – and attended one during prayer. On another day he went down into the cisterns built by Justinian, 'The most eerie place imaginable. You row about in a little skiff to the tune of endless drops through an absolute maze of pillars.'

At Smyrna he was much excited by the mysteries of oriental government and the way this affected his getting a visa. He described the destruction of Smyrna in detail but his sympathies lay with the Turks none the less. There were also visits to dancing dervishes, and camel fighting, and he started to learn Arabic – the classical variety, naturally.

Finally, in February, after he had been on the road for more than three months, he came to Cairo. He was immediately swept up by the Cairenes who had venerated his father 20 years before. He stayed with a number of people, including Allenby, the British High Commissioner.

It was Allenby who had conquered the Turks in 1918, ably assisted by T. E. Lawrence, but Evelyn found that little of the glitter which attended that martial success still remained in the Cairo of 1925. He also found Anglo-Egyptian society a hotbed of gossip and bitchiness, which he faithfully reported to his mother at home.

Evelyn was now, possibly unconsciously, using his letters to sharpen his skills at the kind of political reporting which he would expect to have to do in the diplomatic or imperial service. As pieces of pure political reportage, they are impressive for a young man of his age, though what Katie made of them is another matter. Perhaps she was not actually so scatter-brained as her husband and son were fond of making out. Anyway, for the rest of his life Evelyn in his letters, in addition to the buffoonery, took every opportunity to write her political, agricultural or sociological homilies.

One particular disappointment for Evelyn was his failure to see Zaghlul Pasha, the first great leader of the Egyptian independence movement. Zaghlul was originally a bright young civil servant who became a protégé of Lord Cromer's. He was so attached to Cromer that he made a special journey to England to visit him before he died. When Evelyn arrived in Cairo he arranged to pay a call on Zaghlul but an emissary from the British High Commission asked him not to as it was thought that for Cromer's son to visit somebody in opposition to the British, would embarrass their imperial authority. Evelyn reluctantly complied.

He pottered about Cairo, admiring the Arab quarter, comparing the residential part to second rate Paris, and making arrangements to go up the Nile. In Upper Egypt, amongst other things, he managed to go to the tomb of Tutenkhamen which had just

35

been discovered by Carter and his team. 'I succeeded in seeing the famous tomb. Quite a feat, for round it now there is a sort of murky atmosphere of storm and fury! Talk about the *odium archaeologicum*. The people I was staying with had (according to their version) given Carter every possible help and they certainly did lend him free of charge their expert photographer. Yet he is impossibly offensive to his helpers, and has never done anything for them.'

Eventually he returned home via Damascus, stopping en route in Jerusalem, where he experienced some disgust 'at the general atmosphere of the place like a huge show with various star turns shown by rival showmen. It makes me understand the point of view of the man who said "Religion attracts, but the church repels". For the whole of Jerusalem teems with monks of every sort, greek, rc, armenian, coptic and even abyssinian, who fight sometimes in the literal sense of the word over who is to control some chapel in the Church of the Holy Sepulchre . . . one imagines the old Moslem watching all the quibbling and laughing up his sleeve.'

Evelyn returned to Oxford for the final year's work to qualify him for the ICS. He had already passed the ICS exam, which was open to Indians and Britishers between the age of 21 and 23. Those who passed it then had to spend a year on probation in Britain, concentrating on special subjects such as Hindi, the tenancy laws, the Indian penal code, civil and criminal procedures and so on. At the end of the year there was a final qualifying test which included equitation. Whatever Evelyn's Oxford contemporaries thought of his riding, his Indian colleagues on the course clearly had a higher opinion. During the equitation course the probationers had to attend riding classes at Woolwich Arsenal. The sergeant major in the Horse Artillery there was a disciplinarian who swore loudly, and a fellow Indian probationer, Mr Pulla Reddi, complained to Evelyn about it. Evelyn was reassuring. He told him that the sergeant major meant no offence because he was dark-skinned, and advised him that if he listened to the sergeant major closely he would see that he used worse language on the British. He did. Evelyn also came to the rescue of another probationer, V. N. Menon, during the final exam. Menon was actually thrown and did not want to remount, so they swapped horses; whereupon Menon's fiery animal apparently succumbed to Evelyn's masterful hands, and they both passed their test, Baring second, Menon second from bottom! So those arduous riding sessions with Roger Makins had not been wasted after all.

Since it was by then taken for granted that he was destined for a distinguished career on the imperial stage, the ICS was a natural place to start. However, it is doubtful if Evelyn, or Katie for that matter, ever contemplated a lifetime's career working his way up the ladder of the ICS until he was appointed Provincial Governor or something of that order. If Katie dreamed dreams for her son, then it must have been as Viceroy. He was clearly, by birth and background, Viceroy material. Yet seldom, recently, had there been a Viceroy chosen from the ranks of the ICS itself.

Some of his contemporaries were more suspicious. A number of them believed that the recruitment of Cromer's son to the ICS was a calculated act intended to persuade the young men of Britain that it was still a promising career, in spite of doubts about the eventual status of India and the disturbances caused by Gandhi. It was said that the standard of entry to the ICS had fallen off since the war. Neither British nor Indians in the ICS ever really saw Evelyn as one of them, and perhaps the feeling was reciprocated. 'Baring's dignified behaviour and high social background distinguished him from most of his British colleagues in the ICS at a time when recruitment to this service in the UK was not exactly from the top drawer,' said one Indian who served with him.

There is no doubt, looking back on his life, that his period of service in India had a colossal influence on him in all his subsequent colonial incarnations. It was almost bound to work a spell on any young man.

There is something special about the Indian Civil Service which seems to apply to no other corps of administrators – certainly not in British history. Its traditions are as overpowering as those of any military caste; its history is much more fulfilling. Its characters appear more imaginative, more eccentric, more idiosyncratic. but, at the same time, inspired by a single, common theme which seemed to animate them as rulers of India for two hundred years. These are not the men who rose to eminence in the India Office in Whitehall, but those who presided over the continent in person, yet who, in the words of Philip Woodruff in his magisterial two volume work *The Men Who Ruled India*, 'after ruling millions of subjects, after commanding victorious armies, after dictating terms of peace at the gates of hostile capitals . . . return to their native land with no more than a decent competence.'[1]

Woodruff likens them to Plato's guardians, dedicated since

childhood to model themselves on brave, sober, religious and honourable men. This sounds a bit excessive. Rather than some inherited ideology, it was more likely to be the magic of India herself which captivated them; Woodruff's India has 'the smell of dust thirstily drinking the first rain; the spicy peppery smell of a grain dealer's shop; the reek of mangoes, marigolds and lush vegetation, when the sun breaks through the clouds in August and the earth steams . . . the sound of men's voices in petition, the look on a man's face when he is found guilty, a peasant's emotion when a wrong has been put right.'[2]

The system of administration had a peculiarly Indian flavour, but was so impressively carried out that British colonial administration elsewhere in the empire seemed to ape the Indian experience.

At the base of the pyramid was the Deputy Magistrate and Collector, which was the appointment for the young recruit when, fresh from his final exams, he arrived in India and was placed in the variable wardship of a District Officer. The District Officer was the backbone of British India, lord of all he surveyed, deferred to, if not necessarily respected, by the Deputy Collector under him, by the police officers, by the agricultural officers, by the medical officers, and by the several million native Indians – Hindu and Muslim, Sikh, Bihari, touchable and untouchable, trader, peasant, lawyer – the whole teeming multitude which in some curious, almost inexplicable, way looked up to these few men perched on top of their country; and obeyed. The District Officer in his turn bowed to the Commissioner; the Commissioner bowed to the Provincial Governor; and the Governor bowed to the Viceroy at the very top of the imperial tree, remote, almost regal, certainly noble, and seldom native even to British India.

When Evelyn arrived in India, he found, like every other field officer of the ICS at that time, that he was having to cope with a paradox. The life of the Indian peasant, the cycle of planting and reaping, fighting famine and staunching floods, remained unchanged, as it had done for centuries. 'Do you realize the dull misery of these countless myriads?' Allan Hume, a retired ICS man, who stayed on to found the Congress movement, wrote in the 1890s – 'From their births to their deaths toil! toil! toil!; hunger, hunger, hunger, sickness, suffering, sorrow; these alas are keynotes of their short and sad existence.'[3] It was not quite like that in the 1920s but the basic struggle against the elements was the same, against hunger and thirst, drought, floods and plague.

Yet, though the work on the ground remained unchanged, the whole political context in which it was taking place had changed. From that moment in the 19th century when the British administrators decided to bring western education to India they must have conceded, in their hearts, that it ultimately meant independence for India, with or without a rebellion on the way.

But although this constitutional progress had been gradual over the previous fifty years, the pace seemed to quicken after 1919, and with it – maybe indeed a cause of it – came a changing mood of educated India. The 1918 war was probably the watershed after which the gathering impatience of the Indians meant that the path to self government had to be seen to be an ideal which could be realized in the lifetime of the contemporary Indian leadership. In a matter of years feelings had hardened. In 1918 Gandhi was still speaking of an equal partnership within the empire. Soon after that, however, it became axiomatic among his followers to oppose everything about the Indian government. When the new constitution was unveiled in 1919, with the concept of diarchy – shared rule in the provinces between the old administration and the newly elected native ministers – Gandhi was already in opposition to it. Violent disturbances broke out in various centres in northern India culminating in the shooting of 400 rioters in Amritsar. The inquiry into the Amritsar massacre condemned the British general's action, a verdict reluctantly accepted by the British House of Commons but repudiated by the Lords. As a result Gandhi launched his non-cooperation movement. There were many further outrages of one kind or another, and Gandhi was eventually arrested in March, 1922, and sentenced to six years imprisonment.

In March, 1926, Lord Irwin succeeded Lord Reading as Viceroy. He set out determined to bring about some kind of understanding between the nationalist movement and the governing authorities. The general election of 1923 – the second under the 1919 constitution – had seen the arrival of a section of the Congress Party, labelled *Swaraj* (Home Rule) which had broken away from Gandhi's complete boycott, and secured very substantial representation both in the central assembly and in the provincial councils. Although they entered the legislatures dedicated to a policy of 'uniform continuous and consistent obstruction' of government, forcing the Viceroy to bring in his budget as an emergency measure, they soon became established as a kind of official opposition. However in November, 1927, the Simon Commission was set up to inquire into the working of the 1919 constitution, and reaction to, cooperation with, and criticism of the Simon Commission were to form the main elements of national policies in India while Evelyn was serving his apprenticeship in the administration of the United Provinces.

Evelyn sailed for India in November, 1926, on the SS *Ranpura*. It was a crowded ship with many British families on their way to spend Christmas in India. Among them was the family of Lord Irwin, the Viceroy, and his guests. Evelyn had been asked to spend Christmas with Lord Lytton, the Governor of Bengal, an almost unprecedentedly grand invitation for a young civilian in his first month of service. The other young men of the ICS on the boat were suitably awed. Evelyn seemed to spend most of his time with the viceregal party, which included the Gathorne-Hardy family with whom he got on very well. 'Lady Isobel very amusing,' he told Katie, 'the daughter rather hearty.' The ten ICS men formed a glee club singing group and stood in for the soprano in the ship's concert when that artiste allegedly became too drunk to perform. This leisurely approach to his first posting continued when the *Ranpura* arrived at Bombay, the legendary gateway to India. Evelyn delayed one further day there to watch the MCC under A. E. R. Gilligan playing against an all-India eleven. Then he caught the frontier mail for Delhi and Lucknow, where his life as a young Indian civilian was to begin in earnest, after a brief, gilded interlude with the Lyttons at the viceregal lodge in Calcutta. He wrote to Katie on Boxing Day. 'Here I am in the lap of luxury for a week. The ceremony is terrific. Vast viceregal lodge. Everywhere are swarms of scarlet servants. I shall have my last whirl of gaiety before settling down to the round of Anglo-Indian life, which as a matter of fact, on first acquaintance, doesn't seem to be going to be as trying as I thought it might be.' It was indeed a whirl. He saw polo, racing, the Viceroy, Lord Irwin, arriving in state on the new race course, accompanied by a bodyguard of enormous Punjabi troopers. There was also his hostess, Pamela Lytton, once a famous beauty who had been known as the 'Rose of Hyderabad.' Evelyn thought she was old, which was not quite fair as she could not have been more than 50. 'Her entire energies are devoted to trying to look young. She succeeds fairly well, but the resulting moods nearly drive her ADCs off their heads.' It was hardly an appropriate baptism for life at the district level, but Katie's austere upbringing of her son

managed to prevent his head being turned by such things. In the
New Year he returned to Lucknow to start work.

CHAPTER IV
Lucknow

Life in the United Provinces in those days, or in any of India's provinces for that matter, was an all absorbing undertaking, and it is hard to see how prolonged service in one area – as distinct from Evelyn's more varied later experience in South Africa and the North West Frontier – could not have had an ultimately very limiting effect on a man. Communications in India were primitive to say the least, and distances enormous. There was no air mail and wirelesses were very rare. Cars were still a curiosity in most villages. The British Indians lived ordered if parochial lives in their ramshackle, spacious bungalows, contenting themselves with out-of-date newspapers and the infinite complications of the caste system. This obviously inhibited the development of any deep personal relationships with Indians, but a more prevailing inhibition was the tacit understanding among Europeans, so cruelly but brilliantly exposed by E. M. Forster in *Passage to India*, that an officer of the British administration (and there were very few Britishers about in rural India who were not in some way connected with the administration) must keep aloof from Anglo-Indian friendships lest they gave the impression of personal favouritism.

The Simon Commission was taking evidence, and in Delhi and Whitehall the future of India was occupying the minds of statesmen, but in the districts it was rare for junior officers to be concerned about such matters. Most new ICS recruits would have been reared on a diet of liberal constitutional historians while they were at Oxford or Cambridge, but when they reached India they would have found that, certainly at their level in the districts, nobody bothered much with independence. By the time Evelyn arrived the 1921 civil disobedience campaign was over. Conversations might include occasional contemptuous references to Gandhi but any dealings other than official ones with Indians known to belong to the *Swaraj* movement were likely to be frowned on. The ICS officers regarded members of the *Swaraj* more as nuisances than as heirs presumptive whom they should have been teaching how to operate the system. Consequently each side – the administration on the one hand and the Congress movement on the other – surreptitiously regarded the other as an enemy. The Indians thought that the ICS officers would hang on to power as long as they could, so they struggled with them over almost every issue, seeking to claim political victories over what were more often mere problems of administration. Yet none of this seemed to inhibit the spontaneous welcome which ICS officers almost always received when they visited Indian villages in their area.

The United Provinces – formed by the union of Agra and Oudh – was one of those areas under direct British rule, as opposed to the native states which remained as protectorates under their own princes. The new capital of the UP was Lucknow. It was the centre of the UP administration, which consisted of about 130 ICS officers, of whom 40 were Indians, administering an area and population roughly equal to the entire United Kingdom. They were assisted by the police, medical service, agricultural service and one or two other branches of administration. The provinces were divided up into 48 districts each under a District Officer. Each district was roughly the size of Yorkshire, with a population of about one million. In charge of each district was an ICS officer, usually called District Magistrate and Collector, or District Magistrate and Deputy Commissioner, the double title derived from his traditional dual functions which still obtained – the administration of justice, law and order and security on the one hand, and the collection of revenue on the other. Each district had four sub-divisions, and it was as a sub-divisional officer at Lucknow that Evelyn spent the first year of his service.

Since he worked in the city of Lucknow and not in the open country, the emphasis of his work was as a city magistrate, responsible for smoothing Hindu-Muslim relations, accompanying processions, riot control and so on. On appointment as a sub-divisional magistrate he was given suitable cases on which to gain experience, with powers to imprison offenders for up to one month. He was given acts and regulations to read, and was expected to sit in as an observer of the proceedings of higher courts. He had to employ a native teacher for language and local customs. He was told that at the end of this first year he would undergo a four months course at Moradabad, after which his magisterial powers of imprisonment and sentence would be increased.

After three years of this kind of life an officer would be asked if he wished to apply to join the Indian Political Service, which was a kind of internal diplomatic service covering relations with and between the principal states, the frontier states, and the still largely untamed frontier tribes. Entry in the IPS required an undertaking not to marry for three years more, as the young officers tended to be peripatetic.

After seven years, officers would be asked if they wished to apply for the judicial branch. Naturally many did not, preferring to stay in the administration of their chosen provinces for their whole careers. This is why it is not rare to discover exact contemporaries within the ICS who were hardly known to one other, not because the service was large – it was actually very small – but because the provinces to which they were first posted were often to become the area in which they remained for the rest of their careers. One such was Gwynne, the Deputy Commissioner in Lucknow and District Officer, with whom Evelyn stayed for his first year's service. The character of one's first DO was thought to be important because it could exercise a lasting influence on the outlook of a young officer and thus the whole development of his ICS career. It seems likely that Evelyn was less influenced by Gwynne, however, than by the next District Officer for whom he had to work at Meerut eighteen months later.

Gwynne was a neat dapper little man, dry and precise rather than stodgy. He soon afterwards became Chief Secretary of his provincial administration, and was thought to be much more a secretariat man – more at home in the office – than a District Officer with field work to do. Evelyn's first impressions of him were of 'an inconspicuous little man who is easy to get on with, living in a splendid two storey house occupied formerly by the Nawabs of Oudh, and the building from which Havelock planned his march to relieve the beseiged Lucknow residency during the Indian Mutiny seventy years before.'

In his first week Evelyn listened to his first case, engaged a bearer ('an elderly rascal Rahim Baksh'), retained a *chaprassi* with whom to learn hindustani, and a man to be his clerk in court. He told Katie that the Indians gave the impression of being far more serious than the Egyptians. 'They never shriek with laughter like the Berberine do. Also, reforms or no reforms, after Egypt one gets the impression of how much greater is our prestige than in Cairo. All Indians are far more deferential than Egyptians are. The servants are always bowing and scraping. Their physique is far frailer and their legs compared with those of a Saidi fellah are like matchsticks.'

44

He gradually started to learn about Lucknow. The city had been the capital of the United Provinces for about five years when Evelyn arrived there. It was generally thought to be the gayest and most lively of the provincial capitals, and the United Provinces were considered the most sophisticated of the provinces. It was certainly one of the most attractive cities. The previous Governor, Sir Harcourt Butler, had restored and built up the crumbling architecture and the restoration served to recapture some of Lucknow's old glory as it must have been at the time of the Moguls. In his journal of India, written after he had left, Evelyn wrote that it did not have the beauty of Agra or Delhi but 'a character of its own and a past neither sensational nor glorious.' He was obviously struck, and perhaps comforted by the Muslim atmosphere. Indeed throughout his life he was to show an affinity for Muslims which probably sprung from his father's long association with the Egyptians and the fact that his own first experience of the East was also in the Muslim world on the tour he took in 1924. At one village in the countryside he visited he immediately enquired of the headman, whom he knew to be Muslim, what sort of Shaikhs they were, Quraishi, Farukhi or Saddiqi. 'This question delighted them and we were soon on good terms. Conversation was easy as they clamoured to hear of other Muslim countries I had visited, Egypt, Syria and Iraq.'

In Lucknow there was a common language, Urdu, the *lingua franca* of Northern India which enable Hindu and Muslim to speak to each other. Evelyn plunged into his Urdu studies with his customary heavy and pedantic enthusiasm, learning from a gentleman called Sayid Saduq Husain. Soon he was remarking that Urdu was spoken more purely in Lucknow, 'where the sweepers speak as purely as Nawabs everywhere else.' His habit of speaking Urdu correctly, he once said, gave him a point of contact later with every Indian Muslim in South and East Africa. It was a familiar passion of Evelyn's to speak languages in their most classical mode. Never a man for *patois*, years later he used to regale his African guards in Nairobi with a brand of Swahili which had probably last been heard in the fifteenth century Sultanates of Zanzibar.

Sayid Husain was one of the two men who stand out during his year in Lucknow. 'The ordinary *munshi* who teaches language to every young Indian civilian is an individual with a black complexion, a dirty turban, and a manner as obsequious as that of a Cairo dragoman,' said Evelyn. But not Sayid. Evelyn's first sight of him was clothed in a long white coat with flowers embroidered on it, a drooping white moustache, long grey hair over his neck, white trousers, red and gold shoes, all under a huge white umbrella. The two men warmed to their subject quickly. The teaching sessions soon developed into less intensive, but more enjoyable expeditions to places of interest in the city.

Sayid had some unusual ideas. He believed that Europeans ate their food with a fork instead of with their fingers because, since they lived in rather a cold climate, they did not want to wash too often; therefore their nails became dirty; therefore they could not touch food with them. He said he had translated *Paradise Lost* into Urdu, but did not entirely approve of the piece. He told Evelyn that the language was difficult, and 'undoubtedly, Milton's special intention when writing *Paradise Lost* was that it should be a good book for the MA class.' Moreover, as the inhabitants of Milton's postulated Paradise did not seem to experience any earthly joys, 'Let such a Paradise, I say, go to hell!'

The other character in Evelyn's life was Mr Batting, a large, fat man who had come to Lucknow 35 years earlier as a trooper with the 17th Lancers. His Eurasian wife was even fatter. 'Neither his wife, nor the strong *Chee Chee* or Eurasian accent with which his children spoke English prevented him from professing frequently the greatest contempt for all half castes.' Evelyn asked him innumerable questions. Mr Batting had all the answers. They revisited all the important sites of the Mutiny. 'It was a difficulty story to forget because the life of the English in India has changed remarkably little during the previous 80 years,' wrote Evelyn. 'The men and women who sheltered in the Residency cellars differed little from today.' He found a short inscription on the tomb of Henry Lawrence in the Residency – Here lies Henry Lawrence, who tried to do his duty' – a 'better memorial of the English in India than any of the marble splendours of viceregal pomp.' They made a meticulous reconstruction of the events and battles round Lucknow during the Mutiny. 'The course of the fighting could easily be followed on the ground. But curiously enough I never met an Indian in Lucknow who could remember the Mutiny.' Later, Evelyn did meet such a man at Meerut, but he was a very old headman, aged 90, and could only remember the high grain prices which were obtainable then, and the names of some of the District Officers at the time.

With Batting he saw the scenes of the worst Hindu-Muslim conflict in Lucknow; they went to the butchers' quarter, with

46

narrow streets full of carpet makers and gold-thread merchants;
they tasted mahbad mangoes in the vegetable market (he didn't
like them), watched wrestling matches, with Evelyn, asking whatever questions he could in the middle of the dust and the yells
of the crowd. He learnt that at the start of each fight, a Muslim
called for assistance from Ali, the Prophet's son-in-law, while a
Hindu invoked Hanuma, the monkey-god of great cunning.

Then there were the magistrate's problems, endeavouring to
keep the peace between turbulent sects and communities – a gay
Sunni Muslim festival coinciding with a Shia Muslim lamen-
tation, which had to be arranged for different times of the same
day; or the further complication of seeing that Muslim processions did not get entangled with the branches of the pipal, the
fig-tree sacred to Hindus. 'The wise magistrate goes over the
procession route several weeks before Muharran, accompanied by
a man with a saw; and at that time, strange to say, no one protests against the destruction of innumerable pipal branches. . . .'

Evelyn's work included a variety of other functions. He was
the local excise officer and so had to inspect trading practices. In
Lucknow this meant frequent visits to opium shops. Then, in
addition to the supervision of law and order as a magistrate, he
heard revenue cases, and also aribtrated in civil disputes.

He started to try his first cases after he had been in Lucknow
about a month. He was already being 'assimilated' – or partly so
– into British India. 'I have developed the Anglo-Indian habit of
shouting at my servant and of suddenly bringing out a yell and
a blow on the desk, when in court. In fact I was getting quite
like a *Passage to India*,' he told Katie. 'I can assure you however,
I won't fall victim to any of the beautiful ladies out here, the
temptation is not strong.'

His work would not have been very onerous those first few
months, although exactly how onerous depended on one's District
Officer. When Philip Mason – another contemporary of Evelyn's
in the UP – arrived, his District Officer immediately found him
a polo pony and gave him a book on polo to read. Since the
young civilian normally lived with his District Officer and followed him round, they talked shop almost continuously and the
new recruit was expected to pick up his experience as much by
observation as by delegation.

To Katie, 'The duties of a District Officer are indeed various.
Gwynne spent this morning receiving a deputation of 24 prosti-
tutes. This is a duty which I think your son would carry out

47

admirably when you remember the depraved life he led in London when supposed to have been at Oxford.' At another time there was a great Hindu fair when the 'pious prostrate themselves all the way from their homes to the Temple. The result was that the brutal oppressor coming along in his superior Ford car very nearly ran over a dirty and holy individual who was rolling his naked body in the middle of the road.'

Katie, as always, was fretting at what she thought was the dearth of news from her son (in spite of being informed in one letter that the cold nip had gone out of the air and he had removed his winter vest). Presumably she scolded him, since years later some of her friends were still convinced that she only went out to India in 1929 because she could no longer stand being kept in the dark by Evelyn's non-existent correspondence. If that is what she was saying, it must have been a pose, since she was all that time lovingly copying into a red leather-bound volume every letter she received from him; and the record shows how frequently he wrote. 'You really are a very trying woman,' he wrote after one such rebuke. 'Since landing in India I have become a Theosophist I have been made an honorary Yogi and from tomorrow will sit on the river bank covered with ash and paint marks and pick the fleas out of the coils of hair on top of my head. And I will acquire such soulforce that by sheer exercise of my intellect I shall cause Alice's teeth to rattle in her head, and all your hair to fall out.'

He bought a horse from an army officer, which was allegedly 'an experienced pigsticker,' and each morning at six o'clock would go for one and a half hour's riding instruction with the 4th Hussars. 'They make me go down an appalling line of jumps including an enormous bank without reins or stirrups and with my arms folded. Needless to say I have come off several times.' The horse was for many people the only means of transport in India and even among his colleagues in the ICS Evelyn's battered Model T Ford car was something of a rarity. However, equitation was not just a utility. Apart from the horse racing, which was attended with great gala during various 'weeks' – Lucknow, Meerut, Calcutta, and so on – there was also pigsticking. According to Philip Woodruff, 'pigsticking sweetened men otherwise soured by files, disappointment, and the hot weather, and sublimated their lust for power and women.[1] The young unmarried men were expected to spend their money on guns and ponies, or choose between polo and pigsticking.

Though Evelyn shot occasionally when he was touring, he seems to have chosen pigsticking, though it was not for about another year that he first witnessed a 'kill', whether because he took that time to acquire the skills or because of the luck of the chase, is not quite clear. But one can imagine that he approached the subject methodically and gradually gained a great grasp of its theory without showing any natural physical aptitude towards it. 'I have just seen my first pig killed – a perfectly enormous creature,' he wrote to Katie in March, 1928. 'It was most exciting especially when the pig charges, which this one did several times before we finished him off. I got my spear into it and it came sideways at me. One then has to push it off – this is not too frightfully easy as the pig is a great weight on one, and it is difficult not to leave go of one's spear. He doesn't come head on at one, as one imagines, but when one is alongside and have either speared him or are about to spear him, he turns in on the horse uttering the most extraordinary barking noises. A wild boar is a colossal size, ours measured 30 inches from the toe of his foreleg to the top of his shoulder. He has a pair of whacking tusks, the top ones stick out but it is with the bottom ones (they say) that he rips his enemy up.'

At work, he gradually started being given greater responsibilities. After nine months, he had to take over responsibility for two prisons while the senior prison officer was on leave. He told Katie of two whippings which he had to observe, involving 'a boy who got little more than I got at school, and a man who got 20 of the best on a very lightly clad posterior. Your fat son watches a row of half naked brown and black humanity being dealt out country bread and beans, walks along, asks how the bread is, refrains from touching it, has it weighed, finds out who wants to write a letter, who has a hole in his blanket, whose work is to be changed, who is to go on a nice diet because he has (like other people I know) lost his teeth owing to advancing age.'

About four months after Evelyn arrived, in mid-April, the hot weather was upon them and 'all the females (thank goodness) have, with few exceptions, cleared out.' The women went away in the summer, the older ones home to Britain, the younger ones to the hills. This was not so surprising since in May and June the temperature rose to 120 degrees and life became intolerable until the long rains arrived in about July. One of the reasons why electricity was installed fairly early, was because the heat of oil lamps became quite unbearable during the hot season. Life

49

in the ICS changed during the summer when the women were not there. It was a time for sleeping out on the lawn as far as possible from the house, because all buildings seemed to radiate the tremendous heat througout the night. The temperature began to rise quickly after dawn, and most Anglo-Indians therefore rose about six o'clock. The short tropical twilight also meant that they had to leave their offices by about 4.30 if they were to have the chance of any exercise before dark.

Every ICS officer had to complete two tours of his district each year, the first to inspect the administrative outstations such as the local police stations, the dispensaries, and schools; and the second, lasting for several weeks, during the cooler weather, when the District Officer camped out under canvas, carrying on his normal magisterial functions wherever he was, but also performing his revenue duties. 'I am now in camp,' Evelyn wrote home in November, 1927. 'One has a huge tent, table, chairs, carpets, bath, etc. the whole moving from place to place in bullock carts – with the officer who is settling the land revenue, we walk for miles through the fields in the morning classifying the types of soil. I am becoming most agricultural, distinguish various kinds of soil and talk brightly about crops, rent and irrigation.' It was his first tour and his first real sojourn in the beautiful open country of the United Provinces.

The UP occupied the great North Indian plain stretching from Bihar in the east to the plains of the Punjab in the west. The soil of the Gangetic plain was so fertile that it sustained the highest density of population in rural India – about 500 to the square mile. It was reminiscent of rolling parkland, without palm trees or any sign of desert. Cultivation varied in squares of sugar cane, rice, barley, cotton with clusters of dark green mango trees breaking up the fields. It was flat and dusty, except during the wet months. Because of flooding during the rains, the river beds spread out much wider than the normal water course, with the basin full of patches of wild tamarisk and the long grass where the wild pigs were to be found.

After a year with Gwynne, Evelyn was posted to Moradabad for a course which took place in the provincial police station. To Katie, December, 1927, 'Back at school. Lectures half the day. Young ICS and IPS officers here. It's amazing how childish it makes one feel again. I feel tempted to produce all my private school tricks.' He frequently yielded to the temptation, particularly with a young friend, George Fisher. Fisher was to marry later that year – something almost unheard of for someone so new into the service – and Evelyn was his best man. (He was late for the wedding because a man ran amok in the bazaar with a store of home-made bombs; Evelyn had to take charge and ordered the police to shoot him in the legs. This fate was avoided because the bomber became thirsty and was persuaded to exchange his bombs for a drink.)

Together Fisher and Evelyn sought comfort in a boisterous reaction to the stuffiness of Anglo-Indian officialdom. The army thought that young ICS officers were too intellectual, so Fisher and Baring – 'B', as his friend called him – played the fool and behaved like prep-school boys together. They hit each other in the ribs or fell on the floor in mock rugger-scrums. They mocked the lecturer at Moradabad who was trying to teach would-be magistrates how to tell when an Indian was lying. 'What we need is someone to teach us how to tell when he is telling the truth,' they said. They joked about the martial classes, lampooning the British reverence for soldier/warrior tribes. They made fun of the practice in the ICS whereby you called somebody Sir, if he was *two* rungs senior to you up the ladder, while this form of address was withheld from one's immediate superior.

Socially Evelyn, in particular, seemed to do everything wrong. He was not at his best during the evenings in the club after dinner, though at Lucknow it was actually Fisher who had been reprimanded by Gwynne for not turning up to one such evening. Later Fisher's wife was to get into trouble when her car broke down and a fellow official observed her taking unilateral action. 'Mrs Fisher, Collectors wives do *not* push cars,' she was told. There was always the threat of the 'fishing fleet' at these gatherings – the swarm of marriageable girls who were sent to every social get-together by eager parents. They tried to catch Evelyn, but he told the Fishers that he had no wish to marry any of them and would go home to 'marry one of his own kind . . .'

While at Moradabad he returned with Fisher to Lucknow for the gala week of racing and other festivities. Perhaps Fisher gave him some more social courage, or perhaps he was just getting over some of his shyness. Anyway, he told Katie 'it was the first time I have really enjoyed one of these performances. Young Fisher and I stayed with the Commissioner (Gwynne). Together we roared with laughter, the social activities of Anglo-India being incredibly funny. After years spent as an extremely bad catch in London, it amuses me a lot to see how remarkably polite mamas with marriageable daughters are to me. However I am afraid that the youthful allure of the excellent young bourgeoisie with whom I dance leads me to do nothing more than be exceedingly polite to their faces and then write sarcastically snobbish letters on the subject to Dick Amory [his old Oxford friend then stationed in the army at Meerut]. Also I have been a disgrace by carrying on with the reputedly 'fast girl' of the place, only temporarily out from home, hates India, plenty of powder and paint (such a relief to see it again) and great fun (and blue eyes)! However there is no need to be alarmed as (a) she is going to marry someone else and (b) snobbery that most excellent of failings, protects your son absolutely.'

If Evelyn's solecisms had pained Gwynne or his colleagues during Lucknow week, he had either forgotten them or forgiven them by the time Evelyn departed for a new posting at Meerut. In May, 1928, he wrote to an Under Secretary at the India Office, 'I am glad Baring appreciated my methods of initiation. Without his name and influence he would go far; with them the possibilities of advancement are almost limitless. I like him greatly and have a high regard for both his brains and his character. He lived with me for a year. He has kept extraordinarily fit so far and has thrown himself with zest into the best side of official life in India.'[2]

CHAPTER V

Meerut

Evelyn went to Meerut in March, 1928, as a joint magistrate, known as a 'joint sahib' by all Indians. Meerut was on the main route north to Saharanpur and the foothills of the Himalayas. It was a railway junction with a large Anglo-Indian population, caused mainly by the presence of an English cavalry brigade. It was the centre of good sporting country; grazing areas interspersed with thorn bush, scrub and cactus thickets full of deer, wild pigs, black partridge, quail, sometimes even a panther. The British were in their element, living along wide avenues bordered by old thatched bungalows and spacious gardens full of almond and mango trees and enormous roses. The British cavalry had better bungalows than their Indian army colleagues. They were normally richer. But the civilians had the best houses of all.

Evelyn's District Officer in Meerut was E. H. H. Edye – Harrow and Balliol – who had been a District Officer in the United Provinces since 1906. He was eventually to leave in 1936 having been a District Officer most of this time. Edye possessed altogether a more formidable brain than Gwynne, and had more influence on Baring's thinking. He insisted that his junior officers did their own work. 'If you tell your gardener to shoot a cat, and then hold his hands while he aims at it, you cannot hold him responsible if he misses' was his underlying principle.[1] He believed that most men can be trusted to exercise responsibility and will rise to the occasion if it is offered them. Although he served as a District Officer during a period when that individual's authority was increasingly being eroded by political developments – first the surrender of his direct authority to the overall sanction of a district and municipal board, then the uncertainties of diarchy and approach towards Indian self government – he felt that it was a period when 'a staggering zig zag progress had been made.' In 30 years India had become a happier country. He wrote, 'We are passing on a torch to hands well trained to receive it. The receiving hands might arguably have been trained more quickly and the torch passed sooner. But what is a matter of ten or twenty years in the history of a continent?'[2]

Anglo-Indian life in Meerut was altogether more racy than it had been in Lucknow. During the cool weather there was a dance almost every Saturday night at the club, where tails and white gloves were still the correct dress. The Meerut 'weeks', when they occurred, were periods of hectic social life, with guests living in tents in the bungalow gardens, fancy dress balls, crack polo and pigsticking events.

Again the town was replete with memories of the mutiny, which actually started there. 'Mutiny Line' had bungalows along it with plaques on the gate saying 'Here Mrs . . . and her children were murdered in a well.' At the local church of St Johns there were slots for side-arms on every pew, and British soldiers always took their rifles to expiate the fact that, when the Mutiny broke, the troops were caught in that very church without their arms. Something which would have appealed to Evelyn was a large inscription of the ten commandments on the walls, written in Urdu.

In Meerut Evelyn found himself running the central subdivision of Meerut city the moment he arrived, owing to a shortage of staff. But there were compensations. His authority extended outside the city for a radius of about twenty miles into the countryside, so there was a great deal of rural work involved as well. 'I sit in my court from 11 till 5.30 without a break,' he told Katie. 'I often think of you as I sit with my face gradually going black with rage while two dark gentlemen gibber and squeal at one another in front of me,' he wrote to Ifor Lloyd, an Oxford friend who was reading for the Bar in London. 'I generally wait absolutely quiet and then suddenly without any warning bang my fist down with a most colossal bang on the table, roaring at the top of my voice will you have the goodness to address the court. The dark gentlemen leap about a mile apart, the clerk upsets the inkpot over the files, the witness jumps so high in the air that the *punkah* knocks his fez off, and there is peace in the land.'

As well as being a magistrate, he was also excise officer, rent and revenue officer, surveyor, inspector of police stations, drains, shops. As Mrs Fisher remarked years later, when Evelyn and Fisher were together talking shop it was seldom the beauty of the place, or the collapse of the British Raj which animated them, but the sight of a well covered drain. Evelyn now spent more time out in the countryside than he had done at Lucknow. 'Every village has its mud huts, white mosque or temple, stag-

nant ponds, wells, no grass. Yet an infinite variety induced by
the presence, or not, of water,' he wrote later. In September
they suffered. 'The unfortunate Englishman has been in the
plains since the spring and has few reserves of strength.' Then,
from October until Christmas there was a delightful period of
touring the district, 'when jackals start to brawl at night and
there is the first touch of cold in the early morning ride.' At
night they would pitch their tents by a mango grove and the
chiefs of the local villages would come out to see him and talk
of crops and taxes. He found it much easier to talk to the villagers out in the country, in the evenings, than when they were
overawed by officials during the revenue assessments. Around
Meerut the abject and age-old poverty of the peasants had been
considerably relieved by irrigation. Canals had softened their
worst fears of drought. Prosperity brought confidence, and easier
relations with authority. Further east, 'where the peasants were
not so prosperous, the sight of a man on a horse would make
every woman working in the fields run away as if the devil were
after her.' In the villages round Oudh one was hard put to it to
distinguish the headman from the rest of his impecunious villagers. Here in Meerut, the headman himself would probably
come out to greet him riding a horse himself, totally at ease.
One headman used to write Evelyn long dull poems in Urdu,
which Evelyn used to read and discuss with him at length afterwards. When he left Meerut, he had a pathetic letter from the
headman saying that his successor took no interest in his poetry
and cut his business short.

Evelyn had by then become involved in the world of local poetry
and had attended poetic contests in Lucknow. Urdu poetry was
highly stylised, based on Persian poetry. 'The images are those
of the Persian uplands, not of the hot Indian plain,' he wrote
later. 'The poet praises the rose, the nightingale, and the soft
wind of spring, though in the Indian countryside there are neither
roses, nor nightingales, and the wind of spring is like the blast
of a furnace. To refer to the images of indigenous Indian poetry,
the coming of the rains, the cry of the *poel* or the bloom of the
tesu the red flame of the forest, would have been regarded until
quite recently as a gross breach of taste.'

That year, now that he was settled into Meerut, Katie was
allowed out. As early as March, 1928, Evelyn was suggesting
to her that she find out if the Greys (Lord and Lady Grey and
their two daughters, Nisset and Molly, [Evelyn's eventual bride])

were coming out, as it would be a good plan if she could come out with them.

More detailed instructions followed in April – *first class* under-lined three times, since Evelyn obviously suspected she would try to travel on the lower deck. 'If I hear any talk of a second class passage I will get Alice to do the whole thing. If you push a bit you are certain to be asked to stay at Delhi [with the Vice-roy]. The climate here in the winter is positively cold and even now in late April it is perfectly cool, so bring thick things.'' Katie apparently arrived without them, because she used to go round in an extraordinary quilted coat which Indians rolled themselves up in at night and which looked like two sheets rather shape-lessly sewn together. She said it was forced on her because Evelyn had not warned her it would be cold. To Alice he sent detailed instructions to 'see the old woman properly embarked.' Mean-while, with or without 'pushing', Evelyn had already made his mark with the Viceroy. He went to Simla, found Irwin 'nice man, with a pleasanter staff than Lytton. Simla certainly does give one the impression that one is miles from India,' he added, as if to confirm the unchanging remoteness of the viceregal state.

Katie arrived in January, 1929, for a three month stay. Her visit was looked on as an enormous joke by Evelyn's contemporaries. She travelled round the district in a *tonga* pony cart with a canopy. The Indian servants called her *mamaji* which means honourable mother, and marvelled at the way she spoke about her son, the magistrate. There is one apocryphal story that she distributed coins to children in the street, thus undermining her son's authority; another less apocryphal, that she greeted a caller at Evelyn's bungalow, having just washed her hands for lunch with the words, 'I'm wet, I've been bathing my naughty boy.' She stayed twice with the Fishers, and Mrs Fisher had to buy a new set of underpants for Evelyn because Katie had bought the wrong kind. She also, as Evelyn had predicted, 'got in' at Delhi. The first encounter with Lord Irwin was said to have been at Meerut races, when she was in the next box and he was seen to 'smile wanly' at her over the partition. Anyway, she and Evelyn were both asked to stay. Lady Halifax (then Lady Irwin) recollects that Evelyn was 'very good-looking but extremely shy'.

Evelyn once had to go out on a famine tour, which was one of the most exhausting but rewarding tasks he carried out in Meerut. He was accompanied by his *Tahsildar*, the lowest ranking official in the administration, a Mohammedan of the old school, who 'with his light complexion and neatly painted white beard had the appearance of an old fashioned Frenchman. He was an honest and admirable official but in his heart he looked on Indians as foreigners. His feeling of a somewhat contemptuous benevolence for the country people reminded me of the attitude towards the "fellahin" of a Turkish official of the old regime with whom I once toured the Nile delta. I think that he felt closer to me than to the Hindus of the district; felt that we both represented a conquering race. he of the past and I of the present.'

The Meerut peasant sowed two crops each year. The first, in July, gave him millet and maize for his own food. The second was a winter sowing of wheat and barley which would, if he was lucky, give him enough profit the next year to pay his rent and his taxes, and buy seed corn for the following year. If the rains failed, it would be clear by April when the harvest should be beginning. Then there would be trouble, and the machinery of official famine relief would swing into action. In 1928 in Meerut, the rains failed.

By the following April (1929) it was clear that there might have to be vast remissions of taxes on peasants hit by the ensuing drought. Evelyn was clearly stimulated by the work which he said was 'the oldest that an Indian administrative official has done, under the British, Moguls or old Hindu rulers of Magadha. The facing of a recurring crisis in the never ending fight against the relentless Indian climate, to keep alive a vast agricultural population in the great plains of Northern India.'

They rode out into the countryside through a seemingly endless succession of fields pulverised by the drought. The villagers crowded round them, clamouring for attention. Their insistence exhausted Evelyn. The noise, the dust, the mental effort of trying to apply the same standards to village after village in each of which the scorched wheat and grain seemed at first sight to look just like that in all the others, dazed him. After five days, Evelyn returned to Meerut to make his assessments. It was one of his last tasks because he was shortly to depart on a new posting. But before he did, he one day encountered a crowd of peasants waiting for him outside the Meerut law courts. His recommendations for substantial increases in the remissions had by then gone forward and were accepted. 'I was surrounded and was more warmly thanked than ever before in my life. I was then even more sorry that I would not have the chance to camp in the mango groves of my sub-division during the next winter, for then I should have been on more friendly terms with the villagers, and far closer to them, for they would have realized that I had made some effort to help them in their task of wringing a living in the face of the fierce and uncertain Indian seasons.'

Katie had left before Evelyn went on his famine tour but shortly after she arrived home in May she heard from Evelyn at Simla, the viceregal lodge, where he had again been asked to stay by the Viceroy. He told of the 'most sensational and delightful news.' He had been offered a job for two years as Secretary to the Agent of the Government of India in South Africa. 'You can then come out and live with Sonny (provided you don't interfere) for two years. Little Gwynne made the original suggestion of me. This means that I will definitely be lifted out of the ruck and will come back to a political job. All very nice and a complete change from the *blues* I had last December.'

It was a tremendous opportunity for any young civilian officer who wanted to join the Indian Political Service, and not stay tied to district administration. But, strangely for one so young, and one who was thought (at that stage quite incorrectly) to have been financially so well endowed, Evelyn held out firmly for the best possible terms. There ensued an amazingly laborious correspondence between Delhi and the India Office in London over the details of Evelyn's salary and allowances for South Africa – amazing when one realizes that a great empire had not even then, after 200 years, managed to delegate this kind of detailed administration to the local people on the ground. 'He is one of the most promising of the younger officers in the service and the pay in the junior time scale would seem to be clearly insufficient,' argued Delhi. And a note in the margin of this minute observed, 'If the terms are not sanctioned, I infer from the Viceroy's note that Mr Baring will not go, as his financial prospects in India would be better.'[3] Eventually, after a compromise, his appointment to the political department of the Government of India was gazetted for June 1, 1929, and he sailed for Durban on July 1. Preceding him, a rare harbinger for a young man of his rank, was a letter of introduction from the Viceroy to the Earl of Athlone, Governor General of South Africa, with a similar one to Patrick Duncan, a future Governor General and Minister of the Interior. 'He has just been staying with me in Simla and seems a very nice person. I have good reports of his ability and I hope very much that he will do really well as Secretary to our Agent,' wrote Lord Irwin.⁴ With that, Evelyn arrived in Africa, the continent which was to engulf twenty years of his life.

CHAPTER VI

South Africa's Indians

The Indian problem in South Africa was already sixty years old when Evelyn arrived there, but it showed little sign of abating. It had its origins in South Africa's thirst for cheap labour which had preceded the gold rush and was caused by the abolition of slavery in 1834. This left the Boer sugar-cane growers with a requirement for 35,000 labourers to replace the now emancipated slave labour they had previously been able to import from West Africa. In 1846 W. E. Gladstone, then Colonial Secretary, wrote to the Governor of Cape Colony suggesting the use of convicts to clear the bush, since the natives were apparently unwilling to do the work. However it finally became clear that importing labour was the only answer, and a resolution was passed at a public meeting in Durban in 1851 which declared that it was 'absolutely necessary to introduce foreign free coloured labour' to South Africa. The Indian government finally passed the necessary legislation in 1860, and three months later the first shipment reached Durban, consisting of mechanics, household servants, gardeners, trades people, barbers, carpenters, accountants and grooms – in short, almost anyone except plantation labourers. And this was always to be the case: the immigrants with general and domestic skills and trades outnumbered those intended to work on the plantations, and thus made it inevitable that the Asians would form a settled population and not act merely as contract workers.

Those first Indians who came to South Africa were labourers from Madras. Their descendants still made up the most numerous section among the Indians in the 1920s. They were soon followed by Bombay Mohammedans – merchants who came to trade with the original settlers, selling them *ghi* for their cooking, the sticky rich sweetmeats of their native land, and bangles for the arms and ankles of their wives. When the gold rush started, the number of merchants increased enormously and they soon made up a majority of the Indian population, both in Natal, and further inland in the Transvaal. The Orange Free State never opened its doors to Indian imigration. The seven years after the first shipment saw a tenfold expansion in the sugar output, and immigration figures soared from 6,000 to 30,000.

The first troubles were also not long in coming. With success in commerce came unpopularity. As the Bhara shopkeeper wore a fez on his head he was called an Arab. Men said that the Arab trader 'could live on the smell of an oil rag' – so low were his profits; and they began to talk of an Asian menace. The first consignees who returned to India complained bitterly about the conditions they had worked under in South Africa, and Delhi refused to sanction any more drafts until South Africa could guarantee a better deal. London agreed that Natal's supervision had been 'very lax' and the Colonial Office waded in with the appointment of a Protector of Indian Immigrants in 1870, a precursor of the Agent of the Government of India for whom Evelyn worked in the 1920s.

After eighteen months' further negotiation with Indian immigration still under a ban, a Coolie Commission was formed, and the Indian government accepted the further undertakings proffered by the Natal government. Immigration started again and proceeded more or less unchecked until the South Africans once more became agitated at the number of Indians staying on in the country after their period of indenture had expired. A commission set up in the 1880s confirmed that the great majority of Indians then resident in South Africa had nothing directly to do with work on the plantations, either having completed their indentured work, or having arrived as traders in the first place. The commission of enquiry found that many Europeans were far from keen for future Indian immigrants to be in the country unindentured, and the passage of laws through the Natal legislature started to reflect this growing desire for restriction.

The Europeans seemed to have forgotten how, without Indian labour, Natal as a colony had faced ruin; how it had now become South Africa's leading agricultural state; and how they had given undertakings to the Indian government. Instead they passed laws which further restricted the Indians' civil and political rights, and also inhibited the expansion of their trade. In 1895 a new agreement between South Africa and India stipulated that the coolies must return to India at the end of their second indenture of five years. However, the white South Africans soon again became so agitated that in 1897, in Durban, Europeans rioted at the docks to prevent a further consignment landing from India. On board that ship, accompanied by his wife, was a young Indian lawyer, Mahatma Gandhi.

Gandhi found many disabilities had been put in the way of

61

the Indians, and returned to India to write a series of articles on the situation. The articles met with studied South African disapproval. The restrictions remained; indeed they were extended. Ironically, after the Boer War, the Indians' position did not improve. In his account of the problem, Evelyn gave this explanation:

'When the British came times changed. The young English officer of the Crown colony administration was efficient and insisted on existing laws being enforced. He was incorruptible and could not be appeased by the tactful gift that had usually silenced a too zealous *landrost* of the old days. Finding that the Boer War had worsened rather than improved their position the Indians became bitter. Their condition had been made a *casus belli* by the British in 1899; and had not a corps of Natal Indians served as stretcher bearers in the war under the command of a certain young lawyer from Parbunder named Mohandas Gandhi?

This bitterness began to become a question of importance for Whitehall. These were the days of the early nationalist movement in India, of the first great popular agitation. The India of the new century was becoming very willing to listen to the cry of her sons in the Transvaal. The young lawyer Gandhi had become interested in their difficulties after the peace of Vereeniging. One cold winter's night when he was travelling up to the Transvaal a European police inspector kicked him out of his railway carriage at the Natal town of Pietermaritzburg; he remained shivering on the platform till dawn. It was an unlucky night for the British empire.'

Gandhi initiated a passive resistance movement against the authorities – trial runs for his later campaigns against the British rule in India. Agitation increased. All Indian immigration was stopped in 1911, but the restrictions on those that remained continued. After prolonged talks between the two governments, thousands were repatriated to India, but – as could have been foretold – many more thousands remained and went on expanding, trading, profiting. The more profitable and prosperous Indians started to move out of the shanty towns into the smarter residential areas, and this caused resentment and insecurity among the Europeans.

However, though Gandhi – after organising protests for several years – himself left South Africa to pursue freedom on a more illustrious stage, the troubles for South African Indians continued to grow. After the First World War panic started among the Europeans, who feared that the Indians would swamp the country. Indians were deprived of the vote in Natal and Transvaal. In the latter they were also made to register. Finally, for the whole Union, it was proposed that all Indians should be segregated. In 1924 a further piece of discriminatory legislation aroused the warning of General Smuts, then in Opposition, 'We shall gather on our heads the hatred of the whole of Asia; we shall feel the weight of that hatred in the years to come. . . . We, a handful of whites, are right fencing ourselves, first with an inner ring of black hatred and beyond that with a ring of hatred of the whole of Asia. The Colour Bar Bill is a firebrand flung into a haystack.'[1]

It was this measure which brought matters to a head. One of the first messages Lord Irwin received as Viceroy was from his opposite number in South Africa, Lord Athlone, the Governor General, urging a conference between their two governments which Athlone hoped would lead to the progressive amelioration of the lot of the Indians in South Africa.[2] Capetown was eventually settled on as the venue for the conference, and Irwin chose as his representative, Sir Srinivasa Sastri. After the conference, Athlone wrote again to Irwin, 'There may still be a tendency towards repressive measures by provincial legislatures, but the Union Government, having determined on a liberal policy, will use its best endeavours to keep within bounds.'[3] He went on to urge the immediate appointment of an official Agent of the Indian Government, since public opposition to the Capetown agreement was already gaining ground. He reacted with pleasure in May, 1927, when Sastri's appointment was announced.[4]

The terms of the agreement were that the South African government was to drop its plans for segregation and to give money to Indian education, which had always been neglected. In return the ban on further immigration was to remain and an attempt was to be made to encourage repatriation of Indians by means of a bonus. (The repatriation scheme worked quite well for its first two years but then, as with the other measures, its effectiveness petered out.)

Sastri's post was considered especially important, according to the Viceroy, as 'South African Indians have no recognised or effectual spokesman at present to interpret their views to the Union Government.'[5] His duties were 1) to interpret the wishes of the Indian community to the South African government; 2) to help the Union government with its policy of 'upliftment' of the

63

resident Indian population which had now been officially
affirmed; and 3) to watch over the new scheme of assisted emigration. He was to avoid interfering in the administration of the
scheme, or giving South African Indians the impression that he
was actively cooperating in the policy of reducing Indian
numbers.

'He must also gradually educate opinion,' continued the Viceroy in his explanatory memorandum to the Secretary of State
for India, 'especially in Natal, to regard the Indian as a permanent element of population whose general upliftment would provide the only sure safeguard for maintenance of western standards.
The person selected must therefore have considerable tact and
savoir faire and must be given status which would enable him to
meet Union ministers and other important leaders of opinion
on a footing of equality both officially and socially.'

According to Evelyn, Sastri did much to raise the status of
India and the Indians in South African eyes. He used to refer to
them as the Jews of Africa, who would be again condemned to
become 'untouchable' if they had to return to India. Sastri insisted on his secretary being a fully fledged member of the ICS.
The first secretary, Evelyn's predecessor, was called Tyson. Sastri
and he took up their appointment together in 1928.

Evelyn arrived to succeed Tyson in Durban a year later. His
first impression to Alice was as follows, 'All the young Dutchmen
are now growing up nationalists. The time will soon come they
say, when every Dutchman will vote nationalist. This will mean
a party division on purely racial lines. Such a division would, I
imagine, continue till racialism is forced to die by the emergence
of a really good full-blooded native menace. The latter, I should
think, is bound to come eventually.'

Evelyn expected his appointment to last for not more than two
years – possibly eighteen months – at the end of which he hoped
to be home for his first leave in Britain for five years. He found
the work nothing like as hard as it was in India. To his sorrow
he was condemned to spend most of the year in Durban. There
was a moment of nostalgia, he told Katie, when he wished that
he was 'back in the dust and smells and the odd patches of colour
of the old Indian plain. I can see that I will certainly have to go
back.' His regrets were somewhat softened when he received definite news that he had been gazetted as a member of the Foreign
and Political Service of India. 'So I have stepped rather neatly
in almost without a struggle,' he told Katie. 'Of course I now

64

feel rather sorry that I shall never see my old friends in the UP again. But Meerut wasn't typical and I should have sung a different tune when posted in the Allahabad or Benares districts.'

To Alice he was more expansive about his future, than he was to his mother. He had heard that Barings were keen to have him in the bank, and this had been confirmed to him before he left Delhi, in a meeting with Arthur Villiers, then one of the partners.

'Well now this is interesting. When my mother was in India I was complaining a good deal. Since she left however I became reconciled. Also when I left Meerut I found that I really was immensely popular among the Indian population and received a send off (after only just a year there) such as barely any officers ever get, and this, I flatter myself, without pandering to Indian sentiment in any way.

'The long and the short of it is, then, that I have, modesty apart, a decided talent for district work and would always be a highly successful district officer. Whether I would have the same success in semi-political work in Delhi, where I would dislike the suburban and intriguing life, less hot but less pleasant than a station, where there is not intrigue and there is a close and fascinating touch with the life of the country and often good sport, I do not know. That is why I decided on the compromise of the political service, which would offer the sort of life I should much enjoy and great variety. On the other hand it leads to no very high post in India itself, but I do not think there are many real prospects left for a civilian in India. Does fascination of country, people, language, customs make up for a lifetime abroad with no plum at the end of it? I want to return to India for six months political work before leave.'

As soon as he settled down in South Africa he was making arrangements for Katie to join him there. 'You may arrive in any boat that reaches Capetown January 16 to February 7. So there. I am being very kind to you as I had never meant to let you come out so early. Unnecessary to bring any bedding, nor too much luggage since we live in hotels and want to travel light.' Perhaps he felt that he had indeed been too kind. The next letter said, 'If you arrive before February I shall see to it that you are prohibited from landing as an undesirable immigrant of Jewish origin. So be good and don't be a nuisance. By the way in South Africa it is necessary for dogs of uncertain character to be muzzled so you had better purchase a muzzle. Your vv loving E. ps I do believe in being polite to one's mother don't you?' Or again, the

C

next month, 'My fond mama. How are you you old trout? You are too unintelligent to understand politics here. This letter seems to be nothing but abuse but you deserve it. Your vv loving E.' He commented on some books she sent him, in which one character, 'an excellent fellow' referred to his mother as a 'hell bitch', 'an expression I had not thought of before but find somewhat appropriate. . . . A small but irritating bird tells me that for more mails than one I have not written to my fond mama.' With mail like that one would have thought that she would not have missed one or two – but down into the book they went, every one!

Five months after he arrived Sir Karma Reddhi, Sastri's successor as Agent, became ill, and left for sick leave in India in December, 1929. Evelyn thus found himself in charge of the Agency, performing full duties for an initial period of three months. After some correspondence between Athlone and Irwin and between Evelyn and Irwin, his predecessor, Tyson, was then sent out for a month to help cope with a particular difficulty brought on by the decision of the Johannesburg municipality to attempt to segregate the entire Indian population of the mining city who were, officially, in illegal occupations of their premises. At first Evelyn thought that this would only affect a few Indians, since the great majority should have protection under an Agreement of 1919. It then emerged that the problem was of an altogether different dimension. Apparently, wrote Evelyn, 'there was an unknown but probably large body of shopkeepers who had either started fresh in trade during the preceding ten years or had lost their legal protection through moving to a new township after 1919, for in the city of Johannesburg there were in the eyes of the law as many as eighteen townships. All was alarm and confusion. It became clear that the only method of discovering how many shopkeepers would be affected by the threatened action of the municipality or by a bill passed in Parliament with similar intent would be by a shop by shop visit.' So Evelyn went on his first visit to Johannesburg to meet the leaders of the Indian community.

He had to contend with deep internal divisions between the Transvaal British-India Association and the Congress Party. 'The ill feeling between the two bodies was the curse of the Transvaal Indians,' wrote Evelyn. 'Even in moments of greatest danger it was never completely healed. For it was the reappearance on foreign soil of an ingrained habit of Indians – the habit of splitting into parties on purely personal issues that is to be found throughout India.' A number of small holders presented no trouble because they came from close to the place of Gandhi's birth and regarded his word as law. In the situation which then confronted them, this was extremely useful to Evelyn. 'Whatever the verdict of history may be on that strange character [Gandhi] when taken as a whole,' he wrote, 'it will probably be agreed that on two questions – those of the untouchables and the South African Indians, his motives were disinterested and his opinions sensible. He always taught, even during the time of his imprisonment, that the Indians of South Africa must develop a truly South African outlook and that if ever they hoped to attain the full rights of South African citizenship they must cease to look on themselves as strangers in a strange country. After the 1926 agreement he also urged them to look to the Indian government in moments of stress. So in South Africa I found support from the natural enemies of England and often opposition from those elements (Muslims) which in Bombay itself are the Government's support.'

Eventually the enquiries ended. Evelyn submitted extensive and detailed despatches to Delhi and the Indian case was heard in South Africa before a Select Committee of the legislative assembly. In spite of this, the Bill, when it was subsequently published, was extremely harsh, providing for the segregation in locations, or possibly in special quarters of existing towns, of all Indians who were in illegal occupation of their current premises. The enquiry had shown that there were thousands of these. The Indian government stirred; and the outcome was another full dress conference in Capetown early in 1932, with Evelyn in attendance. The Indian delegation again included Sastri, 'an impressive figure with a long grey coat, high white turban and the finely cut features of a Tamil Brahmin, who understood exactly when to intervene in the discussion and exactly how to make just the right appeal to the generosity of a new and sensitive nation.'

The result of the conference was a masterpiece of negotiation. It had started with the South Africans holding all the cards, complaining that the repatriation provisions of the 1926 agreement had not been properly observed, and threatening to repeal the agreement altogether. The Indians, on the face of it, had little to offer other than more effective assistance for the repatriation schemes. However, according to Evelyn, sitting in on the conference, 'very cautiously the word 'Brazil' was breathed. The

South Africans immediately took the bait. In recent years many shiploads of Japanese had passed through Capetown on their way to Brazil. They were apparently flourishing in the hot coastal regions of that vast and underdeveloped republic.' A new agreement was thereafter quickly concluded in which the Indian government undertook to assist any scheme the Union government might be able to concoct for Indian emigration to Brazil, in return for the South Africans taking no action against the Transvaal traders until the case of all those accused of illegal occupation had been enquired into by an impartial commission. It was a surprising result, but, in the event, fruitless. Brazil had not been consulted in advance, and nobody, least of all the South Africans, seemed to have calculated how long the independent commission would take to enquire into thousands of individual cases. When Evelyn left South Africa a few months later, the Brazilians had already, politely but firmly, indicated that they would not welcome any immigration of Indians to their country. As for the commission of enquiry, it was still sitting four or five years later. Evelyn was to return in 1944 to find the position of South Africa's Indians had deteriorated still further.

Evelyn's life in South Africa was not all spent in the slums of Johannesburg. His mother was with him for most of the last two years of his three year tour. The South African government divided its time equally between Capetown and Pretoria, which meant that everybody who had official dealings either had to have two homes or spend a great deal of time in hotels. Moreover, in addition to Pretoria and Capetown, he also had to frequent Durban a great deal. And where he went, his mother came too. There is a fairly well authenticated story about Evelyn and his mother being asked to leave their hotel in Durban after a particularly rowdy night, though at first glance it might seem strange that the eviction order applied to old Lady Cromer as well. The incident concerned an aspidistra, which was growing in the passage of the hotel. Evelyn's Oxford friends – Dick Amory, Roger Makins and Alec Dunglass – had formed a club whose rules stipulated that whenever one of them saw an aspidistra he must, on a point of honour, destroy it and send proof of the destruction to the other members. His assault on this aspidistra may have been fortified by the fact that it was then 'July Week' in Durban, when everybody, including Lord Athlone, the Governor General, and his wife Princess Alice were there for the races and there would have been much jollification. The Athlones heard about

it through the grapevine of their ADCs who were friends of
Evelyn's, and, according to Princess Alice much later, were
amazed and amused at Lady Cromer's eviction. It was one more
element in Katie's eccentric reputation.

Considering Evelyn's youth and Katie's age, many of their
friends were surprised at what good companions they appeared
to be. One should not get the wrong impression from the heavy
banter of Evelyn's letters. When he was with Katie he was always
extremely considerate and was prepared to spend a lot of time
with her. Not that Katie was a burden. She developed her own
circle of friends in South Africa and, in spite of her years, was still
very mentally alert. Her appearance, as always, was misleading:
very untidy, dressed in black, stockings in wrinkles round her
ankles, by then extremely shortsighted, an unexpected figure to
find as the mother of one of the most eligible young men in South
Africa.

Lady Cromer's presence did not inhibit her son from nearly
getting married. It was the only romantic attachment he seems
to have formed in his life, apart from his subsequent marriage to
Molly Grey. The girl in question was called Mary Cloete. She
was a tall, lissom, auburn-haired girl of striking looks whom Princess Alice was alleged to have said walked like a native woman!
She was unusual meat for a young man of Evelyn's apparently
boisterous appetite. She was a good dancer – particularly of the
Tango, then all the rage in Europe, where it was said she had
even taught the Prince of Wales – she sang, she played the guitar,
she painted.

Mary Cloete and Evelyn met first at a dance at the Cape. They
probably continued to meet casually at the numerous parties
given then, not least by the Athlones. Apart from belonging to a
rich, old Dutch family, Mary was also connected to what one
might call the free-masonry of Government House society through
her sister, who was married to Sir Herbert Stanley, then Governor
of Ceylon. The first prolonged period of contact which she had
with Evelyn was when they were joined by another man, Peter
Buxton, for a trip to the Orange Free State in Buxton's ancient
second-hand Buick. It turned out to be not quite a classic love
triangle – more an isoceles one – since Mary alone of the three
appeared to be emotionally unaffected. Their trip eventually took
them on horseback to some caves in Basutoland – the Buick
having by then fallen victim to the heavy going. At the end of
the trip Buxton proposed to Mary, who refused him and professed

to have been totally unaware of any emotional undercurrents during the trip. If that was really so, the two young men must have remained remarkably in control of their emotions, since she heard much later that Evelyn was already then of a like mind, but had nobly ceded first opportunity to Peter Buxton on the grounds that they were, after all, travelling in *his* car! However, Evelyn was to get his chance too.

Later on he went to stay with Mary at her mother's house – a farm close to the sea near George, Cape Province. Together they explored the countryside, clambering down rocks, swimming in small bays. Mary drew a portrait of Evelyn one evening. According to Mary, much later, their friendship developed without any overt sign of emotion on Evelyn's part. Then one day they took a long walk to a deserted bathing beach. Evelyn had been telling Mary about his prospects on the North West Frontier in India, and saying that his family wanted him to go back to the bank in London. He turned to her and asked what she thought he should do. Why, there was only one choice, she replied. 'Back to the frontier and your exciting life.' He looked at her rather strangely. When they got back to the car he asked her to marry him. She refused. She told him she was already unofficially betrothed to a young man called Robin Byng, who was then her brother-in-law's ADC in Ceylon, but because of his uncertain prospects they had kept it a secret. Evelyn received this in silence, and sat quite still in the car. When he broke the silence he said they must never meet again; it would be too much for him. He dropped her off at the house, collected his luggage and drove straight on. His hoped-for embargo on their meeting was, alas, not to be. Shortly afterwards, Mary was asked to go on a camping weekend with the Birch Reynardsons (he was Controller of the Athlone's household). They had apparently decided that it was time Evelyn and Mary should get married and Evelyn was asked along too. It must have been most painful for him. They did meet again once or twice when Evelyn returned to South Africa in style years later, but the scars of his romance, if there were any, had by then healed well.

Meanwhile, Evelyn had been involved in some protracted negotiations over his future in India. As early as February, 1930, when he had only been in South Africa for about eight months, the Foreign and Political department in Delhi made an official request for his arrival with them in September of that year, to enable him to complete six months training and pass his exams in the IPS before going on leave in the spring of 1931. There were many wrangles, and eventually Evelyn did not leave South Africa for India until July, 1932. In spite of pressure from the Political Department to have him on the North West Frontier as soon as possible, the South African section had won the day. 'The Indian community in South Africa is greatly agitated after the passage of the Transvaal Bill,' said the Under Secretary. 'The Indian public in India and in South Africa would never forgive us if the Indian cause in South Africa were to suffer for want of the advice and intervention of an experienced officer.'[6] Was this another tribute to Evelyn's work or just the rhetoric of administrative convenience?

CHAPTER VII

Dreary Dismael – North West Frontier

Evelyn's last tour in India was at Der Ismael Khan, the centre of the southernmost district of the North West Frontier Province. His parish was four thousand square miles, bordering the kind of rugged country which is the stuff of an Indian romantic's dreams. On the northern edge where the Bhuttani and Marwat ranges of the Himalayas; to the west lay the Sirani and Silaiman hills; and on the eastern edge flowed the Indus, dividing the province from the Punjab and beyond it the great northern plain of India which Evelyn had left three years before.

The North West Frontier Province had been formed by Lord Curzon when he was Viceroy. It consisted of the six frontier districts of the Punjab and six tribal areas. The Indian Political Service carried out all the administration in the province, but it is fair to say that there was much less labour involved in the administration and control of the wilder tribes in the province than there had been in the painstaking and detailed administrative work on which Evelyn had been reared in the United Provinces. The Political Officer spent more of his time on intelligence work than on agriculture. Collection of revenue as in the UP, was replaced by the distribution of payments to informers and other loyalists. A day spent in the open, hawking or shooting partridges, was likely to be just as rewarding, in terms of intelligence, as a day spent in court or sifting through files in the office. Indeed life on the Frontier in the 1930s had changed little in thirty years. As Philip Woodruff writes, 'Here the tribes were still treated like tigers in a national park. They could kill whatever they liked in the park; they risked a bullet if they came outside and took the village cattle.'[1]

The appeal of the Frontier was still seductive to a particular type of officer. Woodruff says that no one suffered more continuously than a Frontier officer from 'that slight mental derangement that afflicted every officer throughout India more or less'; where the company and conversation of colleagues back on the plains were clouded by 'random thoughts and pictures from the world the officer had just left, where it mattered supremely if a hare crossed your path from left to right or the reverse. . . . To some

Frontier officers, the *jirga* (tribal council) and the blood feud were always the reality, the clubs and the polo tournament the shadows.'

The Der Ismael Khan (DIK) district had three towns in it and four hundred villages, with a total population of about a quarter of a million, most of whom were Muslims. The largest group was the Pathans, living mostly in the hills, but in addition the district contained a melting pot of tribes – Baluchis, Jats, Marwats, Bhuttanis, Rajputs, Khokhars, Arams, Aroras, Shaikhs, Khattris, Mochis, Tarkhans, Kumhars, Chibras, Kutanas, and Machis.

It was a wild district with only the barest subsistence economy, based on buffaloes, camels and sheep. The only commercial significance of the area was that it lay across the trade route between India and Khorasan and was therefore passed through by the merchant caravans from Afghanistan. The town of DIK was a small one surrounded by a mud wall with nine gates in it. It also served as the winter headquarters of the Derajet Brigade of the Indian army, consisting of one cavalry regiment and three infantry battalions. In addition to the Deputy Commissioner, there was an Assistant Commissioner (Evelyn) and three extra assistants at certain times. Evelyn's social life was clearly going to be limited; indeed as a posting it was the perfect contrast, not only to the life he had lately led in South African salons and in the back rooms of Indian merchants on the Rand, but also to the refinement and gaiety of British India which he had encountered at Lucknow and Meerut.

On August 14 he arrived at DIK, having taken five hours to cross the Indus in flood. He found he was staying with the District Commissioner and immediately entered fully into the spirit of the rather narrow, rarefied social life of the station. There were only five or six 'civilians', the other Europeans all being soldiers. Life was definitely Victorian; long trousers were *de rigeur* for tennis and week-ends were celebrated with paper chases.

He was at once taken with the district, because, even more than in the United Provinces, he found that the problems which were confronting the natives were ones which had remained unchanged since the time of Alexander the Great. 'The prevailing impression of DIK,' he wrote, 'is one of dust and mud. Its most striking characteristic is the dust cloud that hangs over the whole district. This cloud marks the most important feature of the life of this land. From it may be realized something of its past, and

73

may be guessed yet more of its future. The cloud is the topsoil being blown into the air by the wind. For DIK is gradually suffering the fate known to many lands in antiquity and appearing in modern times to threaten great tracts of the new world. The fertile soil not bound by the roots of sufficient growing things is disappearing. It is being blown away as was blown the soil of the populous lands in Central Asia and Eastern Persia where there is now only sand; as the overcropped prairie states of America and the overgrazed native reserves of Africa are disappearing. A desert is being formed. Slowly but surely since long before the days of its Baluch conquerors the central fact of the life of the district has been a struggle to win for the fields the water that flows in hundreds of streams across the plain or into the Indus from the surrounding hills. This water from the wild highlands to the west never flows smoothly or regularly. For ten months a mere trickle will pass through the thirsty lands. Then suddenly there comes a roaring flood. To tame the flood is a battle; to carry the flood water, rich in silt, is an art – an ancient art.'

Irrigation was achieved by a series of flood dams constructed in the dry weather. Water dominated the culture; it had permeated their vernacular; it created their crops, caused every quarrel, every joy, was the subject of every petition. It promoted riots, and violence. It had divided the people of the district into two types, moulded by the struggles of centuries and by the unresolvable conflict of interest between them. There were the hill people who wanted to keep the water dammed up as high as possible, so that they could siphon most of it off for their crops; and there were the valley peasants, who wanted the hill dams to be broken as quickly as possible.

For centuries the dam-building, which was accompanied by great ceremonial and much rejoicing each time one was completed, had served to hold the water more or less effectively, save in the case of exceptional floods which were too fierce and too high for the dams and broke through them, carrying all the precious silted waste into the wide-flowing Indus. In the few years before Evelyn had arrived in the district this kind of flood had been growing more frequent, not through natural causes but for political reasons.

The area had quite recently been pacified to the north west, where the Waziristanis had remained much less malleable than their less warlike neighbours, the Baluchis. In Waziristan there had been a considerable campaign during the early twenties, but even at its conclusion, the villages on the plain in Evelyn's district still suffered from Waziri raids, kidnappings for ransom, and other depredations such as sheep and goat rustling – the stuff of life on any primitive border. The British retaliated with a tactic familiar to the redcoats who had tried to pacify the highlands after the rebellion of 1715 – building roads like General Wade and positioning isolated forts deep in tribal territory. The forts needed wood, and got it, at the expense of all the hillsides for miles around, denuded by tribesmen eager for a quick profit. The result of so much felling was disastrous. It became more so each year as the force of the torrents down the hills became ever greater, carrying down more earth to silt up the water courses in the plains, and denuding the bare surfaces of the hills so that each season's flow was worse than the last.

'It became a familiar sight to see a pathetic procession of black clad women carrying pitchers and leading donkeys, or camels loaded with jars and old petrol tins, walking many miles from their villages to fetch drinking water,' wrote Evelyn. 'The only remedy lay in the mountains, in the sowing of new vegetation. But no government dared to forbid the Mahsud clansmen to cut wood on their own hillsides.'

However, the district was not always so desolate. Evelyn found joy in the spectacle of the great caravans of traders from Afghanistan – the Pawindas, or walkers who came from the barren stony land round Kandahar. In the autumn their caravans would come down into India, bringing with them their women and children, whom they left encamped throughout the DIK district while they went off in twos and threes to reclaim the money they had lent the previous year. 'There are few scenes more thrilling than the sight of a caravan debouching into the plain from the great pass that cuts the mountains between Southern Waziristan and the heights of Takht-i-suliman,' he wrote. 'The camels still have their long shaggy coats. On their backs are piled skins and dried fruits. In and out of their legs run big prairie dogs. The old men and the women ride, the girls and the younger men walk by the camels. As they see their destination they leap in the air, clap their hands and yell with excitement, the dogs bark, the camels grunt and gobble and rear up on their hind legs and the noise is terrific. The women are mostly unveiled and often good looking, the men are often fairheaded, red faced, looking like friendly bears.'

To Katie, 'Once in the hills one is right away from India and in the atmosphere of Central Asia. You have the feel of a land of the soil, little vegetation, and wandering people. The tribesmen come up to expectation. They are incredibly picturesque, also incredibly dirty. I used to set out with them just before dawn at a pace that was almost a shuffly run. They stopped to pray as the first light came into the sky, laying down their rifles but with their bodies strapped round with cartridges. In the evening they would sometimes dance round the fire letting off their rifles. Their leaders would come up and gossip and give one a round loaf of bread which they had baked with a stone inside it. Altogether a great change from your meek and mild Hindu friends.'

Evelyn was always strongly affected by signs of the submersion of old cultures, or the struggle of ethnic and religious enclaves to survive the dominance of a conqueror. He was also fascinated by Islam and its powerful effect on Asiatic peoples – the rigid and lucid doctrines that the Mullah propounded from the mosque with a determination that brooked no dissent. He recognised its virtues – the insistence on the equality of all true believers, its rejection of idolatry, the fairness of its laws; but he was also struck by the totality of its indoctrination of conquered races, not just in their religious beliefs, but in their everyday life, their literature, their architecture.

On another occasion he visited an old hill station, Shaikh Budir, which stood on a spur dividing the two plains of Dera. He found it an eerie and rather depressing experience. Forty years before it had been a flourishing hill station peopled by the scions of British India. It was in fact the spot from which, in Kipling's poem, 'A Code of Morals', the young officer heliographed his wife 'Don't dance or ride with General Bangs, a most immoral man.' But the arrival of the motor car had enabled the British to go further and higher, and Shaikh Budir stood deserted though intact for Evelyn's inspection – rows of neat bungalows, the rest house, the racquets courts, the church (naturally), and in the very centre, a ridiculous and strangely pathetic reminder of the gaities of Victorian life, a bandstand. 'A single watchman lives in a corner of one of the bungalows and his goats graze on the few green things that grow round the houses. But among all the surrounding hills there is not a single native house. In the hush of a hot and brilliant noon the sense of solitude and hopelessness of the efforts of the English in India is tremendous.'

In January, 1933, Evelyn wrote to Katie, 'My good woman. I get leave in April. The future must then be seriously considered.' Evelyn's ultimate decision on his future in India was eventually decided for him by his health, but at this stage he was still undecided about what to do with his life. The old attractions of life in India were still there, much as he had described them in his letter to Alice Shaw-Stewart some years earlier when in South Africa. On the other hand he recognised that life on the frontier, fascinating though it was, was not going to lead him very far. British India itself was only destined to remain in being another 12 years, and though he obviously could not have predicted so short a life, nothing about the politics of India while he had served in the ICS could have dissuaded him from the view which he had held from the start, that he was taking part in the closing chapter of British rule. Then also he was nearly 30, unmarried and not particularly well off. He was clearly not going to marry a British-Indian — his prejudices in that direction remained unchanged from the days when he had lampooned the antics of the Meerut 'fishing fleet'. Nor would he want to subject a wife 'of his own kind' to life in a hill station, where she would not even have the fascination of the job to mitigate the association with what was essentially a dying concern.

Besides, his mother, now in her seventies, was not getting any healthier. She had contracted diabetes, and was actually one of the first patients to be tried out with an experimental course in the new drug insulin, then being developed at St Thomas's Hospital. On the whole, it seemed very probable that Evelyn was not going to come back to India after his first long leave in England for nearly seven years. But he had not reached a final decision when he left.

He was not to leave without a drama. To Katie, 'The other day when the district officer was away in Peshawar, the prisoners in the jail started to fight one another. In the space of about five minutes, one faction had killed six of the other faction. Your son arrived after the fight was over, but when the victorious faction were waving various implements about, and nearly the whole jail had run away. With his usual caution he sat on the top of a wall and admonished the rioters in indifferent Pushtu. They eventually went inside. I and the English police officer then had to run the jail for the next three days while our Indian jail superintendent recovered his equilibrium. It was great fun. We took some of the stuffing out of them by cutting off all rations for 24 hours which was not popular as it was Ramadan. However, I was a great success with the inmates who were all habituals and about the worst in India as the Pathans are the most violent criminals and the worst of them are sent here as it is the only jail in the province that is not in a Pathan town.'

Evelyn's account of the riot is in fact very underplayed in this letter to his mother. What actually happened was that the jailer had absconded in terror with the keys of the arsenal on his person, so Evelyn could get no arms. He and the young policeman got ladders, climbed to the top of the 12 foot wall, and looked down on the inside into a sea of excitement and noise, with six corpses on the ground. Using a pencil inside his jacket pocket he pretended he had a revolver and, when he had quieted them enough to make himself heard, threatened to shoot anyone who had not returned to his cell within one minute. They went back in and then Evelyn and the police officer had to jump down and disarm the rioters one by one. He used to say it was an example of the 'family' or 'tribal' feud – having killed six successfully honour was satisfied, and they were not bent on murdering a British officer as well. Everybody was very impressed. The Nawab of Dera told Olaf Caroe, then Chief Secretary of the Province, that Evelyn had 'behaved with the courage and calmness one would expect of the son of an earl.'

On March 9, 1933, after six and a half years service, Evelyn left India and proceeded on his first long home leave of six months. He was not to return. Whatever secret thoughts about returning to a new posting he may have had they were outweighed by the double effect of the death of his mother, which occurred while he was sailing home, and the onset of amoebic dysentery while he was on leave. He resigned from the ICS on grounds of ill health.

But the experience of his years in India was both invaluable and unforgettable. It dominated his approach to the colonial problems which confronted him later. It inculcated a feeling for the peasant, for the tribesman, for the chief, and for their perennial problems of custom, cultivation, religion. It meant that his perspective was always focused on the land, and on rural administration. Although the niceties of constitutional politics and diplomacy more often than not preoccupied him in his future governorships, they never entirely distracted him from the land and from the native; nor did they deter him from carrying out that ritual, but basic task of British Indian administration –

touring – which Evelyn managed to continue doing, often with startling effect, from whatever governor's office he was inhabiting. And yet one is left with a feeling that his Indian experience, for all the great benefits and the wisdom he acquired, was somehow incomplete. He was a man who elsewhere left a great mark. India left *its* mark on him but there is nothing of Evelyn left in India. He did not return to the subcontinent until 1972, when he stopped over at Delhi airport while the plane refuelled on its way to Singapore. He rushed out of the plane to try out his laboured and under-used Urdu on the stall keepers crowding round the airport buildings. They looked on uncomprehendingly.

CHAPTER VIII

Marriage and
a Damaged Liver

The six years between Evelyn's return from India and the outbreak of war (when he went to work in the Foreign Office) make up a surprisingly scrappy period in a life which is otherwise composed of long stretches of sustained development and application. But, though scrappy, they contained events which gave rise to some of the most important and lasting influences in Evelyn's life.

His mother died; he got married; he suffered from and was cured of an illness whose after-effects condemned him for the rest of his life to teetotallism and a strict diet. He developed his love of and interest in wild flowers, birds and rockclimbing; he became familiar with high finance and the economics of developing countries; he accquired a more than nodding acquaintanceship with the world of high politics and of Whitehall. Yet for a man who clearly liked to concentrate his mind, who enjoyed getting into a new subject and mastering it, whose 'leisure' pursuits tended to require strenuous mental or physical exertions; these years, spent half in illness and half without a real job, must have been basically sorry ones indeed.

The first blow was the death of his mother on March 4, 1933. At the time Evelyn was in transit from India. Katie died of gangrene in the feet. Her friends suspected that it was caused by a dirty needle with which she used to inject herself with insulin. Paradoxically the insulin treatment had already saved her life. Before she took to it, Katie had been on a strict diet for her diabetes, and it had nearly finished her. 'It may be destroying the diabetes, but it's killing the patient too,' she confided despairingly to a relation.

Her death left a large gap in Evelyn's life, accentuated by the fact that, at the age of thirty, he was returning to a country from which he had been absent for nearly seven years. His Oxford friends might have scattered and got married; and the Ardgowan group, where would they be now? He went to Ardgowan for the summer, during much of which he was feeling ill and low with the amoebic dysentery which was later diagnosed, and which presumably he had caught before he left India.

The author's mother

Evelyn with his father,
Lord Cromer, in 1912

Oxford, summer 1924, taken by Roger Makins (Lord Sherfield). From left to right, *front row*, George Newman, Dick Heathcoat-Amory; *back row*, Niall Rankin, Alec Dunglass (Lord Home), Chris Pitman and Evelyn Baring.

Molly Grey when engaged to Evelyn

Evelyn aged 38 on his appointment to Southern Rhodesia

Above: On Table Mountain in 1948
Below: A family group with Smuts on the left and Van Rynveld the South African Chief of Staff, on the right.

At the end of the summer he returned to London and stayed with his old Oxford and Meerut friend, Dick Heathcote Amory. He joined the bank at Barings. His early work there was hardly onerous for a man who had ruled over vast areas and thousands of people. His responsibilities were elusive, to say the least. He had to read old files and watch the preparation of new issues. He worked with other young trainee bankers – many years his junior – in the acceptance department of the bank. At a time of economic depression the work was desultory. It was made more so by his ill health.

At Christmas, 1934, he went to Northumberland to stay at Howick, with Lord and Lady Grey, whose elder daughter, Molly, had long been a friend of his. Afterwards he used to joke that he always knew what he had been asked there for. On the last day of his stay Molly and he became engaged to be married. Evelyn, who had never had a real home life, was marrying into a closely knit family. Molly and her younger sister, Nisset, were inseparable; indeed the whole Grey family gave visitors the impression that, at Howick, they did not really want or need anyone from outside to enrich their lives. The family was church-going, intellectual, well-read and proud of their standards. Compared with other aristocratic households of the time theirs was modest in style, and perhaps also, for the daughters, a little sheltered. Of the two sisters Nisset was the botanist and horsey one, Molly the more musical. Of course many young men came to Howick – braving, it was said, Lady Grey's capacity for making them feel frightened or uneducated or both – but Molly, who was very attractive and an heiress (since Lord Grey had no son) and had had many suitors before Evelyn came along, had acquired something of a frightening reputation herself, with a sharpish tongue, and a tendency to react with coolness towards any sign of ardour.

Their marriage started uncertainly. Evelyn was terribly shy and gauche for his age. His years in India had not equipped him for the English social life of the 1930s. He had no small talk, and no fashionable social graces, just rather rugged good manners which were still ingrained in him from his days at Winchester. Although he was in his early thirties, his only previous romantic experience had been that impromptu and unexpected proposal to Mary Cloete. Molly, on the other hand, was much more assured, and likely to be impatient with Evelyn's gaucherie. Contemporaries recall that the marriage was not self-evidently a love-match, though they all agree that it ultimately became one. It

was not until after the death of Nisset in Canada during the war,
and during the long years alone with Evelyn in Africa away from
her parents at Howick, that the bond between Molly and her
husband was forged into a union of colossal strength and certainty. Though she was always recognised as a person in her own
right, she filled to perfection her position as Evelyn's consort
throughout Africa.

Evelyn's illness continued to sap his will but now that he was
married he had the drive of his in-laws behind him, and Lady
Grey soon stepped in to take a hand. She sent him to a doctor
at Bristol who diagnosed his amoebic dysentery and prescribed
doses of ematine – a kind of poison which is supposed to poison
the amoeba but not the patient. It is a dangerous treatment which
was then in its infancy – even now patients have to stay in hospital
while they receive ematine. Evelyn had to return to a Bristol
nursing home for the final treatment almost immediately after
he and Molly were married in May, 1935. The treatment left him
with a damaged liver, of which he nearly died and on account of
which he remained low and lethargic. Lunching, at this time, with
an old Oxford friend, Hugh Molson, who scarcely recognised
him, he echoed his mother's view on her treatment, 'It was touch
and go who was going to be killed first – the bug or me.'

He went to Lausanne for treatment from a Dr Jeanneret, who
gave him lots of pills. But he was still too ill that autumn to do
any work, and with Molly he spent most of a rainy Clydeside
winter at Ardgowan – Evelyn taking pills and Molly coping with
her first pregnancy, soon to end in the birth of their daughter
Katharine.

The long days of enforced idleness were not entirely idle, however, nor without advantage. Evelyn applied his mind to wild life
under Molly's encouragement, and with instruction from Lord
William Percy, a brother of the Duke of Northumberland and a
close friend of the Greys. The Percys – Polly Percy was an equal
enthusiast to her husband – started him off on birds, and his
passion for ornithology stayed with him through countless notebooks and hundreds of exotic species around the world. Likewise,
with wild flowers. He bought a *Bentham and Hooker* and a
flower press, and started to tick off the species as he came upon
them. In both pursuits he showed a dedication to complicated
Latin names and generic categorisations, and was much happier
identifying them as such than by their more colloquial names.

Meanwhile, another doctor was at hand; and his treatment

proved to be a turning point. Dr Henry Cohen of Liverpool was recommended to Evelyn by Lord Cranborne, the future Marquis of Salisbury, whose own solicitor in Liverpool was friendly with the doctor. Cohen at the time was Professor of Medicine at Liverpool University. He went on to still higher things becoming Lord Cohen of Birkenhead in 1956. Evelyn, like all other patients – however distinguished – went up to Liverpool to see him, and began an association which changed his life and was to last until he died.

Cohen found him very anaemic, suffering from colitis, and a lack of folic acid. He treated him for these symptoms with various pills and tonics, and recommended him to take frequent exercise and try to live in a dry, cold climate, so that his blood pressure would not get too low. The diagnosis and the treatment sound so simple, that it is hard to appreciate the galvanising effect they had on Evelyn at the time, partly no doubt because of the psychology of Cohen's approach. He treated Evelyn with hope and simplicity, in contrast to the attitudes evinced by his previous doctors. Cohen deduced that it was Evelyn's anaemia which had sapped his will to make a real recovery from the effects of the ematine treatment. The later periods of exhaustion from which Evelyn was to suffer while a colonial Governor were due to his chronically low blood pressure, and the fact that being a big man, he tended to take a lot out of himself in whatever physical and mental struggle he was engaged.

Cohen prescribed Evelyn a diet, and put him off drink, officially only until he had recovered his health. As it turned out the ban was for life. In fact, Evelyn stayed on his diet too, and found, both with food and drink, that as the years passed, any deviation had such a dire effect on his digestion, that, with only one or two lapses into alcohol during the war, he sipped ginger beer, ate boiled chicken and avoided roughage for the rest of his days. And he never ignored Cohen's injunction to take exercise.

Life started to pick up. Evelyn went back to the bank to work full time. He was soon sent for by the senior partner, Sir Edward Peacock, who told him he wished to train him to be his eventual successor. Evelyn was shocked. In his heart, he was already coming to the conclusion that he could not stand city life. Certainly his first experience of life in Barings can only have contrasted unfavourably with the scale of his life, work and responsibility in either India or South Africa – even apart from the absence of the great outdoors. He did not conceal his misgivings, but agreed with Sir Edward that he would have a year's trial as a partner before coming to a final decision. When the year was over he left.

Evelyn did return informally to Barings after he retired from his colonial service in the 1960s, but he never showed that taste for banking which seems to grip so many other members of the Baring family. However, his experience in the bank in the thirties gave him two great advantages later on. First it acquainted him with the world of high finance and, being the thorough man he was, equipped him with a working knowledge of how that world worked, to his later advantage in the economic department of the Foreign Office, and in the shaping of economic policies in Africa during his governorships there. Secondly, he made friends and contacts on which he could call – as he often did – when he became concerned with the development of African countries as a governor and later during his work at the Commonwealth Development Corporation.

So it was not all bad; though it was with a sigh of relief and a spring in his tread that he left the Baring offices in Bishopsgate and went off to become a director of Sudan Plantations. Evelyn had applied for a job there through his friend, Arthur Asquith. His directorship involved spending two months each year in the Sudan, and Evelyn happily applied himself to the task of cotton growing until the outbreak of war.

CHAPTER IX

Letters from London

When war was declared on September 3, 1939, Evelyn moved his family from their London home to Howick. By now Katharine, their eldest child was three and a half, Charlie was nearly two and Molly was expecting their third child, Elizabeth, early in the New Year. Evelyn moved temporarily into the next door house with Alec Dunglass, who had also evacuated his wife, Elizabeth, and her three daughters to the borders. Evelyn and Molly were thus separated for nearly three years. Day after day they used to write to each other with amazing regularity, Molly numbering her letters so that they could be read in the right order if they got delayed or arrived in clusters. When, in 1940, she and her children were sent to Canada, the letters continued across a divide of several days – sometimes weeks – so that the dialogue between them became curiously elongated.

Though Evelyn was only 35 when war was declared, he was unfit for military service. He was very conscious of this unfitness and perhaps secretly rather ashamed of it. Later on, when he became a governor, he was always careful to see that he mastered the punctilio of military ceremonial when he was required to take part in it. Now, in 1939, he lost no time in compensating for his non-military status by at least working for the government, if only behind a desk. In November, 1939 – by the good offices of Roger Makins – he joined the Egyptian Department of the Foreign Office as a temporary diplomat. He settled down to Whitehall work, a life especially flavoured for him by the proximity to high politics which came from sharing a house with Alec Dunglass, then Parliamentary Private Secretary to Neville Chamberlain, the Prime Minister.

His life was a curious mixture. The letters to Molly contained accounts of gossipy dinner parties and descriptions of a social life which could have been extracted from one of Evelyn Waugh's wartime novels; there was also birdwatching, butterfly catching, and botanising – all intermingled with critical asides about the world of politics inhabited by Alec; and behind it all the approaching drama when, after Hitler invaded France, London became the front line. It was then that Evelyn was galvanised into plans to evacuate Molly and the children from Howick. Evelyn himself stayed behind in London.

Occasionally – very occasionally – there were week-ends at Howick, and the family links were further maintained by Lord Grey's rather eccentric trips to London, when Evelyn might be required to find two young men to come to dinner to discuss religious education (he was for years head of the Anglican House of Laity, and a most active if provocative member of the Church of England establishment). Lord Grey was also an ornithologist. Evelyn described a scene one morning in April, 1940, when he was walking across St James' Park with his father-in-law. They saw two unidentifiable ducks in the lake; 'I'll ask the PM, said C [Charlie] turning round as Neville passed [Chamberlain used to walk in the park too] and ask him he did. The old boy looked a bit peckish and said he didn't know. Mrs C looked frightened and the two detectives looked as if the IRA were about to do the PM in. Charlie was furious that Neville didn't know.' On another occasion Alec Dunglass was summoned urgently from his office in Downing Street, to attend upon the PM in the Park. He thought there had been an accident but when he got there he found that Chamberlain merely wanted to show him a scaup which had strayed on to the lake with the other more common varieties.

By the end of April, 1940, the pace started to quicken. Evelyn's letters became more frequent, perhaps with the sense of an impending crisis. For most of the winter he had worked himself into his job with only limited enthusiasm for the Whitehall machine, and he showed signs of frequent irritation with the little things which seemed to excite his colleagues – dramas in the Travellers Club, or the false flurry of minor victories and defeats at interdepartmental meetings. 'I'm feeling fed up with the FO,' he wrote also in April. 'Nature has not fitted me to be a Whitehall bureaucrat.'

The last real fling of the pre-war regime was at Easter that year with Alec Dunglass at his Berwickshire home, Springhill. The party included Roger Makins, so it became a real Oxford reunion. From then on the course of the war was to get grimmer, (Hitler invaded the Low Countries on May 10) and in his letters to Molly Evelyn's fears and frustration, even with Alec, were to show through more and more clearly.

May 1, 1940. 'The FO console themselves with hopes that Neville will fall.'

May 3. 'Universal gloom. I feel anti our rulers. Neville's speech was *far* too complacent. Some pretty nasty stories are going to come back from Norway [the Narvik expedition]. Though I believe that history may well make Winston the villain of the Norwegian piece.'

May 4. 'Roger [Makins] – overworked – tells me to do my best to make Alec feel gloomy in order to dispel the PM's fatal complacency.'

May 8. 'Walked up with Alec much preoccupied. He said the service chiefs predicted chaos in the inner circle without Neville. The Labour Party is exercising political blackmail to clear out the Cabinet deadwood.'

May 9. 'Imperative to have the TUC in the Cabinet.'

May 10. 'All FO leave cancelled. [He had arranged a three-day week-end leave at Howick.] If Hitler has swallowed most of Holland and Belgium in a week I suggest you move away from the coast inland to Heppel. I may be evacuated, being an amateur in the advance party.'

May 11. [Churchill had just taken over the Premiership from Chamberlain.] 'Alec burnt his most incriminating letters in case he was succeeded by Brendan Bracken. He is rather gloomy about Winston as Premier and I have my doubts too. Alec says that in the middle of the debate [in the Commons, after which many Conservatives abstained to show their lack of support for Neville Chamberlain] there was a noise like an air raid siren which was Quintin Hogg who leapt to his feet and screamed five times 1000 to one against Neville.'

May 12. 'Took picnic lunch with Alec beyond Croydon. Three holly blues after a terrific chase to the noise of endless fighters from a neighbouring aerodrome. Alec says he can stand anything provided that Bob Boothby and Harold Macmillan are not put in the Government. [They were.] He is not very pleased at Anthony Eden's appointment. [Secretary for War.]'

May 13. 'Roger told me yesterday that everyone he had met had lost their temper at some time during the day including the Secretary of State. The strain all round is very great. I feel that the new Government is going to be a bit more dynamic but I wish it had two months more in office before the *Blitzkreig* started.'

May 14. 'Alec tried hard not to be catty about the new govt, but could not refrain from saying that Winston had had a very cool and Neville a rapturous reception in the House. I told him there was a serious danger of the House and the country getting completely out of sympathy! I am pleased with the new government. Neville's political epitaph should be that now, 14 months after Hitler invaded Bohemia we are outnumbered 10 to one in the air.'

May 15. 'I must say Beaverbrook makes me blanch a bit [appointed Minister of Aircraft Production] . . . I am glad to see Bobbety [Cranborne] is back. They say that Dalton, himself a very unpopular Old Etonian, will get rid of all the many OEs now in the Ministry of Economic Warfare. . . . I see Rab Butler stays at the FO. I expect Halifax did that. It won't please Roger who calls him the "rt hon Rabbit".'

May 19. 'Richmond Park this morning before the FO. Good view of garden warbler, greenfinch making a queer noise, grand view of a tree pippet.'

May 20. 'News is grim to the last degree. Reynaud and Daladier are on bad terms because their mistresses quarrelled. I talked to Patrick Buchan-Hepburn [later a Tory chief whip who was made Lord Hailes]. The typical Tory MP is quite hopeless, still quite optimistic, more interested in what appeared to him to be the bad treatment of Neville than in the war, unable to see that anyone could think ill of Neville when after these years of his Premiership and all the warnings we are still ill equipped for mechanical warfare.'

May 23. 'Alec says Neville was in despair yesterday and thought it was because he was not used to war. Everything apparently depends on the next few days. I may tell you – in confidence – that June 6 is supposed to be the date of Hitler's timetable for landing his attack on us. I hope you have your plans to move ready. Reading *Rouge et Noir* during air raids. The ladies who share my shelter at the FO are only worth looking at when they have their gas masks on.'

May 28. 'Get your evacuation plans ready, in fact I think it is possible that you should move now, the collapse of the Belgians will speed up the attack on us and there may be a general evacuation of coast areas on the east, in which case accommodation inland might be lost.'

May 29. 'Possibility of martial law coming with the evacuation of coast areas and the banning of private cars. So move in the near future. An awful gloom hangs over Whitehall waiting till the news begins to seep through to the general public.'

88

May 30. 'Alec says that people's minds are now moving very much on the idea of an invasion of Ireland, so don't move to Wales or Cumberland.'

June 16. 'I am afraid the French are through and we will have to face it alone. However, for the week-end I have concentrated on grasses and sedges instead.'

With the fall of France Evelyn moved quickly over plans to evacuate Molly and the children to Canada, probably for the duration of the war. There was not time for any great deliberation, and the evacuation was suggested, agreed, and then implemented in an amazingly short time, the details mostly being arranged through their letters, which, in spite of the blitz and the imminence of invasion, seemed to shuttle back and forth between London and Northumberland with encouraging punctuality and speed.

June 16. 'It makes me feel awful sending you off to Canada but everyone agrees that it is the best thing to do.' He asked for the family's passports (Nisset Dawnay and her four children were also going). He told her he had booked a passage on a liner leaving Liverpool in eight days time, the 26th, and that the allowance Molly could take would probably be £30 a head. 'Darling it breaks my heart thinking of being separated from you and the children but I am sure that it is the best plan, the risks of death are less, of wounds and effect on nerves and starvation infinitely less . . . I adore you. I have never been so happy as when with you and it has been getting better and better and I have been getting happier and happier.'

The family was joined by Lady Waldegrave and her five daughters, and there was even talk of a party of one hundred more children being organised. Alone, Evelyn settled down to a bachelor life of air raids, Foreign Office work, week-ends with his eccentric Aunt Beatrice in Northamptonshire, and the strange, brittle society of wartime London which he used to describe in the most libellous terms to Molly but in which, with his heavy Wykehamist humour and essential shyness, it is hard to visualise him taking a leading part. He reported with gusto on the eccentricities of his friends and relations; his aunt putting out pyjamas for her servants in case they had none for the air raids; Alec Dunglass hunting for butterflies in an Oxfordshire wood and being stopped by the police after a woman had reported his suspicious behaviour; a new colleague in the Foreign Office, whose assistance gave him time for post-prandial naps in the Travellers

Club; fury at being turned out of his office to make space for the 'infernal' Lord Halifax to have a bed.

July 17, advice to Molly. 'Show enthusiasm for Canadian things in general, the scenery, the buildings, it pays every time and it is difficult, if they are like Americans, to lay it on too thick.'

He was hard at work on Egyptian economic affairs and cotton dealing, spending a great deal of his time in the Treasury. At one point the Treasury suggested another financial adviser in the embassy in Cairo, and his name had been put forward. 'It would have been rather a curious turn of fortune to have another Evelyn Baring attacking Egyptian finances. But alas my tummy makes the idea useless.' His cousin, the third Evelyn Baring, ('little Evelyn' as he was called in the bank) suggested that he stood for Parliament as a Labour candidate. 'I said I would because it would annoy you so.' But he didn't.

In August the pressure of that summer seemed to ease slightly, though not in the air, where the Battle of Britain was being fought out each day over the skies above the Home Counties. Evelyn found time to take a holiday, but not before the more cheerful tone of his letters had provoked Molly into saying they might as well now come back from Canada as nothing was clearly going to happen. This, according to Evelyn, was 'a little previous'. He went north to Howick, then on to see Alec who was ill at Springhill, and finally for a fishing and shooting holiday at Ardgowan – which had just suffered from a stray bomb intended for Glasgow. In September he returned to London, where the Battle of Britain was reaching its climax.

September 11. 'I think that an attempt will be made to invade us and that this bombing is the prelude. The disadvantages to Hitler of not invading are so very great.' One letter in which he described how he had rigged up a bed in the area under the pavement outside the house was interrupted by the air raid siren wailing. He continued the letter in pencil. At the end of the raid, with the all clear, 'I *do* love you darling. I really feel happier leading this life knowing how things are between us than I did when we were prosperous and comfortable but not very matey.' 'Who would have thought during the first days of our marriage that we would have thought like this at 37 and 33?'

Evelyn soon settled into a wartime routine. There was bombing almost every night, starting at about 8.30 and continuing until the all clear sounded between five and six in the morning, when he emerged from the arch under the pavement and returned to his bedroom upstairs. After a while his sleeping no longer suffered. He told Molly that the fashionable thing to do was to watch the blitz from Hampstead Heath, 'a wonderful sight I believe, but I am too much of a coward to go myself.' Walking across St James' Park each morning he could see the black patches in the grass marking the final resting place of an incendiary bomb, and there would be the usual gossip with passers-by as to which areas of London – Chelsea, Victoria, or Liverpool Street Station – had 'copped it' particularly badly during the night.

After a year in the Foreign Office, he was asked to stay on as a permanent member. He was not keen. 'My tummy, my income (it would halve it), my liking for country life, my dislike of foreigners and of social life are all against it, quite apart from what you think.' However, he said he would keep it in mind: Sudan Plantations might not survive the war; a second string to his bow was always useful; there was the prospect of playing a small part in rebuilding the world; he was flattered at having made an obvious success of a brand new type of work started without training at the age of 37 and with a rotted liver. 'Heady wine. I know three times as much as an MP, except I miss fresh air and constant bullying by a small attractive woman – the two things essential to my physical and mental well being.'

Evelyn shut up his own house and moved in with Roger Makins. The furniture was sent north to Howick at a cost of £112 after competitive bidding. The keys were left with 'Offer and Offer' – an aptly named house agents. Evelyn remembered even to cancel the clock winder, he said. To Roger he took an oil stove and an iron bed. Roger had just been promoted Counsellor over the head of some other Foreign Office colleagues. There were said to be jealousies.

For the next eighteen months Evelyn worked hard at the Foreign Office, and the letters criss-crossed between London and Canada almost daily. Evelyn reported on various dinner parties (complaining that some courses at the Savoy now cost 7 *shillings*); on the popularity of the rumba (but not for him); on the minutiae of life with Roger Makins (towards the end of 1941 they both moved in with Makins' parents to save money). Molly occasionally agitated to return to Britain, but Evelyn remained firm, 'we'd certainly have been invaded if the air raids of September had worked.'

In January, 1941, he went to see Dr Cohen in Liverpool and returned in a great state of excitement, announcing the turn of his particular tide. 'After having to take more and more dope and pills ever since the spring of 1936 I have now for the first time been told to leave some of it off.' Cohen said he could drink a little light claret and a month later he tried two glasses. Perhaps it was not light enough; he complained of a 'wrong tummy' for two weeks.

He managed to get away from London most week-ends. He went to Norfolk, with the Percys, where he spent a day of ecstasy driving a new tractor, though the furrows he ploughed earned the well-deserved disapproval of the tractor's regular driver. On another occasion he went canoeing up the Stour identifying new grasses in the marshes.

In short, he was content. 'You write such lovely letters that in spite of everything and all the war, I find I feel quite absurdly happy nearly all the time. How true it is what Marlborough (who resembles me in so many ways!!) said, that to the man who is really devoted to his wife, her behaviour is all that matters for his happiness and will easily make up for everything else going wrong – and I may say vice versa!!' And when Molly's sister, Nisset, died in March, 1941, 'I wish I had a quarter of your coolness and self control and power to withstand the shocks of life. What little improvement I have made in this way is entirely due to vou. It is you that have made me realize what religion really means.'

It must have been hard to keep up any kind of emotional life separated by such time and distance. It was not the kind of marriage which would have resulted in their pining and whining about their separation, because they were both essentially undemonstrative people where deeply felt emotions were concerned. Evelyn's letters almost always contain phrases of endearment, which are obviously genuine, yet which as the months wore on become, inevitably, but noticeably ritualistic. 'What fun after the war will be. Think of that. It will be like a theatre after one has stood in a queue for a long time . . .' 'My darling, on June 26 you had been gone a year, a whole large blank year and I feel as if it was a little bit neatly cut out of my life.'

Towards the end of the summer Dr Cohen came to breakfast and ordered him to have a month's rest. He was still not one hundred per cent fit; alternating between sudden bursts of energy and periods when 'I go off badly in warm weather.' He was just preparing to change from the Egyptian to the Economic Department of the Foreign Office, where he would move in 'higher circles'. He went north to Howick, now turned into a hospital, where he was certified unfit for firewatching, and then on to Ardgowan, also a hospital. Aunt Alice, like Mabel Grey, was having trouble with the Matron. She had given up eating butter since the start of rationing, and Hughie, aged 87, had had to follow suit. There were only three more years to go before their diamond wedding, and Alice said she was planning to write a book about their marriage entitled *Sixty Years a Doormat* (in the face of all the evidence!).

Evelyn revisited Ardgowan that December, when his Aunt Beatrice died, and was reassured to find both Alice and Hughie flourishing, in spite of the bitter cold at Ardgowan, where even he had to raid the next door bedroom for an extra blanket and eiderdown. However, he was not really sanguine about their prospects. 'I am afraid we are now in for a holocaust of our elderly relations,' he wrote to Molly; and his fears were well founded. A letter to Molly dated January 24, 1942, ends with his being called away to the telephone. The next one begins, 'I had a hunch something was wrong. Poor Ally died in the night.' Until the end she was indefatigable. Hughie, on the day she died, came upon her dictating letters. 'You have done me good,' he said. She replied, 'At least I've stopped you being a bore.' – a much finer epitaph than 'sixty years a doormat'.

Though Hughie was to live another six months, it was Alice's death which marked the end of Ardgowan for Evelyn. He hurried north for her funeral, which took place in the little church of Inverkip on a bitterly cold snowswept day. There was a huge crowd. The congregation all sang the psalms, though nobody had psalm books. 'For me it is the end of a chapter. I am more like my mother and the two aunts than like any other relations, and all Weymie's children are completely different,' he told Molly. There was a certain amount to be done. Though his memories of Ardgowan were rather gloomy ones they were the only real and constant childhood memories he had. Hughie asked him to be a director of the Ardgowan estate company. 'I agreed as I owe them so much – though an awful sweat. Hughie is a child about money matters. Alice gave him a monthly cheque.' Alice also left Evelyn all her money and possessions in a simple will. Almost overnight he had become a rich man.

Hughie struggled on alone, trying pathetically to carry on all Alice's work and duties. He talked about Alice incessantly, and said he hoped he would not survive the next winter without her, while asking despairingly how on earth he was going to die. He need not have worried. In June he was taken off to a nursing home having wasted away for lack of food, and on the 29th, aged 87, he died. His nephew, Guy, succeeded him; and Evelyn's Ardgowan days were finally done.

Meanwhile there was still the war to contend with and Evelyn's future. After Pearl Harbour he wrote confidently to Molly. 'This means a final and complete victory for us as distinct from a long drawn out and more or less successful draw.' At about the same time he commented on a letter to Lady Grey from Lord Harlech, High Commissioner in South Africa, 'How lovely it would be to be there now.' Within a year, his wish was to be granted.

At the end of June, 1942, he was asked to dinner by a friend, to meet Paul Emrys Evans, MP, then Parliamentary Under Secretary in the Dominions Office. Next day Emrys Evans rang him up and invited him to dinner. Evelyn expected to meet Cranborne there, but the principal guest turned out to be Clement Attlee, Deputy Prime Minister and Dominions Secretary. 'He is curious, and rather shy,' he reported to Molly in that night's letter. 'But we got on well. After dinner he asked me some questions about my past life and then suddenly said he would like to put up my name to be Governor of Southern Rhodesia. You could have knocked me down with a feather. I thought of course that health would make acceptance impossible, but some enquiries showed that Salisbury, except for three months in the year, is cool, dry and bracing, and generally the climate is dry. I saw Koko [Cohen]. So far from turning the project down he was all for it and said that he thought that the general stimulus plus more open air and leisured life might well effect a great improvement. If you want me to say 'no' there is still time to withdraw if you cable quickly.

'Now this is the proposition. It is a five year job but I could probably come back earlier if I find I can't stand the climate. I explained the essential condition of my acceptance was that the Dawnays came home too.' [The Dawnay children, after Nisset's death and with their father missing, presumed captured by the Germans, were virtually orphans in Molly's guardianship in Canada.] The authorities agreed to that, on condition that Molly would accompany him to Africa. The Rhodesians did not want a bachelor Governor. Evelyn explained to Molly that Southern Rhodesia was already three quarters of the way to being a dominion (rather than an old-fashioned colony). 'The governor also has to advise on the vexed question of amalgamation with

Northern Rhodesia, a territory that is still a crown colony, that has a vast native population and – the reason why it is desired – copper.' He had a long talk with the Permanent Secretary, Sir Eric Machtig, with whom he struck up a lasting and close friendship. Machtig predicted that the great clash between segregation and the suppression of the blacks on the one hand, and the British doctrine of trusteeship for the native on the other, was coming nearer, the first spreading north, the second south. Southern Rhodesia would inevitably become the territory in the middle. 'It will therefore be a key job in Africa. This my darling is, I am afraid, a great lure to me. But I shall be guided by you. The overriding feeling in my life is love for you. I adore you and want you to be happy more than I want anything else in the world. What do you think?'

In fact Molly was going to have to make up her mind long before she received these endearing words. It is a measure either of the spontaneity that their correspondence had achieved over the enormous gap in time and distance, or of Evelyn's excitement at the new offer that he overlooked that point in discussing it with Molly. The day after writing to her he sent a cable to her in Magog, Quebec. 'Am offered governorship of Southern Rhodesia. Condition that you accompany me leaving England late September. Climate all right for children throughout the year. Do you agree? If so Malcolm [Macdonald, the British High Commissioner] will arrange early passages home for you and children. I have explained that Dawnays must come too. If you have doubts await letter sent by bomber bag.' The next day Machtig, more cautiously, informed Macdonald that subject to the concurrence of Huggins (Prime Minister of Rhodesia), Attlee proposed to submit Evelyn's name to the King.

Everything then moved fast. Huggins concurred on July 21 and Attlee saw the King on July 22, recommending that Evelyn should also be knighted with the Order of St Michael and St George (KCMG). The same day a cable arrived indicating that Molly had accepted. 'You are an angel, I am still in a daze,' wrote Evelyn, 'Do you realise that I get made KCMG. It really is a bit of a joke. By the time you get back I will be Sir Evelyn Baring.' Exactly a week later Evelyn saw King George and received the accolade. The King would have been aware of Evelyn, at least by name, since his Private Secretary, Sir Alan Lascelles, an old friend of Evelyn's from Ardgowan days, had been lobbying his name constantly to King and Cabinet as a future Viceroy of India – if India lasted.

Evelyn's appointment had been caused by the collapse of the previous nominee for Governor, Lord Huntingfield, who resigned on grounds of ill health before he had even taken up the job. Rhodesia had been without a Governor for months, and Sir Godfrey Huggins, though fretful, had refused to be palmed off with any more Colonial Office veterans. Evelyn could hardly be described as that, though he was not Huggins' first choice. When his appointment was announced *The Daily Telegraph* said he was the youngest man ever appointed to an imperial governor-ship, and described him as 'a man of the world, a good mixer and has the advantage of a fine physique.'

There followed a hectic period of planning, both in London and Quebec. Nobody was allowed to sail on the perilous North Atlantic run without government clearance. Every ship move-ment, and every passenger booking had to be made by the auth-orities. Macdonald was asked to speed clearance for Molly and her brood. The request was complicated by the fact that the American naval authorities were not accepting women and child-ren as passengers on ships which were going to have to sail through areas for which they were responsible. However it was all achieved in the end, and for the second time in the war, Molly and her family found themselves embarking on a perilous ocean journey to an unknown continent, with the minimum of prepar-ation.

Meanwhile in London, Evelyn was going through his own prep-arations. So closely controlled was the British economy that only Mr Attlee, as Secretary of State, could authorise a supply of 250 more clothes coupons from the Board of Trade, for Evelyn to purchase his governor's uniform and three new suits. Molly was allowed the same, and there were fifty more for the staff. Evelyn, after discussion with the Dominions Office, resigned his director-ships and received official guidance on how a governor in Rhodesia would be expected to behave. There was also a hurry in Whitehall to get permission to take with him a staff of five, in-cluding a nanny – deemed an 'unavoidable necessity' by the Do-minions Office, on the grounds that the Governor's wife (in this case an unusually young one with children still at the nursery stage) must be free to travel round the colony with the Governor.

He also had time to meet Rhodesia's High Commissioner in London who reported back to Huggins, 'I have met our new

Governor. He is a very nice quiet man and looks a thinker. He obviously knows nothing about being a Governor and is perhaps all the better for that, as he will be able to learn from you the way he should go. No doubt, however, he will be well coached by the Dominions Office as to the way *they* want him to go before he leaves for Rhodesia.'[1]

Eventually on October 28, 1942, the Baring entourage boarded the *Athlone Castle* in Liverpool – departure date secret – and sailed for Durban. The party was not small. Apart from Evelyn and Molly and three children there was Mrs Parker, Miss Gregor, nanny, Tom Goff, their ADC who had come from being the Athlone's ADC in Canada, and 27 pieces of luggage. When they arrived at Liverpool docks they were met in the dusk by Admiral Bromley and his flag lieutenant. Molly thought they were porters and gave the Admiral her handbag. The six week voyage gave Evelyn a perfect opportunity to read himself in on Rhodesia, devouring copious memos by Lord Hailey and holding forth at great length to his family in order to recapitulate the facts and get them properly stored in his mind. The family remained unconvinced and soon slipped easily into that fusion of pomp and privacy which was to be the hall mark of all Evelyn's governorships. Tom Goff used to regale them by imitating his old boss, Lord Athlone, prompting the thought from Molly that no one can be a hero to his ADC and some speculation as to the stories Tom would be able to tell about the Barings when it was all over. Evelyn cheated at beggar-my-neighbour, and they all went to church in Tom's cabin, which he shared with the Padre, who discomforted Tom somewhat by reading evensong aloud at midnight and erecting a pocket altar on the dressing table. Near Capetown they picked up 35 survivors from a ship sunk by German submarines, but it was the only taste of war during the whole voyage. On December 5 they disembarked in Africa where Evelyn was to remain, basically, for the next seventeen years.

D

CHAPTER X

A Colonial Crown

'The upheaval of the First World War was followed in Britain by a decade of intense examination of her imperial role in Africa and especially in the mixed communities of East and Central Africa. 'Trusteeship' and 'the paramountcy of the native interests' inspired the pronouncements, and to a lesser extent the practice of the Colonial Office. These ideas going back through Johnston and Livingstone to the Abolitionists and Burke, now provided the nearest approach to a coherent theory of British imperialism. This theory of trusteeship encountered, however, another and yet older colonial theme. In the twenties it was still possible, and indeed common, to regard the highlands of Eastern Africa, extending in an unbroken belt hundreds of miles broad from Kenya to Southern Africa, as the last great area in the world ready and waiting for European settlement.'

Thus Richard Grey started his book *The Two Nations*, a study of the development of race relations in the Rhodesias and Nyasaland.[1] Evelyn, before his African career was finished, was to encounter this phenomenon, and be forced to deal with its consequences in East, Central and Southern Africa. Indeed one can say that between 1942 and 1959 the history of British policy in Africa developed as much through him as through any other figure on the colonial stage.

The year 1923 can be looked back on as a crucial year in terms of the subsequent development of Southern Rhodesia and Kenya – the countries which were Evelyn's first and last governorships in Africa. It was the year when the Duke of Devonshire, then Secretary of State for the Colonies, countered the claims of a group of European settlers in Kenya, who demanded an increasing share in the government of the colony by emphatically reasserting Britain's imperial authority, and establishing the primacy of African interests in the colony's future, 'Primarily Kenya is an African territory,' he declared, 'and His Majesty's Government think it necessary definitely to record their considered opinion that the interests of the African natives must be paramount and that, if, and when, those interests and the interests of the immigrant races should conflict, the former shall prevail. Obviously the other communities, European, Indian or Arab, must severally be safeguarded. But in the administration of Kenya His Majesty's Government regard themselves as exercising a trust on behalf of the African population, and they are unable to delegate or share this trust, the object of which may be defined as the protection and advancement of the native races.'[1a] It was the plainest statement that could be made and, though there were occasions during the next forty years (before Kenya became independent under an African government) when the European settlers may have forgotten or chosen to ignore it, it remained the bedrock of British policy.

How different was the policy adopted by HMG towards another small group of European settlers further south in Southern Rhodesia. It makes one wonder how the same government could have spawned two such different policies. In 1922, having freed themselves from the rule of the Chartered Company set up by Cecil Rhodes, the European settlers of Southern Rhodesia held a referendum to decide whether they should formally seek admission to the Union of South Africa, or choose responsible self-government. By 8774 votes to 5989 they chose self-government. The country was then formally annexed to the Crown and acquired internal government, with the British government retaining authority to decide external policy, and also reserve powers of consent and supervision in most aspects of native administration.

In 1923 Southern Rhodesia's white settlers numbered 33,000, of which less than one quarter had been born in the country. However the colony had already acquired a style and consciousness of its own, very different from that of South Africa – even Anglo – South Africa. It typified the spry middle class England of the late nineteenth and early twentieth century. Even though the base of the white population was an agricultural one, the farmers did not sport the easy manners and casual morals of Kenya's aristocratic settlers. Their customs were not those which one might associate with rugged frontiers' men, but with correct unimaginative suburban England; and it was an ethos which persisted and developed throughout the twenties and thirties until the outbreak of the Second World War.

The main issue which preoccupied the early Southern Rhodesian governments and the European settlers who supported them was the question of land, and, in particular the division of land ownership between the 33,000 whites and the 862,000 blacks in the territory. A commission was set up by the British government, under Sir Morris Carter, to examine the distribution of land and to make recommendations about the designation of further areas outside the boundaries of the already delineated native reserves, within which Africans only would be permitted to buy land, and conversely, others within which only Europeans could settle. There was much discussion, and a copious quantity of evidence was submitted, which led the Commission to form the general impression that the overwhelming majority of people preferred some measure of segregation as the best way to ensure the development of the races within the country, giving priority to the interests of each main racial group within its respective area.

Southern Rhodesian land consisted of about 96 million acres, of which by 1925 31 million were already owned by Europeans, and $21\frac{1}{2}$ million were reserved for Africans. The question remained how to allocate the remaining $43\frac{1}{2}$ million, which at that time could be bought by either European or African, though in practice few Africans seemed then able to do so. It was the possibility that they might at some later date be able to do so which agitated the Europeans. In its conclusions the Land Commission apportioned the 43 million acres in the following way – 7 million to be set aside as native purchase areas, where Africans could own freeholds of up to 1000 acres (in the reserves all land was common land vested in the chief), 17 million for European purchase, and the remainder, much of which was very low quality land, to be unassigned, and therefore, officially, available to either race. The proposals were embodied in the 'Land Apportionment Act' which was introduced to the Rhodesian parliament in 1929, went to London for consideration by the Imperial government, and was finally made law in 1931. However the measures, which were designed to achieve segregation, actually brought integration closer, over the years, by creating a class of landless Africans who then became permanently urbanised in their search for work.

The aim of preventing integration between or encroachment of one race upon another, and in particular maintaining the predominant position in the country occupied by the white minority, was being followed in the 1920s and 1930s not only on the land, but to a lesser extent in the industrial field as well. In spite of its small population, by the time Evelyn arrived, Southern Rhodesia could boast a highly organised European industrial scene, with a trade union structure dominated by the railway workers union, which virtually controlled the Rhodesian Labour Party in parliament as well. Its principle objectives were to secure better conditions for its members, and ensure that they were not threatened by the rise of an African working class which would perform the same skilled or semi-skilled work for lower pay. Throughout those years there seemed to be solidarity between the white managerial and landowning class and the European artisans, who jointly believed that the emergence of a poor white class undercut by technically qualified Africans, would be a threat to the whole white position – and therefore a political threat, not just an industrial one.

Between the wars nothing happened in the development of the races in Southern Rhodesia to mitigate the contradiction which lay at the heart of the concept of segregation. True, the conditions in the native reserves were improved, yet Africans continued to move into the European areas where they could apparently improve their conditions even faster. Economic advance and interdependence ate away at the uneconomic certainties of segregation.

The Rhodesia to which Evelyn came was being governed by the United Party, with Sir Godfrey Huggins as Prime Minister. Huggins, who arrived in the colony as a doctor in 1911, had been Prime Minister since 1933. Under him his party pursued a policy of 'differential development,' based on the view that only with segregation could the white artisans be protected, on the one hand, and on the other, African institutions be brought up to a civilised standard. He believed the policy should lead to the construction of two separate social pyramids – black and white – ultimately under overall white control.

Huggins rapidly established himself as the single channel of communication between Salisbury and London (a 'private line' which was to be somewhat less private and exclusive after Evelyn arrived) and during the 1930s a series of acts was passed which strengthened segregation. The other side of this coin was a concerted effort to improve conditions in the reserves, and to make something less of a mockery of the policy of segregation. In fields such as housing, health services, and education, the native areas soon achieved standards which were unknown anywhere else in Africa. Only the urban areas, which were anyway frowned upon as segregational amomalies, were allowed to suffer; yet in spite of this the urban African population continued to increase.

The economic advance of the blacks, however, was providing

a political as well as a financial threat to the whites. The Southern Rhodesian parliament had been elected on a common role since 1911, with voters requiring a property qualification of £150. In 1928 the Cabinet tried to increase this figure to £500, unashamedly admitting that the move was designed to prevent parliament being dominated by the votes of natives who were then, through their ability to buy property in more areas, increasing their capital. The bill was dropped when the government recognised that, though it would successfully keep out those newly enriched blacks, it would just as successfully disenfranchise a substantial number of poor whites. Besides, at that time, there were only 62 black voters to 22,000 whites – hardly a threat. However, the position was not viewed with much satisfaction by members of the Imperial parliament at Westminster. Accordingly, in 1937 a Royal Commission was set up under Lord Bledisloe to see whether or not closer cooperation or association between the Rhodesias and Nyasaland was 'desirable and feasible', in the hope that this would cope with the twin problems besetting London – the increasingly strident demands of the Northern Rhodesian settlers for incorporation into a federation with their more privileged white neighbours in Southern Rhodesia, and the increasingly evident movement in Southen Rhodesia towards some unacceptable degree of white domination under the umbrella of the self rule granted in 1923.

The Bledisloe Commission was set up after a number of crucial meetings in Africa and London. The first main one was a conference at Victoria Falls in January, 1936, when representatives of the legislative bodies of both Northern and Southern Rhodesia unanimously resolved to seek an early amalgamation of their two colonies, and the abolition of the British Secretary of State's reserved powers of veto. After further meetings in London the next year, the Commission was appointed in the summer of 1937.

The Commission heard a great deal of evidence from black as well as white representatives in both territories. At the end, it was unable to recommend anything definite to resolve the conflict inherent in the opposing desires of the whites *for* amalgamation and the blacks *against*. The Commission concluded that the three territories would become 'more and more closely interdependent in all their activities and that identity of interests will lead them sooner or later to political unity. If this view should commend itself also to Your Majesty's Government we recommend it should

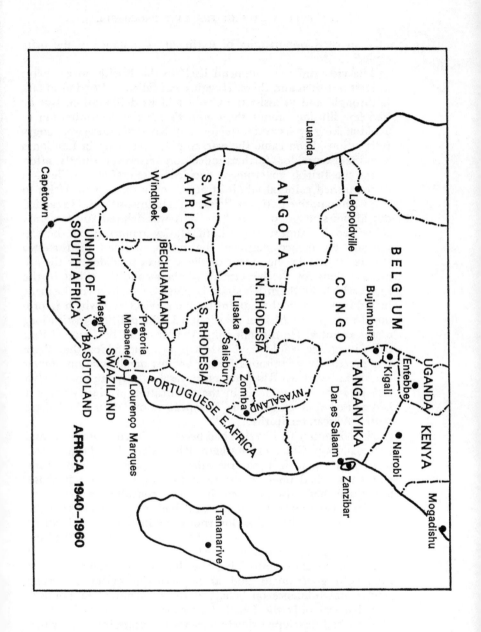

AFRICA 1940–1960

Capetown

UNION OF
SOUTH AFRICA

Windhoek

S. W.
AFRICA

BECHUANALAND

Maseru

BASUTOLAND

SWAZILAND

Mbabane

Pretoria

Lourenço Marques

S. RHODESIA

Salisbury

PORTUGUESE E. AFRICA

Zomba

NYASALAND

Lusaka

N. RHODESIA

ANGOLA

Luanda

Leopoldville

BELGIUM

CONGO

Bujumbura

Kigali

Entebbe

UGANDA

TANGANYIKA

Dar es Salaam

Zanzibar

KENYA

Nairobi

Mogadishu

Tananarive

take an early opportunity of stating its acceptance of the principle.'[2]

The view did not commend itself to the British government; at least not then and there. Huggins was called to London to talk it through, and to assist the Cabinet in its deliberation. But he had few illusions about the Cabinet's private determination to avoid making up its mind. In Northern Rhodesia there were angry resignations. Soon came the war, to give everybody in London a genuine excuse for further indecision. However shortly afterwards the British government decided to send Lord Hailey – a distinguished colonial administrator – on a mission to Africa to study comparative native policies and administrations. He carried out his mission in 1940 but his report was delayed and was only submitted in August 1941. Lord Hailey remarked on the significant divergence between the native policies of the two Rhodesias, not in the extent of the services provided by the administrations for the betterment of their conditions, but in the limits which Southern Rhodesia imposed on African employment in industry and in the administrative services and which it proposed to apply to African association in the political institutions of the country. He did not think that it could be assumed that this divergence would tend to disappear, and added that there was practically unanimous feeling against amalgamation among natives in Northern Rhodesia and Nyasaland. By the time Evelyn arrived in 1942, the delay in the publication of Hailey's report had caused restiveness in the European populations of all three central African territories.

The office to which Evelyn had been appointed – Governor and Commander-in-Chief of Southern Rhodesia – had been constituted in 1923, with a tax free salary of £4,000 and allowances. The Crown had reserved the right to appoint anyone it chose, but there had always been informal consultation with the Rhodesia Government, and Huggins had made it clear that unless he was consulted, the Governor's emoluments would not be increased. The governorship had certain inherent difficulties, since the incumbent was expected to act in two capacities, as a local head of state embodying the domestic sovereignty of the Rhodesian government and as an imperial officer exercising powers and influence on behalf of the government in London.

Evelyn was only the fourth Governor of Southern Rhodesia. The job had developed slowly over twenty years into one which required the exercise of great tact and diplomacy – but at the same time resolve – if anything was to be made of it against the increasingly established position of the Southern Rhodesian government and Assembly. Theoretically, when the governorship was established, the Governor had the power to appoint his executive council; reserve powers to dissent from executive actions proposed by the Cabinet – whose minutes he read though not attending its meetings; powers to appoint and/or dismiss ministers, including the Prime Minister (subject to the party line-up in the Assembly); and obviously considerable influence through being able to advise and comment on the government's policies at all times. However in the previous 20 years the Governor's actual powers, as distinct from his influence, had never been put to the test, and the underlying attitude of Evelyn's predecessors had been to maintain (at almost any cost) satisfactory relations with Southern Rhodesia's Prime Minister, and to hope to influence him against policies which would be unfavourable to the Imperial government, particularly in the field of native administration.

'I regarded my main function as being that of an adviser to both governments, and I felt that my main task was to obtain agreement between them,' Evelyn wrote later to Dr Claire Palley, the Southern Rhodesian constitutional historian.[3] Shortly before he arrived, Lord Hailey in his report said that the development of native policy in the reserves *had* been influenced by the advice given by the Governor – particularly in the field of land settlement and the establishment of native land and marketing boards. But, after 1937, advice and influence was all that the Governor could proffer since, although he was free to acquire information from any department of the administration after that date, he had no actual authority over the departments dealing with native affairs; and the reserve powers which he retained were essentially those which could only be used sparingly on issues of evident and major principle, rather than in the more day to day administration of native policy. Nevertheless, Evelyn was to find that the insistence of the Imperial government in London, through the Governor, that all Rhodesian legislation must satisfy Whitehall that it was not unjust to the African population, provided a continuing corrective to the local government.

CHAPTER XI
Southern Rhodesia

The Barings arrived at Durban on December 5, 1942. They were met by Lord Harlech (formerly Billy Ormsby-Gore) who had by then been High Commissioner in South Africa for a number of years, and whom, incidentally, Evelyn was eventually to succeed. Harlech took Evelyn for his first interview with Smuts in Pretoria, during which Smuts warned Evelyn that Huggins was in a highly strung state and feeling very lonely and isolated.[1]

They then went to Johannesburg to catch their train north to Southern Rhodesia, pausing for matins in the cathedral, where the high church procedures filled Evelyn with gloom and provoked him to put his handkerchief ostentatiously to his nose when the incense was taken round. The arrival in Southern Rhodesia of the young Governor and his even younger wife probably overwhelmed the couple more than it did the citizens of Bulawayo, where they alighted from their train for the formal reception. They had already been impressed by the splendour of the train, with a saloon, two state bedrooms with wardrobes, drawing room, bathroom, kitchen and beds for two servants. Now Evelyn in his cocked hat and plumes, and Molly in a hat which drew the immediate disapproval of the resident Government House Comptroller Colonel Holbech (a great stickler for protocol), were reduced to uncontrollable giggles as they proceeded through the streets of the town in an open car tracked by outriders in the shape of wildly bicycling black youths and observed by thin crowds of Africans who gave sporadic bursts of clapping or cheering. In his opening speech Evelyn told them that Molly's great grandfather was the Lord Salisbury after whom their capital was named, her grandfather was the Lord Selborne who was Governor of the Transvaal in South Africa and always took an interest in Rhodesian affairs, while her other grandfather, Albert Lord Grey, had been a great friend of Rhodes and Administrator of Mashonaland and Matabeleland in 1896. He also had something thoughtful to say about each of the communities – Hindu, coloured and native – who might had had less of a feel for Molly's distinguished ancestry. He was well received; *The Bulawayo Chronicle* next day remarked on his youth, and hoped he could stay a long time.

The Barings then settled down to a new life as a royal family. It was 'cottage industry royalty,' in the sense that Rhodesia was a small community and the household was small, yet the grandeur of their status inevitably set them apart socially. Moreover the importance of Evelyn's political position in Southern Africa could not be underestimated, and was in a wholly different dimension from any political experience he had had previously, either in the Indian Civil or Political Service, or in the Foreign Office.

One of Molly's first tasks, naturally, was to size up Government House, and establish friendly relations with the Dean of Salisbury, who would become a frequent visitor to tea once Molly had assured herself that his Sunday School would not lead to Katharine coming out with any high church 'monkey tricks' to vex Evelyn's low church vigilance. Government House was a little more difficult, because, although the house was attractive and manageable, their staff was accustomed to a gubernatorial couple of much greater *gravitas* than was to be found round the Baring hearth. The Grand Vizier of this little court was the Comptroller, Colonel Lawrence Holbech. He suffered the Barings' eccentricities, not always in silence, until they left, though there were continuous feuds with Tom Goff, their ADC. Holbech was always being disturbed; one night by the sight of Evelyn climbing a tree with six year old Katharine in full view of the natives; on another occasion when Evelyn spoke *directly* to a press reporter on the telephone. He was scandalised when Tom, as ADC, asked a couple called Baxter to dinner and only discovered half way through dinner that he had invited the 'wrong Baxters,' at which the Barings said they were surely preferable to the right ones; or when Tom bought a complete set of football boots for all the African 'houseboys' – fifteen pairs; or when a rather inebriated young RAF officer whisked off the Governor's wife to dance at a municipal dance and they had to stop the band to rescue Molly from her fate. Holbech was observed apologising both *to* Molly for the incident and *about* Molly to the Mayor.

The main household consisted of Holbech and the two ADCs – Tom Goff and a young Rhodesian police officer called Alec Hampshire – and the Barings were always involved in the feuds and dramas which used to sweep through their ADCs' quarters. Poor Tom, who tended to be melancholy and was extremely sensitive, was the victim of Holbech's contempt and Hampshire's efficiency, and was often hard put to it to find practical work to demonstrate his usefulness other than as an old friend and companion for Molly. So he spent most of his time learning Chisisuru, the local language, and designing, making and playing his beloved clavichords. The lines of demarcation in their little court were blurred, to say the least. One day Holbech went to Molly, asked whether she had seen His Excellency's pants, and then produced something which Molly thought looked like the colours that were carried at Waterloo. Together they went out to buy the Governor three new pairs, though they were not so successful in persuading him to wear them.

The running feud between Holbech and the Barings stemmed from the intricacies of the Southern Rhodesian white class structure, which loomed very large to Holbech, and was sustained by a kind of religious obeisance to the Government House rituals observed by Rhodesian citizens. As far as the Barings were concerned they clearly thought that there was little point in making any distinction between one small group of provincially-minded people and another, whether or not they were officials, politicians or in trade – an aristocratic attitude it was natural for them to adopt, but which distressed the ritualist who served them.

Evelyn's life as Governor consisted of a mixture of ceremonial, old style tours to native areas and the white farming areas, and triangular diplomacy between Huggins and the Dominions Office in London presided over by Attlee and then Cranborne as Ministers and the Permanent Secretary, Sir Eric Machtig. The two main areas that concerned him were the question of integration between the Rhodesias, with the strategic future for Southern Africa in mind, and native policy within Southern Rhodesia. Dominating all these questions were his personal relations with Huggins. We shall later see how, towards the end of his time in Rhodesia, he went to South Africa for a holiday and developed an equally close, if not closer relationship with Smuts. His ability to get on with both these men was a crucially important element in the evolution of British policy in Southern Africa during the 1940s. What he learnt from them did much to fashion in Evelyn those qualities of statesmanship which only came into full play as his stature on the African stage grew.

Since Evelyn's was the first governorship over which Huggins had been formally consulted in advance, there was the initial basis for a sympathetic relationship between the two men, a very necessary ingredient if the latent difficulties of reconciling their respective positions was to be overcome. The Barings soon warmed to Huggins – he came down to Bulawayo to stay with them in the small Government House there on their first full visit after six weeks in Salisbury. Their sense of humour seemed to click, particularly where it was at the expense of other Rhodesians, for whom all three had an amused, if slightly contemptuous tolerance. Huggins had trained at St Thomas's Hospital in London, and they discovered one or two mutual friends there. He managed to keep up some medicine even while being Prime Minister – evidence of the easy pace of Rhodesian government and politics at the time – operating in Salisbury Hospital about three times a week, and making a point of keeping his practice going in case he was kicked out of politics. Indeed, in 1943, he was still able to earn an additional £600 from his medical practice – quite a sum of money in those days.[2] Sometimes he arrived to see the Governor smelling strongly of ether.

Huggins' experience of Rhodesian politics had made him rather a cynic and he almost always found himself ahead of white public opinion on native questions, thus reaffirming his suspicion that democracy does not often know what is good for it. But the crucial question, which Evelyn and he never really resolved, was whether his more advanced views on the native question meant that they should merely be better treated and looked after, or governed with a view to exercising ultimate responsibility themselves. He was often troubled by his Cabinet's factiousness, though the Barings thought this was a difficulty partly of his own making since he tended to appoint troublemakers to ministries in order to keep them quiet. Molly thought that he was rather like Malcolm Macdonald, whom she had met in Canada – so nice that you forgot his shortcomings: which in Huggins' case were the absence of a first class brain – aggravated now by deafness – and a lack of tact. However, he was clearly, in the social sense, an ally of the Barings rather than an outsider; and he stood head and shoulders above his fellow politicians. Compared with the imperial giants of London, these struck the Barings as a pathetic collection of town clerks who were totally inadequate for the terrific problems which would face Rhodesia in the future. Before the end of his tour Evelyn felt he had achieved a position of trust with Huggins, and was even managing to get him to do a lot of things indirectly, without Huggins realizing it. Thus the Governor's influence, though not overt, was greatly increased, at least in Evelyn's mind; a development which made him think he was being of some use, having had several bouts of misgiving about his role during the middle period of his governorship.

One of Evelyn's particular successes was to get the British Cabinet to invite Huggins to a Dominions' Prime Minister's conference in London in June, 1944. Rhodesia had never been included before, and the invitation to 'Huggy' as they called him, was the product of some extensive lobbying by Evelyn with Lord Cranborne, who had replaced Attlee at the Dominions Office.

One of the dominant issues with which Evelyn had to deal while he was Governor was the development of native policy. He had to try to influence it against the historical trend towards segregation which had flavoured most white attitudes to Africans ever since the colony achieved internal self-government twenty years earlier.

Evelyn's only previous experience of Africa – white Africa – had been in the Union, and he had then seen it virtually through Indian eyes. He arrived in Rhodesia with a quiet, if cautious determination to use his office as best he could to further liberal policies. But caution was very much his watchword, and in his speeches during the first few months he was so anxious to sugar the pill that he began to wonder whether anybody was getting the hidden message. He decided not to do more than throw out oblique hints until he had established himself on a firm and friendly footing with the government and the administration, and this meant more than merely cementing his personal relationship with Huggins. But the Barings were always receiving shocks to their sensitivities, since they were often exposed socially to hardy Rhodesians, whose bluntness was discomforting to liberal English minds. Molly met a farmer who told her that you had to train Africans exactly as you trained a dog. The Barings came to describe some of the Native Commissioners as the 'MFH variety – plenty of dog biscuit and a good strong whip'. On many occasions, when on tour, Evelyn and Molly were so assailed by the friendly, if raucous and rather coarse, humour of the settlers that they used to retire to their bedrooms disgusted with the uselessness, maddeningness and boringness of colonials. This complaint was not altogether unwelcome to Molly, who had secret fears that Evelyn might want to spend the rest of his working life abroad, while she was still hoping that they would return to England when the war, and Evelyn's tour, ended.

Evelyn was introduced to some of the pitfalls and possibilities of his appointment by Lord Harlech, who after welcoming the Barings to South Africa, brought his wife to stay with them for Christmas in Salisbury three weeks later.

The two men never stopped talking from the moment the Harlechs arrived until they left. Land erosion was one of their favourite topics, but their conversation ranged broadly over the whole gamut of British policy in Africa, with the older man presuming to instruct the young in the ways of the dark continent. They paced the grounds of Government House together, hands clasped behind back like a pair of penguins; sat in the Governor's study together talking at the same time; went driving together, inspecting fields of mealie (maize) and shaking their heads gravely at this or that aspect of the crop. They shared an insatiable thirst for information, and their both being in Southern Africa must have enormously increased the traffic of cables to the Dominions Office (and perhaps also, here and there, opened a Whitehall mind to some new thought about that distant continent).

After his visit Lord Harlech wrote a secret report to Attlee giving a progress report on how the young gubernatorial pair were settling in – with hindsight it looks an odd thing for a neighbouring High Commissioner to report on his colleague's territory, or a guest to report on his host, but from the flavour of his letter to Attlee it is clear he meant no harm. 'The Barings have made a most excellent first impression,' he told Attlee, and Huggins had told him they were all delighted.[3] In a separate message he gave a full report of affairs in Rhodesia. Harlech's report, like all his reports from Southern Africa, was stimulating, wide-ranging and fairminded.[4] There could not have been a more comprehensive curtain raiser for Evelyn himself, who would have seen a copy as it was treated like an official despatch and circulated to interested parties. It was also somewhat prophetic:

'The suggested federation or amalgamation of British central Africa may be in cold storage for the duration of the war but I am clear that it will have a very lively reemergence after the war. For the moment contacts have diminished. Sir Godfrey Huggins flies to Pretoria several times but never to Lusaka. There is an obvious timidity and aloofness between the British territories on either side of the Zambesi. Fears, jealousy, apprehensions, doubts are frankly carried to the point of absurdity. Many prominent people lament that everything now depends on the personal views of two Secretaries of State in Downing Street, neither of whom know Rhodesia.'

Harlech then referred to a statement of Huggins' that England should give up the idea that one could have one single native policy and formal native administration throughout Africa, from Senegal and Khartoum to the Cape.

'A final word as to the outlook of European Southern Rhodesians who just on twenty years ago obtained responsible internal self government but not dominion status. They are essentially permanent colonists bringing up their children as Rhodesians and nothing else, and showing no few signs of the outlook of the several North American colonists before the Declaration of Independence in 1776 i.e. the same impatience at criticism or control from those outside their country. They are emphatically not a country of planters like Malaya or Ceylon or even the West Indies other than Barbados. They are as sharply critical of their own government as of the government of England. They are a comparatively small community, they are both self reliant and ambitious. I am convinced that it would be most unfortunate if their continued good relations with their neighbours and with the U.K. were severely strained because of alleged errors of commission or omission in native policy or administration, particularly would this be so if a clash were to come about as a result of mutual ignorance or miscomprehension of facts. Further it would be unwise to blame the present generation of Rhodesians for the events of history brought about by Rhodes himself in the beginning or for the tragedies of the native rebellions in the last decade of the nineteenth century. Above all it must be remembered that in 1923 the governmental administration of the natives of Southern Rhodesia was in fact handed over by the Imperial government to the European Rhodesians for better or worse. The exercise of the imperial veto over native legislation or legislation affecting natives is difficult and has in fact not been exercised because of those inherent difficulties in spite of the reservations in the present constitution. It is difficult for me to believe that the last word has been said in the better organisation of the multiplicity of separate administrations in the continent of Africa. I have a feeling that the existing boundaries, mostly the result of quite accidental history and the existing units of government and administrative machinery lack quality of permanence. We are doubtless still far from a United States of Africa but there is in this uneasy continent a dynamic potential and the certainty of change and evolution which cannot but be accelerated by the events and ideas which are emerging from this world war . . .'

After this comprehensive review by his guest Evelyn contented himself at the start by writing only to Sir Eric Machtig, the Permanent Secretary in the Dominions Office, and not indulging in the more extravagent epistolary flights of Lord Harlech. Harlech, anyway, with his vast experience and ministerial contacts was at that stage much better equipped to engage the Deputy Prime Minister's attention than was a young Governor feeling his way into his first appointment.

The Baring-Machtig correspondence continued on a top-secret and personal basis throughout Evelyn's tour in Southern Rhodesia. In fact, Evelyn's first message to Machtig, giving his early impressions of the colony, was sent off before the Harlech despatch, but arrived weeks afterwards owing to delays in transit caused by the war. He was soon filling in the gaps in Harlech's essentially broadbrush approach, based as it was on such a fleeting visit in the best traditions of off-the-cuff journalism!

But it was clear almost from the start, and not just from Harlech's own warnings, that the whole question of Central Africa's future, and the possible integration of the territories of Nyasaland and the two Rhodesias could not remain in cold storage until the end of the war – much as British Ministers might have hoped it would be. One of the first things Huggins tackled with Evelyn was the lack of coordination over manpower and the free movement of labour between the territories.

Early in January, 1943, Evelyn told Machtig, 'Huggins nurses a grievance. He thinks efforts are being made to draw Southern Rhodesia further and further away from Northern Rhodesia and Nyasaland. The signs are in the lack of cooperation over manpower policies where Southern Rhodesia has not been kept informed.' Evelyn thought that the cause of his discontent could have been paragraph 477 of the Bledisloe report, which suggested that closer cooperation on various policies would lead to political unity. Huggins suspected that HMG was therefore out to discourage cooperation since it did not want political unity to be introduced by the back door. Evelyn did not think that there was a necessary cause and effect. Closer cooperation could prove to be a substitute for, rather than a catalyst of, political unity, and it would be unfortunate if matters of policy were judged, not on their merits but in accordance with their relationship to the amalgamation issue.[5]

Machtig replied like the wise old Whitehall nanny that he was. He also minuted Eveliyn's despatch with the remark that Harlech confirmed it. 'Our only hope to stave off a pressing demand for immediate amalgamation after the war is to encourage as much cooperation as possible now,' he told Evelyn, and went on to say he would pass on this hint to the Governors of Northern Rhodesia and Nyasaland. He did not want Huggins to start encouraging agitation for amalgamation which 'fortunately had died down'.[6]

The statistics of the area made it clear why there was such pressure for amalgamation. In 1942 Southern Rhodesia's population was 68,000 Europeans, mostly congregated in six municipal areas, and 1.3 million Africans. Northern Rhodesia had the same number of Africans, but only 13,000 Europeans, while Nyasaland's 2.1 million Africans swamped the 1,800 Europeans who held power there. The economic attractions of amalgamation, the formation of a larger market, free mobility of a pool of cheap manpower, had not been lost on the two largest industrial enterprises in the area – the British South Africa Company, and the Anglo-American Corporation, both of whom wanted to harness Southern Rhodesian political and industrial power to the mineral resources of both Rhodesias and the labour of Nyasaland. The plan was anathema to most Africans.

Evelyn had to beware of frustrating these impulses to a point where Southern Rhodesian opinion might turn its back on the Central African scene and reverse the vote of 1923 – in other words return to the idea of incorporation into the Union of South Africa. Soon after he arrived, during a trip to Bulawayo in April, 1943, Evelyn reported to Lord Grey, his father-in-law, on a 'certain drift of opinion towards inclusion in the Union. I'm not quite sure how much this is due to a genuine change in political sentiment and how much to the desire of certain businesses to obtain a wider market for their goods and to join a country that in the modern world is comparatively hostile to socialism,' he wrote.

The preoccupations of the European war were not so great that they distracted Southern Africans from thinking and talking about these issues most of the time. In 1944 Lord Swinton, Britain's Resident Minister in West Africa, toured Southern Africa and reported back to Cranborne at the Dominions Office a conversation he had with Sir Ellis (later Lord) Robins, then Resident Director of the British South Africa Company.[7] Robins was a strong advocate of amalgamation of all Central Africa followed by incorporation of this larger unit into the Union of South Africa. Nobody in Southern Rhodesia wanted union with South

Africa he said, unless they belonged already to a big enough unit to hold their own. Robins said the Northern Rhodesian whites wanted to amalgamate so as to obtain the job security available to Southern Rhodesian white workers through the colour-bar legislation. Swinton added rather shrewdly that he did not see how the colour-bar could last if it started to inhibit industrial development.

Evelyn presided over his first Governors' conference within about three months of his arrival, in March, 1943, and was immediately pitched into a dispute over manpower between Nyasaland and Southern Rhodesia.

Shortly after that he was host to another major and regular conference concerned with the future shape of Central and Southern Africa – the railway conference. It is interesting, in 1978, to look back on the deliberations of the five governments concerned with Rhodesian railways at the time, and see how crucial they were in terms of the longer term development of the area. The participants themselves seem to have appreciated the major strategic issues which lay at the base of their discussions.

Huggins, egged on by one of his most ambitious ministers, a Colonel Guest, argued strongly in favour of Southern Rhodesia owning the whole railway company. It was the largest employer in the Colony – of white labour and black – so that its policies lay at the heart of the Southern Rhodesian economy and its electorate. Harlech proposed that it should be jointly owned by the two Rhodesias, South Africa, and the High Commission Territories. He told Machtig that the situation could not continue where policy of such importance was decided by the board of a big business corporation domiciled in London (BSA). He also argued that sound cooperation on the railways, as the backbone of the developing finances of the region, might take the place of more formal amalgamation – another reason why Huggins would not like it. The conference agreed on a new system of control, which, though it avoided any conclusions about future ownership at least made sure that, regardless of ownership, the railways would function better thereafter. Harlech told Machtig that 'Baring presided with a degree of skill and tact'.[8]

By 1944 it was clear that the war was going to be over within two years at the most. Statesmen in Southern Africa turned with renewed interest to the question of amalgamation, which they felt now could at least be discussed again with representatives of the Imperial government. There are two undated and unmarked memoranda in Evelyn's papers which appear to record an exchange of views between himself and Huggins on the question, probably in July, 1943. The first memorandum shows that Huggins, if it was he, believed the present position was either:

'(a) that the British government having refused to approve a scheme with Northern Rhodesia and Nyasaland, will persist in their refusal (at any rate for a period of years, probably stretching beyond the conclusion of the immediate post-war settlement) or (b) they may be persuaded to reconsider their decision possibly at the conclusion of hostilities. . . .'

He concluded that if (a) was correct, his government should press for a favourable labour agreement, favourable marketing opportunities, and the greatest possible coordination of the development of secondary industries in the three territories so as to induce the development of some kind of common market. If (b) was to be the case it would probably be combined with a proposal to set up a standing council involving all the affected territories, which the Salisbury government should endorse, albeit cautiously.

'Personally I cannot see that the acceptance of the British Government's proposals would have a harmful result. Possibly the Union government might object. But they have declared themselves in favour of pan-Africanism. This term has not yet been too clearly defined. But presumably a movement in two stages is contemplated, first neighbouring states to form some kind of association and then the association to approach one another. The proposal does not seem to clash with stage one.'

This paper is accompanied by a draft memorandum – clearly Evelyn's since there are one or two pencilled addenda in his handwriting. The memorandum must be addressed to Huggins, for a number of reasons, not the least among them that it would have been inconceivable for Evelyn to have written in this indiscreet vein to anybody else in the colony. What is interesting about the draft is that Evelyn is clearly here advising Huggins on the best possible tactics to achieve integration, while at the same time using the opportunity to make some subtle suggestions about how Southern Rhodesia's native policy would have to change, and could change, to become more acceptable both to British and educated African opinion. Evelyn warned Huggins that the Colonial Office's attitude to amalgamation would be dictated by Lord Hailey's report on native administration rather than the Bledisloe Commission. He said that he understood that Hailey had accepted that the provision of material services for Africans in Southern Rhodesia – health, irrigation, agriculture – was equal to and possibly in advance of that for the two northern territories, and that though Hailey had not realised it, Southern Rhodesia could probably also claim the same achievement in education. On the other hand native justice, the severity of the pass-laws and the absence of any local native treasury system were aspects in Southern Rhodesia's disfavour. However, the issue really narrowed down, in Hailey's view, to the likely future employment prospects for an educated native in an amalgamated economy, both with regard to the Nyasaland railway and to any work other than in the mines. Could any assurances be given on these points? Evelyn asked. He recognised that the issues affecting the industrial colour-bar constituted much the most serious obstacle to amalgamation but he suggested that the Southern Rhodesian government should take advantage of the 'cold storage' period to remove the weak points in the native administration (always stressing that the judgment 'weak' was one of Hailey's, not his own) and make more obvious the ways in which Southern Rhodesia provided better services for its natives than were available elsewhere. He suggested sending an administrative officer to Northern Rhodesia to study how Southern Rhodesia might borrow the best of the system of native courts and treasuries run by native councils; as well as simplifying the pass-laws, building a new native hospital in Salisbury, and making a more concerted effort at soil conservation in the native reserve.

The climax to all this preparation came when Huggins was invited to London to attend the Dominions Prime Ministers' conference in June, 1944. He had several hard sessions with Cranborne and also with Stanley, the Colonial Secretary, and the discussions were fully reported back to Evelyn in Salisbury.[9] He told Cranborne how deeply disappointed he had been by the Hailey Report. Cranborne countered by saying – as Evelyn had warned Huggins he would say – that the differences in native policy revealed by Hailey made amalgamation out of the question at this time, but that he was all for closer cooperation between the territories, for instance by extending the governors' conferences. Huggins was not impressed, and complained that the Southern Rhodesians were subsidising Nyasaland's development by using their labour without getting anything in return.

The British ministers tackled him further on the industrial colour bar, which Huggins maintained would not survive in face of the hard economic facts; the need to use coloured labour for jobs now reserved for whites would, quite soon, break it down. That was another reason why he wanted amalgamation now, before his white electorate woke up to the dangers. However, in the end he agreed on a compromise – which entailed a grudging acceptance of a Central African council with a secretariat to promote much closer cooperation between the territories – and said that, though unimpressed, he would put it to his government upon his return.

If the going appeared difficult, it was made better by Huggins being invited to sit in on the meetings of the Dominion's Prime Ministers, and also some of the War Cabinet meetings, which impressed him enormously. He also made a good impression on Cranborne. The outcome was that he got nowhere on the issue of amalgamation, and it went back into cold storage for a few years until the idea of the Central African Federation, was born in the mind of the post war Labour Cabinet, and launched by the Conservatives in the early 1950s. By then, however, Evelyn's time was fully taken up with more pressing affairs in East Africa.

What were Evelyn's own views about the future shape of Central Africa? The tone of his memorandum to Huggins was sympathetic, and seemed to align him firmly with his Prime Minister on the amalgamation issue. He took care not to associate himself with any of the criticisms of native policy, which were all tactfully attributed to Lord Hailey. Was his attitude based on a surreptitious hope that he could coax Huggins before his trip to London into making concessions on native policy, by presenting them as necessary if tiresome prerequisites to the much greater prize of amalgamation? From his other contributions to the issue it is clear that he recognised that it was Southern Rhodesia which would have to change before the geopolitically attractive idea of amalgamation would stand any chance of success.

CHAPTER XII

The View from
Government House

From Evelyn's and Molly's letters home from Southern Rhodesia we know that he endorsed the distaste for much of Southern Rhodesia's native policies which was implicit if not explicit in the Hailey report. The whole of his governship was geared to seeing how he could use his office, albeit obliquely, to influence attitudes among Rhodesian whites, to loosen the hardening assumptions which were already taking Rhodesia towards a segregated society. According to Sir Humphrey Gibbs, who was a great friend and became Southern Rhodesia's last colonial governor before the declaration of independence, Evelyn's liberal views, and his courage in putting them forward and pursuing them as Governor, won him more respect with the younger generation than with those with whom, or through whom, he mostly had to work. Already, by May, 1943, after only six months in office, the official censor had intercepted a letter which crops up rather cryptically in the Public Records under the heading 'Unpopularity of Sir Evelyn and Lady Mary Baring' and then quotes an extract from the intercepted letter which read, 'Some people think that . . . will occur as they think that Sir E and Lady M are taking so much interest in the natives.' The entry has the words 'destroyed under statute' stamped all over it, so we will never know more than that the official censor thought it important enough to send back to the Dominions Office.

It does seem that Evelyn used his office much more to concentrate on native policies and administration than the European settlers were accustomed to expect from His Excellency, whom they traditionally regarded at *their* Governor, appointed to give garden parties for them and to leave concern for the natives to the Chief Native Commissioner and his administrative officers. Once at an *ndaba* of chiefs, in the presence of Evelyn, a chief let out a string of grievances. The Native Commissioner in whose area this occurred was given a rap over the knuckles. 'We were always careful to keep the Governor out of the trouble spots,' according to one senior member of Huggins's staff at the time.

If that was the attitude of most senior members of the native administration, they must have had considerable difficulty adjusting to the way Evelyn went about acquainting himself with and involving himself in every aspect of native policy. The first key was in touring – a practise born of his old days in India – which galvanised him to penetrate parts of Rhodesia seldom visited before by even a Provincial Commissioner, let alone a Governor. The second key, as part of the tour, was his voracious appetite for information, which involved endless, rather heavy-handed conversations with everybody whom Evelyn thought could add something to the little black notebooks he kept with him. His technique was to take the 'expert' aside and tell him all he – Evelyn – knew about the subject, asking him along the way if that was correct. The purpose of this seemed two-fold – partly to impress the official with the expertise of the Governor, partly to get him to volunteer more real information now that he realized he could not fob off this knowledgeable Governer with the usual ritual platitudes reserved for visiting dignitaries. Evelyn was not above feeling slightly pleased with himself for what he obviously thought were virtuoso performances.

His touring started almost immediately he arrived in the colony and Evelyn was soon haranguing chiefs about the virtues of agricultural reform, rotational grazing and other methods of soil conservation, such as contour ridging. Sometimes their meetings were informal affairs in front of the District Officer's house, with a few chiefs sitting round (one Commissioner apparently used to keep his chiefs waiting outside his house for days or weeks to ensure their acquiescence in a particular line of policy); on other occasions it was a grand affair. Evelyn used to appear clothed in white uniform, crowned with the tall cocked hat and the white feathers, his Star of St Michael and George glistening on his chest. In front of him would squat several hundred chiefs in their best suits, crowding into the shade of jacaranda trees, with their wives at the back in bright cotton dresses. There would be innumerable speeches from the chiefs, and Evelyn would make the speech he almost always made, emphasising the few main points about crop rotation, soil conservation, stock control. Then he would descend from his platform and talk to as many chiefs as they could fit in.

One *ndaba* was held in a district near Gokwe which had never been visited by a Governor before. Evelyn wore his plumes, but the chiefs and headman, many of whom had travelled as far as 150 miles to attend, were more primitively attired than their mission-educated fellow countrymen near the European areas, and came one by one to squat down in front of Evelyn and converse with him – the squatter and the nine-foot-high plumed figure of white presenting a fitting tableau, and confirming for the Africans their image of Evelyn's absolute power. The Chief Native Commissioner confided to Molly afterwards that many of their petitions would be granted whatever their wants, since otherwise they might think the *ndaba* had lost its point, and next time would not bother to travel the 150 miles.

In July, 1943, Molly and Evelyn went on a prolonged tour along the Zambesi, accompanied by the local administrative officer and his wife, Mr and Mrs Ross Tapson, who were just the sort of characters the Barings preferred to the more cloying society which fluttered in and out of Government House. Mr Tapson had been on the move in his district for about sixteen years. He knew all the spoors, which fascinated Evelyn; and he dealt fairly, if harshly, with the natives under his control. On one occasion, when he had sent instructions to a chief to prepare a rest camp for the Governor's party, they arrived to find it scruffily prepared. He instantly ordered the natives in his own party to burn it down. After that no further rest camps were scruffily prepared. He used to refer to the Governor in quasi-superstitious terms for the Africans' benefit – in that area they had not been christianised – talking about 'The Great One' and telling the chiefs to hide their faces and look down as they were in the presence of one 'Who Came From High Places.' Down by the banks of the Zambesi, after an *ndaba*, he provided 1600 tribesmen with beer, upon which they danced for three days and three nights without stopping even for something to eat.

There were also tours of the game reserves, which became a regular feature of Evelyn's African governorships. The first one, without Molly who was ill, was in the Wankie game reserve in August, 1943, when he went with a warden into a hide built next to a drinking place and saw almost all the animals of the Rhodesian bush at a sitting – all the African species of buck like koodoo, eland, duiker, sable, klipspringer, stembuck, water buck, and also giraffes, zebras, wildebeests, lions, buffaloes, and as a final display, a herd of 18 elephants. On their way back to camp Evelyn and the game warden were chased by an angry cow elephant, having ventured ill-advisedly out of their car to take photographs. The story of the governor's escape was not allowed to circulate in Salisbury, but Evelyn claimed to have thoroughly enjoyed the thrill of such a danger as he had not experienced since his pigsticking days in India. His tours to Wankie were always on foot, owing to the petrol shortage. He would arrive by train and then trek off into the bush with a warden, followed by a party of bearers carrying, in pride of place, a pannier full of live chickens which would be killed one by one for the Governor's special diet. The tours were not always to the native areas. The touring in a European farming area followed a fairly familiar pattern – staying with the local commissioner, and holding three meetings a day in village halls full of farmers, with cream buns and milky tea for refreshment.

Evelyn's concentration on native affairs yielded a small dividend, he believed, when Huggins's government added £50,000 to the vote for African administration in the 1944 budget, something which was apparently unprecedented, not least because it went through parliament without a murmur of opposition. He was also, at the time, stepping up his warnings to Rhodesian municipalities to tackle the problem of native areas before Rhodesia suffered the fate of South Africa, where the expansion of African shanty towns, unplanned and undesired, had already created an insoluble social difficulty.

Evelyn soon seemed to recognise that there were two different aspects to African social policy – rural and urban – and that the urban question was one which was both more urgent, in terms of the needs, and less popular in the sense that any new policy initiative had to be financed by European ratepayers contributing to the municipal budgets. Although his touring brought him more in contact with the administrative officers in the field, with chiefs, headmen, and the familiar question of soil management and peasant agriculture which he recalled from his days in India, it was the situation in the towns of Rhodesia that provided the more critical illustration of the differences of race, culture and standard of living which were increasingly to aggravate Rhodesian society. And the pace of change there, and hence the importance of new policies, was much faster than in the timeworn procedures of rural colonial administration.

In May, 1943, Evelyn sent a despatch to Machtig about the conditions of natives in the towns.[1] He first pointed out that many of them were non-indigenous Rhodesians, having come from Nyasaland, Northern Rhodesia and Portuguese East Africa. Salisbury contained about half the urban African population of the entire colony, and he described in great detail how the native housing there was constructed, what materials were used and what the cost was, what recreation facilities were available, standards of cleanliness and so on. One can imagine his little black note-book fairly bursting its binding after some visit to an African housing location accompanied by assiduous officials pouring facts and figures into the emperor's ear. He described the rather patch-work approach to native housing which was shown by the Salis-bury Municipal Authority, but ended by concluding that public interest was increasing, and opinion was 'changing with surprising speed'.

This change had been heralded by another Land Apportion-ment Act passed in 1941, which sought to encourage municipali-ties to create housing areas for natives working for ratepayers, by replacing the shanty towns with proper housing and by regular-ising the very haphazard series of tenancies held by those Africans who resided on white freeholds within the municipal areas. By the end of 1943 Salisbury had 40,000 Africans living in the mu-nicipal area, while Bulawayo had doubled its African population to 34,000 in the space of the previous seven years – mostly under the economic influence of the war, which was providing more employment for Africans within the industrial centres of Rho-desia. This influx had, naturally, not been matched by any cor-responding growth in the provision of adequate housing for the Africans. Only Salisbury had set aside any land for African hous-ing, and even then only whites were allowed to build the houses for blacks. Moreover, the Land Apportionment Act sought to en-shrine the continued semi-segregation of housing, whatever extra provision was made for African locations, and to see that the con-tinuous influx, even under the pressure of the rising economic power of the African worker, did not result in Africans being enabled to move into a housing area formerly occupied only by whites. As in South Africa, European opinion remained un-comfortably bedevilled by the contradiction that, though their traditional view of blacks was of a stable rural population, living in tribal reserves under the authority of the chiefs, the colony's, and European's, economic needs required an expanding non-rural, non-tribal African population which had escaped from the comforting continuity of African rural life. Consequently the European ratepayers begrudged subsidising this kind of housing for Africans, because it cut across all their preconceptions of what the African's role in Rhodesian society should be.

In May 1944 he wrote to Paul Emrys Evans, advising him that the most interesting feature of the current parliamentary session in Salisbury was the ease with which the estimates for an increase in the native affairs and native education budgets had slipped through.[2] He pointed out that the Rhodesian Labour Party's attitude towards natives was not likely to be confused with that of the British Labour Party, since, though it adopted fine sounding sentiments, its leader had agreed with Huggins's view that the native living in white areas of the colony would remain a drawer of water and hewer of wood – 'scarcely a liberal point of view.' Another and serious future danger for the country was the divorce between European and native agriculture implied by the administrative segregation of agricultural development, and the likelihood therefore of competition between European and native crop producers, which could only be avoided by the development of a good selling cooperative scheme for African farmers (a very similar problem was to await him in Kenya ten years later).

Evelyn's view of the importance of developing African society and institutions across a wide front, not just politically, had already developed by the time he arrived in the colony, probably as a result of his observation of the breakdown of British authority in India. As early as January, 1943, after only a month in Salisbury, he made a speech in which he said that the misfortunes of the British administration started in India in the nineteenth century with the ideas of *laissez faire*.[3] The cause of the subsequent troubles in India was the failure to carry on economic development of Indian society at the same speed as organised secondary education. The growth of race antagonism, born of an educated but unemployable indigenous population, destroyed good will. This, he thought, had, up to the present been avoided in Britain's African colonies, largely because progressive use had been made of indigenous authorities (central and local) like tribal councils, chiefs and headmen, for which people had felt respect before the British came. His underlying view was that the structure of African society should not be Europeanised in form if the form had outpaced any change in the substance. Thus he always strove to work social changes through the familiar and established structure of African society, unless or until the tribal or local institutions reached a point where they were clearly not capable of any further development.

This of course was not a view entirely consistent with the prevailing desire in London to impose on British colonies a political structure which corresponded closely to the Westminster model. Reaffirmation of the authority of chiefs, or of the importance of tribal loyalties, was looked on askance by more liberal thinkers, as evidence of a desire to keep the African down, backward, irresponsible. Evelyn was much influenced by what he had seen in India of the unbridgeable gulf which had developed between the educated, and therefore westernised, Indian, and the peasant. Indeed, in October, 1944, in his farewell speech to educated Africans in Salisbury, he made this his main point. He told them that the vote for African education had increased by 40% the previous year, but then went on to say that nothing could be more disastrous than a breach between educated and uneducated Africans. 'I have lived several years in eastern countries and seen the bad results of such a breach – the growth of a class of educated people who are too proud, too foreign in their thoughts and ideas from their fellows, to be able to raise the general level of life in their country. If you truly profit from school, you will just use your knowledge to help your uneducated fellows to be better farmers, to build better houses, raise better cattle, mend bad customs. So don't be too hasty to condemn everything that is traditional in African life.'[4] He also counselled them not to be too impatient with the political authorities' and the Europeans' apparent indifference to African affairs. If they looked in *Hansard* they would see the increasing interest being taken in native affairs.

Meanwhile, behind the political and public front, the Barings were developing a Government House lifestyle which, before Evelyn's African career was finished, was to earn him the sneering soubriquet of 'Last of the Viceroys'. Certainly it was unusual in comparison with the other post-war Government Houses occupied by career colonial servants with less money and older children than had Evelyn and Molly. In one sense, their age was the key, since Evelyn's marked youth on assuming the Salisbury governorship, and the fact that he had three extremely young children with whom he was accustomed to romp at the beginning and end of their day, singled him out from most other colonial servants then strutting the gubernatorial stage. Molly was determined to see that his home life provided a constant factor, enabling him to escape from the pressures of work, and helping the children to accept the disruption of living abroad, or, when they subsequently went to boarding school, of trying to be at home during the holidays in places half a world apart. Government House life was in reality Howick life, and if this meant that it obtruded more, permeated the quasi-official atmosphere of a Government House, that was probably all for the good. It certainly gave the locals something to talk about, and the newspapers to write about. But one can see why it came to be regarded as viceregal. The tone was set at Molly's first big dinner party, shortly after their first Christmas in Salisbury, when, after dinner, she and Tom brought out their clavichords and played duets while the guests politely listened, and Evelyn, not so unobtrusively, went to sleep (once or twice in Africa he actually went to sleep *at* dinner, as his mother had done in Cairo). At half past ten punctually Evelyn woke up just in time to say good-bye, and the guests all left; not everyone's idea of a rollicking good evening under an African moon.

Because .of the war the Barings probably found conditions rather similar to that experienced by Rhodesians under international sanctions thirty years later. Butter was rationed, and meat difficult to find, with mutton unobtainable. Electric light bulbs were practically non-existent and Government House, being only equipped with 40 watt bulbs, was almost dark after sunset. But there were compensations, naturally, for the highest in the land; with fourteen African houseboys to look after them indoors, and a garden staff which had shortly before been cut from 18 to 10 and which provided the supplies for the 26 vases which Molly found herself arranging in the house every day. One day Molly decided to relieve the gloom of their dinner parties by introducing rowdy games after dinner – acting and other kinds of uninhibited drawing-room buffoonery. It was a great success, even overcoming the initially starchy misgivings of the Grand Vizier Holbech.

Evelyn's somnolence during these evenings was hardly surprising, given the nature of his daily routine – rising about 6.45 to go out, with any guests who could brave it, to ride the Salisbury police horses for an hour or so, followed by a romp with the children; breakfast at 8.45, followed by a long morning in his office; probably guests to lunch; a visit after lunch to a farm, a municipality, African location or anything else which Evelyn might be interested in, or an expedition to make a speech or open something – the staple fare of most men holding dignified public office. By the time the guests came for dinner – clavichord or party games notwithstanding – His Excellency was ready for bed.

When Evelyn went out on a visit, he almost always overdid it, to the mixed admiration and consternation of officials in attendance. Those concerned with the timetable were normally left in despair, as he finished a day's tour of farming lands at 9 p.m., long after dark, through insisting on climbing some hill in the vicinity;

or examined the railway workshops exhaustively for the whole of one day and then expressed a royal desire to return to the fray the next day.

Friends – real friends rather than acquaintances – were few and far between. One couple were the Humphrey Gibbs' who farmed near Bulawayo, and were to succeed the Barings in Government House some twenty years later, when Gibbs became the last Governor before the Unilateral Declaration of Independence. Apart from the Gibbs' however and a very few others, the Barings avoided intimate relationships with fellow Rhodesians, and not just because the nature of the office kept them apart, as it might a minor royalty. There was something of a cultural gap between them and the Rhodesians, which partially explained why Molly assiduously arranged her entertaining so that the guests were permanently occupied, eating or competing – but not conversing. One day an army parson came to lunch, and put their own suspicion into words, when he told them that he did not find the Rhodesian mind up to the English one. General knowledge and culture were completely lacking in the young men who came to the barracks at eighteen to be trained for the army. He held discussion groups which they seemed to enjoy, but the moment the subject left a purely practical range they were lost. The boys had mainly been educated in South Africa. As, at that time, there was no university, no learning was attracted to Rhodesia, and therefore there was no intellectual substratum, and certainly no intelligent conversation in private homes. The Barings wondered gloomily what would be the result in another generation, in a country where the climate conspired against thought – hadn't Bernard Shaw said that the curse of South Africa was its climate? – which, coupled with cheap labour reducing the need for ingenuity and imagination, induced a life of no reflection and all action. Mind you, Molly was clearly not quite so immune from these influences as one might suppose, since she started taking flying lessons – to Evelyn's barely concealed consternation – and also took part in and won the Salisbury show jumping competition, riding a police horse and following a man who gave himself concussion after a crashing fall at the gate fence.

Mostly, the Barings diverted themselves socially by seeking out interesting eccentrics. One man came from South Africa who was mad about compost, and who nagged Evelyn night and day about the evil done by people 'who ought to be shot' for burning their mealy stalks. The rest of the family were driven mad by his attentions. Tom Goff and Molly christened him the 'Loud Speaker' – but Evelyn, ever searching for that elusive ten per cent of new information, weathered the other ninety per cent waffle without appearing to notice it. In Sir Evelyn's and Lady Mary's Government Houses, there were always going to be surprises; but they were surprises one might more naturally expect of an English colonial palace.

CHAPTER XIII
Promotion

By mid-1944 Evelyn had grown into his governorship. Though he was still only 41, he had fashioned a distinctive style and largely overcome the inhibitions which had grown up through the caprices and omissions of his predecessors. London was well pleased with his performance, and clearly Huggins was also, to judge by his reaction when the Cabinet in London suddenly decided that Evelyn should move on. Huggins was furious at being deprived of a Governor with whom he had established a close, reliable and useful relationship. Evelyn was naturally thrilled, since he had already come to the view that Rhodesia was too small a place for his energies, and that the pace of change and of political life generally was too slow. This attitude had not taken long to develop once the initial novelty of being a constitutional colonial monarch had worn off. His period in the Foreign Office had convinced him that he would never be happy except at the hub of affairs, and ensured that he was only going to enjoy being Governor of Rhodesia for so long as he could convince himself that he was at the centre of things. In a Rhodesian context that would always be true, but it soon became clear that much of his work involved the whole Southern African scene. Rhodesia was not going to be a satisfactory centre for very long.

In Rhodesia Evelyn found that, with his Indian experience, he had a ready-made advantage when dealing with the administrative world of which the Governor in a colony – even a self-governing one – was the nominal head. He also found that his Baring's and Foreign Office experience had equipped him to bring to Rhodesia a wider perspective than the settlers had been used to. They must have been initially surprised and impressed by the young Governor's range of speeches on the international economic order after the war, on commodities, on the role of gold and so on. Moreover, Evelyn managed to develop a convincing, if never very light-footed, style of speaking. His health seemed to have almost entirely recovered in the Rhodesian climate, particularly since he could periodically fortify himself by tours to the high country, with cold mountain air and lots of exercise to add to the fortnightly liver injections he used to receive at Government House. By August 1943, after about nine months, he was getting a little

E

restless, thought he had found out almost everything there was to know about the colony and wondered how he was going to fill his time during the next year. Molly suggested he should learn Russian. It was a recurring nightmare of hers that he would be posted next to some still more obscure colony, but every time Evelyn received a letter from one of his Foreign Office friends he felt so frustrated at being out of things that she was reassured that he would not accept another backwater.

One day he felt so well that he tried, at a Government House *thé dansant*, to have a little drink which was definitely not *thé*. He promptly started hiccups which continued for seventy two hours. Doctors were called; doses administered; Tom Goff lurked behind every corner springing out on Evelyn with a great yell in the hope of frightening the hiccups into submission – all to no avail. The Governor went on hiccuping. The family went to church without him, and though the hiccups temporarily ceased in the excitement of watching a rugby match, it was not until he went off on his own for a whole day to a tobacco farm that he finally shed them. The moral of the incident, they all decided, was that Evelyn was not yet in a state to enjoy even one whisky and soda.

Early in July, 1944, Molly wrote to her mother to warn her that, if she was going to be in London, she might find that Bobbety Cranborne had some news for her. The censor saw to it that she said no more. What she was hinting at was the fact that Evelyn had by then been told that his next appointment was to be in South Africa as Lord Harlech's successor. It was not for a month that Molly felt free to write more fully, which was perhaps just as well, since Huggins had only just been told, and his dismay at the news would have been considerably aggravated if he had also heard if first unofficially. Smuts had asked for Evelyn after meeting him a second time, and getting on extremely well with him during a holiday which the Barings took in South Africa in March of that year. London deliberated, and decided that the 'insult' to Rhodesia of moving Evelyn on after less than two years in Salisbury was outweighed by what they regarded as 'the great advantage to the empire as a whole'. Evelyn was obviously swayed by the fact that the request and the pressure came from Cranborne, rather than Attlee, his predecessor at the Dominions Office.

Cranborne was Molly's cousin, and Evelyn had developed a close friendship with him while spending week-ends at Hatfield before and during the war. Evelyn had valued Cranborne's judgment (though they were to disagree over later African policies) and in his early days as a proconsul relied on him to be ministerial mentor within Churchill's wartime government. More interestingly he felt that he had a chance of saving the three British protectorates – Bechuanaland, Swaziland and Basutoland – which, as he put it, 'might be lost by someone with an eye to his own future and therefore anxious to get a good chit from Smuts' (who was agitating for their incorporation into the Union).

The term of his new appointment, at that stage, was to be 'for the duration of the war,' but it was recognised to be somewhat elastic and would last for at least two years. Elastic it certainly was, since the two years stretched eventually to seven.

Molly and the family were in some ways sad to leave Rhodesia – since, politics apart, their conditions in Pretoria and Cape Town were going to be inferior to the standard of life they enjoyed in Salisbury. The 'long grass' life, their camping expeditions on the *veld*, would all be more circumscribed, certainly as far as the children were concerned, though they could hope for some touring in the High Commission Territories. The diplomatic atmosphere in Pretoria and Cape Town, even without the spasmodic anti-English attitude of the Boers, would compare unfavourably with the admittedly dull but friendly and very British atmosphere of Salisbury, where there were ADCs to answer the telephone, shopkeepers falling over themselves to hang on to Government House patronage, and the other inestimable advantage of the minor royalty status which attached to the representative of the Crown in a British colony.

Evelyn, on the other hand, was to benefit greatly from the change. He had established a convincing reputation of being the most discreet man in the colony, and he had so thoroughly won Huggins's confidence, that he even used to draft some of his Cabinet briefs for him. But the prospect of jousting with Smuts was clearly more attractive to somebody of his age and cast of mind.

The reaction to his departure seemed to be one of almost universal regret. Both the *Bulawayo Chronicle* and *Rhodesian Herald* commented on his early promotion, recalled that he had been their youngest Governor and enthused about the breadth and depth of his speeches. *The Labour Front*, organ of the Southern Rhodesian Labour Party, said, 'We have never had a more sympathetic Governor . . . There is no secret of the fact that he was unpopular in certain quarters because of his sympathy with our African population. . . .' *The African Weekly,* one of the few papers written by and for blacks, commented, 'We shall surely miss his genial personality. It is common knowledge that he rendered first class service to the African people from the very heart. He has throughout his career enjoyed the confidence of the African people. An agreeable surprise to the African people was the way he showed a healthy disregard for outworn precedent. When he went to the native areas many Africans flocked round him just to talk to him, and when he went to their homes he wanted to see their wives, mothers and children. He was named Vilidhela, which means he who points the way to others.' From South Africa too there was a welcoming editorial in the *Cape Times,* which said, 'South Africans, many of whom are almost morbidly inclined to look for an air of conscious superiority in the families of the higher nobility of England, were impressed with the simple friendliness of the great Lord Cromer's son.'

Somehow, in the two months between the announcement of his promotion and his formal departure from Rhodesia, Evelyn found time to pay an official visit to the Belgian Congo. It took the form of a minor African state occasion, with Molly accompanying him, and had been laid on so long before that there was no question of his cancelling it owing to the suddenness of his impending departure. Their progress through the Congo was positively imperial. Its style seemed incongruous in view of the desperate struggle which the two parent imperial powers were waging together in darkest Europe – a fact which it would have been hard to determine from the resplendent occasions, the white plumes and uniforms bedecked with sashes and medals, guards of honour, artillery salutes, royal trains, banquets, speeches in French, and marzipan Union Jacks, which accompanied their triumphal progress through the region.

On his return, and barely a week before he had to leave Rhodesia, Evelyn jotted down a few 'notes' for Machtig, arising out of his Congo trip. Considering that he had spent most of his official visit talking with great enthusiasm in French to whichever Belgian official was attached to him it is not surprising that his 'notes' took up fourteen foolscap pages, dealing with every aspect of the Belgian Congo – European population, labour, social life, native authorities, towns, education, health, agriculture, native trade and Asiatics. The Dominions Office was thrilled with his offering, 'This is a brilliant letter,' said the minute. 'Sir Evelyn Baring's interest in anthropology, in forestry, in agriculture, in African tribal customs, his insight into political feeling and his power of vivid and humorous description encourage one to await his impressions of the High Commission Territories with eagerness.'[1] Clearly those early experimental despatches to Katie were now beginning to pay dividends.

The closing weeks in Salisbury were hectic. Farewell visits and speeches had to be made almost to excess, to compensate for the offence which Rhodesian opinion took at Evelyn's premature posting.

In his closing despatch to Machtig, sent on October 21, 1944, four days before he departed, he was quite optimistic:

'European opinion is on the move. It is my misfortune to leave the colony at a moment when it is impossible to state what the final results of this stirring of conscience and awakening of apprehension will be. Before the war the staff of the European administration of African affairs was ludicrously insufficient. Now a big increase has been made without any criticism.'

He went on to describe various measures of civil and legal administration, in fields in which the Europeans were now taking a more active and expansive role.

'The test of the durability of these intentions will come if, after the war, trade flags, revenue declines and "economise on the native" becomes the cry.'

He then dealt with native education and health services and the plans to provide more indirect rule of the native areas through native authorities and the chiefs, but he cautioned that the present Chief Native Commissioner had a long way to go before this conviction could be given practical form.

'No progress of any sort has been made on amendment of the pass-laws or the relaxation of their administration. The only hope appears to be that when the overcrowded compounds in the towns are being cleared and the vast majority of natives live in the native urban areas the offences of pass-laws may become less numerous. This was the experience of the Belgians in the Congo. Huggins is trying hard to stimulate more native housing outside unplanned urban areas. Huggins maintains that restrictions on the advance of native workmen are breaking down and will still further relax in the future. Clearly future developments must depend on the views of the rising generation and the soldiers who will return from the war. Among many young Rhodesians a growing feeling of nationalism is noticeable and an increasing desire to be proud of their country. As a part of this desire may sometimes come the wish to feel that White Rhodesia's administration of its black subjects is something to praise, not something to be excused. The only home these young men know is in Africa. In this they are no different from the young men and women of the Union. But the attention of the young South African is fatally diverted by the never-ending squabbles of Boer and Briton. I sometimes feel that it is in Southern Rhodesia that the young have the opportunity to do what has never yet been done; work out a mode of life for a mixed country. The tide of bitter feeling has not washed away the pass-laws or the industrial colour bar but it is nevertheless a strong tide. People will, however, listen to the Prime Minister when he discusses native affairs. It is important that in the future the Prime Minister of the day should be encouraged by advice, questions, informal notes to act on the following lines: minimum wages for natives, more native housing, build up native authorities, and encourage the establishment of a government organisation to market all native crops.

I will conclude with some general observations. When I arrived Huggins was in a vaguely disgruntled mood. His feeling was a compound of fear that Southern Rhodesia was so small that her interests might be ignored but uncertainty concerning the action to be taken on the recommendation of the Bledisloe Commission, resentment of the fancied lack of appreciation of his genuine desire to keep the British flag flying in South Central Africa and Southern Rhodesia out of the Union. In particular he knew that when allowances were made for her size Southern Rhodesia's war effort compared very favourably with that of the Union and he felt that for this the colony should be given credit. During the last two years he has reached a more contented frame of mind. In spite of the rejection of amalgamation proposals he returned from London very pleased. Recently there has been a set back. The legislative changes in Northern Rhodesia have made him remark that the inclusion of Africans in the Legco would probably shut the door on amalgamation for ever. Secondly, it would be idle to deny that he was greatly annoyed by my transfer.

Three general suggestions: 1) Do everything possible to make the new Council a success. 2) Tactfully emphasise the growing sense of nationalism among young Rhodesians. There may be a side to this sentiment critical to the British government – the powers they retain in their attitude to amalgamation – but there is also another side resentful of patronage by the Union and fearful of absorption in it. The movement is in any case too strong to check and might possibly, I believe, with good fortune, be used to help to maintain South Rhodesia as a buffer state between the Union and Colonial Office territories. 3) Continue to give Huggins as much information as possible on the aims of policy in the British government. He greatly appreciated the manner in which he was taken into the confidence of the Cabinet during his visit to the U.K. But living as he does in a small country full of false rumours, curious ideas sometimes get into his head. The last time I saw him he told me that he had come to the conclusion that the real reason for the rejection of amalgamation was a feeling in London that if Southern Rhodesia was allowed to administer Northern Rhodesia and Nyasaland, it would be impossible to continue to refuse to allow the Union to administer the three protectorates. But in spite of all this Huggins is by far the best man in the country. I have the highest opinion of him and I believe that the majority of Rhodesians share this opinion. He is definitely a leader of and not a follower of public opinion. He is completely sincere and devoted to the British connection.'[2]

There remained the farewell broadcast, and a closing speech to a Government House garden party, a function which always seems to come closest to holy communion among British colonials living abroad. His farewell broadcast, directed specifically at the white population of Rhodesia was, for a Governor, fairly blunt:

'It would be to the advantage of a country such as Southern Rhodesia if more was known of the ideals and methods used and patience shown by the great oriental and African administrators of British history in their dealings with people of other races. You are the rulers: and good rulers should know much about those they rule. You often complain that Southern Rhodesia is misrepresented. But I hope you will not think me ungenerous if I say that I have noticed among Rhodesians themselves some lack of knowledge of the facts. How many of you know the difference between native reserves and native areas, or that the largest irrigation schemes south of the equator for Africans are to be found in your own Sabi valley? Do you realize you have probably the best system of rural clinics in

Africa – a curious contrast to the most inadequate native hospitals in Salisbury and Bulawayo?[3]'
There was more of the same kind. To his garden party guests, he varied the theme only slightly, but the underlying message was the same – an appeal to the best Europeans to become more involved with the affairs of the whole country. 'I hope the new generation will regard political life as an honourable and important career,' he said. He hoped they would preserve the British connection and appealed for a greater sense of urgency in dealing with native affairs. 'On most other matters Rhodesians are able to get a move on – but not when it comes to native matters. If young Rhodesians can grow up to take the trouble to learn the facts and particularly to realize that natives are human beings, then all will be well with your country.' These sentiments sound pretty banal in the 1970s, but uttered at an all-white garden party in wartime Rhodesia they would have offended many an ear. *The Rhodesian Herald* in its leader column endorsed what the Governor had to say – albeit coolly – by saying that he had shown a ready ability to get to the roots of many questions which, as he reminded them in his broadcast, 'many of us are somewhat inclined to view superficially.' However a letter from Humphrey Gibbs was much less detached. 'Dear HE and Molly B, We are losing real friends. What a difference the last two years has made to the Colony to have a couple who took such a real interest in everything that we are trying to do – not just figureheads – and could throw out such a lot of helpful advice.'
On October 26 they steamed out of Salisbury in the royal train. Their luggage had now grown to a mammoth 104 packing cases. Evelyn had put on his full dress uniform and had received a mounted escort the whole way from Government House. Hundreds of people turned out, many in tears. They stopped at Bulawayo for the night, where the farewells were rather more jolly and less maudlin, until Huggins came for his final breakfast with Evelyn. He was clearly very upset. After a long session with the Governor he came to say goodbye to Molly, not his usual robust self, so often full of chaff, but fidgety and bewildered. He blurted out, 'You know this is all very upsetting when you are trying to run a country,' and then bolted out of the room.
So Evelyn's first major colonial appointment was over. What had he achieved? He had stamped himself firmly on the minds of senior mandarins and ministers in Whitehall. The quality and persistence of his communications from Africa seemed to have

pleasantly surprised them. With the exception of Lord Harlech, the days when Britain's Proconsuls provided the London government with comprehensive but individual reporting of local affairs had already been superseded by the development of wireless communications. The exigencies of the war, and the need to minimise cable traffic, presented Evelyn with an excuse to indulge himself in his favourite pastime of imbibing and then imparting knowledge to interested listeners.

Secondly, the quality of his diplomacy, and his dealings with Huggins, in addition to the first and obviously dramatic effect he had had on Smuts, must have persuaded Whitehall that his talents were being wasted in what was a relative backwater in Rhodesia.

Third, his presence in Southern Africa, through his dealings with other governments at the railway conferences, at the Governors' conferences, and with his visit to the Belgian Congo, gave him a wider reputation than that possessed, for instance, by his fellow colonial governors in Nothern Rhodesia and Nyasaland. All these were external advantages which he had acquired during his sojourn in Salisbury.

And what about the internal scene? A study of all the governorships of Southern Rhodesia, both before and after Evelyn, suggests that his own period of office was indeed distinctive. Obviously his youth marked him off from all the other colonial servants nearing retirement, or senior officers from the services, already retired, who occupied Government House between 1923 and 1965. More significantly though he was there at a time when the war might have been used as a valid excuse for not stimulating any movement in Rhodesian politics, whether in native affairs or in the wider question of amalgamation or integration, the records show that these questions were exhaustively worked on during that period. By the time he left it was clear that the amalgamation issue was settled for at least another 10 years – then only to reappear in the guise of the Central African Federation, and not as part of the immediate post-war settlement for which Huggins had hoped in 1941. But it was also clear that the Rhodesian polity had made a small start towards recognising that the native problem was not something which could be left to the simple nostrums of a farming philosophy, and that the alleviation of the Africans' social conditions, even before one considered their political advance, was going to take up time and money which could only be provided by whites.

Finally Evelyn, in spite of his youth, and comparative inexperience had in the space of two years impressed London enough for him to be appointed at the age of 41 to a position which, at that time, was the most important imperial and diplomatic appointment in Africa. He was returning to Pretoria in style.

CHAPTER XIV
Smuts

Evelyn's job as High Commissioner in South Africa had two distinct sides to it. In the first place he was a diplomat, behaving as an ambassador, accredited to a foreign country though in this case one which was also a fellow member of the Commonwealth. His work therefore consisted of all the usual duties of an ambassador: representing his country's views to his host government; taking part in the continuing dialogue of Anglo-South African relations; reporting to London on the state of affairs in South Africa, its politics, economics, native questions, and likely prospects; entertaining distinguished visitors from the United Kingdom; and finally carrying out some functions as the assumed, if untitular, head of the large English speaking community. The other part of his job was as a traditional Colonial Governor of the three High Commission Territories – Bechuanaland, Basutoland and Swaziland – all of which had Resident Commissioners and locally based administrations responsible directly to Evelyn. His colonial, as opposed to diplomatic, duties involved touring those territories, and dealing directly with the Dominions Office about their development and their economies. The Dominions (later Commonwealth Relations) Office held traditional responsibility for them, rather than the Colonial Office, because it was recognised that they were in a special relationship with South Africa, and it was believed that the best way of ensuring that British policy in the Territories was sensitive to the proximity of South Africa was by having the Dominions Office responsible for them.

Life for the Barings was different and more restricting than it had been as uncrowned king and queen in Salisbury. For a start, Evelyn had to be much more careful what he said – indeed he could say practically nothing in public, which was rather an inhibition after the carefree days of speaking his mind to all and sundry in Southern Rhodesia. He also had a far more formidable network of protocol to contend with than anything devised by Laurence Holbech, since the diplomatic and official community in Capetown and Pretoria seemed to think of very little else. When they first arrived the Barings found that, as the newest head of a mission (apart from being also the youngest) they were the junior members of the diplomatic community and had to pay courtesy calls in order of precedence on all the other missions and members of the government. It was called 'doing the protocol' and woe-betide you if you attempted to ask anybody to your house until these social propieties had been observed. On a more personal level the come-down from Salisbury was immediately noticeable in Pretoria. They had exchanged a Government House for a large villa in a row of houses where they could hear the gramophone playing next door. Evelyn led a real office life as though he was in London. They wore town, rather than country, clothes and had to endure an unending series of lunch and dinner parties. Pretoria was worse than Capetown, where at least there was lovely scenery, sea and mountains, and a house which was set in a beautiful garden on its own under the Table Mountain and about ten miles from the sea. But they also had to suffer the twice-yearly ordeal of packing everything up and moving house between Capetown and Pretoria. Since neither of the official High Commission houses was left furnished when the inhabitants moved on to the other, they had to take all movable contents with them; and, of course, the office files.

Evelyn's work in the Territories, his touring and his great personal crisis over the Seretse Khama affair will be dealt with in later chapters. In Capetown and Pretoria, however, he was mainly concerned with the dealings between the two governments on a number of extremely important external issues; such as the start of the United Nations, (whose charter Smuts helped to draft); the arguments over the future of the South West Africa mandate; important bilateral agreements between Britain and South Africa, over the supply of uranium for the secret new atomic weapons programme and the economic support provided by the gold agreement and other loans at the time of Britain's economic crisis, in 1947; and the row between South Africa and India over the Smuts Government's treatment of South African Indians.

Underlying all this, and perhaps in the longer term more important, was Evelyn's analysis of the developments in South African politics which led, while he was still there, to the eclipse of Smuts, the return of an Afrikaner Nationalist government, and the first steps on a path towards *apartheid* which set South Africa on a thirty-year course from which she has not yet been deflected.

For the first four years of Evelyn's tour, however, General Smuts was the dominant political figure. It may or may not have been diplomatically useful for the British Government that Evelyn developed a special relationship with the old Boer; certainly it made life more interesting for Evelyn, and for Molly for that matter, who found herself beguiled through many a fascinating dinner party sitting next to the old man. Smuts was, by then, in his mid-seventies. It was almost incredible to think that as long ago as 1901 he had been appointed the Supreme Commander of all Boer forces in Cape Colony at the age of 31, at the height of the Boer War, and had taken a hand in the peace negotiations at the end of that bitter struggle. He had been a cabinet minister since 1912, Prime Minister for the first time in 1919, and in and out of office ever since then. But he was not only a giant on the South African stage. Apart from being given command of United Kingdom troops in East Africa in 1916, he was made a member of the Imperial War Cabinet in 1917 – the Committee of Imperial Defence – and, almost alone of South African statesmen, was capable of looking outside the *laager* and concentrating most of his energies on the great global developments which shook the world in the first half of the twentieth century. Shortly before the 1947 Royal Tour of South Africa, Evelyn had to send home a pen-sketch of Smuts for King George's benefit. In it he said, 'He is a great figure who dominates Cabinet and Parliament. His vitality is unimpaired and his shrewd political intelligence and subtle brain have never lost their hold on events. In caucus he is as impatient of criticism as ever, and gives little encouragement to younger recruits among his followers. In Parliament there is a general feeling that he is somewhat prefunctory in his treatment of both Houses and that he reserves his more full dress speeches on international affairs for more favoured audiences in London.'[1]

Though Smuts had asked for Evelyn to be posted to South Africa as High Commissioner, and obviously enjoyed the exchanges of views they had together, their relationship did not inhibit him from continuing to have direct and frequent personal dealings with both Churchill and Attlee when they were Prime Ministers of Britain. In this, Evelyn was merely acting as a postbox, particularly when Smuts was taking part in the discussions about the shape of the post-war settlement However he had to keep himself briefed about the issues which animated the Prime Ministers, which meant that he could feel close to that centre of things for which he had developed such a taste during his time in the Foreign Office. He could hardly have complained of being out of things, when during his first years as High Commissioner, in addition to all the issues which specifically affected Southern Africa and Anglo-South African relations, he was able to listen in on conversations about the future shape of the whole world.

The relationship between the two men had really begun when Evelyn took his family to see Smuts in March, 1944. The Barings were on holiday from Southern Rhodesia, and were, at that time, quite unaware that they were going to be posted subsequently to South Africa. When Evelyn arrived in Pretoria in October, 1944, he found Smuts heavily engaged in discussion with London about the future structure of the proposed United Nations organisation, which Smuts believed should be based on a nexus of the great powers ready to act in concert against any other aggressor. Smuts was against the proposed unanimity rule, and, in the light of subsequent South African attitudes to the United Nations – and the much rehearsed arguments about whether or not that country should unilaterally leave the organisation – it is interesting to quote from his letter to the Dominions Secretary in London:

'Resignation from the organisation should not be allowed, and if a member purports to leave the case should be one for punitive measures, such as economic ostracism or exclusion from benefits enjoyed by members. It would be desertion and might almost be looked on as a hostile act. One of the greatest weaknesses of the old League was the freedom and impunity with which members resigned as soon as they differed from the League's decisions. Membership of the new organisation should be a position of honour and privilege and economic advantage, and leaving it a corresponding disgrace and substantial loss. This is an important matter for the future of the organisation and I hope it may be possible to embody some such provision in the new instrument.'[2]

(South African attitudes to the new organisation, when it was established without these provisions, were to be sorely tested in its very first session over the case of South West Africa, and the Indian campaign against the Smuts' government policies towards South Africa's Indian population).

Smuts was also very exercised about the tendency of the 'Big Three' coalition to break up before a post-war settlement had been achieved, and constantly urged Churchill to preserve the strength and influence of the Commonwealth and Empire as an equal partner in every sense with the United States and the Soviet Union, whom he feared was being allowed too much scope to manipulate a post-war settlement to her advantage. When Attlee took over as Prime Minister, Smuts warned him also against the Allies giving in too much to the Russians, particularly over the Russian desire to keep Germany in a depressed condition. Attlee replied that Britain was not receiving the full support of the United States. (To Churchill, who lost the election, Smuts wired, 'To those whom the Gods love they send both joys and sorrows.')

On his return from the San Francisco conference which set up the United Nations, Smuts gave Evelyn a full-length formal interview, an account of which Evelyn cabled back to the Dominions Office.[3] His view was that the maintenance of world peace now depended on the closest cooperation between the 'Big Three', employing the most modern weapons (this was a week before the atomic bombs exploded over Japan). However the United States, he said, was only just out of isolationism, and its leaders were inexperienced in world affairs; the Russians lived in permanent suspicion of the rest of the world and were led by men who were in some senses ruffians; so that, if power were left with these two nations alone, there would be no effective action. The British Commonwealth was a mature institution, with great experience all over the world, and should play the part of the honest broker, its capacity for this role being so great that it might well actually, if not apparently, be the dominant actor on the world stage. Though he disapproved of the Australian and New Zealand proposals to internationalise the administration of British colonies, he believed that all members of the Commonwealth were still proud to belong to the group, which must, as a group, continue to be active in world affairs. If, through lack of leadership or informed interest by the United Kingdom, the group came to play only a secondary role, the disruptive forces in the world would gain the upper hand.

He then turned to the United Kingdom, where the Labour Party had just won such a colossal victory in the general election. He saw an irony in the fact that the choice had been seen as one between two parties with divergent internal, but single foreign policies, whereas the opposite was really the case. The Labour victory would have no ill effect on Britain's internal structure. The Labour leaders were good and sincere men. Britain would gain from the nationalisation of sources of power, particularly electricity and the railways. But the external dangers were: 1) lack of experience; 2) that Labour leaders and their supporters saw Russia through rose-tinted spectacles. Bevin was all right, and experience of diplomatic negotiations with Russia might destroy his illusions about that country, yet this would take time, and then it might be too late; 3) The need for a strong personality to deal with the Russians. Attlee was a good man but he lacked personal vision and the quality of international leadership. He feared that Britain would weaken under the effect of Soviet intransigence, and doubted if strong leadership would continue to be given. Was there anybody left to stand up to Stalin, a 'ruffian of genius'?

The Barings occasionally visited Smuts and his wife socially at their own home at Irene, where the old couple lived in conditions which Molly thought primitive, if not downright insanitary. The house had a tin roof and everything seemed very dirty, in spite of the presence of a daughter-in-law and a baby grandchild. Mrs Smuts confirmed this impression by advising them always to wear black pyjamas as they did not show the dirt! They all thought it must be a remarkable contrast for Smuts to visit all the grandees of the world and then return to his tumbledown squalor. Smuts himself clearly charmed both Evelyn and Molly – Evelyn with his wide range of interests, his sweep of history and, of course, his passion for walking up Table Mountain, (and the desire shared by both of them to show how they could outwalk younger men); Molly because of his provocative paganism and the fact that he evidently found them both a younger and more attractive couple than Capetown diplomatic society normally threw into his lap. Smuts confessed to being a follower of Christ, but of no church. He used to taunt Molly with the fact that christianity had failed to stop any war. Now the world would be ruled by fear instead, and perhaps that would have more success. Yet what the Barings found irresistible was his unquenchable optimism, and his evident joy in life, even at his advanced age. Molly once described him as one of those people you would like to revive after they were dead just to see what they were like. Perhaps he also warmed to the Barings because his own followers no longer seemed to appreciate him, either through fear or the fact that he was hanging on to power too long, at the expense of the younger men; or, in the case of his cabinet ministers, because they complained that he would soar away from the business in hand into flights of literature, ethics or history which meant little to them, and inhibited their more immediate business. (Evelyn, on the other hand, was obviously delighted when Smuts concluded one session with the words, 'My dear Baring, it is always delightful to have an exchange of ideas with you.')

Since an election in 1943 Smuts' government had been a co-alition composed of three elements. The first was the old South Africa Party formed by Botha and Smuts in the early 1900s; the second was the Labour Party, drawn from urban constituencies; and the third was the Dominion Party, all from Natal constitu-encies, whose members represented the extreme 'British' point of view in South African politics. Throughout the twentieth cen-tury Anglo-South African relations had been chequered, starting with the trauma of the Boer War. The continuous friction be-tween the Afrikaner and the English speaking community in South Africa was normally the barometer of external relations between the two countries, since there was a natural inclination in London to see South African affairs only through the eyes of the English speakers' community. In political terms this meant that there were effectively no black politics to talk about, so that the greater part of Evelyn's political work consisted of analysing and reporting on the state of affairs in the white polity.

White politics in the 1940s still took their cue from a starting point in 1910, after the Boer War peace settlement and the grant of self-government. There was a feeling then that a return had been made to the days before the Boer War and the Jameson Raid, when Rhodes and Hofmeyr, leaders of the English and Afrikaner communities, seemed to have been working together towards a vision of a united South Africa, which was so shattered by the fighting of the Boer War. In that false spring of 1910 the grant of self-government seemed to have assuaged the Afrikaner urge to free themselves of British domination. But it only took two years for the Afrikaners to split, in a way that they have been splitting ever since, when in 1912 Hertzog broke off from Smuts and Botha to form the Nationalist Party of true Afrikaner-dom. From 1924 until 1933, he was in power in alliance with the Labour Party, but after 1933 he rejoined General Smuts in a 'fusion' government set up to cope with the economic crisis caused by South Africa staying on the gold standard when the British had come off it. Once again the extreme Afrikaner nationalists, under Dr Malan, went off into the political wilderness taking their Afrikaner Party with them.

The days of the fusion government between the two surviving giants of Afrikanerdom seemed to promise to wipe out the effects of Hertzog's earlier break with Botha and herald a new period of Anglo-Boer cooperation more complete than anything since 1912. It was not only the outbreak of war which broke up this harmony, but the persistent growth – within the whole Afrikaner community and not just the rump under Malan's leadership – of that bold, unyielding republican nationalism reminiscent of Kruger's day, which was based on a constant fear that the Boer nation would lose its identity under the flow of people to the towns, the influx of new European immigrants and the weakening effects of English-speaking liberalism. These Afrikaners believed that the threat to white supremacy, which accompanied the increased industrialisation of the country and the parallel flow of natives from the tribal areas into the towns, could only be overcome by a strong undiluted Afrikaner community dedicated to preserving their supremacy. They believed that the English speaking South Africans would have to be totally absorbed into this *laager*, or be content with being kept firmly from political power, as were the Uitlanders of Kruger's time.

Earlier in the century the black population of the country had been largely neglected by white politicians. Smuts, when in opposition, once said to Lord Athlone, the Governor General, 'I never turn my attention to native affairs until I have to.' Smuts preferred to walk the world stage, which is why, on the outbreak of the Second World War, the fusion government split, with Smuts wanting to ally South Africa with the British and Hertzog to remain neutral. Smuts obtained a majority of only 13 in the debate; but it was enough for him to secure a coalition government. The Hertzog party once again went into opposition, joining Malan in the fold of a single Nationalist organisation. The 1943 general election enhanced Smuts' hold on power, probably because the Nationalists during the war expressed much sympathy for Nazism, and for totalitarian ideas. However as the fate of the Axis powers deteriorated, they seemed to revert easily to a faith in parliamentary democracy, though outside parliament they continued to be affiliated with some unsavoury quasi-Nazi organisations.

In January, 1945, Evelyn sent a long letter to Cranborne, his Secretary of State, in which he gave his first impressions of South Africa after an absence of twelve years.[4] He said one of the most noticeable shifts was in the number of Afrikaners who were now living in the towns. He warned of the evil influence of the *Broederbond*, a secret body of carefully picked Afrikaners which was attempting to infiltrate its followers into important positions in the civil service, the armed forces and public bodies. It had obtained a stranglehold both on the Dutch Reformed Church and on the teaching profession, and he saw little chance of any move towards liberalism on colour matters among those attending Afrikaans schools.

A few months later, Evelyn told Cranborne's successor, Lord Addison, that though the disputes between the two sections of the European population were currently in the forefront of the minds of most South Africans, the really important problem for the future was that of relations between Europeans as a whole and Africans.[5] He divided the African population into four categories: 1. Africans permanently resident in rural areas, which could not support a very large population; 2. Africans permanently resident in the towns, by then numbering more than a million; 3. Africans who worked temporarily for white farmers, some of whom had temporary tenancies of a small plot of land and; 4. Migrant town workers, who left their families in rural areas. 'As a result of the anomalies these differences created in standards of living, and the operation of a 'ruthless industrial colour bar' there are increasing indications that the Union Government may expect trouble.'

In the meantime, he had to educate Britain's new Labour government to the strains and pitfalls of Anglo-South African relations – helped by the fact that Attlee was no stranger to them and Lord Addison had worked with Smuts in the First World War. But there was a number of issues on which the Labour Party in Britain was not so prepared to accommodate the South Africans as were Labour ministers, and Evelyn was kept [quite] busy giving advice to the two governments on how to steer a survival course through these difficulties. One of the more familiar rows, for him, was the dispute between India and South Africa over Smuts' treatment of the South African Indians. Evelyn was called upon by the British government to see what he could do to conciliate. Smuts' position was regarded as relatively liberal in South Africa. It was liberal only in the sense that the Nationalists favoured either expulsion or complete segregation of all the Indians; mere limitations of the kind envisaged under the latest Acts were regarded as quite ineffective – as indeed they had been shown to be during the previous forty years.

Another long-running saga in Evelyn's early years concerned the South African government's plans to incorporate South West Africa, which they controlled under the old League of Nations mandate. In September, 1945, Evelyn reported back to London on the visit paid to Pretoria by the Administrator of South West Africa who came to talk with Smuts about the territory's future, and particularly the future of the 10,444 German nationals there, who faced possible repatriation.[6] Evelyn had been told that these Germans could have seized control of South West Africa in 1939 had not the Union government despatched a contingent of special police. The Smuts view was that, since the formation of the United Nations Organisation did not specifically involve any change in the relationship between the Union and South West Africa, it would continue to be administered as an integral part of the Union, but that the South African government would, in time, consider its longer term future. Two months later Evelyn told his Secretary of State that it was taken for granted that the territory would eventually be incorporated, and the main question now was what kind of administration it would have when it was handed over – i.e. would it become just another province of the Union like the Transvaal, or would it remain as a self-governing colony. The inhabitants were largely in favour of incorporation, but according to Evelyn, the 'extreme racialism' of some of the Germans [who had not been repatriated] had aroused such antipathy in the Union that only a small minority would be likely to agree with Dr Malan that they should not be repatriated to Europe. The Dominions Office advised Lord Addison that 'it would be difficult to oppose incorporation, particularly as we intend to resist pressure to incorporate the High Commission Territories.'[7]

However the British Cabinet marginally shifted its line by May the next year and told Smuts that Britain would support the plan for incorporation 'if the consent of the natives as well as the Europeans was sought and obtained by methods agreeable to the United Nations' – something which even British ministers must have known was almost inconceivable since the files show that even officials were confused about how to define 'agreeable'. When, later, the UN rejected South Africa's case for annexation, Evelyn reported that it came as no surprise and Malan's immediate call for a withdrawal from the United Nations was not supported by the pro-government press.

One of the most important, and most secret, negotiations in which Evelyn was involved was the agreement between Britain and South Africa for supplies of uranium to make Britain's future atom bombs. The nuclear weapons programme was then being contemplated in the utmost secrecy by the Attlee government, though no final decision to go ahead was taken until some time later. In December, 1945, Evelyn received a top secret message from Attlee which said that, as a result of some private talks between Sir John Anderson and Smuts, the British wanted to propose formally that they should take out an option for all South Africa's disposable surplus uranium for a specified number of years in the future.[8] Evelyn went to see Smuts, who replied, a week later, that he was willing to enter into an agreement, but that he was still ignorant of the economic possibilities. This message caused a flurry in London. The Cabinet cabled back to Evelyn immediately, demanding to know what Smuts meant. Attlee did not want to tie him down to a price, but was thinking in terms of an agreement for at least ten years. The top secrecy of the project meant that they could not open the question with the other Dominions, and it was obviously vital for the United Kingdom and Canada to develop atomic energy and not be dependent on the Americans. It was looked on with great urgency, since South Africa had the largest supplies in the Empire.

A month later Evelyn received another long explanatory memorandum, setting out the background for him to conduct his secret conversations with Smuts.[9] It was vital that there should be the earliest production of atomic energy in Britain, explained the memorandum and 'we are pressing forward as rapidly as possible.' There was to be a joint Anglo-American approach to uranium and thorium supplies, with Britain responsible for Commonwealth sources. A combined development trust had been set up, which involved agreement with Belgium for the large uranium supplies in the Congo and with Brazil and Holland for supplies of thorium. There was now a risk of shortages for research and development requirements. The British were negotiating with the Americans for a full exchange of information, so it was important that they had a contribution of their own. 'Our ability to make a substantial contribution to the raw material pool may prove to be a decisive factor in our continuing to obtain our essential requirements from the Americans, whose full co-operation will be indispensable to us until our own programme has developed further.' Evelyn replied that it was best for him to take it up then and there with Smuts rather than wait either for Smuts to come to London, or for another British representative from London to come out to him (although this did happen subsequently in May, 1946, when Evelyn took Lord Portal to see

Smuts, and the latter gave him assurances that Britain's supplies were firm).

A year later another agreement, almost as crucial to the post-war order as the nuclear one, passed through Evelyn's hands. This was the Anglo-South African gold agreement. The main negotiations took place in London, but in October, 1947, Evelyn wrote to Machtig to report on a conversation he had held with the Governor of South Africa's Reserve Bank who had just returned from London. Evelyn said that the South African bankers had hoped to conclude an agreement with Britain that would be honoured by a Nationalist government, so the main idea behind the agreement was to provide Britain with an inducement to assist gold production in South Africa. The Nationalists, he said, would have opposed both a loan of gold to Britain and any undertaking to sell a set quantity to the British. So the agreement had to incorporate a rather subtle scheme for giving general encouragement to gold production while at the same time securing for a single customer most of the gold which would be produced.

Smuts' dealings with Churchill had been much more direct than with Attlee, with the result that Evelyn's role was more as a messenger between them, than it was to become after the British election in 1945. Throughout the first two years of the Labour government, the strain of the acute British economic crisis was felt directly in South Africa, as a series of international loans for Britain had to be negotiated. At a lunch with the Barings one day during the negotiations, when there had been no telegram from London, Smuts said, 'Is there no news today? What do you think they are doing? Faith is one thing, but make believe is quite another and they are like children, playing at make believe.'

It was ironic for the British government that they had, so soon, to come back to an involvement in South African affairs. When Evelyn sent his first *tour d'horizon* to old Lord Addison, upon his appointment, the 76 year old minister rather wearily replied by saying that he had indeed read Evelyn's message twice but 'for the present I can only live in hope that the many difficult problems you indicate will not force themselves to the front for we certainly have plenty on our plate to be going on with.' Addison had his wish granted; but his successors did not.

CHAPTER XV

Royal Tour

In 1947 King George and Queen Elizabeth, with the two Princesses, Elizabeth and Margaret, carried out a nine-week Royal Tour of South Africa and the three High Commission Territories. The Barings were naturally involved, though less so in the South African part than in the visits paid to Bechuanaland, Basutoland and Swaziland. Evelyn had not had any particular hand in the origins of the tour, but was clearly hoping, like everybody else in the royal party – and in the British government for that matter – that the tour would yield some diplomatic benefit in future relations between South Africa and Britain. In spite of the passage of forty years, these were still much coloured by the hangover of the Boer War, and in 1939 had not been greatly helped by the deep divisions caused by Smuts' decision – on such a slender majority – to take South Africa into the war on Britain's side.

Long before the Allied victory was achieved Smuts had been pressing for a Royal Visit immediately after the war, and had proposed 1946 as the date. King George had refused to come so early, saying that there would be too much to do in the United Kingdom; so that the two governments agreed on 1947. The tour was thus not conceived as a special trip to save South Africa for the empire. All the Dominions would be visited after the war to thank them for their contributions to the Allied forces.

Evelyn and Molly were saved most of the preliminary planning because they were on home leave for the second half of 1946 and only returned to South Africa on the SS *Caernavon* – accompanied by all their family – two weeks ahead of the Royal Family in HMS *Vanguard*, Britain's last battleship. The King and Queen landed at Capetown in the middle of February, having survived a rougher journey than the Barings, such a storm blowing the day before their arrival that only the Ladies-in-Waiting – Lady Harlech and Lady Delia Peel – survived the morning service in the ship's chapel, and even then the candles were swept off the altar. Onshore there were to be equal dramas – trivialities, really, but the sort of inconsequential details of royal occasions which assume colossal significance at the time. The South African flag was both upside down and flying at half mast as the King stepped ashore – a mistake on both counts, but the sort of mistake people took to be portentous.

The first few days of the visit were marked by much ceremonial shadow boxing with the Boers, before their prickly nationalistic attitudes shook down into some kind of *modus vivendi* with the British party. It was not easy going, though the essential normality of King George helped things along. Evelyn regarded him as the 'apotheosis of the ordinary man', and when he was beside Smuts – who was without any doubt one of the twentieth century's olympians – the King seemed to fade out into insignificance. However, this essential ordinariness enabled him to overcome, or overlook, the protocolaire nightmares which hovered about all the early ceremonies. At the main banquet, where Molly found herself sitting next to Dr Malan, the opposition leader and future Nationalist Prime Minister (whom she had never seen before in all the two years they had been in South Africa, such was the lack of contact between the Nationalists and the British), Dr Malan would not take part in the singing of God Save the King, which followed immediately after the rendering of *Die Stem*, the South African national anthem. At the end of the banquet it was not played at all, until Colonel Stallard, leader of the Dominion Party, leapt to his feet and started singing it on his own, at which point everybody else joined in, including the orchestra.

However, the South African reception improved on each day of the visit: so much so that by the time the King and Queen had been in the country five days, the Governor-General's office was beseiged by Nationalist MPs, who had refused to attend any of the opening ceremonies, but now were asking if they could, after all, be included on the invitation lists (for all future functions) when the King returned to the Cape for his second visit in April. The Nationalist papers tried to overcome these contradictions, and the evident success of the tour, by remarking what charming people the royal visitors were, but reminding their readers that no true South African could possibly be interested in them as King and Queen.

The King and Queen themselves were encouraged by their reception, but worried that they were not being introduced to enough people. In part, this was because Smuts had permanent precedence – a position to which he clung, partly because he liked it, and partly no doubt because, like Evelyn, he was at his worst at the hyper-refined kind of bunfights which answer to the description of Royal Garden Party, or receptions, on this kind of occasion. ('If this is pleasure, give me pain,' Evelyn observed morosely, cooped up in a little pen at one garden party, where, when the King and Queen departed, he was submerged in the rush of the guests to pinch crockery and cutlery as souvenirs of the occasion). Another worry, for the ladies of the bedchamber, and no doubt within the bedchamber too, was that Princess Elizabeth did not seem to *smile* like her mother.

Soon the Royal Party left the Cape and proceeded 'up country' in the White Train, from which Evelyn, still in Capetown, received a letter from Sir Alan Lascelles, the King's Private Secretary, 'I am probably over-inured to shouting in the streets and kindred emotional manifestations, and therefore inclined to undervalue them; but I can honestly say that I have been unexpectedly impressed by the welcome given TM everywhere in SA so far and that I believe it expresses a good deal more than ordinary excitement over the circus that has come to town – what one might call the "headline" excitement aroused by a visit from Charlie Chaplin or any other merely popular figure. I am beginning to hope, in fact, that this visit may have long distance results of real value.'

The colour problem fell upon the Royal Party in a small way the moment they reached the British Protectorates, where Evelyn and Molly rejoined them. It arose over the question of native investitures. When King George had held a native investiture in the Union the previous week, he had not been allowed to pin on the medals himself, much less shake hands with the blacks. Instead he had to hand the medals to an official of the native department who stood beside him, so that the King's pure white hands at no point came in contact with a black man. Nothing was said openly to Evelyn about it, but some Union officials approached Lascelles and said they hoped very much that investitures held in the High Commission Territories would follow the same procedure. Lascelles then wrote to Evelyn, putting the point and hoping he would agree. Evelyn quite firmly said that agreement was out of the question; if the King was not going to shake hands with the Africans, he was not going to shake hands with Europeans either. Thereupon the King, of course, agreed to shake hands with everyone, and to pin on the medals himself, an act which promptly secured headline treatment in the local papers.

The highlight of the visit to Basutoland was a *pitso* attended by between eighty and one hundred thousand tribesmen, which was the biggest gathering anybody could remember since another

pitso in 1904 convened by Molly's grandfather, Lord Selborne.
The tribesmen collected in a bowl of ground, with the horsemen
at the rear. The King and Queen occupied a small stone pavilion
with a thatched roof and iron railings, while the Paramount Chief
sat in a smaller pavilion opposite, accompanied by the four sons
of Moshesh dressed in magnificent leopard skins. There were
speeches from Evelyn and from the Paramount Chief, whose plain
appeal never to be transferred to the Union had had to be watered
down in the final version to keep it more or less unpolitical. Then
the King spoke and was thought to have struck just the right note
of paternal and royal protection. Finally came the investiture,
and it was plain for all to see that the King's own hand pinned
on the medals.

On arriving in Swaziland, Evelyn and Molly were greeted by
a worried Resident Commissioner with the news that the Royal
Family had been preceded by a plague of bees caused by the
local farmers burning the *veld*. Indeed, when the King met an
old Boer farmer he was startled by a swarm of bees flying out
from under the farmer's top hat when he took it off. They had
apparently been attracted by the hair oil he had put on for the
occasion. The King dined out on the story for days. In Swaziland
the bees had to be swept up in bucketfuls every half hour from
the rooms in the royal guest house. Nobody need have worried,
because it rained all night and so there were no bees in attendance
the next morning at the vast concourse of 12,000 Swazi warriors
who danced and swirled in front of the King and Queen. The
Royal Party drew a very favourable contrast between the freedom
and openness with which they had been exposed to the Africans
in the High Commission Territories, and the slightly peremptory
way in which the King while in the Union had been whisked
down lines of Zulus hemmed in by droves of European police
guarding against the possibility of an 'incident'.

Evelyn missed the next part of the tour in Bechuanaland because he caught tick-bite fever, and retired to bed with a high
temperature. While the Royal Party were there, with about
another three weeks to go before they returned to Capetown to
embark on HMS *Vanguard*, Lascelles had a disturbing cable from
the Admiral in command. It appeared that there had been a
slight mutiny in Vanguard's crew, while the battleship cruised
off Durban. The mutiny was caused by overcrowding on the
lower deck, brought about because of the intense compression in
the living quarters, not just because the Royal retinue occupied

all the senior officers' cabins, but because the ship had also had to take on an extra 18 midshipmen from the Dominions as well. The mutiny was, of course, hushed up at the time – it would have created a terrible impression during the tour, particularly as *Vanguard* was the pride of the Royal Navy, being the latest, and as it turned out, the last, battleship ever to be built. It was all settled before the King and Queen reembarked at Capetown, but the *cognoscenti* might have guessed later that something had gone wrong, when the King arrived back at Portsmouth, because the Cabinet advised the King against holding the usual end-of-voyage investiture on the quarter deck. King George, though disappointed, agreed. Having himself been reared as a young midshipman, he quite understood the point.

Before the Royal Party left, Evelyn and Molly were invited to several private sessions with the King and Queen. At one moment the King was so impressed with Evelyn's command of Afrikaans, that he suggested he should be the next Governor General. Evelyn countered this by suggesting confidentially to Lascelles that they should cash in at once on the tremendous personal success of the Queen by sending out her brother, David Bowes-Lyon, as Governor General. Both these proposals were insensitive to the likely reaction of the Boers, but they had the same root – dissatisfaction with the current Governor General, van Zyl, by then an old man in his mid 70s. The King was particularly forthright, 'What's the use of our coming out to buck things up if an old chap like that is going to let it all down again?' he asked the Barings during their farewell dinner *en famille*. 'He only has a few old cronies of his own to dinner occasionally and never, never does his job as it properly ought to be done. It is perfectly absurd.' As usual, when he was vexed, the King's voice would rise to an angry crescendo before suddenly giving way to a disarming smile and the words, 'Don't you think so?'

At dinner the Queen asked Evelyn what he really thought the results of the visit would be. He told her that he did not think it would change any votes, but that it very likely would make the Nationalists less extreme and more disposed to be friendly to the English. The Queen had by then quite capitvated Evelyn. According to Molly in her letters home he found her bewitching, with the most fascinating mind, not intellectual but astute and quick and '300 per cent feminine.' The farewell evening ended with the King rummaging about rather sheepishly in a pile of cardboard boxes and then dumping a box on the table with the words, 'This is all for Evelyn. You didn't know you were going to get that, did you?' as Evelyn unwrapped the KCVO ribbon and star. It was one of the King's little jokes because he knew that Evelyn had been privately tipped off in advance by Lascelles that he was going to get the honour. Evelyn – slightly embarrassed – laughed too and said it was a great surprise and thank you very much.

On the next day they sailed away in the *Vanguard* and everybody settled down to a feeling of anti-climax and some tentative post mortems. It was clearly going to be some time before anybody could precisely describe what the results of the visit would be. The Barings met the Administrator of the Orange Free State, the only member of the government party on his own State's executive council, who told them that he thought the visit had been very successful in the Free State, not because it would have changed many votes (the election result the next year showed that not to be the case) but because the bitterness between the two people – English and Boer – seemed to have gone completely. If that lasted it would be extremely valuable. He said that the Nationalist speakers who had always said that the English were political intriguers and that the King and Queen in particular were stuck-up snobs, simply could not now get a hearing among their own people.

Sometime before, in December, 1945, when the war-time coalition finally broke up Smuts was left with a commanding majority of his party alone. In spite of his age, there was no sign of any intention to give up. The Prime Minister still usually walked home every evening to his farmhouse at Irene – nine miles. Nobody expected an election until 1949 (it came in 1948). In the meantime Evelyn was slowly getting on better terms with Smuts' opponents, the Nationalist politicians. He had learnt Afrikaans, and made rather a hit one evening when he sat next to Mrs Malan and was able to carry on what he described as an 'uninteresting conversation' in Afrikaans for the whole of dinner. However, he also paid a goodwill trip to Bloomfontein, one of the hearts of Afrikanerdom, where the good will was not entirely reciprocated. The Nationalists boycotted all the functions to which he had been invited. 'The visit was not without its humorous side,' he told Machtig. 'Both the provincial and the city councils avoided my polluting presence.'[1]

By 1947 the country was clearly in an election mood, and,

when he was not touring his territories, or negotiating Anglo-South African loans, Evelyn tried to get around the Union and assess the prospects for the coming contest between Smuts and the Nationalists. Early in 1947 he was telling Machtig that South African politics would become pretty gloomy in the run-up to the forthcoming election. 'Europeans, other than Liberals, have become more obstinately attached to the technique of domination . . . the rising sound and fury of the Nationalist campaign is giving most members of the government some anxious moments.'[2] In May he warned that, though no sensible person would attempt to make confident statements concerning the future course of Union politics, Smuts' ministers felt they were losing ground in the countryside and possibly in the towns as well.[3] He went on to say that there were signs that the main lines of division between the South African parties were changing. At present they divided on the question of South Africa's attitude to the British connection and to the Crown. In future, it looked as though they might divide less on that, or on conventional left-right questions of political economy, and more on the treatment of non-Europeans. He referred to a 'very lucid' speech made in parliament by the 'fanatical and important Nationalist figure' Strydom, who had 'declared without contradiction by any member of his party that if a European race were to remain in South Africa the colour instinct must be preserved, that for the two races there must be "separation in every sphere" and finally that the Europeans must be masters and remain masters in South Africa.' He was reporting on the first official unfolding of what by the time of the election had become the orthodox Nationalist doctrine of *apartheid*.

Late in the year Addison was replaced as Commonwealth Secretary by Philip Noel-Baker. Evelyn once again went through the customary salutations, and set about briefing his new Secretary of State on the nature of Afrikaner politics. There was a didactic streak about him which relished these opportunities to instruct his ministers in the deeper aspects of South African tribal culture – white and black. (He taught his son, Charlie, Latin before breakfast every day because it was not taught in South African schools). He told Noel-Baker that the only cement which held Smuts' party together was a common hatred of the Nationalists. 'In the United Party's ranks are convinced socialists and uncompromising supporters of private enterprise, backveld farmers and representatives of the cosmopolitcan urban life of the Rand, supporters of Hofmeyr's principles who believe that salvation can only be found in great and early concessions to non-Europeans, and personal followers of General Smuts whose thoughts and feelings on questions of colour are sometimes indistinguishable from those of the Nationalists.' He predicted that the general election would take place in the second half of 1948 and that the United Party prospects were bad, though slightly better than they had been a few months previously. The Nationalists had gained votes from the United Nations criticism of South Africa, but 'many, but not all white South Africans – at least in the towns – have a bad conscience'. They did not know what to do about it, but this had the effect of slightly mitigating the widespread anti-British feeling on which the Nationalists based their strength.[4]

The United Party of Smuts went into the election in May, 1948, with 89 seats, over the 49 held by the Nationalist Party of Malan, and another 15 held by smaller parties. When the votes were counted Smuts was out and Malan in. Malan had scraped home by five seats over the United Party, though he did not possess an overall majority, holding only 70 seats in the 150 strong chamber. The victory of the Nationalists, which was to ensure them power for at least thirty years, had in the end come as a surprise to the country, since it had appeared that Smuts was regaining some lost ground. According to Evelyn's despatch it even surprised the Nationalist leaders.[5] Indeed, Malan's majority was only assured by nine seats of the dour Afrikaner party, original followers of General Hertzog, with whom Dr Malan had extremely strained relations owing to his refusal to have any association with the *Ossewa Brandwag*, an extremist sect of Afrikaners to which most of the Afrikaner party belonged, which had openly hoped for a Hitlerite victory in the war, and which stood for the violent overthrow of parliamentary democracy in the Union.

However, *Ossewa Brandwag* or no, Dr Malan was in power. The question everybody asked was, what now? Evelyn plunged into a major despatch, which he sent off on June 12, some two weeks after the election, his main point was that, though there were a number of causes of weakness in the United Party's performance, the decisive factor in the election had been the constantly repeated theme that it was a 'Hofmeyr' election, that if J. H. Hofmeyr came to power after Smuts retired, the supremacy of the white man would come to an end as a result of his liberal views and his emphasis on the need to secure political as opposed to merely economic advancement for the Africans. As a result, the Nationalists, for the first time, had won the support of a considerable number of English speaking voters. Evelyn went on: 'To find explanations for the Nationalist victory is comparatively easy. To forecast future political events is difficult. General Smuts and his advisers believe that Dr Malan's government will immediately begin to create conditions favourable for a second and more decisive electoral victory. Should provincial elections next year be favourable to the Nationalists it is possible that the new government will decide to force a general election some time during 1949.

It would be rash to argue that because during their first year in office the new government are conciliatory in negotiations with the United Kingdom it follows that they will maintain this attitude in future years. At present the government are weak and dependent on English speaking votes; could they obtain a larger majority in Parliament their attitude might well change for the worse. Reasonable parliamentarians and men who have absorbed Nazi ideas are both in the Nationalist ranks. There are indications that the country will soon buzz with rumours of the establishment of a totalitarian state. To my mind the abandonment of constitutional government by the Nationalist's leaders is improbable. The presence of a great non-European population is an argument against causing too deep a split between the two divisions of South Africans of European origin. But the possibility of violence should not be entirely discounted. The men of violence are there, and should things go badly for the government their views might in the last resort prevail.'

The Nationalist victory had an immediate effect on Evelyn's own future. It seemed that his thrice weekly lessons of Afrikaans, and those tentative if uninteresting conversations across the dinner tables with Mrs Malan had had their effect. One of Malan's first acts was to ask for Evelyn's tour to be extended beyond its expected expiry in November, 1948. In July Machtig wrote to say he was glad Evelyn was prepared to stay five years in South Africa since it was very important in view of the new government.[6] 'There is no reason for despair of an adequate working arrangement with them. They have done nothing so far to harm us,' he wrote, reflecting the great apprehension which London felt on hearing news of the Nationalist victory, and remembering the previous periods of Nationalist Afrikaner rule in the Union, and the difficulties for the Empire and Commonwealth which they normally seemed to bring in their wake.

However Malan did attend the Prime Ministers' conference early the next year, and returned home pleased with his visit. Meanwhile in the Union, Evelyn had to settle down to justify the decision of both sides to extend his tour – the Nationalists who had requested him as being the man they knew, and the British ministers who had consented to his staying on as the man who knew. He found the new social atmosphere in Pretoria often an electric one, particularly at formal functions where the Governor General was involved, and the republicanism of the Nationalists had to be restrained in the interests of protocol. But at least to start with he found that his relations with Afrikaner ministers seemed to prosper, though without any of the intellectual stimulation he had received from his sessions with Smuts. Smuts, incidentally, he used to find depressed, but Evelyn still set great store by his advice.

However, although the Nationalist ministers continued to welcome the way Evelyn spoke Afrikaans to them, it was not long before he realized that he was not likely to be able to moderate their policy by a single degree. Even if the Seretse Khama affair had not blown up there were other issues which heralded the end of the short political honeymoon – not just on Anglo-South African relations, but between the English and Dutch speaking South African communities as well. At one moment Molly was reporting home that Evelyn, after two weeks lunching almost every day with Nationalist ministers, could hardly keep the venom out of his voice he now disliked them so much. The passage of a series of contentious acts of parliament, restricting liberties and basic rights, had caused as violent a deterioration between English and Dutch as anything since the Boer War. And the prospect for the natives was even worse.

Owing to the time Evelyn devoted to the Territories, in the scrutiny of white South African politics, and his residual interest in the Indian community in South Africa, his preoccupation with the blacks of the Union was less than it might have been. Certainly, however, he kept abreast of the situation with which the natives were having to contend. He occasionally visited the worst areas of urban slumland, often with Father Trevor Huddleston as his guide. Father Huddleston, who was stationed in the Comunity of the Resurrection in Sophiatown, outside Johannesburg, almost immediately became a great personal and spiritual friend of the Barings. But though Evelyn absorbed all the facts of the native situation in the Union, he was not the kind of man who developed an emotional involvement without being able to concentrate more closely on the subject. He had little such attention to give to the Union's blacks, compared to the time and energy he lavished on the African population in the Territories. To these he could offer something more concrete than sympathy. In the Territories there were Africans for whom he was responsible and whose future he could influence dramatically for better or worse. With the Africans in the Union he was in no such position. Without any doubt, though he performed his diplomatic functions conscientiously, his heart during all those years was always in the Territories.

F

CHAPTER XVI
Transfer

By far the most important aspect of Evelyn's tour of South Africa, both at the time, and in the light of subsequent history in Southern Africa, was the debate over the future of the High Commission Territories – Bechuanaland, Basutoland and Swaziland. Even while he was still in Southern Rhodesia it became clear to him that after the war there was likely to be a demand by the Union to have them incorporated in South Africa. Indeed one of the reasons why Evelyn felt like accepting the job, and prolonging his time in Africa against his family's inclination, was because he felt that he would be able to stand up to Smuts on the issue, and looked forward with some relish to doing so. So he approached the question firmly convinced, even before he acquired corroborative evidence, that the Territories' future did *not* lie within the Union, and that every diplomatic effort from his office should be geared to seeing that they survived outside the Union, in spite of the fact that they were at the mercy of the South Africans if resort were ever had to economic or military force.

The character of the three territories varied considerably. Basutoland was a colony with a population of 495,000 blacks and 1600 whites; Bechnanaland (151,000 blacks, 1700 whites) and Swaziland (121,000 and 2200) were protectorates. The crucial difference between a protectorate and a crown colony – particularly crucial for tribesmen – was that the soil of a crown colony was British soil and the inhabitants of the colony British subjects, whereas the soil of a protectorate and its inhabitants were not.

Basutoland had been recognised as British territory in 1868 at the request of Moshesh, the founder of the line of Basuto chiefs. Bechuanaland, in the form of the paramount chiefs of the three main tribes, concurred in a treaty of protection in 1885 on the basis that they would rule their own people according to custom, and the territory was brought formally under the administration of the High Commission in 1891. Swaziland remained nominally independent until 1890, when it was jointly administered by Britain and the South African Republic. After the Boer War HMG reassumed full control of the area through the High Commissioner and a Resident Commissioner.

In the South Africa Act of 1909 the possibility of handing over the three territories was contemplated, on the assumption that the Union would remain an integral part of the Empire. This assumption itself was later nullified by the passage in South Africa of a number of acts which eliminated the possibility of action by the Imperial Crown in respect of external affairs. This was an important innovation, because the South Africa Act expressly stated that the Protectorates could not be brought into a state of subordination to the Union government unless the King, acting on the advice of the Privy Council and following on addresses from the Houses of Parliament both in Britain and the Union, agreed to transfer to the Union government any of the High Commission Territories, subject to the terms and conditions in the schedule to the Act. However, during the debates on that Act, Liberal ministers of Asquith's government made it clear that they fully expected incorporation to occur at some date, and in the case of Swaziland within the following ten years. The Act itself did not specify what safeguarding procedures would be necessary before any such transfer, but a memorandum attached to it made clear that HMG undertook to consult native opinion in the Territories before any transfer could take place. There was no suggestion that the consultation was to be binding; and the vagueness of the Act – like so many acts – and the widely held assumption in 1909 that transfer *would* take place eventually was thereafter to be a source of continual diplomatic dispute. From 1913 onwards there was almost continuous pressure from South Africa – from Smuts, Botha and Hertzog in their various capacities – to have the Territories incorporated in the Union. These requests were repeatedly turned down by British ministers. In 1934 the South Africans passed some particularly racialist legislation, which restricted the black franchise. In the following year the British government published a White Paper setting out its views about transfer, which said:

'All our information goes to show that at present native opinion in the Territories is very strongly opposed to transfer. Britain is pledged that no transfer shall take place until inhabitants, native as well as European, have been consulted, and the British Parliament has been given an opportunity of expressing its view.

It appears to the British Government that the results of such consultation would be embarrassing and undesirable from every point of view. We believe that the Union Government, in the words used by General Hertzog in March, 1925, would indeed not wish to incorporate the Territories in the Union unless the inhabitants of the Territories, native as well as European, are prepared and desire to come in.

The policy of both Governments for the next few years should be directed to bringing about a situation in which, if transfer were to become a matter of practical policies, it could be effected with the full acquiesence of the populations concerned. In particular it appears to us to be an eventual condition that the closest possible cooperation should be established between the Union Government and the advisers of the Territories, and that the native population should feel that the Union Government are working in concert with the local advisers with a real and generous desire to develop and improve conditions in the Territories.'[1]

This White Paper caused considerable unease in the Territories, particularly since after his talks with British ministers in London, General Hertzog gave the impression that he expected transfer to begin in two years. Further discussions in London brought about a suspension of the agreement for financial assistance by the Union government, though in 1938 the two governments set up an advisory conference of officials to consider matters of joint concern. The Union government was also asked to prepare a memorandum setting out its proposals for transfer. The memorandum was prepared, but then war intervened and it was agreed to postpone further discussions of transfer for the time being.

The three Territories had naturally escaped all the rigours of colour bar legislation passed in South Africa between the wars, so that by the time Evelyn arrived in Southern Africa there was a distinct difference in the rights and advantages enjoyed by inhabitants of the Territories as compared to the natives in every province of the Union. However, if politically and socially they were in a favourable position, they were economically at the mercy of the Union, and their dependence on the Union's markets and its transportation system was almost absolute. Their most important export was manpower; some 60% of their adult population could only find employment in the mines and other industries of the Transvaal and in the farms and households of the Transvaal and the Free State.

The war only put a partial damper on the question of transfer, and in 1943 the records show Cranborne discussing the subject in an exchange with Harlech.[2] In April, 1945, Evelyn reported to the Secretary of State on several speeches by Smuts which showed that, although the Union had no wider territorial ambitions to the north, they definitely coveted the British territories and intended to ask for all three once the fighting was over.[3] Possibly the opening shot would depend on Smuts' election plans, since it would be good for him to succeed where Hertzog in the 1930s had failed. 'We will soon be faced therefore with a most difficult problem,' he warned. Smuts had made much of the great influx of labour from the Territories, but, Evelyn suggested, an adequate counterpoint to that was to ask whether the flow of Irish workmen to Glasgow was proof that Irishmen were panting to rejoin the United Kingdom. He added that all was not well with the Union's native policy which was clearly going to remain based on white political supremacy. Britain should therefore press ahead with its own native development in the Territories to emphasise the difference, since, 'We should never sacrifice the true interests of Africans to a desire to remain friendly with a United Party Government [Smuts' party] in Pretoria. It will therefore be difficult to reconcile a proper native policy with keeping on good terms with English speaking South Africans.'

In September, 1945, Evelyn reported to Machtig that every educated African he met within the Union was opposed to the idea of the Territories being incorporated.[4] This arose originally through a chance dinner-table conversation which Molly had with the African wife of a don at Fort Hare, the African university. She spoke so strongly to Molly against transfer that Evelyn visited her in her home the next day to acquire the names of as many educated Africans as possible, such as newspaper editors and teachers. He intended to visit as many as he could, in order to be able to use African opinion in the Union as an additional argument against transfer. By then he was convinced that transfer was inconceivable, but it is interesting to note that the view in London, at least as held by Cranborne – then leaving the Dominions Office after the British general election – was very different. In Cranborne's farewell letter he said of the Territories that he did not really know the answer but, 'it is a real brute. I had always had in the back of my mind the idea that we might do a deal with the Union over Swaziland and keep the rest, at any rate for the present. Swaziland, geographically even more than the other Territories, might quite properly be taken

over by them and we never made much of a success of it, whereas
Basutoland, and perhaps to a slightly lesser degree Bechuanaland, are good going concerns. But the situation has lately become much more complicated. Smuts has pledged himself publicly
to ask for all the Territories and it will be very difficult for us
to put him in an awkward position after all he has done for us
in the war.'[5]

After the result of the British election Evelyn had a momen-
tary feeling of relief that there would be no question of a back-
door deal on the Territories between Churchill and Smuts, as
had seemed likely some time previously and had been hinted at
in Cranborne's last letter. But then he started to worry that the
new Labour ministers would be tactless in the dealings with the
South Africans and provoke them by lecturing them on their
native policy. It was not long before the question of transfer was
once again raised for the Labour government to answer in the
House of Commons. Attlee was discouraging about the idea,
without being totally negative. The main Afrikaner newspaper,
Die Burger, came out with a strong leader calling on Smuts to
make a statement on the question. It was clear from Attlee's
answers, it said, that HMG was not at all eager to permit transfer; the South Africa Act had already made provisions for the
eventual take over; the British government had no objection to
the principle but wanted to satisfy itself on the native policy of
the newly formed Union. It went on to claim that the Union
now, in spite of her own critical food position, was helping to
prevent starvation in the Protectorates.

The Dominions Office minute on Evelyn's despatch dealing
with the leader said, 'We know from the High Commissioner's
despatches how much the natives of all three Territories fear the
idea of absorbtion in the Union. If their wishes are respected
amalgamation or transfer is nothing but a Nationalist pipedream.'[6] One notices in all the official documents of the day that
the hypothetical possibility of transfer and the soundness of its
juridical basis, were still respected. This was in spite of the fact
that it was being made clear by Evelyn that, in Southern African
terms, transfer was inconceivable to all blacks. Yet the British
government, though tacitly accepting his premise, remained reluctant at the time to spell it out too forcefully, either for fear
of offending Smuts, who had been a good ally in the war, or for
fear of undermining his position and inducing an incoming
Nationalist government to take over by force or by economic

blockade what they regarded as theirs by right. In both cases Britain would be impotent to prevent it.

In April, 1946, Evelyn sent a long memorandum to Lord Addison, the Labour Secretary of State, dealing with the fact that Smuts was coming under pressure on transfer from Dr Malan and the Nationalist opposition.[7] He summarised Dr Malan's views as follows; that it was wrong to maintain that transfer needed the prior approval of the natives since the Act made no mention of prior consultation or approval; that the only reason for delay in 1909 was a military one, which anyway lapsed in 1912 when South Africa assumed responsibility for her own defence; that South Africa, now having responsibility for checking famine in the Territories, should also have commensurate power over them and that this was only being withheld because of British lack of confidence in South African native policy, which was none of their business anyway. To these points Smuts had replied that Britain *had* undertaken to consult native opinion, but not to be bound by the need for African consent to a transfer; that good headway on the subject had been made before the war, and this would be resumed; that he thought there would be no insurmountable objections when he raised it again, which he fully intended to; and that the United Kingdom Parliament would have to be consulted, but his own view was that the Territories were an indivisible part of the Union. Evelyn noted that the *aide memoire* to the 1909 Act had committed HMG carefully to consider the views of the natives, and that such a process would currently be bound to show total native opposition to the idea; moreover the famine argument was answered by the fact that Britain herself was using her good offices to alleviate South Africa's own wheat and maize shortage; finally, the lack of confidence in South Africa's native policies was widespread and not just held by the natives of the three Territories. To illustrate this he also sent a memorandum of unqualified opposition to transfer put together by leaders of African opinion within the Union who, he said, 'include in their number most of those Africans who play a leading part in politics and in those few professions which are open to a South African with black skin.'[8] This effectively answered Malan's suggestion that the only opposition to transfer came from pliable Africans in the Territories who were being told what to say by their chiefs.

It is a tribute to the sensitivity of the issue (or could it just have been the Treasury using any excuse it could find to avoid

spending money?) that the British government was extremely reluctant to agree to Evelyn's pressing recommendation to remove
the headquarters of the Bechuanaland administration from
Mafeking.[9] Evelyn failed to convince the Dominions Office of his
case. 'Once public opinion knows of the move and is stirred to
press for transfer, both we and Smuts will find ourselves on a
slippery slope,' it said.[10]

It is extraordinary to note how, even in 1946, in their private
discussions, British officials and ministers were cautious about
the question of transfer, still paying rather more than lip service
to the possibility that the South Africans might eventually incorporate the Territories. The threat of Smuts' impending demand
hung over their deliberations, and in December, 1946, a draft
White Paper was prepared, dealing with HMG's attitude to any
claim by the Union.[11] 'If any proposal for the transfer of these
Territories, in terms of the South Africa Act, 1909, is put forward,
the Government would not make any decision until the inhabitants of the Territories, native and European, had been consulted,
and until Parliament had been given an opportunity of expressing its views,' it said, significantly avoiding any commitment to
comply if consultation unearthed a negative opinion from within
the Territories. However, it was clear that no British government
could in fact have contemplated handing them over if the process
of consultation established (as all the evidence suggested that it
would) that native opinion was overwhelmingly hostile to the idea
of transfer. It was their weakness on the ground, their desire not
to make Smuts' life more difficult with his Nationalist opposition,
and possibly their need to foster good relations with South Africa
for other reasons at the time, like the gold and uranium agreements, that persuaded ministers in London that it would be
wrong to be too categorical about the future of the Territories.
However their attitude must have induced a great deal of unnecessary insecurity in those Territories at the time.

In October, 1947, Evelyn sent another warning about the situation to the incoming Secretary of State, Philip Noel-Baker.[12] 'The
High Commission Territories are dependent on South Africa.
They are inside the Union customs ring. Their people go to work
in the Union mines and industries, and their trade both ways is
largely with the Union. Unfortunately their separate existence is
an irritant to many South Africans. It was hoped that the Africans
of the three Territories would, as the years passed, come gradually
to accept the idea of transfer to Union control. But in the event

objections to transfer among the Africans of the High Commission Territories and indeed among many Union Africans as well, have increased and apparently may still increase yet more. Recent events have not diminished the force of these objections since fundamentally they are based on a feeling that, to use the words of a Bechuana chief "The British treat Africans like men and the South Africans treat them like children." Our main difficulty is to maintain a reasonable standard of administration in the Territories, two of which are very poor and all of which are next door to a rich and developing country. The great need for each Territory is the development of some wealth-producing unit.'

After the 1948 election the British naturally expected the Nationalist government to demand the incorporation of the Territories. But the demand did not come immediately. The delicacy of the issue was one of the reasons why Evelyn was so incensed at the Seretse Khama affair, which he thought was jeopardising the position for all three Territories. Seretse's marriage to a white woman and the subsequent difficulties over British recognition of the marriage, engendered a great deal of feeling in the Union, which Dr Malan exploited by making speeches saying he would demand the incorporation of the Territories early in 1950. In October, 1949, after a particularly aggressive speech by Malan in Blomfontein, the British government cabled a message to him which had to be delivered personally by Evelyn. It urged him not to bring forward the question of the Territories at the moment because it would be quite impossible for the British answer to be yes, and suggested that he should wait for some time in the future when a change of position *might* be possible. Malan was extremely angry and harangued Evelyn, saying he had waited for twenty years already and if he waited any longer he would wait for ever. The British should not think they could treat South Africa like a colony. When Evelyn murmured about the entrenched clauses in the Act, Malan said that it was ridiculous to wait for the natives to say yes, since they would say no or yes according to what the white man told them. At this, Evelyn drew out his new trump card, and replied that it was not for the white man to persuade them, but for other black men – their own brothers and fathers and relations already in the Union. This novel idea seemed to take Malan rather by surprise and the meeting ended with no further discussion. That was more or less the last that was heard of the subject, on that level, until Gordon-Walker came out as Commonwealth Secretary in February, 1951, when Malan again made his point, only in such a maladroit way that Gordon-Walker was easily able to deflect the thrust.

When Evelyn left South Africa he gave an address to Chatham House in November, 1951, in which he dealt publicly with some of the aspects of transfer which he had until then only been able to discuss privately in his despatches and cables to his minister.[13] He said that it was sometimes suggested – by the South African authorities – that since the Africans could not form a sound opinion on where their future interests lay, the administration of the Territories should have actively persuaded them to accept transfer. 'After seven years in charge of the three Territories my own view is that the merits and demerits of transfer can be understood by Africans and that their decision cannot be influenced by European government officers,' he said. He pointed out that most male Africans in the Territories had at one time worked in the Union, and would all have a better understanding of the condition of life of Africans in the Union than would any European. The only people who could persuade the Africans of the Territories to accept transfer would be the Africans of the Union, who would not be likely to do so. But he ended by pointing out that, both on geographical and economic grounds, it would be impossible to cut off the Territories from relations with South Africa, nor would it be wise to try to do so.

His own contribution to the three Territories' subsequent emergence as independent black states was considerable. Apart from using his diplomacy to prevent an open confrontation on the question between Britain and South Africa – one which he felt Britain might easily lose – he set about organising the Territories' economies and administrations so that they became not only more or less self-sufficient but also areas where the natives were so plainly more free and more fairly ruled than they could hope to be in the Union, that no British government could have visualised handing them over, and no Union government would have dared to seize them.

The central fact remains that throughout his tour Evelyn had to contend with pressure from Smuts and then Malan without any very obvious, let alone firm support from London. In the Commonwealth Relations Office of the time (formed after the merger of the India and Dominions Office) it was unusual to find anybody who thought the High Commission Territories would become independent; some kind of dependent relationship with the Union was always assumed. It was not until the early 1960s that independence came to be seriously considered; and it is illustrative of this that in their local intelligence summaries Bechuanaland administrative officers had to report on the state of African opinion towards the question of transfer until as late as 1959, indicating that the question was still officially an open one. Of that Evelyn must have been aware. When Smuts died Evelyn was on tour in Swaziland; and for all his fondness for the Field Marshal, his first reaction was that he would now sleep more soundly in his bed over the question of incorporation.

CHAPTER XVII

The Marriage of
Seretse Khama

The row over Seretse Khama in 1948 and afterwards involved a quarrel within the Bechuana royal family over the choice of queen for the chief elect, and was very much in the tradition of the Bamangwato, the largest tribe in Bechuanaland. Though the tribe numbered less than half the population of Bechuanaland it was the major tribe in a loose collection of about twenty other smaller ones, and its chief therefore was regarded as the main African leader in the Protectorate. At the turn of the century the Great Khama's son, Sekgoma, had been exiled for 23 years because he chose a wife of whom his father disapproved. When Sekgoma died in 1925, his son, Seretse, was only four years old. A struggle for power and for the succession ensued, and Tshekedi Khama, another of the Great Khama's sons, then aged twenty, was recalled from college to be acting chief of the Bamangwato tribe.

Tshekedi decided to bring up Seretse as his own son, and he set about administering the territory with great energy and efficiency. Before the war there was only one incident which marred what otherwise had become, in the eyes of London, a model career as a modern African chief, and that was when he ordered a white youth to be judicially flogged for a sexual assault on a black girl – a case which caused his temporary suspension as chief. Evelyn clearly found him an exemplary leader of the Protectorate, and admired his enterprising leadership of the Ngwato native authority.

On his first tour of Bechuanaland, Evelyn was so impressed with Tshekedi, with his ability to argue well and to take a point, that he and Molly could not help wondering, rather ironically, what a really intelligent African like he was must think of some of the Europeans he came across in the government service who were supposed to belong to an altogether superior race – or certainly behaved as if they did. In a letter home to Molly in August, 1948 – barely a month before the first sign of trouble for Tshekedi – Evelyn described a trip to Bechuanaland in Tshekedi's company, 'We tagged on to Tshekedi who appeared in a bright white and red jeep truck. He charges in and out of the trees and over the bumps as hard as he can go. Travelling in his territory is faintly like an Indian state. He runs a real government with his representatives posted as controllers of the non-Bamangwato "the lesser breeds without the law" who make up ¾ of the population of this reserve.'

Seretse had first come to official attention some three years earlier in August, 1945, when Evelyn wrote to Machtig to tell him that he had agreed to a proposal from Tshekedi to let Seretse read law at Balliol. He referred to Tshekedi as 'an altogether exceptional ruler and even something of a statesman'. Seretse's Balliol plans had emerged a year earlier, when he was still at the Witwatersrand University, and Tshekedi had collected the tribal chiefs together to work out the transfer of power to Seretse, since they had decided it was time for him to take over the chieftainship. Seretse had had misgivings about such an imminent take over, and said he wanted to work under his uncle for two years before he assumed the reins of power. Tshekedi replied that one year as understudy was enough, at which Seretse said that he wanted to go to read law at university in the United Kingdom. To this the elders agreed; and it was accepted that he would return to take over the chieftainship of the tribe in December, 1948.

On September 20, 1948, Tshekedi received a letter from his nephew announcing his intention to marry an English girl, Ruth Williams. He wrote, 'I realize that this matter will not please you because the tribe will not like it as the person I am marrying is a white woman. . . . In spite of what they might do or say I shall still return home whenever you say to serve them in any capacity. I realize that it was my duty to have asked your consent before I had done this thing but I knew you would refuse and it would be difficult for me to disregard your advice and that is why I notified you when it was all done. Please forgive me . . . please don't try to stop me, father, I want to go through with it.'[1] He went on to say he had known his fiancée for a year and had proposed to her in June. They were to be married on October 2.

Tshekedi was hurt and confused. He had been looking forward to Seretse's return to take over the chieftainship so that he could be free to devote himself to his pet educational and agricultural projects. He had been regent for twenty years; he had had enough. He knew that Seretse's behaviour was now going to cause trouble in the tribe, and outside it. There were established procedures for a chief choosing a wife, which depended at all stages on there being no objections from the other chiefs or elders of the tribe.

Seretse was proposing to flout them; not just to flout them, but to introduce the vexatious element of a mixed marriage into the argument as well. This opened up all sorts of complications externally – not least because at Mafeking, in the Union, which was still then the administrative headquarters of the Protectorate, mixed marriages were about to become illegal under new laws introduced as a result of the Nationalist election victory. Moreover Tshekedi also saw a mixed marriage in a tribal society as a disaster, a potentially divisive element, which would give rise to feuds and plots within the tribe which would inevitably be exploited by the South Africans.

He promptly asked the Resident Commissioner to prevent the marriage and recall Seretse to Africa. On a less official level, Tshekedi's law adviser, Douglas Buchanan, wrote to his brother John, an Anglican parson, asking him to contact the Archbishop of Canterbury to get the marriage stopped, and to warn Ruth's parents that ostracism and misery awaited her in Africa if she went ahead with he marriage. There was no time to lose. Indeed it had already been lost, since Seretse, who apparently was surprised at Tshekedi's attitude, having expected paternal support, advanced the date of the wedding to September 25. There followed an extraordinary episode which does no credit to the Church of England, when the Vicar of Campden Hill, London, where Seretse and Ruth intended to marry, said he had been advised by the Bishop of London that he could not hold a marriage service until he had consulted the Colonial Office. Tshekedi wired Seretse saying he had asked the Commonwealth Relations Office to arrange for his return; but it was already too late. The couple had married.

There were now four parties to a dispute which was to continue unresolved for several years. First there was Tshekedi, the acting chief but not the only authority within the tribe, who was violently opposed both to the marriage, and to Seretse's succession unless the marriage, and therefore his flaunting of tribal procedures, was annulled. Secondly, there was the tribe itself, which started by reacting in the same way as Tshekedi, but came to see the issue less as one of mixed marriage or Seretse's flouting of tribal procedures and more in terms of a straight choice between Tshekedi and Seretse for the future leadership of the tribe. Thirdly, there was Seretse, who now showed that he no longer held any of those earlier doubts about his readiness and determination to assume the chieftainship. Finally, there was the

British government. That description concealed a wide range of different attitudes between the local men in the Protectorate, the High Commission staff in Pretoria, and the Commonwealth Relations Office and British Cabinet in London. But the basic differences within the British view were between the desire to do what was right in the best interests of the tribe (whatever they appeared to be at any one time), the preservation of British authority in the tribal area, and the need to keep the situation from souring Anglo-South African relations, when the future of the territories was already such a sensitive and contentious issue after the Nationalist victory in the election of 1948.

Evelyn had been notified of Seretse's letter on September 23. He immediately sent a telegram to the Commonwealth Relations Office, seeking any help that could be given, since, in his view, the marriage would be disastrous for the tribe and for Seretse personally. Another telegram came from his office, recording the smiliar views of Sillery, then Resident Commissioner in Bechuanaland.

There was some inter-office discussion on how, or whether, the marriage could be stopped. There was no reason to suppose that the marriage would not be valid in the Protectorate, so there was little that could be done. At this stage, the Commonwealth Relations Office studiously tried to avoid committing itself to one side or the other, though opinion within the Bechuanaland administration was resolutely against the marriage, as was the High Commission office with Evelyn at its head. Their trouble was that they had no legal grounds, at that stage, for objecting to the marriage, which they recognised had to be a matter for the tribe.

Indeed it was an early complaint of Tshekedi that he was not able to call on the full support of the British authorities, which he expected to help him uphold his, and the tribe's, authority; and moreover, that he was not even able to elicit from the British what their attitude to the situation was, and what advice they had given Seretse in London, once it was clear that the attempts to stop the marriage had failed. Looking back on the affair, it seems conceivable that if the British administration had lent their full support to Tshekedi at the start they might have got away with less fuss, even though they would have been intervening in the affairs of the tribe.

It does also seem as though Evelyn was less alert to the implications of the affair than he should have been. At the time of Seretse's marriage he was intensely preoccupied with the other two territories, and with the continuing developments of the first few months of Nationalist government. His much-cherished Swaziland forestry scheme was coming unstuck, and there was a serious outburst of ritual murders in Basutoland. He was also hoping to return to the U.K. in October or November for discussions with the government; and then a period of leave. At one moment this trip was cancelled because of difficulties in Southern Africa; then it was reinstated. However, before he left for Britain, he did decide that Ruth Williams, by then Seretse's wife, should be prevented from entering the territory should Seretse ignore everybody's advice and come back with her to Bechuanaland before he had confronted the tribe. Noel-Baker, as Secretary of State, agreed that this should, if necessary, be stated as the view of HMG, on the grounds that her presence in the tribal reserve would be a disruptive influence, which could well give rise to disturbances.

However Seretse, without Ruth, returned to Bechuanaland late in October and the royal family of the tribe gathered together on November 13 to consider the position. There were fifteen of them present, including Seretse and his uncle. Only one of them acquiesced in the marriage. A big *kgotla* (public meeting) of the tribe followed on November 15, attended by about 3000 people from every district of the tribe. It went on for four hours, with 85 speakers, of whom only seven were in favour of Seretse's marriage. Tshekedi, as acting chief, summed up the decisions of the *kgotla*: Ruth Williams was not acceptable as the wife of the future chief; they hoped she would be refused admission to the tribal areas; Seretse was to stay with the tribe; and if he returned to Ruth in the United Kingdom he would be doing so entirely on his own responsibility and against the decision of the tribe. Seretse then asked for a farewell *kgotla*, perhaps to play for time, because there were signs that many younger tribesmen, who had not been able to attend the first *kgotla*, were better disposed towards the marriage, and he already sensed that although many tribesmen might have been hostile to the marriage, when they realized that Seretse would go into exile, and Tshekedi would continue as acting chief — or even become chief — their opinions would swing round in favour of the younger man. Tshekedi had been strict and not all of them appreciated his hard-driving enthusiasms.

At the second *kgotla* the tribe again confirmed that they wanted Seretse to abandon Ruth. They were not sure how, since they were not particularly conversant with, or concerned with, English divorce law. Although Khama's dynasty was christian there was a tradition of polygamy in the tribe which enabled them to accommodate the idea of Seretse discarding his first wife and moving on to a second one – a fellow tribeswoman – whose off-spring would be more acceptable as future chiefs. When asked at the subsequent official enquiry how the tribe thought Seretse could 'get rid of his wife', Tshekedi said, 'We felt it was a matter of negotiation, we did not think it could be done by law, but possibly with an explanation of the position in South Africa, with explanations to the parents of this woman and herself we might have got the couple to realize that the step taken was not in their interests.'[2]

On 4th January, 1949, Sir Walter Harragin, who was acting for Evelyn while the latter was on leave, received a report from the Protectorate administration on the second *kgotla* which showed three groups within the tribe: (a) those who without qualification approved of Seretse's marriage, 1%; (b) those who were disinclined to accept the marriage but at the same time would not reject it for fear of Seretse leaving, 20%; and (c) those who were solidly behind Tshekedi and would not in any circumstances accept the marriage, 79%. This was admitted to be a very rough calculation, but the assessment of the second group was that its members wanted a change in the leadership of the tribe and the marriage seemed to make this impossible.[3] Moreover, they were disturbed by Seretse's threat that if he could not bring his wife to the reserve with him he would leave permanently. Sillery, the Resident Commissioner, endorsed the report with the comment that there was almost solid disapproval of the marriage among the Bamangwato and the lesser tribes who made up the majority of the reserve. He made it clear that it was his wife and not Seretse's claim to be chief, which was at issue.

At that early stage the British position was to maintain the strictest neutrality in the dispute so that, in Harragin's words, 'it could never be said in the future the government had influenced the decisions in any way whatsoever.'[3] Indeed, before Seretse left the reserve to return to England he received a letter from the Government Secretary at Serowe which impressed on him that, in leaving the Protectorate at that juncture, he was not in any way renouncing his chieftainship and that he could be given an undertaking that the government would give him facilities for returning at any future time, provided, of course, that he did not come with an army or join a fifth column in the reserve.

So Seretse returned to his law studies and Evelyn returned from his leave to be brought up to date with the situation. Tshekedi, in the meantime, had drawn up a confidential report for the administration, in which he expressed his concern at the deterioration of affairs in the tribe, in particular the increasing insubordination among younger members of the tribe. He recommended strong and urgent administrative action to support the decision of the tribe. It was not until April that he received an official reply indicating that the administration would *not* implement the second decision of the *kgotla* which dealt with the request to exclude Ruth from the territory.

The British authorities were still attempting to preserve some neutrality in the dispute and 'await developments'. One might ask why they chose to adopt a policy of such unmasterly activity, when in so many other respects the British were only too ready to exercise their imperial authority. They could have moved to support Tshekedi, and in doing so would have been seen to uphold tribal authority probably to the great relief of most of the Bamangwato and its acting chief, whom everybody agreed had been a first class leader. If their refusal were animated by the view that they could not take this kind of action simply because Seretse had married a white woman, it is hard to understand the position they adopted after the next *kgotla*, when the tribe came to accept Seretse as its next chief, white woman and all. Indeed, the final position Evelyn adopted on the Secretse affair laid great store on its damaging effect on Anglo-South African relations, particularly with regard to the future of the High Commission Territories, for the very reason that Seretse *was* marrying a white woman. So the early view of the administration was clearly not as favourable to Seretse as was liberal political opinion in Britain. There the popular projection of the dispute was of Seretse being persecuted by a wicked, old-fashioned, illiberal uncle who was over-exercising his authority to prevent a marriage which was nothing to get excited about in terms of the mores of post-war Europe.

Although the official documents on the case are still closed to public view, from the papers available in Evelyn's collection it appears that he personally did not get actively involved in the affair until it was too late. By then a third *kgotla* had been held, in June, 1949, which resulted in a decisive shift in the power structure within the tribe, and made it impossible to underwrite Tshekedi's authority against Seretse as Evelyn might have been able to do initially. Certainly there is no mention of the case in any of Molly's letters home between January, 1949, and July, when it blew up in their faces. Equally certainly, Evelyn did not think there was a serious enough situation within the tribe to merit a visit either to Mafeking, or to the territory – something he was always inclined to do if there was a hint of trouble brewing.

Some of the fault here must lie with the Bechuanaland administration. It was, even in contemporary terms, a particularly tightly knit branch of the imperial service. All officers had to sign a document recognising that miscegenation was a disciplinary offence, so that they were not likely to take a friendly attitude to Seretse's mixed marriage even apart from its disruptive effects in the tribe. Moreover there were strained relations between Sillery, the Resident Commissioner who had recently arrived in the Protectorate, and a core of his senior administrative officers who had been there all their lives, had intermarried, and regarded Sillery with not unmerited disdain. So the advice which Evelyn would have been receiving from Mafeking and Serowe is not likely to have alerted him to the serious implications of the affair.

In the interview Evelyn had with Tshekedi in April the acting chief made the following points to him: 1) that Seretse had shown himself incompetent ever to be chief; 2) that he could not reside in the reserve as an individual if he was not recognised as chief; 3) that Ruth should be excluded; and 4) that a third *kgotla* would be advantageous. Tshekedi told Evelyn that he felt the third *kgotla* would show Seretse once and for all that opinion was unalterably against him.[4] Ironically, the third *kgotla* was to be Tsekedi's undoing.

CHAPTER XVIII

The Crisis of Seretse Khama

On May 24, on the eve of Seretse's return to the Protectorate, and exactly a month before the vital third *kgotla* was held, Evelyn received from Sillery the latest assessment of the situation within the tribe. 'I am still persuaded that the bulk of responsible opinion in the tribe, though not pro-Tshekedi, is opposed to the marriage and to the accession of Seretse married to a European. This opinion is no doubt held with regret as the appeal of the blood royal is very strong and might still in the long run, since public opinion is volatile, refute my present opinion. There are still of course a number who want to see which way the cat will jump.'[1] He went on to say that the affair was no longer a simple affair of mixed marriage. This aspect had now been subordinated to an old and bitter game of tribal politics played by violent and unscrupulous men. This assessment of the situation could not have been more disastrously wrong.

On June 24 the third *kgotla* was held. About 3500 tribesmen attended it, many, perhaps most, from Serowe, Seretse's home area. It lasted four days. Both Seretse and Tshekedi made impassioned personal appeals to the assembled tribesmen and the meeting ended in tumultuous support, by acclamation, for Seretse. As a result of the decisions of the *kgotla* Tshekedi – though still acting chief – announced he would go into 12 months exile in the territory of a neighbouring chief taking some headmen with him and much of his cattle. Now a completely new situation confronted the authorities, and Evelyn immediately sent for Seretse. Their meeting in Pretoria in early July gave rise to considerable misunderstanding between them since it was followed soon afterwards by a fundamental – and until now unexplained – change of policy on Evelyn's part. Seretse's clear impression when he left the meeting was that he would be installed within three weeks, but that the High Commissioner would prefer Ruth to arrive in the reserve after the installation. He cabled Ruth to that effect. Evelyn's account of the meeting is not all that different, since, in a despatch to the Commonwealth Relations Office, he recorded that he had said he would welcome now some indication of Seretse's plans and policy *if he should be confirmed* in the appointment.[2] He suggested to him that there should be no witch hunt, that he should avoid bad advisers and heal the breach in the tribe if he became chief. Though there were, built into those notes, the usual qualifications – the *ifs* were underlined in Evelyn's despatch – there can have seemed little doubt that Seretse was going to be confirmed chief, otherwise why would Evelyn have bothered to send for him, let alone give him friendly advice about how to behave once he had become chief? What Evelyn meant, presumably, was that Seretse's confirmation had to go through three stages before he was fully appointed – first designation by the tribe, second, acceptance by the High Commissioner and third, approval of the Secretary of State.

Sillery by now was advising Evelyn that Seretse had to be installed as chief (though Ruth should remain in the U.K. until he was actually installed). In the Commonwealth Relations Office there was a view, put forward by Patrick Gordon-Walker, the Parliamentary Under Secretary, that he should be allowed to be chief, but that the powers and functions of the chieftainship should be temporarily exercised by somebody else. This initially found no favour with the Bechuanaland administration, though it subsequently formed the basis of the plan for direct rule which was ultimately imposed on the tribe.

However, in spite of the encouraging signs at his meeting with Evelyn, things then seemed to slip speedily away from Seretse. In the first place Tshekedi and his followers issued a statement explaining their self-imposed exile on the grounds that they questioned the legality of the steps Seretse and his supporters had taken to proclaim himself chief and Ruth Williams queen. They called for a judicial enquiry. Everything then happened very quickly. Tshekedi's statement was on July 5. On July 8, Liesching, who had succeeded Machtig as Permanent Secretary at the Commonwealth Relations Office, suggested to Evelyn that the powers and functions of the chieftainship might temporarily be exercised by a council including neither Seretse nor Tshekedi (Gordon-Walker's proposal). On July 11, Evelyn replied, advocating a judicial enquiry along the lines suggested by Tshekedi, and recommending that they should all play for time, if that was possible. Indeed, in the few days between Evelyn seeing Seretse, and his writing to Liesching, everything changed, and the changes were so crucial in terms of later developments in the Seretse affair, and so inexplicable at the time – certainly from Seretse's point of view – that much of Evelyn's letter of explanation to Liesching is worth reproducing in the original.[3] The Forsyth referred to in the letter was Douglas Forsyth, Secretary of South Africa's Department of External Affairs. He was a wise and frank friend of Evelyn's and held a key position in the South African government. He had been Smuts' right-hand man during the war, and now more or less ran South African foreign policy because Malan, who was both Prime Minister and Foreign Minister, was ignorant of external affairs, and relied almost entirely on Forsyth's advice.

TOP SECRET AND PERSONAL

'My dear Liesching,

I feel I owe you some explanation of the recommendation made in my despatch No. 197 of the 11th July about the Seretse affair in the Bechuanaland Protectorate. In deciding on future action we are faced by a choice of evils. On the one hand refusal now to recognise Seretse as Chief on the ground that an African married to a white woman is not a suitable person to fill the office would open us to accusations of having surrendered to representations made by the Union Government and of having flouted the views of the tribe. On the other hand to recognise Seretse as Chief during the next few months and completely to reject the representations made by Dr Malan would lead to a head-on collision with the Union at the worst possible time and for the worst possible reason. The High Commission Territories are so dependent economically on South Africa and their very existence gives rise to such strong feelings among South Africans that it has always been our policy to avoid such a collision if avoidance is possible without paying too great a price.

My first reaction to the news of the tribe's decision was to recommend the recognition of Seretse. I thought that we should face as soon as possible the inevitable storm of criticism in Southern Africa. I have always felt and I still feel that where there is a straight and an unavoidable choice in our Territories between fostering the interests and preserving the confidence of Africans on the one hand and the maintenance of good relations with the Union on the other hand, it is our relations with the Union which must be sacrificed. This is the advice I would offer if consulted on a request by any South African Government for transfer of the High Commission Territories against the will of their inhabitants or for application to those

Territories of such South African practices as an economic colour bar.

I have, however, with great reluctance and after much thought come to the conclusion that in this case I should not advice on these lines.'

He explained that Tshekedi's decision to leave the reserve, with 43 headmen would have serious consequences for the tribe, and suggested that still more time was needed to show that the tribe *really* wanted Seretse, and that he was fitted to be chief.

'As regards the Union the situation is the gravest which has faced us since I first came to this country. When I was first informed of the result of the Serowe meeting I knew that there would be official protests and a loud public outcry. I then thought that South Africans would be less troubled by Seretse's position as chief than by the fact of a European woman and an African man living together as man and wife on the Union's borders. I believed that a result of the recognition of Seretse while he is married to his present wife would be a great impetus to the demand for the transfer of the High Commission Territories.

On the 7th July, however, I obtained my first opportunity of seeking Forsyth's help. In Cape Town he had discussed the whole matter with Dr Malan. Dr Malan had discussed the question with Ministers and was greatly worried and distressed. He spoke freely to Forsyth.

Two points emerge. First, official recognition of Seretse as chief so long as it implies the residence in Serowe of his English wife and the performance by her of the duties of the first wife of a chief is what really matters to the members of the Government and probably to most South Africans. The mere residence of Seretse and his wife in Serowe without official recognition is objectionable to them, but in Forsyth's view of subsidiary importance. He hopes that it might be avoided but it is the recognition of Seretse as chief which will be the match to set off the gunpowder. Huggins has also written to me taking exactly the same point of view.

Secondly, the political consequences in the Union of recognition would be far more serious than I had realized. Recognition would naturally assist the fight for transfer, but this will not be the sole or the most important result. Nationalist feeling has already been inflamed as a result of the disputes over the Citizenship Bill. The more extreme Nationalists will use the Seretse incident to add fuel to those flames. They will argue that our action demonstrates the folly of allowing the existence side by side in Southern Africa of two systems of Native administration diametrically opposed to one another. They will go on to say that South Africans should not and cannot remain associated with a country which recognises officially an African chief married to a white woman and they will make Seretse's recognition the occasion of an appeal of the country for the establishment of a republic, and not only of a republic but of a republic outside the Commonwealth. Dr Malan is desperately worried and feels that he could not successfully oppose an extremist offensive on these lines.

Forsyth shares his view and believes that if we recognise Seretse the extremists will override the more moderate Nationalists. They believe that Seretse's recognition would enable them to exploit colour feeling in order to sever the tie with Great Britain without exasperating English-speaking South Africans. They would appeal to the whole country on a common South African dislike of the application in the High Commission Territories of British principles of Native administration and on a common South African abhorrence of race mixture. They would thus fight the battle for a secessionist republic with the ideal war cry and at the ideal time; and Forsyth, following the hints dropped by Dr Malan during their conversation, believes that they would succeed.'

Evelyn added a further paragraph suggesting that some proposals for defence cooperation between Britain and South Africa might be jeopardised by the affair. He went on:

'These are Forsyth's views and I have never known him speak with such feeling. To argue that this incident on the edge of the Kalahari might lead to the complete secession of South Africa from the Commonwealth may seem far-fetched. Yet I am afraid that what Forsyth says has the ring of truth and I believe him. The following are my reasons: —

Forsyth is by nature cautious and not alarmist, inclined, if he makes a mistake, to under-rate rather than to over-rate.

If the result of recognition of Seretse had been merely a fillip to the campaign for transfer, Dr Malan would have been pleased. His distress shows that something more radical is in the wind.

In all these circumstances I feel on one assumption that we must play for time. I am well aware that if we do so we shall be accused of weakness and of behaving like Mr Micawber. Yet the political results of recognition would be so serious, and the effect on the tribe of a quick decision, if wrong, would be so bad that I have no other alternative.'

Evelyn said that the Bechuanaland administration believed that the tribe would accept an immediate decision to disquality Seretse from the chieftainship on the grounds of Ruth's unsuitability as a white woman to be a chief's wife. But they recognised the difficulties, and, instead, he proposed a small committee of enquiry to investigate Seretse's suitability as chief. By playing for time they would postpone a confrontation with the Union. Moreover, it was possible that Seretse would become tired of Ruth, or that the tribe might harden their minds against him. He concluded:

'I recognise the disadvantages of the proposal I have made, but the consequences of recognising Seretse would be so serious that we should, I believe, do everything we can to avoid a collision on this issue with the Union.'

Evelyn's recommendation to play for time was a compromise, based on his assumption that the U.K. government would not be prepared to declare that Seretse could not be recognised as chief because he had married a white woman. In London, Noel-Baker, the Commonwealth Secretary, said he felt he was not adequately informed, and queried some of Evelyn's observations. What was the reaction of the native press in the Union, for instance? Would the Nationalists take the occasion to occupy the High Commission Territories by force? On what grounds did he think HMG could base a decision to refuse to recognise? The Cabinet were in a quandary. They were assailed by all liberal opinion and also by the official opposition for their handling of the affair. They were anyway unversed in the intricacies of the tribal politics of the Bamangwato. They saw the issue as one in which a British Cabinet was about to refuse to recognise an African as chief because he had married a white woman – on the face of it solely to appease white South African Nationalist government and reactionary African sentiment in a Protectorate where Britain's imperial rationale was to wean the Africans away from such primitive reactions.

In the face of such confusion, Evelyn's advice almost *had* to be accepted, since ministers had neither sufficient confidence in themselves or their own judgment, nor apparently the knowledge, to go against it. It was an unusual situation for a Proconsul, and this was clearly appreciated by Liesching who sent Evelyn a remarkable letter of support – remarkable because he appeared to be egging Evelyn on, urging him to consolidate his position.[4] In a 'private and personal' letter written in longhand, he thanked Evelyn for his 'extraordinarily valuable reports over this terribly difficult Seretse problem. I cannot go into detail as time is too short, but I should like you to know that among ministers here there has now developed a complete unanimity against recognition of Seretse with Ruth as his wife. It was very difficult to estimate how ministerial opinion would go on this and Creech Jones (Colonies) has come out entirely on the right side. My S of S has been very sensible from the first. Your reputation here is exceedingly high, as well it might be, and your judgment is trusted to an extent which has never been exceeded in the case of any High Commissioner I have known.'

The same could not be said with the Conservatives. Lord Salisbury was staying with Evelyn at about that time, and Evelyn discussed the affair with him, hoping to get sound advice, and suggesting that it was worth sacrificing Seretse in order not to bedevil relations between South Africa and the United Kingdom. 'Bobbety' would have none of that. 'That was the argument of Caiaphas,' he remarked pointedly. Evelyn was badly shaken, but his pragmatism prevailed.

On July 20, Evelyn sent a further reply to Noel-Baker's enquiries.[5] He said he did not wish to press the Secretary of State to refuse now to recognise Seretse, but he did urge him to play for time. He said that the only people who would benefit from recognition would be the extremist wing of the Nationalist party. ' "The thin end of the wedge" argument in native affairs would be strengthened and by a false move we might damage both our case for retaining the High Commission Territories and the cause of all Africans in South Africa. I therefore strongly push the proposal for an enquiry.' He recalled that the South African High Commissioner in London had been sent to see Noel-Baker the previous month to give semi-official representation that the marriage would be considered a grave infringement of basic principle and that he hoped Britain would refuse recognition.

A few days later Evelyn heard the result of the Cabinet decision and on July 31 he wrote to Molly, in England, 'I received a telegram from the Cabinet. It was more satisfactory than my wildest hopes. Not only did they accept the proposal for a judicial enquiry but it is clear partly from the telegram, and partly from a letter Liesching wrote to me, that they accept the main point i.e.

the impossibility of recognising Seretse as long as he is bound to Ruth. I took a plane, gave the press the slip, spent a busy energetic day in Mafeking. I saw Tshekedi and Seretse, put the enquiry proposal to them and they took it well. I encouraged poor little Sillery who is feeling pained and worried.' Evelyn also found support from an unexpected quarter – Father Trevor Huddleston. 'When I put to Trevor the point whether it would not be immoral to refuse to recognise Seretse because by this action the break up of his marriage would be brought nearer, he brushed it on one side and is very strongly against recognition.' So that made two Caiaphases!

Evelyn immediately announced the setting up of the enquiry under Sir Walter Harragin, High Court Judge of the Territories, with two assistants. Meanwhile, Ruth Khama had quietly arrived in the Protectorate, without any fuss. The Nationalist government now started to make openly hostile noises, in the hope, no doubt, of influencing the British government in the way it set up the formal enquiry and its terms of reference. In September and October Dr Malan, the Prime Minister, made a number of speeches condemning the marriage and calling on HMG either to repudiate it, or to face the consequences of a demand by his government to incorporate the High Commission Territories into the Union in the New Year. The South African government then made this position even more clear by declaring Seretse and Ruth prohibited immigrants – an act of interference which could have prompted Evelyn to make a stand against them then and there if he had thought he could prevail.

The enquiry in November took place first at Lobatsi for Tshekedi, then at Serowe for Seretse. Harragin ruled that he would only make two findings for the High Commissioner; the first would be whether or not the *kgotla* was properly conducted, and the second, whether, having particular regard for the interests of the tribe, Seretse was a fit and proper person to discharge the functions of chief. Within the second finding, however the question of his marriage was obviously of such vital importance that evidence given with regard to it would be relevant.

The hearings ended on November 18, with no published verdict, while the tribe continued chiefless, with Seretse and Ruth living quietly in Serowe, and Tshekedi arranging his departure. Evelyn had clearly been hoping that Ruth would find life in the reserve much less exciting than she had expected. He worked on the assumption that she had thought Seretse a grander person than he turned out to be, that she had thought she was marrying into something akin to an Indian rajah state. Evelyn hoped that the proceedings of the enquiry would build up a great deal of damaging evidence against her – certainly in tribal terms. This had shocked Sillery, who had become rather sorry for Ruth – that is until he found her one day at the local railway station playing pingpong and drinking gin with what he described as 'some very low class Europeans, who might even have been commercial travellers.' Anyway Evelyn, and presumably most of the High Commission staff, were wrong when they calculated that Ruth would be only too happy to get out of Serowe at a reasonable price. This incorrect assessment of her attitude led indirectly to a number of policy miscalculations a few months later.

Harragin's findings were never published but were given to the British government in December 1949. His conclusions were:

1) The kgotla held at Serowe between the 20th and 25th of June, 1949, at which Seretse Khama was designated a Chief of the Bamangwato Tribe, was properly convened and assembled, and its proceedings conducted in accordance with native custom.

2) That having regard to the interests and well being of the Tribe, Seretse Khama is not a fit and proper person to discharge the functions of Chief.

Harragin's reasons for 2) were partly based on the external consequences of a Seretse chieftainship – its effect on the Union and so on – and these Evelyn officially rejected. But he endorsed the finding on the grounds that recognition of Seretse as chief would undoubtedly cause disruption in the tribe and, on December 10, he telegrammed a recommendation to Noel-Baker that Seretse should not be recognised. Later that week Evelyn arrived in London for extensive discussions about the affair.

From now on there is a curious internal contradiction in the way the affair was handled. We have seen from Evelyn's letter to Liesching that, though he was mindful of the disruption in the tribe caused by the defection of Tshekedi and his experienced headmen and for that matter by Seretse's previous flouting of tribal custom and procedure, it was the *external* effect of the affair – within the Union – which clinched the argument against recognition of Seretse. Yet that was never officially acknowledged. Naturally HMG did not want it to be thought that they took the decision for fear of the external consequences – even though they had – and therefore they clung to the residual *tribal* reasons for non-recognition. It was because of their sensitivity on this point that they preferred not to publish Harragin's report. But what of Evelyn? He too, apparently, sought to play down the external reasons and to concentrate entirely on Seretse's *tribal* unsuitability. There was some casuistry apparent; because the grounds chosen for Seretse's unfitness to be chief were that he had shown himself to be irresponsible in contracting a marriage without the tribe's consent, and thus to be unmindful of their interests. Yet the tribe itself by then had already forgiven him for this in the decisive vote it registered at the final *kgotla*.

The talks between Evelyn and the Commonwealth Relations Office eventually concluded that the report would not be published and that Seretse and Ruth would be summoned to London *after* a decision as to the future had been reached, but in time for him to be consulted about a White Paper which would be published later. It was intended that Noel-Baker should see Seretse personally to try to persuade him to relinquish the chieftainship voluntarily; while Tshekedi would also not be allowed to return to the reserve. Noel-Baker would also offer Seretse an allowance on condition that he kept out of Bechuanaland altogether. If Seretse did not accede voluntarily it was clear that he was going to have to accept exile involuntarily.

The government thought that both Seretse and Ruth would come to London, and Evelyn was adamant that she should not be left behind in Bechuanaland. However, in view of the government's plans for the couple, Sillery was naturally unable to furnish Seretse with a written guarantee that Ruth, if she were to go to London, would be allowed to return. So Seretse went alone, much to the administration's surprise and disappointment. Evelyn's response to this development was again a misguided one. He thought that the British government would merely have to put pressure on Seretse in London to make Ruth follow him. As it turned out the pressure failed. Seretse's visit to London was a fiasco which Evelyn felt was mismanaged from start to finish by the government; but for which he cannot escape much of the blame himself.

The sequence of events was as follows: on February 3 Evelyn arrived in Johannesburg from London. He had strongly pressed the government firmly to exclude Seretse from the territory and disqualify him from the chieftainship for ever, but Noel-Baker wanted to avoid taking such an uncompromising stand.

On February 6 Seretse told the tribe at a *kgotla* that he had been invited to London, and the tribe advised him not to go, and certainly not to take Ruth with him if he went. He went alone and though Evelyn advised the Commonwealth Relations Office to insist on Ruth's presence, Noel-Baker ignored this, saw Seretse on the 16th and merely asked him if Ruth would come later. Noel-Baker then went on to suggest to Seretse that it would be in the interests of the tribe that he should voluntarily relinquish the chieftainship; and that, should he do so, he would receive an allowance of £1100 per year while he and Ruth were living elsewhere than in the Protectorate. Seretse did not respond to this suggestion other than to say the tribe might feel he had 'sold out' on them. He also insisted that he could make no decision without first returning to Africa to consult the tribe.

Evelyn's advice, from South Africa, was that Seretse should be told in no uncertain manner that, if he refused to stand down voluntarily, he could not be recognised under any circumstances. His exclusion from the reserve would then become both essential and easier to justify. However, Noel-Baker was then replaced in a Cabinet reshuffle, and when Seretse returned to the Secretary of State's office two weeks later (March 3) he found Patrick Gordon-Walker (formerly a junior minister in the Department) in the chair. Gordon-Walker could not bring himself to be entirely open with Seretse, and to tell him there and then that, if he refused to resign, he would not be recognised anyway. It was only when Seretse continued to refuse the offer of £1100 that the Cabinet decided finally to accept the gist of Evelyn's original advice that he should not be recognised as chief, that he should be excluded from the territory, and that direct rule should be imposed on the tribe for at least five years. Seretse gave a press conference saying he had been tricked. He had been invited to Britain without strings, he said, and only after he had arrived was he told he would not be allowed back.

Gordon-Walker now had to move quickly, in the face of mounting political difficulties. Two days later he made a statement to the House of Commons that Seretse was to be excluded from the reserve for five years; but he would not disclose the contents of Harragin's report. The imbroglio was further aggravated by the fact that the government's decision to ban Seretse for five years – Evelyn had advised against putting a time limit on it but Gordon-Walker overruled his advice – was leaked before Seretse was officially told of it. Consequently the Conservatives were fiercely critical. Churchill particularly concentrated on the point of honour – or rather dishonour – involved in the possibility that

Seretse did not know he was to be excluded from returning when he was originally invited to London. The British press was generally critical. A leader in *The Times* said, 'If the Bamangwato do not object to a white consort and the prospect of a half-breed succession it would not seem to be for the Imperial Government, pledged before all the nations to respect the equal rights of all races, to overrule them in their own domestic concerns. There, if principle were to prevail over expediency, should be an end of the argument . . . [Transfer considerations] are acutely perplexing to HMG. But they do not touch the rights and wrongs of the case. No good can come of compromise involving injustice to individuals if its aim is to blur the outline of the truth.'[6] Even the South African press thought the government had handled the affair deplorably.

Evelyn privately thought he might get the sack for the affair, and appeared to Molly to be more worried during the ensuing week than he had ever been about anything before. He was critical in private of the government decision to ask Seretse back before they had really made up their minds what to do – hoping that he would accept the bribe, and not thinking through the consequences of his not doing so. But could that have been because ministers had been led to believe previously by the High Commission that Seretse and Ruth would be susceptible to that kind of offer? Evelyn, accompanied by four senior officials of the Bechuanaland government, went to Serowe on March 13 to explain to the tribe the terms of Seretse's exclusion. The *kgotla* was completely boycotted, and abandoned. Evelyn sent orders to 24 headmen to meet him in half an hour. All refused. At a press conference that day, rather shaken, he said, 'We had to stop the development of one of the biggest and worst dynastic feuds there has ever been,' and pointed out that there were only 18,000 Bamangwato in the reserve, compared to a total Bechuanaland population of 100,000.[7] He then received a wire from the Cabinet asking if it would be all right for Seretse to come back into Bechuanaland to complete his lawsuit against Tshekedi and live not in his reserve but under another chief, at least until Ruth had her baby. Evelyn advised against it, without much confidence that his advice would be accepted, and prepared to resign if, at the end of it all, the government caved in and reinstated Seretse as chief. He argued most strongly that direct rule would be undermined while Seretse was on or near the scene. He was also worried that the government appeared ready to reconsider the expulsion order and the five year ban, and felt that public opinion might interpret this as the first step towards recognition of Seretse. Though he may not have known of it at the time, he was right to think that the government were not entirely happy with his advice. Attlee, as Prime Minister, took the almost unprecedented step of going behind Evelyn's back and writing directly to the District Commissioner at Serowe, asking for his views on the affair.

Evelyn was in a quandary because, although he was fully prepared to resign over the narrow point about Seretse, he did not think that Nationalists demands for the Territories would be properly fought by any successor, and it was that issue which he saw all along as his main objective in South Africa. He was distressed because he could not answer the criticism in Britain which grew from a widespread belief that he and the government had yielded to the Union on a point of principle. Though he felt it *was* a matter of principle that Seretse should be allowed to marry whomsoever he liked, it was not a matter of principle that he should then be recognised as chief if the political consequences of that recognition were going to be disastrous for his people. Evelyn in fact would probably have been against Seretse becoming chief even if the Union had not been indirectly involved in the affair, since he tended to take the same view as Tshekedi about the tribal disruptions likely to ensue from a mixed marriage.

Meanwhile the affair was still being exploited by the Conservatives. The Tories were annoyed that Gordon-Walker's five year moratorium on Seretse would land them with the ultimate decision, if they regained office; and they pressed their attack. Smuts, however, visited the Barings that week and told them he had written a private letter to Churchill telling him not to play with dynamite. He warned that if Seretse were recognised it would be the end of the Commonwealth as far as South Africa was concerned, and there would be a united and overwhelming demand for the Territories which would be extremely difficult to withstand.

The affair had now entered its last phase and had become simply a struggle between the tribes and the British authorities. The basic argument between them was that the tribe wanted a chief and an end to direct rule, while the British remained firm in their refusal to rescind Seretse's or Tshekedi's exile. The tribe remained equally firm in its refusal to cooperate with the administration, and in May the DC was shouted down at a *kgotla*. There was a danger that the absence of the two leading Khamas would reopen other dynastic feuds which were never far below the surface with the Bamangwato, but for the moment they seemed to be more united behind Seretse than they had ever been.

The administration suffered another blow when Nettleton, the acting Resident Commissioner, died early in August. Evelyn wrote to Molly, 'Sillery has offered to come back at once from leave, but I am trying tactfully to put him off until the end of September, since I do not want him to arrive and dither in the middle of the Seretses' departure, which takes place this coming week. There have been endless complications and I am having one hell of a time.' (Sillery was eventually removed on Evelyn's instigation.) Finally, on August 20 he felt he was over the worst. 'We succeeded in getting the Khamas out and the press was bitterly disappointed there was not a scene. They did their level best to manufacture one. I had Forbes [Mackenzie, an administrative officer] bring Tshekedi down here suddenly after picking him up in the middle of the night. I had a successful talk with him and he and Seretse published an innocuous statement in spite of many misrepresentations. All the same we are not out of the woods since Seretse and Tshekedi now think they will both resign the chieftainship and both come back as private individuals. For the moment everyone is so relieved at the complete absence of a row that I received a row of congratulations, not very well deserved, including one from Clem [Attlee]. I will be relieved to be rid of the Seretse problem next July. (Malan and I are now practically blood brothers!)'

When Colin Legum, of *The Observer*, saw him next July, he thought he was still 'very rattled' and uncharacteristically rude in refusing to answer any questions about Tshekedi. The centre of pressure on the British government had by then shifted. Tshekedi, having originally been cast as the villain of the piece in opposing Seretse's marriage, was now attracting much more support in appeals to the Secretary of State to allow him back into the reserve. The affair came up again in a debate in the House of Commons in June 1951, when the Tories laid a motion of censure against Patrick Gordon-Walker. At about that time, probably in preparation for the final debate on July 31, when Evelyn had returned from South Africa and was sitting in the officials' box in the House of Commons, he wrote a memorandum on the affair, which, from its wording, was obviously not intended for Labour ministers' eyes – but was either for Liesching, or more probably for Lord Salisbury and Alan Lennox-Boyd, the senior Conservative politicians responsible for Southern African policies. The memorandum shows how he eventually hardened his position to exclude Seretse for ever from the chieftainship, and that he took this view basically because he set great store by the advice he had received from Smuts about what the consequence would be:

'10. The plain fact is then that if we are to maintain our rule over these three enclaves in South Africa we cannot recognise an African Chief with a white wife. The evidence is very strong that if we did so the Union Government would turn the economic screw and would in this have the support of nearly all white South Africans and Southern Rhodesians. This was true in 1949. It is doubly true today since owing to our recent actions in West Africa we are more unpopular in Southern Africa now than we were then, and since recognition now would appear to be not only an error but also a surrender by a Government of white men to pressure by black men.

11. I have equally little doubt that in the end our present Government would give way under economic pressure from the Union. Then the ill-feeling caused among Africans further North by the abandonment of the High Commission Territories would be far greater than that caused by a refusal to recognise Seretse. On the other hand I suggest that refusal to recognise is more like refusal to give your opponent a knuckle-duster when you are about to fight him than it is like appeasement. We know that Mr Malan will ask for the transfer of the Territories soon, and we know that his request will be refused.

12. But I fully realize the bad results of a refusal to recognise. The marriage of an African Chief to a white woman in a small territory dependent upon rich and powerful neighbours where the ruling people are fanatically opposed to mixed marriage is to present a choice of evils. Refusal to recognise is, I think, the lesser evil, but it is still an evil. It has become a greater evil than was necessary owing to the promise in the White Paper to review the position after five years.

19. These views are not merely my own, they are also those of the leading Basuto and Swazi whose interests are vitally affected and who have consistently expressed views against the recognition of Seretse. I should also add that the estimate of reactions in the Union to Seretse's recognition is that of General Smuts, and he gave this estimate before the recent constitutional changes in the Gold Coast and therefore at a

time when our relations with South Africa were better than they are now.'[8]

The references to West Africa in Evelyn's letter were inspired by a governmental statement envisaging the early progress to independence of the Gold Coast. This was greeted with much criticism and alarm in South Africa, since it was the first practical step towards relinquishing control over any British-governed territory in Africa. Evelyn's letter, I suspect, was actually addressed to Lord Salisbury, since the latter, on becoming Commonwealth Secretary when the Conservatives regained office in October, 1951, soon announced that the government intended to make Seretse's non-recognition permanent, and that it hoped this would settle the disturbances in the tribe and leave the way for the Bamangwato to choose another chief – after which it would be possible to allow Tshekedi back into the reserve along the lines of Evelyn's advice.

Five years later, in September, 1956, Lord Home, the then Commonwealth Secretary, announced that Seretse had renounced all claim to the chieftainship for himself and his offspring and on that basis was being allowed to return to the reserve. Subsequently he formed a political party, which won a majority in Bechuanaland's first election under the constitution which was to steer it to independent status as Botswana, at which point Seretse became its first president. By then the tribe had stated that his descendants were equally eligible for the chieftainship of the tribe. So for Seretse at least the story had a happy ending, if not for Evelyn. For though the affair no longer remained his primary concern after July, 1951, he felt that his reputation in Africa never fully recovered from the damage caused by the whole saga. Certainly, on two successive occasions when he was offered a distinguished appointment dealing with African affairs his instinctive reaction was to refuse. Fortunately the first of these offers – the future Governorship of Kenya – was one he was eventually persuaded to accept.

CHAPTER XIX

The Territories

Much the pleasantest time Evelyn spent as High Commissioner was when he was touring the three Territories. His lifelong interest was in the countryside – people and problems such as soil erosion and conservation, tribal customs, general agriculture, stock developments, forestry, irrigation, indeed all the constant and recurring elements of peasant life in primitive countries.

As he was to find later in Kenya, there was an urgent political reason for the Territories to develop soundly-based (if modest) agrarian economies, to demonstrate their relative independence of the industrialised and formidable South African economy around them, and to show Africans both in and out of the Union that this could be done. The first thing he did after being sworn in as High Commissioner in Pretoria in October, 1944, was to arrange tours of Basutoland and Swaziland before the government caravan moved down to the Cape after Christmas. He decided Bechuanaland would have to wait until the end of the parliamentary session the following June.

There were basic similarities in the conditions of all three Territories. During the war they had been starved of funds for development, and with a much reduced administrative staff, had been left to tick over as quietly as possible – leaving the existing tribal and agrarian structure largely untouched. The danger now, however, was that the return of many natives from military service would not only over-burden these undernourished economies, but also disturb the existing system of tribal discipline and authority, which was not likely to be gladly accepted by men who had seen something of the wider world. Basutoland seemed already to be beset by rows between the Resident Commissioner and the Paramount Chieftainess – the former full of zeal for reform, the latter a strong-willed old lady of little education but supported by her subjects. So Evelyn decided to go immediately to Basutoland and then on to Swaziland shortly before Christmas.

Accordingly, Evelyn and Molly set off for Maseru in November, 1944. They were pleased to find a country which contrasted so vividly with the suburban refinement of Pretoria. It was wild and hilly, rather reminiscent of Scotland, with the Basutos' houses built of stone, rather than with mud and wattle as was mostly found elsewhere in Africa. It was nice to be back where Evelyn was 'His Excellency', though the informality of the Territory compared favourably to what had been experienced in Southern Rhodesia, and nobody stood on much ceremony with the Queen's representative. The moment they were in the Territory they were met by the Paramount Chief, a great lady with whom Evelyn was to have a number of fairly turbulent dealings. (Lord Harlech had always referred to her privately as Her Amplitude). She and her chiefs had been leading a determined rearguard action against the Resident Commissioner's attempts to deprive them of their ancient rights to impose and then to appropriate fines on their subjects – a device which had naturally kept them rather better off than the tribesmen. The Resident Commissioner, Colonel Arden Clarke, had been trying hard to establish some kind of tribal treasury which would bank the fines and put them to general revenue purposes, but had met with such opposition that he had invoked the direct support of his new High Commissioner. Arden Clarke also told Evelyn that his dealings with the chief were seriously impeded by the activities of a group of Roman Catholic French-Canadian missionaries, who had made a series of important conversions among the chiefs. This meant that they were inevitably allied with the chiefs in their resistance to Clarke's reforms, since the effect of the changes would be to diminish chiefly authority.

Evelyn started off with a stern lecture to the great lady. He told her that his government's policy was to maintain the influence of the chiefs but that they, for their part, must join in responsible government, and sit as salaried court officials paying fines into a treasury, rather than pocketing the proceeds. This did not go down too well, but Arden Clarke was pleased with such direct support, in contrast to the high-flown lectures on the duties of the aristocracy and the lessons of the French Revolution, with which Lord Harlech used to harangue the royal house of Moshesh.

Evelyn reported the visit to Cranborne, 'I found the country very dry, and on all sides hope was expressed that I would bring rain. I had read of the (successful) efforts of my predecessor in this direction. Accordingly I did my best. But, being rather an inexperienced witch doctor, I lost all sense of proportion and produced such a violent storm that there was a washaway on each road to the station, I myself failed to catch the train and was marooned in Maseru.'[1] He said the old system of native courts, which Arden Clarke and he were now trying to change, had become dangerous, since the many Basuto who had worked in the Union and returned home would not put up with the present state of affairs. He estimated that the Paramount Chief was getting about £9000 a year from pocketing fines, in addition to the £2000 which she received from the British government. Apart from the judicial aspects, the control of the chief's authority was essential to save Basutoland's soil which he believed was the vital task of the future. Cranborne agreed that the current practice of native courts was 'really indefensible these days.' He sent Evelyn's despatch to Harlech, who wrote back with a typical comment on the passage dealing with the difficulties over the missionaries. 'Baring has put the political issue admirably. We must save the chieftainship in Basutoland from itself and from the reactionary teaching of the Roman Catholic Church. It was Cardinal Richelieu and the Abbés of the Court of Versailles that destroyed the House of Bourbon and the French monarchy. And it was Rasputin and the Holy Synod that destroyed the Romanoffs. The House of Moshesh will follow suit unless we modernise and liberalise it. But make no mistake, we are up against the Quebec clergy, quite as much as the short-sighted selfishness of the Regent. [The Paramount Chief was regent for her young nephew.]'[2]

The House of Moshesh seemed to respond more favourably to the Baring-Clarke pressure than they had done to Lord Harlech. Next year Evelyn was able to send a more favourable report to his Secretary of State, Lord Addison. 'Last year there was a hint of organised passive resistance from the chieftainship. But once the new scheme replaced the old "placing", the days of the old regime were numbered. This the Paramount Chief dimly perceived. She was surrounded by bad advisers. She was confused by many of the new proposals. As a result she was silent, sulky and noncooperative. But there has been a truly remarkable change over the last year now that the national treasury is established. She is now surrounded by a new and far wider set of councillors. She is much more cooperative in action and forthcoming in conversation. These improved relations are of great importance since our object is to reform and not to overthrow the chieftainship. In the past there was a danger of a tyrannical oligarchy. In future, there will be the fear of too early a destruction of the chieftainship, since the district councils are not an indigenous institution and many of the Basutos also live and work in South Africa.' The Paramount Chifetain had told him that her spirit of cooperation would mean that the Resident Comissioner and she would be like 'two oxen under one yoke', a piece of imagery which amused all and sundry, considering her huge girth, and the fact that she was thought to weigh about 16 stone.

But Evelyn's worries about discipline in Basutoland were not over, and during the next two years he found he was repeatedly having to be called in to deal with an outbreak of ritual murders, which appeared to be sponsored by some of the chiefs to compensate themselves for their loss of despotic authority. A particularly nasty aspect of it was that the victim had to be taken alive before she was ritualistically dismembered. The Colonial Office commissioned a distinguished anthropologist to advise them on the phenomenon (Evelyn having said that he must not be a South African). Evelyn confessed himself at a loss to know how to deal with it – other than to try the culprits – not least because there was evidence that christianised and educated Basuto were involving themselves in it too. The anthropologist had nothing much to offer, and eventually after 19 gruesome murders Evelyn, in September, 1948, had to go up to Maseru to administer a good old-fashioned ticking-off, which he subsequently described in a letter to Molly in England. 'It was clear that the chiefs were organising these crimes and that the old girl is deeply involved. So I put on my smart blue uniform and went down to the first day of the Basutoland national council's session and I made them a terrifice speech praising the work of the chiefs in every other respect but speaking frankly on ritual murder. Later I gave a further long lecture to the old girl and about fifteen of the leading chiefs. They presented a petition complaining that the police did not consult the chief of a district before they started their investigations – naturally since in 18 out of 19 cases chiefs of one grade or another have been involved. I replied by a very vigorous counterattack saying that the continuance of the murders proved that the chiefs were either guilty or ineffective. Their eyes really popped out of their heads. I thought the old girl was going to cry. This would have been awkward as I wanted to give her a further lecture more or less alone [which he did] . . . saying that if the murders did not cease the results to her personally would be very painful indeed, and remarking "I have spoken" dismissed them on the spot – very proud and haughty like.' All this while his stiff blue Governor's coat and tight braided overalls were giving him acute fibrositis in his bottom.

An aspect of Basutoland much more interesting to Evelyn than ritual murders was that of soil conservation. The problem of soil erosion in all three Territories had been taken seriously for some time, and annual progress reports were sent in on areas which had been terraced, the length of the banks, the type of contour grass strips which had been sown, ploughing experiments, tree planting and so on. Swaziland was the first territory where the tribesmen had been advised to limit their stocks of cattle – something of a heresy to Africans who regarded the size of their herd as an important and economically vital status symbol. In Bechuanaland too, special trees had been implanted from North America with roots which helped to strengthen contour ridging, and the planting of particularly tenacious species of grasses. The basic problem of all three Territories was overstocking of cattle, particularly in areas with limited water resources. In Bechuanaland this had led to a concerted programme for the provision of more water supplies; in Swaziland for more dipping tanks, more strip planting of grass, demonstrations of contour ploughing and the planting of more than two million trees. All these measures however had been slowed down owing to the shortage of staff during the war, and Evelyn's main task was to reactivate them before it was too late, and to see that the 100,000 acres which had been virtually reclaimed in the programmes before the war were not allowed to slip back to their old state.

In Basutoland, which he tackled first, the problem had already assumed threatening proportions by the mid-thirties. Here the main cause was not so much overstocking – though that contributed indirectly – as the uncontrolled run-off of storm water from the overgrazed slopes of the mountains. Basutoland had never had any kind of forest cover to check these cataracts, and so the first programme entailed a massive tree planting campaign, which Evelyn decided he had better inspect personally. This involved riding right across the country, for Evelyn to acquaint himself with every feature of the problem. He and Molly set out in January, 1946, for one of the two or three most spectacular official tours they had ever been on, or were likely to go on. They started on New Year's Day, after a *pitso* attended by about five hundred tribesmen all mounted and clothed in coloured blankets. This host accompanied them to their first night's camp, where there was much dancing and slaughtering of oxen, and the hillsides must have looked rather like the night before Agincourt. Their cavalcade then continued – about a hundred horses strong – along a series of passes through the mountains between 8,000 and 10,000 feet high, with Evelyn walking, rather than riding, so that he could collect the host of wild flowers which they found in this botanist's paradise, and also so that he could inspect more closely the state of the soil.

Their imperial pony trek lasted three weeks, by the end of which the ritual Basuto cry of *pula* (rain) had become so ingrained in Evelyn's mind that, upon his return to civilisation, he accosted the startled white mayor of Maritzburg with the Basuto greeting. However, he found his trip rewarding, not least for the fact that at every *pitso* he held along the mountains, he was told there had never, or not in living memory, been a visit from a High Commissioner. Once, a chief said the last High Commissioner who had visited there had been Lord Selborne, 40 years before. When told that Molly was his granddaughter he looked at her and snorted, it later being discovered that this signified disappointment that such a grand lady should be so small. It may equally have been surprise at the contrast in dress between the two High Commissioners. Lord Selborne in 1904 would have dressed the part. On the other hand Evelyn's trekking uniform was an old and purloined rugby club sweater with blue and white horizontal stripes and other stains.

Evelyn reported that he found the agricultural situation in Basutoland precarious. Food was scarce, and the Basuto had sustained themselves by eating rather than exporting the previous year's wheat crop. Until their harvest people would be totally dependent on grain imports from the Union (a point made repeatedly by the Union government during the arguments about transfer). He sent Machtig a long homily on grass, which must have startled that essentially urban mandarin, describing the various strains, the effect of erosion and suggesting a programme of strip grazing, diversion furrows for water courses, and strict grazing control – all essential measures of conservation, but ones which were not going to be at all popular with the Basuto.

The second Territory Evelyn visited, and the one which caused him least trouble, and where as a result he is remembered most lovingly, was Swaziland. At the time Swaziland was still thought of as the Territory which was most likely to be handed over to the Union. There had been rumours of a back-door deal between Smuts and Churchill, which Evelyn feared but which Cranborne seemed to view with equanimity. In his first report Evelyn emphasised the serious deficiencies in the country's economic and administrative situation. It had largely been left to its own devices internally, with the result that it was ill-adapted to the conditions of the modern world under the command of a Paramount Chief. The Swazi suspicion of Europeans was derived from bitter memories of land alienations. They also had a weakness for contemporary witchcraft, and these two characteristics made it likely that they would respond rather more slowly than the Basuto to [the same kind of] reforms in tribal leadership and management. There had been continuous meetings between the Resident Commissioner and the young King Sobhuza, accompanied by his council and the queen mother. 'The maintenance of continuous pressure on Sobhuza and his council and the avoidance as far as possible of a change in the persons exerting that pressure are essential until the native courts proclamation has been passed and the native treasury established,' Evelyn said.[3]

He found Swaziland a much more backward country even than Basutoland. For instance he estimated that only about 25% of children were at school; in Basutoland this figure was nearer 70%. There was a 50% rate of infant mortality, and much witchcraft in the large heathen population. 'The heathen Swazi on the road with his dyed hair, shield, knobkerry and stabbing assegai is a superbly picturesque sight. The price paid is the horn of the witchdoctor filled with human flesh.'

The most important issue in Swaziland, however, as elsewhere, was land – not just soil erosion and the need to improve the agrarian economy, as in Basutoland, but in political terms as well. The Swazis shared with the Africans of the Union and Southern Rhodesia a grievance derived from an inequitable division of land earlier in the 20th century, presided over, ironically, by Molly's grandfather. Consequently, according to Evelyn, 'there was a feeling of resentment and suspicion and a tendency when any new proposals are made by the Government to ask themselves what are the white men going to get out of this.'[4] This would be their attitude both to the establishment of native courts and a native treasury, and to any measures of stock control for soil conservation which struck at the roots of a Swazi's position, since cattle were the coin with which he paid his bride price, his bank and a measure of his importance in the tribe. The Swazis were pleased with the fact that, as a cattle-owning people, they owned more cattle per head than either the Basuto or the natives of Rhodesia.

The white settlers in Swaziland were an uneven lot of farmers. There were many rich Johannesburg families who were referred to as 'cheque book farmers'; but Evelyn preferred them to a group of small-scale largely migratory Afrikaner sheep farmers, described in a later despatch as 'a curse to the country, who pay no tax, start innumerable fires, and most of their land lies idle.'[5] A land settlement scheme was in hand to buy out European farmers and eventually make available to Africans about half the land area of the country. There were about 27,000 who had lived a precarious life as squatters on European land and who would eventually come into small holdings of five to 15 acres each. If all this in Evelyn's first report sounded rather pessimistic, that was not Cranborne's impression in London. Apart from agreeing that the health services' position was 'clearly deplorable' he commented that it was not as depressing as might have been feared, and certainly a contrast in tone to Lord Harlech's despatches. Lord Harlech's observations had clearly encouraged British ministers to think that the country was in such a hopeless state that it might just as well be handed over to the Union anyway.

When Evelyn inherited Swaziland from Harlech it was certainly considered to be the backward child in the family of High Commission Territories; and it took him some time to get it going. On his second tour in 1945 he was still reporting the effect of the previous year's crop failure – 3000 bags of maize per month having to be brought in from the Union (more political capital for the South Africans). However the land position had improved. The Swazis now owned half the country, as compared to a third only a few years previously. No Europeans could buy land any more, whereas the natives could buy into European areas – a position which had not obtained in the Union since 1913, nor in South Rhodesia since 1930. The main objective of development, he now felt, should be to plant more forests and to reduce soil erosion. Such schemes would both produce extra revenue and more employment for the natives, of whom only 10,000 out of 200,000 worked in the Union. Forestry, indeed, was to become Evelyn's main preoccupation in Swaziland and the huge forests which grew up, after many a setback, the main monument to him in that country. He pursued the idea with enormous energy over a period of about four years, before he could be certain that the projects were properly financed and established. He found that, though Swaziland had an unusually good supply of water, its economic development was being impeded by a sort of vicious circle. Those with capital were reluctant to invest because of inadequate communications; yet South African Railways refused to build a line to Swaziland because there was not enough traffic to justify it. The only way he could see to break the circle was by large-scale forestry development.

He already knew a certain amount about the suitability of Swazi conditions for forestry. He remembered from his time in Natal 20 years earlier that a Dr Craib had revolutionised forestry there and he noticed that there was bracken on the hills, tree ferns in the valleys, and moisture in the soil – ideal conditions for large scale planting of wattle and pine. He sought out Dr Craib, and, at the end of much negotiation, persuaded a company to invest in a 35,000 acre timber project in an area known as Piggs' Peak.

With his new Resident Commissioner, Edward Beetham, Evelyn struggled – successfully – to persuade the Swazis to exchange some of their existing settlements for new ones, as the former land was required for forestry. In view of their suspicion of the Europeans, and their senisitivity over land, it took all the authority and cooperation of the Paramount Chief, King Sobhuza, to persuade them to do so.

After a great deal of further negotiation the South African finance for the forestry project failed and Evelyn had to call on his old friends in the city to join together in a consortium to back the plan. But for the second, bigger, project the city seemed to cool off, and there was no sign of excitement among potential investors. Evelyn tried hard to interest the Colonial Development Corporation in the idea, and its Chairman, Lord Trefgarne, came out to see for himself but returned to London without any great enthusiasm for the project. In 1948 Evelyn wrote rather soulfully to Molly describing the area he hoped would become a Swazi forest, 'high wilderness of grass and granite outcrops. Like the Empty Quarter in South Arabia. High and grassy and you feel exhilarated crossing them and have the sensation of walking at the top of the world. Empty except for some wagons and wild ragged Swazis herding sheep. Perhaps the whole plan will go flat and Swaziland's wild green hills will remain untouched. Perhaps, though, we shall have mile upon mile of horrid prim plantations, but then real development and prosperity for Swaziland.' He sometimes had misgivings about the whole thing – certainly on aesthetic grounds. In another letter to Molly he likened the hills of Swaziland to his beloved Cheviots – which are thrillingly treeless to say the least – and said 'Alas, having sweated my guts out to establish Peak Timbers [the forestry scheme] I now feel that we have raped Africa. In most of the kloofs the bush has been cut, fires have burnt many of the grassy slopes prepared for planting and already there are mile upon mile of neat little pits each with its beastly little pine tree.'

However, early in 1949, the second scheme seemed to be stillborn. Craib was in despair, but Evelyn was still hopeful that a way would be found; and he was right. Suddenly in June, 1949, the plan came on again so swiftly that the 100,000 acre Usutu forest was almost a *fait accompli* before anybody realized it. The CDC backing the project felt that it was going to be even larger than had first been envisaged, with an expected annual turnover in five years time of £5m – an enormous sum for Swaziland whose total annual budget was only £500,000. Moreover, the CDC had, in the course of their studying of Swaziland, become much more generally interested in all three Territories. Evelyn also persuaded them to exploit the fact that Swaziland was, for its size, probably the best-watered country in Africa, by joining in the establishment of a Swaziland irrigation scheme which resulted in a most successful cultivation of sugar-cane. Both enterprises contributed enormously to the development and prosperity of the Territory and are still doing so. It was hardly surprising that, when Evelyn departed in 1951, it was King Sobhuza who sent him the warmest and most genuine sounding message of good wishes. They remained firm friends for life.

Evelyn had been in South Africa almost a year before he was able to get away for long enough to justify a trip to Bechuanaland – the biggest (275,000 sq. miles compared to 11,000 for Basutoland and only 6,000 for Swaziland) and most distant of the three Territories. Of all the Territories it provided most evidence of political progress, which was just as well in view of the fact that in a country three times the size of Great Britain its great physical distances would have gravely aggravated any serious political disturbances. The people were divided into eight tribes under a well developed system of native authorities ruled by the chief-in-council; schools were organised by tribes, not missions; and many social reforms had been achieved within the tribal system – for instance there was no longer any system of bride price at weddings, and the control of native treasuries for the collection of fines had been working smoothly for years before it was even mooted in the other two Territories.

The most ambitious tour Evelyn and Molly carried out in Bechuanaland took place in July, 1947, in the area of the Okovango Swamps – a huge tract of marshy land in the north west

corner of Bechuanaland closest to Angola, which had seldom
been visited by any white man. The reason for the trip was to
determine British policy over a threatened and serious dispute
over water resources, (and thereafter possibly the spectre of transfer) which concerned the River Okovango. This river rises in
Angola and enters Bechuanaland at its extreme north west corner.
Every year when the rains came it flooded. It would take the flood
waters about five months to creep down into the Okovango
Swamps, so that when the rest of the country – and the Union –
was in its dry season there was this vast flooded area which remained under water for months until it all trickled away into the
drying sand of Lake Ngami. The area flooded every year was
roughly 4,000 square miles.

Two years previously the Union had sent a parliamentary
delegation to motor rather gingerly round the edge of the swamp
and see if anything could be done to exploit this vast amount of
water. The visit was followed by a series of unofficial but extremely ambitious proposals to bring the water down and change
the whole agricultural pattern of the Transvaal and Bechuanaland. Evelyn decided that he should go through the middle of the
swamp and see for himself – something which had not been done
by more than six European men since the beginning of the century, and apparently never by a woman (Molly was to come too).
The tribes who lived in the northern area were accustomed to
travelling the 250 mile journey in their dug-out canoes, but it was
recognised to be one of the wildest, most deserted, and most un-
charted areas of the world – just a tissue of channels and promon-
tories when in flood, varying in depth from two feet to twenty,
which forced the game to swim from island to island to look for
food. The plan to go across the area in a barge was conceived by
the local District Commissioner and attracted enormous opposition from Evelyn's office in Pretoria. It was only after prolonged
discussions with doctors, policemen, and others and an agreement
that a search party would be sent out if the barge and its flotilla
did not arrive at its destination quite soon after the expected
eight days, that they all got under way.

For Evelyn the trip was really made enjoyable by the presence
of a professional naturalist, who took him off every morning and
evening to show him trees, birds, insects, game spoor, dung (his
latest hobby), ferns (another one) and anything else interesting
which came along – accompanied always by an armed police
corporal to shoot any angry hippopotamus or leopard. The flotilla

must have looked rather picturesque, consisting of two barges, propelled by six paddlers in each, fourteen two-man dug-out canoes with baggage, and a fat round tub of a boat bringing up the rear, which was nicknamed the 'Red Navy' and became a potential source of embarrassment throughout the trip. The only things they saw for two days were crocodiles, which were probably equally surprised by the spectacle of the large barge flying a Union Jack and transporting two very English looking people sitting in deckchairs and wearing solar topees. At times they glided through the water like so many picnickers punting up the Cam; at other times, in the reed beds and long buffalo grass, the barge took some strenuous poling to keep it on the move. As evening approached, they would look for an island big enough to accomodate the entire camp, and the chickens which had been brought as live provisions were let out of their cages for a run. After eleven days and nights of this eerie odyssey, with numerous excitements and incidents of the kind one would expect on such a journey, the intrepid explorers arrived at the District Commissioner's headquarters at Maun, thence to proceed by more conventional road transport along the Zambezi to the Victoria Falls. They were safe; and Evelyn was able to write a full politico-geographical report for his masters in London.

Not all Evelyn's touring was carried out in the Territories, though it was only in them that he could combine the passison of a naturalist with the purposes of an imperial administrator. Occasionally he would go off to wild places in the Union, for botanical trips, or mountaineering, or game watching. On his return from one such combined operation in the Northern Transvaal he wrote Molly such a descriptive letter that it tells all one needs to know about the flavour of most of his safaris:

> High Commission House,
> Bryntirion,
> Pretoria.
> 13.7.48.

'My darling,
Here I am back two hours from Dongola and in tremendous form though my tummy is a bit queer and I have nearly killed myself. Darling it is a most wonderful place and exceeds all expectations. Also Forbes Mackenzie is the perfect bush companion. He is quite unmoved by anything, he has lots of bush

craft, he is very good on birds – I learned lots of calls from him – he is becoming a botanist, he knows about all animals, spoor, your old friends the droppings etc, he loves you (obviously regretted your absence and was full of references to our B.P. camping trip) and does he go right up to elephant oh boy oh boy! Well imagine a huge area of Mopani, and our old friend the Kalahari vegetation. It is arid soil of 7" rain per ann. on red granite. Through the granite burst black diarite dykes and kopjes. At one place the granite itself is in a hill just like the Matoppos, bare sheets of stone and curious twisted trees in the crannies and our old Matoppos friend the big black Verreaux eagle nesting in the crags. Beyond that to the east a sudden change to pink Waterberg rock. Away to the west another change into the white cave sandstone [typical] of Basutoland. Here are the sensational white and red krantzes and flat topped nearly impregnable table mountains of the lowlands we passed through on our way to the Moteng Pass. Then along the river a strip of silt growing enormous trees festooned with creepers, surrounded by dense undergrowth and full of baboons and vervet monkeys. You suddenly leap from the arid Mopani country with its light grass covering and bare rocks to the conditions of an Indian jungle and beyond them miles of sand and a little water.

. . . We lived in some luxury. Bob Evans is a bit of a Lord Emsworth he is full of devices and always goes around with a revolver and bit of khaki cloth tied round his mouth presumably either to keep the dust out or to stop his lips from becoming chapped. His wife and family usually met us for lunch and produced a table, chairs, crockery, admirable food from the frig. and the general appearance of a shooting lunch at Longleat over twenty years ago. There were a 19 year old girl and a 17 year old boy. Neither uttered but each leapt to his or her feet the moment a plate was to be taken away or a chair moved. So like the Baring children. Mrs B. E., who is really rather nice, was also usually put in her place when she spoke then remained silent. So like my wife. We fed on huge paw paws and immense fresh pink grape fruit, but the party was very sedate.

. . . Well the very first day I saw an auger buzzard (big tropical and white crested) on a baobab tree and a fine big Gom Pau (karpoor). Later we got a superb view of two white Martial Eagles, one under a tree eating a baby duiker. We saw a splen-

didly situated saddle bill stalk and nest, a Goliath Heron on
the river, thought of Maun as we heard the Fish Eagles call
and listened to a fine chorus down by the river under giant
Acacia Albida with bluish foliage and huge twisted purple
pods.

. . . Below this is 'Elephant's Alley' an awkward bit where the
road enters thick riverain bush just below a rock wall. Just
outside this we saw our first four elephant, but I had no camera.
Next day there was a solitary bull in Mopani his behind stick-
ing out and looking like a boss of granite. I set off with Forbes
and sympathised with you as his legs are so long and we had
to make a big circuit. I had forgotten how exciting it is, the
thrill of finding the spoor across your recent tyre marks, of
dung steaming when you kick it open, of the smell of elephants
and the tremendous rumblings of their tummies. This last gave
us where this one was and next thing he was one side of a big
Mopane bush and we the other and I could see how red his
eyes were and we stared at one another and I hadn't got my
camera drill straight yet and I think muffed my photo. The
day after was a dies mirabilis. We left in perfect weather and on
the river just where the sandstone country was beginning we
found them in the palm bush near the big river trees and got
well among a herd of 12 bulls. The palm leaves make noiseless
movement v. difficult, but then the elephants make plenty themselves. We got all sorts of shots at all kinds of angles and distances. We went on down to a large island and the confluence
of the Slachi and the Limpopo, a lovely wild spot full of bird
song and giving a good sight of the white grey and black plover
with yellow wattles which we last saw when boating down the
Zambezie with Tapson from Binyas. The trees are covered with
Conbretum Microphyllum the pink flowered creeper which
comes out well in B. E.'s film. . . . In the evening we were not
far from our old elephant place when I suggested that we
should make a detour to see if they weren't about half a mile
west of their morning haunt. . . . The light was failing and
the wind was wrong but Forbes and I just made for them and
I hope got some reasonable ones partly of the herd on the move
and partly of a straggler. Finally they ran off to the river trees
and one turned round and faced us. He began to flap his ears
and agitate his trunk. Thinking he was behaving a bit like my
old girl friend in Wankie I was decidedly windy. Not so Forbes,
so after some hesitation I crawled up and got some head on but

I don't think they will come out. Then I went up the hill
ending by climbing a real Table Mt overlong and watched the
herd disappear in to the setting sun. Alas it all came to an end.
We flew away sadly and felt like the baobab trees which when
the Natives have pulled off the bark too much suddenly die
and collapse in what appears to be a mass of old rags. . . .
Hug all the brats and nieces from me.

Your adoring

E'

At other times his letters showed he had not lost his wartime flair
for social reportage. [June '46] 'Here you have the repentant
debauchee. I went round the works of the big wine grower's cooperative at Paarl. I felt that to drink nothing would be churlish.
So I drank plenty; we all talked Afrikaans and were boys together.
But I paid the price in two really bad nights and had to cancel
this morning's climbing.'

Two months later, on a party into Johannesburg, home of
white South Africa's progressive white minority, 'Here were a lot
of fat well-fed people all bursting with liberal theories, all completely urban in their experience of life, nearly all a bit ignorant
of the facts, all without exception quite ignorant of the Afrikaans
language, all very self-opinionated and all eager to gain the
pleasure of damning the sins they are least inclined to. They all
cursed the Dutch. But after all, the old Dutchman, intolerant,
corrupt and prejudiced, as he is, was the man who tamed the
wilderness, fought the natives and made the country in the past,
and is the man who fights the droughts dust and diseases of the
high veld farms today.'

On meeting one of the belles of Durban in his day, now an
'ageing bitch', 'Don't let us send Charlie to South Africa while he
is young and unmarried. I think it was only the direct intervention of providence that stopped me marrying a South African.'

Notwithstanding his passion for the great outdoors, Evelyn's
life in Pretoria and Capetown seemed to discover hidden reserves
of energy and enthusiasm in him, and not just in the social life
portrayed above. Nicholas Monsarrat was one of his information
officers and described Evelyn fully in his autobiography. He said
Evelyn seemed to have the perfect attitude to his subordinates,
'This was to teach them, control them, praise them when appropriate, blast their stupid heads off when they made a mistake, *but*
– and this was the biggest "but" in this area, widely neglected by

other practitioners of authority – always to draw the mantle of
personal responsibility over the battlefield when something had
gone wrong!' On two occasions, when Monsarrat had erred, the
outcome was a biblical kind of lecture, 'followed by a soothing
telegram to London, making the point that Monsarrat was doing
his best in difficult circumstances and still enjoyed the High Commissioner's full confidence.' Evelyn's world, he said, was somehow
typified by his habit of climbing to the summit of Table Mountain, a 'world of strict endeavour, efficiency, good conduct and
the honourable discharge of duty.'[6] Yet there was time for clown-
ing too. Sir Morrice James, formerly on his staff, recalled later
in a personal letter a scene which typified Evelyn's rather ponderous sense of humour:

'I remember him some hundreds of feet underground at Sterkfontein in the Transvaal, holding a hurricane lantern up in a
cavern to which I took him with Patrick Duncan then private
secretary to explore one Sunday. Patrick and I went for a swim
in an underground lake by the light of this lantern, whilst
Baring harangued in Afrikaans the several hundred bats which
were milling around the roof: 'Batte van Sterkfontein! Ek is
die Britse Hoe Kommissaris. . . .' I can hear him intoning this
now, in his impeccable New College accent.'

After two extensions to his tour Evelyn was ready for home, and
Molly even more so. In fact he was still a young man, (he was
only 47 when he left South Africa for good in 1951), but Molly
and he had made it quite clear, when he was asked to stay on for
the second time, that he must in 1951 be guaranteed a full nine
month break at Howick – with no interruptions. In October,
1950, a rumour reached the Barings that he was to be offered the
governorship of Kenya, which Evelyn dismissed briskly as ground-
less – too briskly his family thought, since he clearly wished that
it was true, while suspecting that it may have been a still-born
idea owing to the row about Seretse. Anyway, a few months later
in London, he had a chance to talk to James Griffiths, the Colonial Secretary. Evelyn to Molly, 'He realizes all about the nine
months [sabbatical] and spoke only of possibilities on or after the
middle of 1952. He explained that he might then be no longer in
office but could we discuss again in the autumn. He asked whether
I had ever been to the far east so I pipped in and told him of my
health. He then asked about East Africa and said he was about
to visit it. As Percival (Liesching) said, no definite offer but plenty
of hints. I got on splendidly with Griffiths who is a Welsh miner

and we talked about rugger for ages – much better than coping with old Wykehamist dons [a crack at Gordon Walker].'

The outcome of this rather oblique promotional quadrille was that Evelyn left South Africa for good in July, 1951, with no formal next appointment, though it was clearly in one or two minds that he would go to Kenya to succeed Sir Philip Mitchell. The 'dry Wykehamist don', Gordon-Walker, visited Evelyn in South Africa in March, 1951, and they got on better than Evelyn expected. When he left, the Secretary of State wrote saying, 'I hope it won't be necessary to call on you again [in case they were unsuccessful in finding a successor for Evelyn before his appointment ended], and I will do all I can to find a place for you suitable to your abilities.' Before Evelyn left South Africa he sent Gordon-Walker one final despatch outlining what he thought had happened during his seven years and would happen in the future.[7] It was fairly stark:

'The Afrikaner people feel they are too few in numbers to preserve their identity unless they are the dominant group. English speaking South Africans they regard as allied to a people who give self government to Africans and whose missionaries have attacked Afrikaners ever since the first years of the nineteenth century. They also feel that when their opponents are in power the vested interest of the goldmines count for too much. The only alternative is then a monopoly of political power in the hands of those who are nationally minded.

Young nationalists do not learn to think. They strive to be loyal to the family, the state and the church. They trust and obey their leaders and they distrust anybody who exercises his or her critical faculties. Young men and women of this type are coming in increasing numbers from the nationalist schools and universities and the comparison with prewar Germany and Italy, or indeed with Russia, is obvious . . .

The country's rulers think with the blood, and emotion prevails over reason. It is easy to criticise the nationalists, but their strength should not be underrated . . . The strength of the nationalist hold on power may be best explained by using the South African slang expression to 'white ant' i.e. to undermine someone. By exploiting the apathy of the English speaking voters, the complacency of the men who surrounded General Smuts, and the aloofness in his later years of their great opponent, they gradually gained adherents. The small secret and well organised Broederbond followed with great success its policy of infiltration, until the nationalist doctrine was heard from every pulpit and expounded in the classroom of every Afrikaans medium school.

If the nationalists' aims are fulfilled the non-European will be deprived of all political rights; the maximum of separation of races in every walk of life will be enforced by draconian legislation. Residence of African women in towns will be discouraged by tightening up the administration of the pass laws, by a possibly deliberate slowness in providing houses for urban Africans and by the cancellation of unemployment benefits for the greater part of them. The English speaking South African will be treated better. He will be allowed to lead a happy life and to become rich, provided he steers clear of politics. But public life in Parliament and in Government service will gradually become the preserve of the ruling section who, inside their own fence, will no doubt preserve the greatest equality opportunity.

If, on the other hand, the English speaking South African is willing to accept *in toto* the nationalist creed, to forget all his links with Britain, his loyalty to the crown and all other things British, and to become in fact an Afrikaner of British origin, he will be readily accepted. Once he has grasped the nature of the fate in store for him, he may come to understand also the method of avoiding it. The nationalists are the heirs of Krugerism who have caught some of the infection of Nazi Germany. Their appeal is strong. In South African history the only other appeal which has successfully opposed it is that of a patriotism for South Africa as a whole. The call to wider patriotism and to the defence of individual liberty can alone provide enthusiasm sufficient to roll back the nationalist flood.

The conclusion is that for the first time since 1910 South Africa has stepped back in time. It is now dominated by an oligarchy. Its rulers are strongly entrenched. They control the thoughts and ideas of many young Afrikaners. They evoke strong feelings and are served with devotion by many. The Ministers of today are at the head, less of a political party prepared for alternating victory and defeat at the polls, than of a movement probably determined to retain power permanently.'
It was a prophetic message.

He went on to suggest that a republic would probably be declared, there would be a weakening of the pro-British sentiment, and relations would suffer. Moreover, if the ideas of white African nationalism spread north over the Limpopo there would be trouble in Rhodesia. Whatever one said of the United Party, under their rule there had been some change for the better in Africans' conditions; not so now. 'Nearly all the nationalists fear and hate Africans. As a result they cannot refrain from threats and insults. They not only refuse to share power but also in all activities of government they treat Africans harshly. They have closed minds. The theory of apartheid dominates nationalist thinking and nationalist feeling, yet as a programme of action it is useless and little more than a pipedream.' He then turned to the wider lesson for Britain. 'To despise or ignore the strong and expanding force of South African nationalism in 1951 would be as unwise as it was to decry in March, 1933, the power of Hitler to do harm.' On the other hand South Africa would still be of vital strategic importance in war time, through its location and its raw materials, and was destined to remain far and away the strongest industrial power in the continent. 'Nationalist fanatics control a strong and important country. However unpalatable may be the political and social theories of the present rulers, it will be useless to attempt to draw a complete cordon sanitaire round South Africa and to cut ourselves and our African dependencies off from that country.' But two conclusions followed from this – first, that Britain should encourage the proposed federation of the two Rhodesias and Nyasaland, but also take steps there to prevent the infiltration or immigration of South African 'white ants'. Secondly, if Britain willed the end of maintaining the High Commission Territories under her control she must also will the means. The first was to develop the natural resources of the Territories, the second to maintain reasonably friendly relations with the Union, and hope and wait, that the opponents of nationalism would eventually come back to power.

With that final note of tempered pessimism, he went off. Howick, a whole year of Howick, beckoned, after seven of the hardest, but probably most interesting years of his life. In spite of the Seretse Khama affair, which still rumbled on and still troubled Evelyn, the plaudits at his departure were unequivocal. *The Financial Times* in London said there had never been a more successful High Commissioner. Leaders of Indian and African opinion in the Union all made known their regrets at his going. From Liesching, 'The PM read your last despatch with great interest and minuted that it was very good. I shall miss you sadly'; from Gordon-Walker, 'It is largely yourself we have to thank for the friendliness which in spite of all the difficulties still pervades our relations with the Union government'; and from Huggins, a short, typical note, 'I see you have left for England. I hope you will turn up in Africa again'. It was not going to be long before he did.

CHAPTER XX
Kenya – the Build-up

When Evelyn left South Africa the Labour Government was still hanging on to office. He had received no specific offer for his next job though Griffiths had obliquely sounded him out about East Africa – certainly enough to raise his hopes that he would eventually become Governor of Kenya. There had also been speculation in Nairobi's *East African Standard,* as early as September, 1950, that Evelyn would succeed to the Governorship. After his experience in Southern Rhodesia and South Africa it seemed a natural appointment, for Kenya had about 60,000 white settlers in its population of 6 million and a considerable Asian community as well.

However, these matters were superseded by the British general election in October, 1951, which returned a Conservative Government. The result was much to Evelyn's private relief – he had been tempted to plunge into the campaign on the Tories' behalf, so disgusted was he with the Labour Government's handling of the Seretse affair. Nevertheless, an offer from the new ministry was not immediately forthcoming, and it was some months before Alan Lennox-Boyd, the Minister of State (No. 2) in the Colonial Office, told Evelyn that the Government wanted to appoint him to Kenya.

The appointment was finally clinched in March, 1952, with a private letter from Oliver Lyttelton, the Colonial Secretary: 'Dear Baring, I had a word with the PM yesterday about Kenya. His reaction was immediate and warm. The wheels of the official machine will therefore now begin to turn and you should hear from us again before long.' The news was not made public until April, when it was welcomed by the Kenyan press, which emphasised the breadth of Evelyn's African experience, and also the useful knowledge of financial affairs which he would bring to the job. The Kenya African Union, on the other hand, representing the African politicians' view, expressed concern at the appointment after Evelyn's 'disastrous handling of Bechuana-land affairs', which were 'so closely identified with the policy of appeasement of South Africa'.

There was no sign of urgency by anybody concerned with the appointment. London, after all, was still totally unaware that there was any need for urgency. Some time later it was suggested that the delay in Evelyn's arrival in the colony was due to another illness. It is true that in January, 1952, before he was appointed, he had a bad accident with an axe and had lost a lot of blood, which provoked the rebuke from Lord Hailey, 'May I suggest that you are too valuable to be allowed to have misadventures with axes.' But in reply to Hailey at the end of March, Evelyn was still able to say he was due to go to Kenya sometime during the second half of the year, possibly September.

But, if it was not clear that he should have gone out in the spring, why did he not at least go out in the summer when the change for the worse in Kenya became more clear? Why was this interregnum between Governors in Kenya not brought to a speedy end? There is a great deal of documentary evidence to show that it did *not* become clear in London, or even *much* clearer in governing circles in Nairobi, that there was any urgent need for the new Governor to arrive before the end of September.

Yet it is interesting to contrast the almost casual, unconcerned way in which Evelyn's arrival was being prepared that summer, and the Government's lack of appreciation of deteriorating security in the Kikuyu areas, with the severity of the crisis which broke over Kenya from almost the moment that Evelyn arrived. Before tracing the developments which were taking place in Kenya prior to his arrival, it is worth dealing with the situation as it was being presented to Evelyn at the time.

In June, 1952, (a week or so before they met in London, upon Mitchell's retirement) he received the first full length letter from his predecessor.[1] It could have given him no hint of the gathering storm. 'There really is a genuine feeling of desire to cooperate and be friendly at the present time. I have not had a chance to talk to Africans yet but I hope to do so before I go' wrote the retiring Governor, before branching off into a rather more involved exegesis about how Evelyn should behave towards divorced people in the colony – something for which Kenya had developed rather a special reputation. 'It is of somewhat unusual complexity especially as we have the amateur champion out here, who has, I think, been divorced by five if not six husbands. The Delamere household is another not very simple one particularly on the occasion of royal visits. The situation in which Lord Mountbatten's sister is technically disqualified from coming to Government House, as her husband is, while Prince Philip is here is not without its difficulties' (Prince Philip and Princess Elizabeth had been in Kenya in February, 1952, when they heard the news of King George's death). Mitchell went on to counsel 'rough and ready rule. Take no notice for garden parties, unless an open scandal, but apply the rules for lunches and dinners.'

The letters from the Governor's private secretary, Henry Howard, were much in the same vein, though justifiably, since he was solely responsible for the personal side of Evelyn's arrival. Howard asked if Evelyn minded the fact that both the Controller and the Assistant Private Secretary were divorcees. More correspondence followed, dealing with the need to order a new cellar – always a hallmark of the change of regime in Government Houses; opening shows; addressing dinners; was Princess Alice to come for a function during the winter months, (the only problem was not Mau Mau, but the effect of the altitude on Lord Athlone's heart); Evelyn's attendance at the police reserve ball; the self-sufficiency of Government House in ducks and geese; the impossibility of having a garden party until after the 'short' rains; and finally a list of the Baring's luggage which had been sent on by sea and which, had grown apace since the departure for Rhodesia ten years earlier. Finally, in a rather nervous aside, Howard wrote: 'You are no doubt being kept informed of the difficult political situation through which we are going.'

Howard's letter was dated September 9, only two weeks before Evelyn arrived. It was not exactly Evelyn's first intimation of troubles in Kenya, but he clearly had *not* been kept very fully informed. To understand the reasons for that we have to go back to what had been happening in Kenya during 1952. It was not so much that there was a gathering state of insurrection which had been generally unnoticed in Kenya; it was more a case of those people in the highest authority, both during Sir Philip Mitchell's closing months as Governor, and by the acting Government after he left, questioning the validity of the facts which were being put before them by the administration with whom the Mitchell regime had become rather out of sympathy.

The Mau Mau rebellion with which Evelyn had to cope in 1952 was an uprising in the Kikuyu tribe – Kenya's largest, most industrious, possibly richest tribe, and the one whose tribal areas were closest to Nairobi, the capital, and whose politics during the fifty years of British settlement had always been the most complicated and sophisticated, as well as most involved with the Europeans. One of the main reasons for this was because a great part of the land taken over for European settlement in Kenya

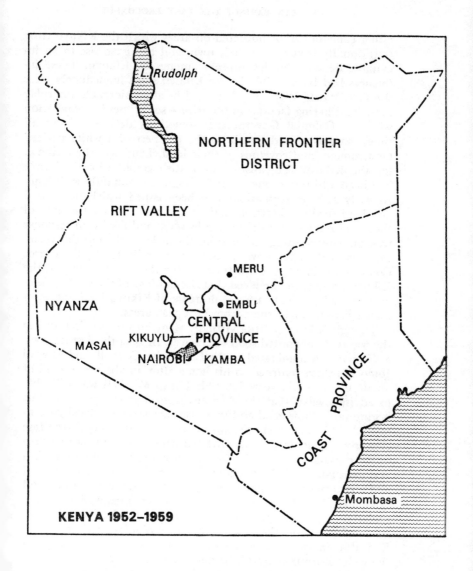

L. Rudolph

NORTHERN FRONTIER
DISTRICT

RIFT VALLEY

MERU

EMBU

NYANZA

CENTRAL
PROVINCE

MASAI

KIKUYU

NAIROBI   KAMBA

COAST PROVINCE

Mombasa

KENYA 1952–1959

either came out of or bordered on areas which the Kikuyu tribe traditionally regarded as their own, and this gave rise to an inevitable demand for *lebensraum* among the Kikuyu. These influences had been visible in the Kikuyu since immediately after the First World War, and there had been considerable interplay between differing factions in the tribe – sometimes in cooperation with the Colonial Government; sometimes defiant; but at all times nervous of and hostile to the prospect of a white settlers' Government, and covetous of their land. Land was the talisman for the Kikuyu. The history of British colonisation in Kenya had been a history of measures dealing predominantly with land. As early as 1897 regulations had been issued which prohibited any land dealings between natives and non-natives; the area of the tribal reserves was delineated in 1905; and finally, in response to some concerted agitation from the Kikuyu during the 1920s, the area of the reserve was examined and adjusted by the Carter Commission in 1933. Unfortunately for the future, many of the Kikuyu erroneously believed that the findings of the Carter Commission had resulted in a net decrease of Kikuyu land and even some eviction of tribesmen from European areas.

Though Kikuyu politics virtually went into suspension during the war, they re-ignited soon afterwards. In 1944 the first African, a Kikuyu, was nominated to the Legislative Council, and in 1946 Jomo Kenyatta returned to his home after an absence abroad of about 16 years. Six years later Sir Philip Mitchell was still able to advise Evelyn that the Africans were 'largely apolitical, but beginning to show good ability operating a system of local government'.[2] This was a classic misjudgment of the mood of those elements, particularly in the Kikuyu tribe – amounting to a fifth of the population – which after the war rejected the paternalism and gradualism of the colonial government, feared the political and territorial encroachment of the white settler community, and gradually formed a series of political front organisations whose underlying purpose was to seek ultimate freedom from white rule, whether of the indigenous or colonial variety. Jomo Kenyatta, in spite of, or maybe because of his long sojourn in the wider European world, became a leading figure in this movement, though he was by no means the only manipulator of Kikuyu dissent. More probably he exploited the unity formed through oath-taking ceremonies, than actually inspired this particular technique himself. The oaths started harmlessly enough – though to the European mind any such witchdoctory was distasteful.

Oathing was very much part of the Kikuyu tradition, and a typical ceremony would include human and goats' blood mingled into a sort of paste, with other animal organs. It was not so much the grisly nature of the oath which bound the Kikuyu to it – though it terrified them into submission – as a feeling of bondship not dissimilar to that felt by other members of secret societies with strange initiation rituals.

By 1952 the Kikuyu had a divided leadership. On the one hand were the chiefs – appointed officials, but nevertheless respected and authoritative figures within the tribe; on the other, the unofficial leadership, mostly in the Kenya African Union and Kikuyu Independent Schools Association (KAU/KISA), which included Jomo Kenyatta, the best orator and most forceful figure, though by no means the most industrious. There was a clandestine network of local committees, whose loyalty was cemented by oathing ceremonies. The KAU/KISA had penetrated the teaching profession, where it was pitted against the mission establishments. It had strong political muscle, posing a challenge to chiefly authority and far exceeding the ineffective political representation of the two Africans in the Legislative Council (LEGCO) which was all that was permitted under the colony's constitution.

This unofficial leadership of the Kikuyu went through a variety of incarnations as the power base changed, and as the political relationship with the colonial administration evolved with it. But the District Commissioner in Nyeri was reporting to his masters in September, 1951, that they were 'all the same old stiffs working under different guises in order to increase the number of public meetings they can hold and the amount of money they can extract from a gullible public'. That comment typified the administration's approach to Kikuyu affairs, and it partly explains why the situation deteriorated so seriously and suddenly. It was not just because the administration was insensitive to the real influences at work within the Kikuyu and so made no attempt to respond to it, but rather because, even when it did perceive the surface manifestation of unrest, its attitude to the Kikuyu remained patronising. There was also a low state of morale within the administration during the closing years of Mitchell's governorship. Apart from the fact that Mitchell himself had given up touring, the Kikuyu areas had also suffered a debilitating turnover of its administrative officers, with the result that few of them spoke Kikuyu or knew much about the tribe. Moreover, the 'membership' system of the constitution meant that the administration was for the first time having to account for its conduct to the settler community's elected members in the Legislative Council. Whereas before they had perceived their duty to be to work for the best interests of the colony and to be accountable only to the governor and through him to the Colonial Office, they now found they were exposed to the scrutiny of settlers' representatives, who had always been regarded as a rather irresponsible element in Kenya.

Reports from the administrative officers in Kikuyu areas, of oathing, general defiance, and one or two attempted murders, led to the proscription of Mau Mau in August, 1950. But a year later the Attorney General, Mr John Whyatt, was referring to 'alarmist reports' from the Provincial Commissioner of the Central Province which included most of the Kikuyu, and shortly afterwards Mitchell himself circulated a message stating that reform was the major security measure. But the reforms were not forthcoming except in the form of a request for a royal commission to study the vexed question of land, which was not actually announced until after Mitchell had gone. Mitchell's view was that he had seen similar periods of unrest before in his long service in East Africa, and he maintained that the *general* political feeling was better than he had ever known it.

Throughout the summer before Evelyn arrived the pressure from settlers and from the administration grew in strength. A comprehensive report on the Mau Mau organisers, alleging a central direction, was sent to Whyatt in May, but did not reach the acting-Governor's office until mid-August. Mitchell had left in June, still breathing sweetness and light into the Kenya scene, at a time when the Mau Mau were said to have introduced a 'double killing' oath – I promise to kill, and if I do not, the oath will kill me.' It is by no means improbable that the administration and the acting government were by now so out of sympathy with each other that the former were exaggerating the significance of their intelligence, while the latter were applying an increasingly – unduly – sceptical approach. This scepticism was encouraged by the fact that the administration's claims were being backed up by settler opinion, which had always in the minds of the government performed the role of a permanent and rather hysterical opposition.

Pressure from the settlers continued, under threat of taking the law into their own hands if the government did not show itself more responsive to the dangers of a Kikuyu revolt against settlers and government, about which they claimed ministers were being warned by the police. Eventually, during August, the acting governor, Henry Potter, and Whyatt started to plan the introduction of some more severe legislation – though still short of a full state of emergency – which would give them powers of detention and conviction on the basis of evidence by affidavit. This would have protected witnesses from having to be exposed to intimidation if they appeared in the witness box. On August 17, Potter warned the Colonial Office – for the first time officially – that 'he would soon refer some proposals for drastic legislation to them'.[3] Whyatt followed this up with a more optimistic assessment, suggesting that, armed with such legislation, they should succeed in checking the growth of Mau Mau before too long. On September 16 he flew to London with B. R. Davies, the member for African Affairs, to seek Lyttelton's permission to present the new bills to Legco.

Surprisingly, while they were in London they did not see Evelyn, in spite of the fact that he was due to arrive in the colony only two weeks later. Indeed, he was not even *at* the deliberations with the Secretary of State, though he was required, only two weeks later as Governor, to give the Royal Assent to the legislation which Whyatt had come to London to get cleared. After his meeting with Mitchell in June, Evelyn had been kept in touch by Howard and Potter, and presumably by the Colonial Office, who, as we have seen, were not themselves being troubled by any exaggerated reports from within the Kenya administration.

In August Evelyn offered to arrive earlier if it was considered necessary, but both Whyatt and Blundell, at different times, told him that there was no need, and the Colonial Office were against any move which smacked of panic. In fact there were minor administrative inconveniences about any hurry which probably weighed heavily with the Colonial Office. Apart from Evelyn's own private desire to stay in Britain a full year – made all the more pressing by the fact that his son Charlie contracted a mild case of polio in July, 1952 – the Colonial Office relied on these periods of interregnum in colonies to try out acting governors. Potter was being given a trial run for a later governorship (as Resident in Zanzibar). There was also the desire of the finance departments to avoid having to pay for two governors by discouraging a successor from arriving before his predecessor had exhausted his terminal leave on full pay. None of these provides a very convincing reason for the delay in Evelyn's arrival in

Kenya, but collectively they explain why the question of a more hurried changeover of governors was left unconsidered until it was too late to do anything without making it look like a panic measure.

It was not only Potter who was finding his feet in Nairobi. Whyatt, too, was a comparative newcomer. He had only been Attorney General for about a year, and while nobody questioned his integrity and intelligence as a lawyer, by training he was ill-equipped to take on administrative responsibility for law and order, police, immigration and so on. By most accounts Whyatt's personality presented an added complication, since he clearly decided that the weight of his duty lay in the legal rather than the administrative field. With an acting governor expressing the kind of diffidence shown by Potter, and with his Attorney General applying the strictly legalistic attitude to the unrest which Whyatt considered appropriate, it is not surprising that they did not perceive that a state of emergency had crept up on them until it became evident even to them that the courts had ceased to function properly because of intimidation of witnesses.

With hindsight one can more easily examine the build-up within the Kikuyu tribe towards the point when the state of emergency was declared; one can see the flaws and miscalculations in the administration's analysis of and response to those developments. At the time, however, certainly as far as Evelyn was concerned, it was neither historically nor administratively possible to go behind these events and test them against more stringent analysis.

We can now query whether Jomo Kenyatta really merited his demoniac reputation; whether he had anything like the control over Kikuyu developments with which he was being credited; whether the Kikuyu leadership, with or without Kenyatta, was quite the collection of gangsters that they were depicted; whether there was anything special about the Kikuyu psyche which impelled it through clandestine conspiracy to an outbreak of such apparent bestiality; whether, indeed, it was possible to generalise with such confidence about a whole tribe of whom the European experts had known nothing until only seventy years before. At the time, however, there was no such capacity for detachment in the minds of white people. Horror and fear seemed to grip the European imagination, and was transmitted as vividly to the minds of the British public, which had all its secret fears about the black man confirmed. The settlers, the administrative officers, academics, policemen, and most of the missionaries, accepted that a section of the tribe had lost its head and become psychotic; had reverted to an earlier primitivism. Though Evelyn did not totally accept such theses, he heard their voices; and there were no other voices to hear. He acted on the advice he received, and the things he saw within the context of that advice. It is clear that Evelyn — arriving as a new Governor — had virtually no alternative but to respond to these warnings, since he could not have afforded to take the risk, and did not know enough about the colony to put the Kikuyu developments into a different context from the one which was presented to him by all those in a position to advise.

H

CHAPTER XXI

Emergency

Evelyn arrived in Kenya on September 29, 1952, saying, 'It is much too early at this stage to say I have formulated a plan for combating the disturbances.'[1] Waiting on his desk was a memorandum from Davies, the Chief Native Commissioner, which concluded that Mau Mau dominated three districts and showed no sign of abating – indeed that security was deteriorating in spite of the imposition of curfews, collective fines, and the infusion of more police into the area; that Mau Mau was spreading into a wider geographical area; that it was intensely anti-European; and that though there was no direct evidence to implicate Jomo Kenyatta, there were many factors to suggest a close association between him and his organisation.[2]

Almost immediately he was sworn in, Evelyn set off on a tour of the troubled Kikuyu areas, where murders of Africans by Africans were running now at about twenty a week. He returned much shaken by what he had seen and heard, and convinced that the English press had been right to urge his earlier arrival. His first reaction was depression at the fact that none of his advisers had anything positive to recommend by way of a solution – neither the police, nor the administration, nor the government. He felt that no one really knew the Kikuyu except for a few missionaries, because so few whites could speak the Kikuyu language, relying instead on Swahili, the *lingua franca* of East Africa, which is adequate on an every day basis, and for giving orders, but does not enable one to get at all close to any understanding of a tribe such as the Kikuyu.

He described the tour, many years later, to Marjery Perham. 'Five days after I arrived I started a tour which I will never forget. The first place I visited was a town called Kandara which was south of what was then called Fort Hall, the original home of the Kikuyu people, and I rode through the main street to have a meeting in the school at the top and there the people stood in shops and houses. I've never seen such faces, they were scowling, they looked unhappy, they were intensely suspicious. It was an expression I saw a great deal during the early years of Mau Mau.

'My first meeting was an entirely African meeting, there were African civil servants, there was the local chief – Kenya chiefs are not hereditary they are appointed – and local headmen, there was a teacher who had resigned from the Kikuyu independent schools, there were African teachers from missions schools and government schools. They all, with one voice said the same thing – that there had been a complete breakdown of law and order, there was a murder every night and unless you proceed against the people who are doing this our position in the future is perfectly impossible. The same thing was repeated to me in other places. I went up near the forest where I found there was a very strong leader named Njiri, who had repulsed the Mau Mau people when they came up and had a number of supporters. It made me realize that there was, among the Kikuyu, at any rate a fairly strong minority who were against this movement. I went on to Nyeri where I had a more European meeting but you know, people often say it is difficult for missions to combine, but I got the Roman Catholic bishop, Cavalera, an Italian, and the head of the Presbyterian teacher training establishment at Tuma, both giving me exactly the same replies, word for word that the Africans had said. And I said – who do you mean? Kenyatta, they all said. If you don't get Kenyatta and those all round him and shut them up somehow or other we are in a terrible, hopeless position. I went on the next day to the European farming areas, first near Mount Kenya and then Rumuruti which is a great ranching area. And when I was in the middle of the meeting there someone came in and told me that chief Waruhiu, who was one of the three leading men in the Kikuyu country – Waruhiu, Njiri and Ndere, who was murdered afterwards at Nyeri, were the three leading characters – had been murdered on the high road by a hired assassin who didn't even know him by sight, between Kiambu and Nairobi in a very public place. And I thought, well, if we want to take extreme powers, this is the occasion. And I went back and I sent a letter and telegram describing the situation as I found it.'[3]

His two top secret messages to Lyttelton, dated October 9, were as follows:[4]

'Following information gained during a short tour of the most troubled areas of Kikuyland, both the reserves and farms, and a recent sharp increase in the tempo of crime, I have regretfully come to the following conclusions, 1 quite apart from their political views most of the KAU (Kenya African Union) leaders, including Kenyatta, are the planners of the Mau Mau movement, an organised conspiracy exists and Mau Mau crimes committed are either the result of direct instigation by the KAU leaders at Nairobi or arise indirectly from the initiative of local Africans inflamed against loyal Africans and Europeans by speeches and messages from their leaders. 2 My main reasons for this conclusion:

1) the pattern of events, speeches, the shuttle service for instructions, widespread oathtaking, finally murder, assault, boycott. Before it the areas were quiet.

2) Jomo Kenyatta, when he chooses, has induced most Kikuyu to obey him, he practically stopped the drinking of European beer by Africans in Nairobi. Yet his denunciation of Mau Mau crimes is ineffective and has often, I'm told, by Kikuyu, been accompanied by sayings and gestures making clear he did not mean what he said.

3) Kikuyu chiefs, African administrative officers, Kikuyu teachers, missionaries of three denominations, all said KAU (particularly Jomo Kenyatta) were backing Mau Mau and JK allowed his name to be inserted blasphemously, in hymns and prayers as part of the strongly antichristian movement which has gone a long way in some areas to empty mission schools in favour of Kikuyu independent schools and churches in favour of the Mau Mau religion.

4) I conclude therefore that we must remove Jomo Kenyatta and several of his henchmen during the next few weeks. If we do not 1) the chiefs, headmen, government servants and missionaries who still support us will cease their support and may be killed. 2) trouble will spread to other tribes more warlike than the Kikuyu and who provide men for the Kenya police. 3) there will be reprisals by Europeans. During the last few days the killing of chief Waruhiu (perhaps one of the three leading Africans in Kenya) and two murderous attacks on Europeans have produced a temper bound to lead to reprisals and then almost to civil war unless the leaders of the Mau Mau are removed during the next few weeks. 4) If we do remove them I believe that the indoctrination of tribes other than the Kikuyu will cease and even among the Kikuyu there are a. sufficient centres of resistance b. so many followers of Mau Mau who have joined from fear alone, that the position can be regained.

5) I am informed by all my advisers that the arrest of Kenyatta may well be followed by much violence. Greatest danger at the moment is that this may lead to European reprisals. If we

proceeded against Kenyatta under the new Special Districts Ordinance, the violence I anticipate would develop during the 14 days' grace. If alternatively we would obtain sufficient evidence to deport, the same violence would develop during judicial enquiry at Nairobi. Our information is that this violence would start the moment hands are laid on Kenyatta, there would be reprisals, loss of life and it would then become necessary to declare a state of emergency.

6) The most likely way of avoiding bloodshed would be to declare an emergency and then immediately remove Kenyatta and his followers by executive action under the emergency regulations.

7) If this operation was staged about October 23 we would have time to build up adequate police and military forces. I believe that the risk of trouble is very great and we should be too strong rather than too weak.'

Evelyn also wrote to Lyttelton to explain a little more of the background. He started by recognising that, although the newspapers had exaggeratel their reports, they had only done so by suggesting that Mau Mau was a colony-wide movement rather than restricted to the Kikuyu areas within an arc of about 100 miles radius north and west of Nairobi. Evelyn calculated about 5% of the movement were fanatical African nationalists, 20% thugs, and the remaining 75% joined from fear.

He believed that a number of facts, taken together, led to the unmistakable conclusion that they were facing a planned revolutionary movement, which, if not stopped, would lead to administrative breakdown, followed by a great deal of bloodshed, even to civil war. 'I myself do not think that it would be true to say that every single act of violence has been planned at the centre. But there *is* a plan, a rather ragged and a rather African one, but none the less formidable for that.

'I hope you will not think I have been carried away by panic on the part of excitable Europeans here. I have reached my conclusions very unwillingly and fully realize that the strong action I recommend will cause you much political trouble for which I am very sorry. But . . . if we wait, the trouble will become much worse, and probably lead to the loss of so many lives that in the future bitter memories of bloodshed will bedevil all race relations. I have in South Africa seen too much the effect of these memories to take any risk of letting Kenya go the same way.'

Five days later, on October 14, Evelyn heard that the British cabinet had approved all his proposals. The emergency operation was planned to go into effect on October 20, with the extra battalion flying in that night and a cruiser stationed off Mombasa. By midnight on the 15th everything was tied up and a mood of excitement, tinged with relief, settled over Government House as its inhabitants waited for the zero hour, when 138 of the suspected ringleaders would be arrested and detained without trial. In Government House itself the Barings found themselves surrounded by security, with an armed ADC sleeping outside their bedroom, two police cars shadowing them if they went out, every door locked at night and the house inside and outside patrolled by armed guards – so much so that the beleaguered family were unable to get to early service on the Sunday morning because they were locked into their palace. The family all rather enjoyed the drama, because at that stage everyone, including Evelyn, seemed to believe that after the initial shock the emergency was unlikely to last more than a few weeks.

So, within a fortnight of his arrival in the colony, the new Governor found himself grappling with political and military questions on a scale much greater than anything he had had to cope with hitherto. Even though the breakdown had not spread to the colony as a whole, it infested the two major provinces, both adjacent to Nairobi. All Evelyn's experience would have led him to postpone or prevent this state of affairs if he had had the power to do so; yet one should not therefore assume that, when it came to the point, he was very fastidious about the exercise of imperial power. The preservation of the imperium – of imperial control, without which the sound administration and development which he so cherished could not take place – was always the bedrock of his service. He would no more contemplate letting things slip out of the control of the administration than he would think of resigning from the service because he did not like dealing with soldiers.

Twenty five years later, however, with Kenya already an independent commonwealth country of fourteen years standing; with Jomo Kenyatta the grand old man of Anglo-phone Africa; with the age of empire now firmly behind us, it is possible, indeed essential, to examine whether or not he had any alternative to the declaration of a state of emergency. It is occasionally argued now that the declaration produced a reaction which turned Mau Mau into a mass movement, and prolonged the battle by many years, at a cost of many lives. Certainly Evelyn and his advisers

thought that the insurrection would be shortlived once they had
removed the Kikuyu leadership – so indeed did the Director
General of the Security Services, Sir Percy Sillitoe, whom Evelyn
asked to come out to advise the Kenya Government on setting up
an efficient system of intelligence. They were all hopelessly wrong.
They thought that witnesses would come forward and cases could
be tried once the leaders were locked up. That happened eventually but only very slowly. The main reaction to the emergency
and to the detentions, was a hardening of the whole atmosphere
within the Kikuyu tribe and a commitment by both sides to a
long guerrilla war of attrition – not at all the two or three weeks
wonder which Evelyn had hoped for at the time. This was a
reflection of the atrocious intelligence which was available, and
the absence of any great understanding of the Kikuyu tribe among
administrative officers and even from Dr Louis Leakey, on whom
everybody relied for wisdom about the Kikuyu. He told Evelyn
that Mau Mau was like a fire made of kindling wood and not of
coal, which burnt with intense violence and was unstoppable,
but would presently abate with equal speed.

Evelyn was swept up in the events after he arrived; indeed the
momentum of murder, arson, and intimidation seemed unstoppable to most of his advisers. One imagines, however, that he
would have tried to go behind the advice he received, and to test
it against his own instincts, particularly as his first impression of
the quality of his advisers was very low. There is some anecdotal
evidence that he did for one moment decide to make contact with
Kenyatta – it would have been the obvious thing to do if he had
had time – and had instructed the District Officer where Kenyatta lived to make the initial approach. This overture was then
discontinued when chief Waruhiu was murdered, since that murder finally convinced Evelyn that he must act, and act quickly, if
he was ever again going to be able to rely on any loyalist Kikuyu.
In the now inevitable struggle for the heart and soul of the tribe,
any overture to Kenyatta would have been interpreted as a sign
of weakness. It was at Waruhiu's funeral that Evelyn saw
Kenyatta for the first and only time before he was detained. They
faced each other across the grave, and Evelyn was conscious of
some of what he felt was the demoniac force of Kenyatta's personality. But they did not speak. The two men had to wait nearly
twenty more years before they actually met.

We cannot speculate on the outcome of such a meeting, had
it taken place. My own view is that a Baring/Kenyatta meeting,

and any aftermath, would only have shown up how powerless within the Kikuyu Kenyatta actually was. It would have shown how his oratory and stature naturally pushed him forward for leadership but how, both within the senior if rather shifting councils of the KAU movement, and certainly outside it in the mass of opinion, his reputation would not have withstood the effects of overt contact with the Governor, unless Evelyn had been in a position to deliver something in exchange. That would have been a most unlikely possibility given the very delicate balancing act Evelyn had to play between the various forces arrayed in the colony. Apart from this slender evidence that Evelyn tried to set up a meeting with Kenyatta, there is no other sign that he tried to question the inexorable advice he received from his officials. The situation had gone too far in their eyes, and the evidence that they were right was mounting daily in the tally of murders, intimidaton, cattle garrotings; and it was there to be seen by Evelyn in the eyes of the Kikuyu he met on his first tour.

Evelyn now had to settle down and take stock of the situation in which he found himself, only three weeks after his arrival. The first obvious objective was to insulate the rest of the colony, as much as possible, from the infection in the Kikuyu areas. There was really no insecurity elsewhere in Kenya. Could that last? The task was complicated by the fact that the Kikuyu were not just the biggest tribe in the colony, with their areas situated near Nairobi, the industrial, economic and political centre of the colony; they were also adjacent to the areas of white farmland, the famous White Highlands, and the European population were actively and emotionally involved in the affair – so that British public opinion became emotionally charged as well. Evelyn was to find that he could not divorce the question of Kikuyu security from the rest of the colony's business, because there were so many Kikuyu both in Nairobi and working on the European farms. He thus had to take account of the constant danger of white retaliation for some Kikuyu atrocity. The administration and the settlers had traditionally been at arm's length from each other, yet the support of both was now vital to any successful policy. What bedfellows would they make?

It may be asked why Evelyn paid so much attention to settler opinion, and did not instead concentrate on winning the battle against the Mau Mau with simply the forces of police, army and administration which were at his disposal. The answer is threefold. First of all the white settlers were too often within the danger area – as farmers and employers – for Evelyn to ignore their presence and their potential. Secondly, they were, on account of their agricultural output, a vital element in maintaining the Kenyan economy, both to help pay for the emergency (almost all of which had to come from the Kenya treasury and not from Whitehall) and to provide the basis for the longer term economic development with which Evelyn hoped to tackle some of the Kikuyu's underlying grievances. Finally, the settlers could not be ignored because they made a great deal of noise which was heard only too readily by friends and sometimes relations in the British House of Commons. Besides, the antics of some settlers made good, not to say explosive copy, for the hundred or so representatives of the world's press who had descended on Nairobi when the emergency was declared.

Then there was the administration – the District Officers, District Commissioners and Provincial Commissioners, with their central secretariat in the office of the Chief Native Commissioner. Again they represented a vital constituency. Without their support, Evelyn's policies for overcoming Mau Mau would stand no chance of success. It is not that they were likely to be recalcitrant or disobedient; just that, in a fast moving situation, the administration, accustomed as it was to a more leisurely pace and certainly to a high degree of delegation and independence on the ground, was not going to be an easy organisation to seize by the scruff of the neck and redirect down new paths. There was an added complication. Traditionally each District Officer was master of his area, with the District Commissioner and the Provincial Commissioner above him feeling the same, at their respective levels. The emergency undermined that hierarchy with security forces operating across provincial boundaries.

Finally, in increasing strength, Evelyn was going to have to cope with the military – a new animal for him and one which never sat very easily by his side during the four most active years of the emergency. These were the four groups with which he had to work – the loyal Kikuyu, the settlers, the administration, and the army: all vital, all different, sometimes though seldom united in a common purpose, mostly reflecting shifting alliances which only came together in the office of the Governor – and sometimes not even there but in the distant reaches of Whitehall. These were the elements Evelyn had to contend with in the immediate battle for the heart and mind of the Kikuyu tribe. Behind this preoccupation, of course, there were other, more permanent

themes such as the economy, and the future agricultural and
constitutional development of the country. The emergency was
not colony-wide, in the security sense, and the Kikuyu, though
the most industrious and intelligent of Kenya's tribes, were only
one among many others – including several almost equally populous like the Luo and the Kamba. But it would be difficult to
think of any major issue which came up to Evelyn's desk during
those first two or three years which was not almost completely
overshadowed by, and therefore affected by, the course of the
struggle within the Kikuyu. The first two or three years of his
governorship were going to be the most testing of his career.

CHAPTER XXII

The Darkest Days

The emergency which was declared on October 21, 1952, did not officially end until January 12, 1960, after Evelyn had left the colony, but the army was actually withdrawn from operations on November 17, 1956, when the police reassumed full responsibility for law and order. The full-scale counter-insurgency campaign was always confined to Nairobi and its two adjacent provinces – Rift Valley and Central. For the first six months there was only a rudimentary coordination between the various organisations involved with security – police, army, administration – and security did not improve. A series of particularly savage murders of Europeans, and loyal Kikuyu, and attacks by armed gangs both within the reserve and in the Nairobi area on police stations and other government posts, showed that Mau Mau gangs – sometimes up to 100 strong – had the initiative in all but a few places.

The Kikuyu tribe as a whole was united in its underlying support of the political objectives of Mau Mau. Only a small proportion was happy with the use of force; many others however were prepared to harbour and supply the minority; and if not prepared, they were soon intimidated into doing so. There were several thousand terrorists under arms, and most of the loyalists, who were being formed into home guards, came from the older members of the tribe. The Mau Mau objective was to destroy the loyalist element and forge a unity between the Kikuyu and the neighbouring Embu and Meru tribes, after which they believed that they would be able to turn in strength on the European population. Because Mau Mau never convincingly won the struggle within these tribes, they never turned on the Europeans as part of an overall plan. What European murders there were – under thirty – were normally caused by the demands of supply, morale or prestige. They were what would now be called 'targets of opportunity' rather than well thought-out tactical objectives. But they were almost always of a particularly bloodthirsty and brutal kind, with the result that Evelyn had to cope with a reaction of fear and fury which far outweighed the military significance of the murders.

In spite of his initial optimism, it soon became apparent to Evelyn that the emergency declaration was not going to produce any overnight improvement in security. He found himself engaged in an endless series of encounters with settler groups demanding a quick solution and envisaging the annihilation, or at least the decimation of the Kikuyu tribe. His counsel of patience was ill-received. There built up in many settlers' minds the idea that Baring was 'wet' and 'weak' – that what they needed was some stern figure with an iron will, who would not flinch from the unpleasant measures which they believed to be necessary.

A month after the emergency had been declared, on November 24 Evelyn wrote to Lyttelton to tell him that the situation had taken a turn for the worse.[1] There had been a series of raids on lonely white farms, which showed that the young Kikuyu had reorganised with a second tier leadership, and – equally serious – had access to weapons. He warned Lyttelton that they should now expect armed resistance in the forest and an increase both in oathing, and in attacks by armed gangs intent on killing the European occupants of lonely farmhouses. To counter this development the security forces were moving over from a strictly police operation to something more resembling a small scale guerrilla war. He asked Lyttelton for a Director of Operations with the rank of major general, suggesting Bernard Fergusson (of Chindit fame) if he was available. General Cameron, the local army commander agreed. The request was conventional enough, in the sense that it followed the guidelines for a command structure in colonial emergencies which had been circulated by the British cabinet as a result of lessons learnt in Malaya. But both Lyttelton and the War Office were unconvinced and, early in December, Evelyn had to fly back to London to press his case with Winston Churchill, the Prime Minister.

He lost his case – though he later felt he should have pressed his arguments to the point of resignation. Instead he was only allowed to appoint Major General Hinde as a personal staff officer. Hinde was well known and liked – perhaps almost too well liked – by the settlers, and his appointment certainly served to reassure them, but it had no beneficial effect on the state of security. The military situation continued to show no sign of improvement during the first few months of 1953, and Hinde's position remained far from secure in Whitehall, even after Evelyn finally managed to have him made Director of Operations.

Evelyn's nadir, in public esteem, was reached in January, 1953, when no obvious military progress had been made. The security forces were still suffering from lack of coordination; and the difficulty of fighting a rough and barbaric enemy without resorting to equally rough and barbaric methods was putting an almost intolerable strain on some sections of the local security forces, and more particularly, on settler opinion. After a savagely horrible murder of a complete family of Europeans – the father, mother and seven year old boy – there was a demonstration by white settlers in the grounds of Government House. Michael Blundell, the settler's leader, had heard of the plans for a march on Government House and had rung up Evelyn to warn him, also requesting that the African *askaris* (armed police) on guard duty be withdrawn from the front of the house in case they became a provocation. Between 500 and 1000 marchers arrived, left their cars at the bottom of the 200 yard drive and tramped up to the stately porch of Government House, assembling on the large gravel square in front of it. Unknown to Evelyn the Commissioner of Police had cordoned off the gravel with a detachment of *askaris*. This provoked an immediate outcry from the marchers, who objected to being corralled by 'dirty niggers', shouting 'we're not the Mau Mau', and calling for the Governor.

Inside, Evelyn was sitting in his office. He sent for Michael Blundell and told him he would not see the crowd; it would set a bad precedent since he would then be obliged to see any crowd of any race or faction which marched on Government House. A message was sent out to the demonstrators saying that two representatives would be received by the Governor. The two spokesmen were then received by Evelyn, and reported back to the crowd that he had been quite reasonable but had requested that they disperse. This was greeted with more shouts of defiance and demands for the removal of the *askaris*. Some settlers advanced on the cordon and stubbed out their cigarettes on the *askaris'* bare arms; others broke through the cordon and started trying to storm the front door, which had been barricaded on the inside with tables and chairs from the cypher clerk's rooms, but nevertheless was soon bending ominously under the pressure from without. Eventually Michael Blundell and another leading settler, Humphrey Slade, stood on chairs and succeeded in pacifying the crowd and dispersing them. When Blundell returned to Evelyn's office he found him still sitting where he had left him, reading a book – the hagiographers have it that it was Thucidydes. Evelyn apparently looked up, and simply said, 'Well done.'[2]

After a few months the Commander-in-Chief came out to inspect the situation from Cairo, meeting the Colonial Secretary in Nairobi. They both told Evelyn that Hinde would have to go. Evelyn protested, because he got on well with Hinde, and knew that his departure would cause him further trouble with the settlers. But he recognised that Hinde might not have been the best soldier for the job. In the end a compromise was agreed, in which a senior general would be appointed as Commander in Chief, with direct access to the War Office and no longer subordinate to the headquarters in Cairo. Hinde would become answerable to him. The appointment, personally selected by Winston Churchill, was General Sir George Erskine. From that moment, the counterinsurgency operation – as a purely military endeavour – acquired some consistent pattern, and started to improve gradually over the months ahead.

At the start of the emergency the police were short of manpower and anyway not equipped for that kind of operation. This meant that the army was held back to augment the police, and consequently had to delay any plans for offensive operations against the Mau Mau in the forest. When General Erskine arrived in June, 1953, his orders were to take the military measures required to end the emergency.[3] The Governor was instructed to help him but was to remain responsible for the government of the colony. There was to be no martial law, and the conduct of the security forces was to be governed by the emergency regulations. Some areas however were designated as prohibited, within which the security forces were allowed to use their weapons freely, without fear of the consequences.

Erskine's arrival reinfected the forces with an offensive spirit; and also led to the establishment, for the first time, of a list of priority objectives to be followed. Forces were to be concentrated, whereas before they had been dissipated in small packets throughout the affected area. Erskine found that parts of the Central Province in or near the forest were firmly under the grip of Mau Mau – almost resembling small republics. He asked for reinforcements, and a third brigade arrived in September, 1953, enabling him to start offensive operations against deep and well-defended Mau Mau positions in the Aberdares Forest. He established bases in the forest up to a height of 6000 feet, and carried out complementary harassment of the terrorists within the reserve.

For the first time since October, 1952, the incidence of terrorism started to decrease. As though to emphasise the recivilisation of the area, a magistrate used to travel with the army columns for speedy trial and convictions of prisoners. A surrender offer published in August, 1953, produced 815 surrenders by the end of the year. However, though it was clear that the planned fusion of Mau Mau with the Embu and Meru tribes had failed, Mau Mau was still operating as a serious military force in the field. Moreover in the reserve there was still no sign of a breakthrough in weaning the Kikuyu away from their passive support for the movement.

The key clearly lay in Nairobi. According to Erskine, Mau Mau had established a reign of terror over the city, the movement's main supply base. At the turn of the year, he decided that his principal task for 1954 would be to eliminate Mau Mau control in Nairobi.[4] Then he would be free to concentrate on building up an effective Kikuyu home guard and on reestablishing the police as the main security force in the reserves and settled areas, developments intended to free the army to operate more actively in the forest areas of the Mau Mau heartland. The operation to clear Nairobi, codenamed 'Anvil', took place in April, 1954, and resulted in the rounding up of 65,000 members of the Kikuyu, Embu and Meru tribes. It was seen as the turning point of the campaign.

After 'Anvil' the security forces gradually extended their activities outwards from Nairobi, all the time widening the secure area and pushing further into the Kikuyu reserve with a policy of creating protected villages. Meanwhile, Erskine had given instructions to prepare for deep penetration into the forest between December, 1954, and April 1955 – in the dry period between the rains – and tracker combat teams were selected for this purpose, to act as the spearhead of larger formations. Throughout 1954 Mau Mau was given no chance to recover from the shock of 'Anvil', and by January, 1955, a new surrender offer was prepared to coincide with major operations in the Aberdares Forest and on Mount Kenya, the last redoubts of the Mau Mau. When Erskine left in April, 1955, he felt that the Mau Mau emergency had entered its last phase, with many of its leaders killed, and the rank and file 'mostly concerned with personal survival'. He concluded his official despatch as follows: 'There are still some determined leaders in the field, but I'm sure that the security forces will be able to eliminate the last terrorists from the forest in time. Meanwhile a large part of the colony will be able to return to a peaceful development.'[5]

The task of his successor, Lieutenant General Sir Gerald Lathbury, was therefore to devise military measures which would
locate and eliminate the large number of terrorist gangs which
were still roaming in the forest. One tactic was to deny them
access to their sources of supply in the reserve; another to create
'pseudo gangs' of rehabilitated Mau Mau, who would go back
into the forest and hunt down their former colleagues. This
phase, assisted by bombing from RAF planes, continued on a
diminishing scale until the army was withdrawn from operations
in November, 1956, when the military side of the emergency
virtually came to an end. In military terms, the campaign against
Mau Mau followed an exemplary strategy, which reached a
successful conclusion in a comparatively short time when compared to other counter-insurgency campaigns of this kind.

Seretse and Ruth Khama

Above: With Mau Mau fighters in the Kenya forest in 1956
Below: The Kenya War Council: *left to right*, Sir Frederick Crawford,
Evelyn Baring, General Erskine and Michael Blundell.

Above: A family group in front of Government House, Nairobi.
The author is seated on the right.
Below: Howick

Evelyn with Jomo Kenyatta in the garden of State House, Nairobi in 1972.

CHAPTER XXIII

'Baring Must Go'!

The arrival of Erskine soon showed up the previous lack of military strategy. Evelyn had an overall political strategy for the colony but it did not cover the military practicalities of how the Mau Mau rebellion was to be finished off. He concentrated instead on more positive long term plans for the period *after* it was finished, and on not letting the counter-insurgency campaign inhibit the chances of such a long term plan being successful when the time came.

He naturally had to be kept involved in every phase of the fight, since nothing Erskine suggested could be entirely divorced from the well-being of the colony as a whole – indeed all political factors were of necessity something for the Governor to decide. But his main influence on the course of the military battle was in seeing that the non-military elements on whom the security force had to rely – the police, administration, settlers, and loyal Kikuyu – were phased into the operation in the most constructive way.

The strain of the emergency, and of having to conduct his life on so many tiers, was compounded by the strange official and personal relationship Evelyn had with General Erskine. It resulted, after a visit from Lyttelton and Harding, the CIGS, in January, 1954, in the establishment of a War Council, complete with a separate secretariat presided over by Mr (late Sir) George Mallaby of the Cabinet Office, a civil servant of great seniority, well versed in the intricate ways of statesmen and soldiers at war. The problem with Erskine could have been much worse if the two men had been different personalities, because the terms of Erskine's appointment seemed to be a prescription for disaster. Whereas the Governor of a colony was traditionally also the Commander in Chief – as Evelyn had been until Erskine's arrival – Erskine's own instructions made it clear that he was not subordinate to Evelyn where military requirements were concerned. Indeed, though Evelyn retained full responsibility for the government and administration of the colony, he had to give priority to those plans Erskine considered essential; and should the two reach an impasse, they had to appeal individually to their respective Secretaries of State for a ruling. A man more conscious of his status, or more alarmed by any erosion of his authority, might have resigned the governorship rather than submit to the arrival of a senior army officer, who in certain respects, would be able to override him. Evelyn did not. If the campaign could only be waged successfully by the appointment of a senior general and the surrender of some of his own powers and authority, so be it. Erskine used to joke about his special instructions; that he kept them permanently in his spectacle case, ready to be produced at war council meetings if he was unable to get his way. But though the preparations for 'Anvil' – the swoop through Nairobi – provided one occasion on which an appeal to the Secretaries of State was contemplated, it never actually happened since, by the time Lyttelton arrived in Nairobi early in 1954, Evelyn and the General had already resolved their differences.

Erskine was a soldier's soldier, who never became popular with the settlers. His unpopularity blinded them to his sound military strategy, which has been much underrated by historians. Erskine was a lonely man and dedicated himself entirely to the military task before him. His wife did not accompany him, partly because he felt it would be wrong for her to be there when junior ranks were not allowed their wives, partly because of security. 'If they are going to eat an Erskine, they will only eat one,' she was rumoured to have said. The settlers resented his formidable body-guard of military police vehicles, failing to understand that the propaganda effect of his assassination would have been infinitely greater than the death of one more settler. They compared him unfavourably in that respect with Hinde, who drove about protected by a single African policeman. He was never popular with the administration either, because his own analysis of the situation assumed far greater support for Mau Mau among the Kikuyu than the administration had contended. Even his attitude to oathing, as shown in his official despatch, showed an attempt to get behind the superficial approach to the Kikuyu which often seemed so prevalent with the administration and police.

Erskine was even harder on the settlers, 'I frankly loathe this place and the job,' he told his wife after they had been separated for a year. 'Kenya is the mecca of the middle class, so I have been told. I have coined a new phrase, a sunny place for shady people . . . I hate the guts of them all, they are all middle class sluts. I never want to see another Kenya man or woman and I dislike them all with few exceptions.'[1]

Erskine's relations with Evelyn were always correct, though

there was an inevitable contrast between the general's 'no non-sense' military approach, and Evelyn's endless ratiocination before every decision. 'Half the trouble is that all these civil servants and police sit in their offices behind barbed wire fences and so do not know what goes on in their districts' was Erskine's first snap judgment. This was mirrored in his first analysis of Evelyn, in which he showed that he had already perceived the strain which was to get the better of Evelyn during the next year. June, 1953: 'Baring is a very sick man and I do not believe he will last...'[2]

Erskine's attitude to Evelyn suggests that he thought he was running the emergency, while having to carry a senior political figure who was both ill and indecisive, and therefore frustrating. 'The governor has been away for three weeks and I expected him to come back rested and fit. The odd thing is just the reverse has happened. His meetings (which I never attend) were always fairly long winded and now go on for longer and never reach a decision.'[3] 'I have had a difficult time gingering up HE to act. I always have to make up his mind for him. That may be not quite fair but that is what it feels like ... I should like to see Sir Edward Twining, Governor of Tanganyika, governor of this place. I like Baring very much and the whole family are charming, but he can make no decisions and that is fatal. I don't feel in any way optimistic on the long term policy. I am sure I can put down the gangs in a reasonable time, but I can't do much to alter the outlook of the Kikuyu tribe as C in C except to knock them on the head when they are troublesome, and that is no answer to the real problem though it is an essential preliminary.'[4]

In January, 1954, the question of Evelyn's unfitness to continue the job, ostensibly because of illness (which was in reality only exhaustion and depression), but, one suspects, more because of widespread complaints about his indecisiveness, reached a head with a visit to Nairobi by Lyttelton and Harding, the CIGS. The possibility of replacing Evelyn with a military governor, much as Templar had been in Malaya – an example everybody invoked – was very much in the air. Indeed it had obviously already been mentioned to Erskine as soon as he arrived some months previously, when he wrote to his wife, 'I'm sure there is no question of my being governor, I should hate it.'[5]

Although there appear to be no records of any cabinet discussion about Evelyn's replacement or temporary suspension, it was clearly being discussed in Whitehall. The Colonial Office was hostile to the idea of a change. However, there appears to have been – in Lyttelton's mind at least – some recognition of the fact that Evelyn was proving a questionable governor. He had tried to help by bringing in Sir Frederick Crawford, as deputy Governor, to lighten Evelyn's load. Everybody still seemed to assume that Evelyn would be the best Governor for Kenya after the emergency, if somehow he could be got through this most testing period.

Blundell had visited London after the coronation and had discussed the problem of Evelyn with Lyttelton. Blundell told Lyttelton it had always been his policy to back Evelyn as he thought he would be a good Governor after the emergency. His support would continue, provided steps were taken to strengthen Evelyn during the emergency, since, although Evelyn was the only governor who thoroughly understood the Kenya situation, he was too flexible and indecisive. Lyttelton apparently concurred with this view, though neither of their opinions reached Evelyn. Harding also recollects long discussions with Lyttelton in February, 1954, about the wisdom of replacing Evelyn with a military governor, while they walked up and down the verandah of Government House, Nairobi, immediately outside Evelyn's own office, in which, presumably, he was sitting. Erskine was aware of the talk too, even if Evelyn was not, 'I gather everybody wants to do something but nobody knows what to do. Baring is a sick man and I do not think he can possibly carry on. The settlers hate me just as much as I hate them and I do not reckon I'm a starter.'[6]

In the end it was decided that Evelyn should go off on six weeks sick-leave starting in March, 1954. He was desperate to visit Cohen, his doctor in Liverpool, to see if, after a complete rest at Howick, he would be likely to recover his energies and optimism enough to face the strain. There was a spate of rumours that he would *not* return, denied by the Colonial Office but firmly believed in the junior ranks of army and administration. His actual return was delayed until towards the end of June, 1954, and there is some evidence that Lyttelton for one was convinced as late as May, 1954, that Evelyn would never go back.[7]

Apart from the exhaustion he felt as a result of his weakened liver, Evelyn had clearly come close to the limits of his endurance by the early months of 1954. Since he arrived in the colony, apart from the day-to-day pressures involved in trying to fight a counter-insurgency campaign, he had also been drawn into the fierce in-fighting of Kenya politics. There was the unremitting lobbying of a very active and volatile group of elected settlers' representatives. There was also the whole saga of the Kenyatta trial, which I will describe later; and the beginnings of a long-running dispute with Whyatt, the Attorney General, over the role of justice in the emergency.

As early as April, 1953, Evelyn had to receive a delegation from the settlers, several of whom had already said in public, 'Baring must go.' Their leaders were Michael Blundell, Wilfred Havelock and Humphrey Slade. They were demanding summary justice, wider death sentences, movement controls, forfeiture of Mau Mau land, and an inner cabinet which would include some of them. When Evelyn saw them, he told them he would resign if they wanted him to, but warned them that he would then be replaced by a military governor who would have no truck with settler politics. Evelyn told them he would refuse to carry on if they were going to attack everything that was done, and make it difficult for the government to carry on the war. After that meeting the pressure eased off for a while, though Nairobi was soon to witness notices saying 'What no Governor', and there was another spasm of criticism when Evelyn made a speech criticising the Europeans for too much arrogance and the Africans for too much suspicion. In Rhodesia he had also been unpopular for some of the things he said, but there he had had no real executive responsibility, nor did he have to spend his time in the political market place coping with everyday pressures. That was a job for Huggins, the Prime Minister. Evelyn badly needed a Huggins in Nairobi; instead, he did acquire Sir Frederick Crawford as Deputy Governor in June, 1953, at about the same time as Erskine, and thereafter a great deal of the day-to-day load was taken off his shoulders.

These two new arrivals were very popular with Evelyn. The Barings thought Erskine had great charm, though perhaps a bit of a 'bounder'. He impressed them as being in a different class from everybody else. Molly reported home that he had been very nice to Evelyn, and asked his advice on innumerable points, but did not give the impression that he would necessarily take it. (He was also very correct in his relations with Evelyn, only venturing to call him by his christian name in his farewell letter two years later.) His arrival initially inspired Evelyn with the hope that he would no longer have to consider the operational side, and his family hoped that Erskine and Crawford had come in the nick of time to save him from succumbing to complete exhaustion.

But they achieved only a temporary respite for him. There were always going to be things which could not be delegated, and one which at this time caused Evelyn considerable worry was the Kenyatta case. The trial of Jomo Kenyatta was not explicitly planned when the emergency was declared in October, 1952. Although all the administration and the police seemed convinced that Jomo Kenyatta was – as Erskine later put it – 'the father and mother of the whole movement,'[8] it was agreed by Evelyn and his legal advisers at the time that they had no hope of trying him, unless some witnesses came forward. It was hoped that they would do so under the influence of the emergency and it was left to Somerville, the Chief Crown Prosecutor, to advise Evelyn if and when a case against Kenyatta could be made viable. Although it must have been clear to the government law officers that there was increasing political demand for a trial of Kenyatta, there was no pressure from Evelyn for them to hurry up and prepare one. Yet it was an unavoidable fact that the longer the government was unable to mount a trial, the more slender appeared to be the pretext for declaring the emergency, even though the number of atrocities since then gave it some retrospective justification.

Eventually evidence was obtained which the Crown felt enabled it to charge Kenyatta with being the manager of Mau Mau. The evidence was pretty thin, however. Kenyatta was no doubt guilty by association with the spirit of Mau Mau, but almost certainly not of the technical management of its operations before the emergency – at least not so far as the evidence could adduce.

There were considerable dangers for Evelyn and his government if they did decide on a trial which would result in acquittal. It would appear to world opinion, already highly critical of the emergency, that there had been no real justification for such a step. The settlers would almost certainly take the law into their own hands, presenting the security forces with a choice between ignoring their activities, or else suffering from overstretch as they tried to police white anarchy as well as black rebellion. It would give an enormous boost to the morale of the Mau Mau, as well as tip all the Kikuyu waverers on to the side of the rebellion.

As early as November, 1952, Evelyn was writing to Lyttelton in terms which showed the importance he set by the trial of Kenyatta and five other Mau Mau leaders. 'If witnesses will repeat in open court what they have said on affidavit to magistrates, convictions should be obtained. *Every possible effort has been made to offer them rewards* [my italics] and to protect them, but no-one can tell what will really happen when they are confronted in court by Kenyatta's formidable personality. If they speak they will disclose a degree of close connection between the Kenya African Union and the Mau Mau movement greater than has ever been mentioned before in public. We hope that, if there is a conviction, we will be able to lift the emergency regulations in areas other than the two Kikuyu provinces.' The reference to *rewards* is interesting in view of the controversy which surrounded these witnesses several years later. One of them recanted, saying he had been bribed, and was promptly convicted of perjury.

A retired High Court judge from Kenya, Mr Justice Thacker, was chosen to take the case, even though it was to take place in a magistrates' court. The reason for his selection was apparently that the Attorney General did not think that any local magistrate would have been able to stand up to the heavyweight attack of the British QC, D. N. Pritt, who came out to defend Kenyatta. Thacker convicted Kenyatta – sentencing him to seven years hard labour for managing Mau Mau. But he was careful to explain his rejection of the defence evidence by saying that he had done so from his long experience of the African as a witness. By implication he was protecting himself from any subsequent appeal, since there was no point of law on which Pritt could criticise the sentence, only on the fact that the judge's assessment of the prosecution and defence evidence was very biased.

The publicity given to the trial however seems to have gone to Thacker's head. He apparently asked for an honour after it was over, an unusual request, and he also seemed to engage in somewhat improper discussions *during* the trial. What is more strange, Evelyn seems to have been a party to them. Apparently Thacker informed the Governor that, should he reach a conclusion that Kenyatta was guilty, his own life in Kenya would not be worth a penny; he would have to leave the country. What arrangements would be made to facilitate this process? While making all allowances for the unusual circumstances of the trial, it was an irregular request to make and should have been countered noncomittally. Not surprisingly there is no record of such a conversation in the files, and Whyatt, the Attorney General, has no recollection of such an overture from Thacker, which clearly did not go through the legal department. Be that as it may, Thacker received an *ex gratia* payment of £20,000 from the Kenya government, drawn against some special emergency fund on Evelyn's own instructions. One can only speculate about this payment, but one does not need to suggest that the case against Kenyatta had no hope of being proved to conclude that, nevertheless, Thacker had an eye for the importance of his judgment and sought to capitalise on the situation, and that Evelyn, acting with unusual cynicism and ruthlessness, saw that he could not afford to take any risk.

As if that was not enough it was then discovered that Kapenguria, the place of the trial, had in the indictment been sited in the wrong province. This gave Pritt leave to appeal. Evelyn was furious at the prospect of a retrial, particularly no doubt in view of his private transaction with Thacker. Apart from the fact that he desperately wanted a conviction, and a quick one at that, he had the previous November asked both the Legal and the Lands departments of the government to iron out the ambiguous position of Kapenguria, which was considered to be in one province for administrative purposes but was actually located in another. The answer he then received was absolutely wrong, based on an omission to minute an order-in-council passed some years before. It was a legal fiasco. 'If I was the governor I should sack the Attorney General and that is exactly why they would never make me governor,' Erskine remarked to his wife.[9] In fact Whyatt eventually retrieved the situation when Pritt's appeal for a retrial was thrown out by the Privy Council in August, 1953. But it must have added to the strain on Evelyn's nerves.

CHAPTER XXIV

Law and Disorder

The fiasco over the Kenyatta trial must have added to Evelyn's growing discontent with his Attorney General, John Whyatt. As the emergency progressed Evelyn found himself caught in something of a vice between the security forces' desire to take the war to the enemy, and Whyatt's principled insistence that their actions must be within the law. The response from settlers and many members of the administration was to press for the law to be changed. Whyatt's opposition to every move in this direction was persistent and uncomfortable, but it did not reach a crisis until after Evelyn came back from his long break in mid-1954, when he discovered that he had a new Police Commissioner, Mr Arthur Young. The 'Young affair,' as it came to be known after Young's sudden departure in December, 1954, was perhaps the most dramatic clash of personalities involved in Evelyn's governorship during the emergency – and no doubt took its toll on his peace of mind. It could not have taken place had not the Attorney General been maintaining the principled if unsympathetic and at times over-legalistic stand that he had been taking ever since Evelyn arrived.

Whyatt was a devout Roman Catholic, a deeply emotional though undemonstrative man, who was never at ease with Baring. Evelyn was equally uneasy with him. Whyatt disliked and distrusted the self-confidence with which Evelyn would approach a problem, saying 'I think I know how to play this hand' and splaying his fingers out on the desk in front of him. Evelyn, who was never very strong on paper and disliked formal memoranda, deplored the incessant flow of minutes and memoranda from Whyatt, raising formal objections to this or that plan and warning him portentously of its legal (or illegal) consequences. Later in his governorship, Evelyn developed a more intimate relationship with Whyatt's successor, Eric Griffith-Jones, which showed what a formidable partnership could be made by a Governor and his Attorney General working closely together, rather than through the formal bureaucratic machine. In Whyatt's day however, with the situation complicated by the war council's security committees and other official paraphenalia, there seemed never to be an opportunity for Evelyn and his Attorney General to forge that kind of relationship, even if their personalities had allowed them to do so.

The early troubles arose on account of cases of brutality, even amounting to murder, which were committed by the security forces. It was always a nightmare of Evelyn's that, unless the war against Mau Mau was seen to be prosecuted with firmness by the official security forces, both settlers and probably some elements of the administration would start to take the law into their own hands. A delicate balance had therefore to be preserved. Malpractices had to be stamped out and atrocities by loyal forces punished, but not to the extent of creating in the minds of Africans a belief that they were being punished for obeying their orders to pursue terrorists with vigour. The most common occurrence was when a suspect was 'shot while attempting to escape,' often in circumstances which made that cover-story most implausible. There was also fairly general concern from early 1953 about the formation of settlers' commando groups, which were privately raised groups, ostensibly working with their local police stations but often having a measure of independence which was not enjoyed by any of the forces in uniform. After Erskine arrived he issued a formal message to all members of the security forces saying he would not 'tolerate breaches of discipline leading to unfair treatment of anybody.' Erskine, in private, thought that the 'MCC rules,' as he called them, were completely crippling; but under his firm control the army nevertheless maintained its high standards. Of course it was not emotionally involved in the Mau Mau uprising in the way the local people had become.

It was thus the attitude of local forces – the Kenya regiment, the all-white locally recruited infantry battalion, the Kikuyu guard, and some local police officers – which proved most troublesome. After Whyatt pressed one or two cases involving members of the Kenya regiment, Erskine told the commanding officer, 'I am not going to get any more of your men off a murder charge.' His warning seemed to suffice. He recognised that Whyatt's point was correct in principle, but thought he was pushing it too far in view of the circumstances. More often it was Evelyn who found himself in the invidious position of having to support the administration against Whyatt's demands for enquiries and prosecutions. In his view he could not so destroy the morale of the administration by witchhunts that they would cease to be an effective force. He recognised that he would have to rely on the administration for the government of Kenya, that he could not govern Kenya by British bayonets and colonial policemen alone. When it came to a choice between asserting Whyatt's rule of law, or losing the trust of District Officers or Commissioners, he tried normally to protect his administration. In the process he lost the confidence of both sides – at least temporarily – since the administration seldom knew of those incidents in which he had supported them and only knew when he had sanctioned enquiries which led to the suspension or sacking of local police officers.

It was the relationship between the administration and the police which lay at the root of the great argument of principle which preoccupied Evelyn and his new Commissioner of Police, Arthur Young, during the second half of 1954. Young was appointed after a parliamentary delegation had visited Kenya early in 1954, shortly before Evelyn went on his sick leave. The MPs came home with the unanimous recommendation to Lyttelton that a new Commissioner of Police was needed. Arthur Young was at that time Commissioner of the City of London Police. His appointment derived from general concern over allegations of police brutality in Kenya, and from a desire to establish a police force which was going to have the confidence of the African population in the period after paramilitary operations ceased. Lyttelton arranged with the City of London for Young's secondment for up to a year, without any reference to Evelyn, who was having a complete rest at Howick. Young suggested to the Secretary of State that he should see Baring before he left for the colony, to which Lyttelton replied that Evelyn was anyway likely to retire through ill health without returning to Kenya, so there was no need. 'He is too intelligent for his job,' Lyttelton told Young. 'He sees too many possibilities and can't choose any of them.'[1] The Europeans, he said, owed little allegiance to government and certainly none to the governor himself who was frequently abused and at least once was the subject of an abduction plot. So Young prepared to go out to the colony without seeing Evelyn. He was to find, rather to his surprise, that Evelyn was already back in harness in Nairobi when he got there. A stormy six months' relationship ensued.

Young did not get off to a very good start. Before taking up his full time appointment he had paid a lightning visit to Kenya and had returned to lobby the cabinet for a change of governor and Commander-in-Chief – this before he had ever met Evelyn. He told Oliver Woods, the Colonial Correspondent of *The Times*, that Kenya lacked both a leader and a plan.[2] The new War Council made it difficult to appoint a Templar-type figure but he was going to lobby Anthony Head, the Secretary of State for War, to get a better Commander-in-Chief out of him – he wanted General Stockwell – and he was also on the hunt for a better Governor, perhaps somebody like Oliver Franks. It is hard to believe Evelyn's Whitehall intelligence did not give him some news of these intrigues, and of the newcomer Young's part in them.

The basic problem centred on Young's belief that he had been sent out to Kenya to create a constabulary based on the idea of the 'village bobby'. This immediately clashed with the administration's view that, even at the best of times, in a colony the administrative officer was the emanation of power from the centre, with the police forces subordinate to him in his area. At this particular time, with a colonial administration actually fighting an armed rebellion, it was inconceivable that there should be any tampering with that principle. Evelyn, even if he *had* got on well with Young or had been party to Young's appointment and the apparent philosophy behind it, was bound to side with his administration over this point. It was fundamental to the District Officer's view of life, which he had acquired so strongly during his formative years in India. This argument became overlaid with the extra points of friction thrown up by the emergency – atrocities committed by loyal members of the security forces, Young's access to the Governor, his non-membership of the War Council and so on.

Young took as his text a White Paper on the Kenya police, published two years earlier. This had recommended police independence from the administration. The administration was naturally hostile to this idea, arguing strongly that if the police did become independent, there would have been two centres of power, which would have been confusing to the Africans. Besides, it was argued, the District Officer had always represented the central power in the field. An independent constabulary was well known to be a bastion of Britain's parliamentary democracy, but would have been totally out of context in the enlightened dictatorship of a Crown Colony.

Young was undeterred by these arguments. 'I set my heart on an independent judiciary but realized that the pressure of the emergency would delay my coming to terms with it,' he said later.[3] Unfortunately for him and for all the other actors in this particular scene, it was really his only *raison d'être* in Kenya – the explanation for his temporary appointment. This led to his attaching too much importance to it, against all the evidence that the state of emergency was an inauspicious time to suggest such a radical change in administrative practice. He felt he knew all about states of emergency since he had been Templar's Police Commissioner during the Malayan war. 'Unlike my relations with General Templar in Malaya, Baring treated me not as a colleague but as a subordinate official about whom no special consideration applied,' he later recalled. 'He was pleasant and courteous but never frank and warmhearted.'⁴ His private view of Evelyn was that he was devious and ill.

Young found that a number of police enquiries had unearthed cases of atrocities by tribal chiefs and even by some Europeans. He immediately abolished the practice of allowing the white vigilante patrols to carry weapons. Eventually, eight cases, seven black and one white, were assembled by the police for prosecution by Whyatt. Young and his deputy called on Evelyn and warned him of the material they had in hand, which was also in the hands of the Attorney General. Evelyn was obviously in a quandary. If the prosecutions of the loyalists were proceeded with, he felt he might lose the enthusiasm, if not the cooperation, of many junior members of the administration at a vital juncture in the emergency. Yet he could not simply sweep the cases under the carpet, particularly with Whyatt and Young ready to resign and expose the business if he did so. However a lifeline was to hand, in the form of an amnesty offer which was being prepared as part of the next package of surrender terms to be put before the terrorists. Mau Mau members were to be offered an amnesty which would mean that, if they surrendered before a certain time, they would not be prosecuted for any crimes that they had committed and would have to face nothing worse than detention. Evelyn explained to Whyatt and Young that it would only be fair to extend this amnesty to members of the security forces, and consequently such crimes as those under consideration would have to be absolved.

Young, undeterred, pressed on with his enquiries, and his attempts to persuade the government to adopt his view of the constabulary. He nearly swayed the Executive Council of Ministers. Only Evelyn and Dick Turnbull, the Chief Secretary, were against it from the start (though Young always felt Evelyn had been in favour of the idea until he was nobbled overnight by Turnbull). Though Evelyn had always avoided putting matters to the vote, this time the argument was so acute, that he had to do so. Young lost his case by a majority of one. The Ministers' conclusions were read to Young by Evelyn:

'An essential element of the new status-of-the-police proposals [Young's] is that the police should not be regarded as the agents of the government, but would exercise an independent and impartial authority on their own personal responsibility. Does that fit in with present day circumstances with Kenya in the midst of an emergency and almost every citizen subject in some degree to the orders of the government and to its emergency regulations? It is clear that during the emergency at any rate decisions on executive acts must be government decisions at whatever level, and that in so far as the police may be asked to carry those decisions into effect they do and must act as agents of government. A lone wolf status is not possible in present circumstances although on the other hand no-one would wish or contemplate interfering with a policeman's duties under the law or for instance interfering with his right to bring or not to bring a prosecution in the courts.'[5]

The last sentence had a peculiar poignancy for Young since he had had occasion to draw Evelyn's attention to an offence of his own. This arose after Evelyn had received an appeal from the Provincial Commissioner, Mr C. M. Johnston, who had failed to dissuade the CID from pressing a convincing case against an African chief. Young received a statement from his Assistant Commissioner which appeared to be pretty damning, it read as follows:

'On the occasion of a recent visit of the Secretary of State for the Colonies accompanied by His Excellency the Governor, to South Nyeri, HE drew me aside for some ten minutes to discuss the chief Mundia case. HE said that his discussion with me was off the record and while he would not give me any directions in the matter he considered it would be politically most inexpedient to prosecute a loyal chief who had taken a leading part in the fight against Mau Mau. He said that a loyal Kikuyu would find it difficult to differentiate between killing Mau Mau in the heat of battle and killing the government's enemies out of battle. He said that one should take into account the difference of mentality between loyal Kikuyu and, say, European security force personnel who were well able to realize the wrong of taking the law into their own hands. HE repeated that if there was a strong *prima facie* case against Mundia he would, of course, have to be prosecuted but that if a conviction were doubtful he felt that it would be politically inexpedient for the case to go forward.'[6]

Of course in terms of the argument then going on with Arthur Young, Evelyn's intervention over Chief Mundia was very damaging. It illustrated in a nutshell what Whyatt and Young had been complaining of – the primacy of the executive over the constabulary. Evelyn was clearly also conscious of his mistake, since after his final meeting with Young he sent for the CID officer concerned and told him that what he had said at Nyeri that day had been wrong and that he would instruct Mr Johnston, the PC, to make a similar statement.

A few weeks after the War Council rejected his proposals Young resigned – as it had by then become fairly clear he was determined to do – and returned to Britain, intent on alerting the Colonial Office and the Secretary of State to what he thought were dangerous tendencies towards a 'police state' within Kenya. The Labour opposition stirred. Two backbench MPs, Mrs Barbara Castle and John Stonehouse, were both keen that his reasons for resignation should be published, but they never were. His resignation letter ran to thirty paragraphs, and the opposition clearly hoped that Alan Lennox-Boyd, the new Colonial Secretary, would inadvertently refer to it in the House of Commons, necessitating its subsequent publication. Lennox-Boyd avoided that trap, no doubt aware that, as Young contended later, 'If my report had been published the Governor and Colonial Secretary would have been in a very hazardous position.'[7]

Young's departure drove everybody into quick post mortems, and hurried meetings with the press. Evelyn saw the Nairobi correspondent of *The Times* and gave him the full background, including the incident about chief Mundia and the allegations against himself. He admitted his indiscretion but said that he was unaware at the time of a feud going on between the administration and the police – (a questionable defence in view of the private appeal he had received from Johnston). He contended that Young had only added his complaint about the chief Mundia case to his reasons for resigning, because his original threat to resign if the War Council's decision on the status of the police went against him, looked rather thin in the light of Evelyn's offer that the status of the police in the long term should be looked at by a working party.[8]

Young, in the meantime, was seeing Oliver Woods in London, claiming he would insist on Lennox-Boyd publishing the reasons for his resignation, and that he would do so himself if Lennox-Boyd refused. He was bitterly disappointed, he told Woods, with his reception in Kenya. Having been loaned by the City of London at the request of the Prime Minister, he found when he got to Kenya that he was subordinate to a Minister of Defence who was utterly useless, and he had not been a member of the War Council, or even invited to its deliberations when police affairs were being discussed.[9]

The last word was from Erskine in a confidential comment to his wife. 'There is a lot of trouble going on, partly brought to a head by the Young/Governor row and the trial of a number of loyalists and home guard. All this could endanger the operation because of home guard defections – so I am interested. The Governor is terribly wobbly and it is an uphill job keeping him up to the bit.'[10]

CHAPTER XXV

Surrender:
The Turning Point

General Erskine's private view of Evelyn was widely shared. One of the general underlying criticisms of the Governor during those first two or three years of the emergency was that he was indecisive, that he was not clear in his own mind how he wanted to prosecute the war against the Mau Mau, and that he was more or less at sea in the rough and tumble of a counter-insurgency campaign. The criticisms, in isolation, are merited. From an early stage in the emergency Evelyn was probably conscious of his inexperience, and also of his inability to put across what it was he was hoping to achieve. This was not altogether a difficulty of his own making, however. His own objective was never just to defeat the Mau Mau; nor just to restore the *status quo ante,* whenever that might have been, though that was clearly a view held by the settler community and some members of the administration. When he arrived in Kenya he had no formed long-term views about the future of the colony, and at least for the first months, little time to develop any. Yet there was no point in somebody like him being governor unless he did think beyond the defeat of the rebellion. Moreover he always saw himself as a developer and an improver. Earlier in Rhodesia and in the High Commission Territories he had shown that he possessed an abundance of such long term vision. Was it likely to be still-born in Kenya just because he was faced with an armed rebellion by one of its tribes numbering only about a fifth of the black population?

However, he had a difficulty. It was going to take time to develop such views while all around him swirled the preoccupations of the military emergency; it was going to take time also to persuade other people to think ahead beyond the next security objectives. Moreover, he alone could decide when there would be much point in propagating his longer term plans for Kenya. By Africans, with the evidence of the emergency regulations before them, they were unlikely to be believed or even listened to. In the case of the Europeans there was also a danger that his views of the future could cause a collapse of morale among just that part of the indigenous population on which he had to rely.

J

These Europeans were not just partners in security, or a community capable of making much political noise. Their economic power in the colony was considerable. As the *Oxford History of East Africa* put it, 'Their farms and plantations produced most of the country's exports and the greater part of its marketed food supplies, while they were prominent – perhaps dominant – in commerce, industry and the professions.'[1] They were not an element whose views about the future could be ignored.

Thus what came to be known by Evelyn as the 'second prong' of his policy took some time to emerge from the dark arsenal of counter-insurgent activity, and even longer to infect the administration with its purposes. But with hindsight one can now see that, however indecisive and ill-cast Evelyn appeared to be in the politico-military environment, there were actually deep, longer term strategies being worked out within him which, ultimately, burst forth on Kenya and equipped it for the path to independence. Though independence actually happened quicker than Evelyn expected, it would have been impossible without the achievement of his 'second prong' policies during the 1950s. Paradoxically, within a seven year governorship, he could not have achieved what he did had it not been for the emergency, which gave him the power to introduce a whole series of social and economic changes in an unusually short time.

In fact the second prong consisted of a number of prongs, all calculated to provide a future for Kenya which would make it worthwhile for all communities to overcome the Mau Mau infection. It was composed of a number of agricultural, economic and political developments which actually did take place in spite of the distractions of the fight within the Kikuyu. If one compares the Kenya which confronted Evelyn in 1952, with the state of the colony when he left seven years later, the changes are indeed remarkable, and it is evident that they all started to occur while the emergency operations were still in full spate. Singular among those developments was an agrarian revolution which transformed the face of Kenya. It was the chief element in the second prong attack, and it could only have been put through with such speed and efficiency by the almost ruthless application of emergency regulations. The other profound development which Evelyn masterminded was the changeover from the rigid colonial constitution he inherited – where a straight colonial administration was confronted by an unofficial majority of settlers within the parliament – to the gradual development of cabinet-style government in a multi-racial polity, through constitutional changes calculated to foster active African involvement in the political life of the country, which before 1952 had been dominated almost entirely by the white settlers.

However, while these longer term developments were being prepared, a more explicit sign that things were looking up came with the major surrender offer soon after Evelyn returned, much refreshed, from his long sick leave in the summer of 1954. The arguments which surrounded the offer served to crystallise the forces with which he had to contend, both within his government and in Kenyan society at large, and which had nearly brought him down the year before. But after his break Evelyn seemed able to cope with them in a way which refuted the demand for his retirement made by the London *Sunday Express*, with the words, 'A man in poor health is not fit for the task.'[2] Though he was always going to find himself prone to massive bouts of exhaustion, his physical and psychological reserves were never again stretched as they had been in early 1954.

Upon his return to Kenya he was presented with statistics which showed that for some months the military situation had been improving. The point had clearly been reached where an active military policy had to be accompanied by a more active and specific policy of political encouragement; hence the new surrender offer. But before he was able to announce the surrender terms in January, 1955, Evelyn had to contend with one of the major crises of his regime. There had been an earlier surrender offer in 1953/54. Evelyn and Erskine at every stage had had to cope with settler opposition to the idea of any negotiations with the terrorists. When Lyttelton visited Kenya in February, 1954, he tackled Blundell head on, 'Do you want to finish the emergency or do you want revenge?' Erskine was privately convinced that many of the settlers wanted revenge with a capital R. However opposition to the surrender terms was not confined to the settlers. Elements of the administration were also unhappy about it. After a protracted series of negotiations during the first four months of 1954, a major surrender was aborted by an unscheduled encounter in the vicinity of the gathering of the gangs. The security forces, however, had acquired much useful intelligence, and also valuable lessons about how to conduct the next offer when the time appeared ripe. It was to do so some six months later.

In January, 1955, Evelyn told his Council of Ministers of the new surrender terms which had been prepared. There were two issues which caused much disquiet. One was the basic principle of dealing with the Mau Mau at all – the 'reprieve or revenge' argument put so starkly a year before by Lyttelton. The second, much more difficult question arose out of the need to incorporate an amnesty for loyalist forces in the same package, along the lines foreshadowed by Evelyn in his uncomfortable talks with Young a few months earlier. Whyatt had insisted that there could be no amnesty for loyalists whose cases had already started to be investigated. That left about 20 cases of loyalist troops and Kikuyu guards who would be included in the package offer. Evelyn told his Ministers that he intended to make two speeches praising the loyalist forces while condemning malpractices, in the hope of putting the whole offer into a more understandable context. But there was much disquiet. The settler ministers, and some of the senior colonial office ministers who had come up through the administration, objected to the fact that loyalist should be tied into the same statement as the terrorists, since whatever they had done had been in the course of combating Mau Mau terrorism. Whyatt was adamant that, unless the statements *were* synchronised, the clemency towards the loyalists ceased to be an act of state, and merely became discriminatory, letting a few people off the law. Against that the administration was warning Evelyn about the effect of the Kikuyu guard coming to believe that they were going to be prosecuted for everything they had done in their enthusiasm to fight Mau Mau. There were already cases of their having handed in their weapons, and one or two police posts in the reserve had had to be closed down because the Kikuyu guard had thrown in the sponge as a result of the rumoured prosecutions. Evelyn's last hope was that he would be able to make two announcements rather than the one. His fear was that, if Whyatt insisted on a single announcement, his Council of Ministers would crack up and there would be resignations. This would have broken up the anyway rather fragile ministerial structure which had been brought in by Lyttelton during his visit the year before, and which for the first time had introduced the idea of elected members – white settler representatives – holding responsible office as ministers of the colonial government.

There was much to-ing and fro-ing. The argument among the Ministers became so fierce that Evelyn had to refer the whole thing to the British cabinet in London, though by then he had endorsed Whyatt's stand and was merely enlisting Lennox-Boyd's support to browbeat the dissident settler ministers into submission. When the terms were eventually announced there was an outcry from the settlers. In February the Nairobi correspondent of *The Times* was reporting confidentially that opposition to the terms had spawned demands for lynch law and for members of the security forces not to serve a government 'which had treated them so badly'.[3] The settlers' members also stepped up their pressure for the removal of Wyatt, for whom they had been gunning since the emergency began. Whether it was that pressure, or Evelyn's final weariness with Whyatt's studied legalism, is not clear, but when the Attorney General went on leave that summer he did not return. He was appointed Chief Justice of Singapore.

Whyatt had certainly left his mark on Evelyn's first three years. He had resisted when the settlers wanted some form of summary justice, and he would not consent to alter existing legal procedures to shorten the time between arrest and sentence. He had prosecuted cases regardless of whether the accused were members of Mau Mau or of the security forces. He had insisted, presumably to the point of resignation, that the surrender offer had to include the amnesty for loyalists. He won all these points, though at great cost in personal relationships, and high feelings. He always tended to overreact. He had, indeed, been known to lose his temper at Executive Council meetings; his normal reaction to an enquiry by Evelyn was to say 'out of the question; against the law', almost snapping it out and showing no inclination to see a way round, but all the time deriving some sense of virtue from his legal decisions. He even accused the War Council of which he was not a member, of being an illegal body, which perhaps, according to strict construction, was the case. But it somehow typified his approach. However, though Evelyn was obviously relieved when he had gone, he recognised his integrity. *The Times* correspondent reported confidentially the gist of a private conversation in which Evelyn said that 'Whyatt was right from the very beginning and had not deviated from his principles.' 'This was quite a tribute,' commented the correspondent, 'as Whyatt's principles resulted in many headaches.'[4]

CHAPTER XXVI

The Second Prong

Once the major surrender offer was under way the other elements of the second prong could be pushed ahead. With terrorists surrendering at the rate of about 100 a month, they were adding to the large population of detained Kikuyu who were gradually being rehabilitated in a network of camps scattered throughout the colony. The government's intention was to rehabilitate as many of the 80,000 as they could, feeding them back into their districts on an intensive basis of supervision and probation. There would always remain the 'hard core' of what were considered to be irreconcilables, who would have to remain in exile for the foreseeable future; and for them the government prepared agricultural settlements far removed from civilisation, where they would eventually be joined by their families. One of the earliest sites chosen for this scheme, which was expected to have to accommodate anything up to about 12,000 Kikuyu (the numbers later came down quite sharply) was Hola camp, of later notoriety.

But the main element of the second prong was, without doubt, the total revolution which occurred in Kikuyu living and working habits as a result of the emergency. At the start of the emergency the Kikuyu tribe did not live in villages but were scattered in small family groups throughout the reserve, with their huts surrounded by agricultural land on which each tribesman farmed – sometimes as many as 20 or 30 different strips. There was no local community in the social sense, nor any local services such as water, lighting or communications. The state of Kikuyu agriculture was poor, and suffered acutely from overpopulation overstocking, soil erosion and the usual damage from primitive agrarian habits. When the rebellion broke out it soon became clear to the Kenya government that security would be much improved if the Kikuyu could be collected into protected villages, as had been done with great success in the Malayan emergency. It soon also became clear that this would provide an ideal opportunity to eliminate the fragmentation of the land tenure system which had bedevilled Kikuyu agricultural production but which in normal circumstances could not have been changed without much upheaval and years of tribal unrest.

It was on this basis that the 'Swynnerton Plan' was formed. Roger Swynnerton was an official in the Department of Agriculture. His radical ideas for African agriculture first surfaced in a memorandum written in 1951, and formed the basis for his department's submission to the East African Royal Commission on Land early in 1953. The vast potential of African agriculture had come to be perceived when material was being prepared for the Royal Commission, which showed that, given a chance to consolidate, there were in the African areas as many acres of potential land for all the lucrative cash crops like coffee, tea, sisal and pyrethrum, as there were already under cultivation by European settlers, who until then had held the monopoly. The objective was to create family holdings which would be large enough to keep the family self-sufficient in food, and also enable them to practise alternate husbandry and thus develop a cash income. The agriculture department was always ready to face up to the prospect of considerable displacement of families as a result of these measures, though for that very reason its ideas were not so popular with the provincial administration. So it was only when Evelyn and his Finance Minister were able to get money from the British exchequer, and use the excuse that it should form part of the grand strategy against Mau Mau – the second prong – that the plan showed any sign of being adopted. In spite of the efforts of his most able Finance Minister, Ernest Vasey, however, they only managed to obtain a grant of £5m. for African agricultural development, and none for their programme of expansion in African education. This formed the basis of the Swynnerton Plan.

There was obviously a danger, since all this money was going to be concentrated on the Kikuyu, that the other tribes would interpret it as being a reward which could only be won by rebelling like the Mau Mau had. In fact, on a strictly agricultural criterion, the plan was similar to the World Bank plan for African agricultural development, which had as its first rule that one must choose an area of good agricultural potential. The Kikuyu area was the most fertile in Kenya; so the Kikuyu area would probably have been chosen anyway. But of course there were also political advantages in being able to choose this tribe and overturn its hallowed practices under the guise of emergency procedures. The danger of souring the other tribes was foreseen by Evelyn, who made certain that land consolidation was also introduced elsewhere before the increased prosperity of the

Kikuyu farmers came to be wrongly interpreted as being a by-product of the rebellion.

In drawing up his plan Swynnerton assumed that twenty years would be needed before consolidation would be complete. However, the pressure of the emergency, the infusion of funds, the short-circuiting of traditional African administrative processes, and above all Evelyn's enthusiasm as Governor, enabled the scheme to be pushed through with unprecedented speed. By the time Evelyn left Kenya thousands of new holdings had been created, and, according to the Oxford History, by mid-1962 nearly 300,000 farms had been consolidated and enlarged, covering some 2.4 million acres and amounting to slightly more than half the high-potential land in the African areas.

The Swynnerton Plan inspired Evelyn more than anything he had had to cope with since he arrived in the colony. Now at least he was tackling problems which were familiar to him but were also central to his whole philosophy of life as a creative imperial administrator. On his return from London in mid-1955 he enthused about the fact that for the first time his discussions in Whitehall had dealt with the practicalities of reconstruction and not about military matters. The next stage of the plan, having organised the redistribution and consolidation, was to raise enough capital to ensure that the new small holders got off to a flying start in their voyage into the deep waters of a cash economy. The resources needed were far beyond anything Evelyn could expect from the British treasury.

In 1956 he was writing to Lennox-Boyd; 'A very important event is the success of land consolidation. We must give ourselves plenty of time before the final title registered by the Registrar of Titles is issued. We are going over from the well known world of tribal ownership to the little known world of peasant ownership, and few people in Kenya understand the troubles and dangers of a population of landowning peasants.'[1] There were important questions as yet unresolved, as over the merits of long leaseholds or freeholds, and what should be the minimum subdivision allowed full title. But within three years, he predicted, that they would be in a position to take the irrevocable step of issuing permanent title for the first time to some Kikuyu farmers. It was to be a revolution indeed.

After consolidation there was no time to lose in which to organise efficient farming. To show the necessary dividend, Evelyn calculated that he had about 18 months between 1957 and 1959 in which to get it established. Phase one of the Swynnerton plan had cost £7 million of which the British government agreed to provide £5 million as a grant. Most of this money went into communal capital projects. But, towards the end of Evelyn's time, there was a considerable demand for more investment by individual farmers on their new holdings. However, until they achieved freehold title to their plots, which was not to be until 1959, neither the Land Bank nor commercial banks were very ready to lend money to African farmers. Some other source of captial had to be found.

It was here that Evelyn's old training in banking, the many contacts he had made and maintained from those days and his sessions in the Economic Department of the wartime Foreign Office, now came into their own. In October, 1958, he wrote to Eugene Black, Chairman of the World Bank.[2] His letter is really the foundation document for Kenya's agricultural prosperity during the 1960s and 1970s. 'Land consolidation has changed the face of the countryside and enormously increased the intensity of farming. Now on all sides the main demand is for rural credit. If we can lend a man with his new holding sufficient money to establish a farm of a pattern suitable to the locality, he should do very well. He will need a cash crop on the higher altitudes of tea or pyrethrum, middle altitudes coffee, and lower ones a range of other crops like pineapples. He must also be able to buy good stock such as Gurnseys.' He went on to say a major loan was now essential, since it could be tied to moves to exploit the process of consolidation, as well as further measures for soil conservation on the new plots, and good farming practice such as crop rotation. He asked Black to discuss the subject in full with Vasey who was shortly to visit Washington. They needed nearly £4 million over 10 years, which nowadays sounds a small sum but was then a major undertaking for a small exchequer like Kenya's.

With African land and agriculture moving so fast out of the tribal and subsistence context into a phase of intensive and profitable farming, Evelyn was presented with an opportunity to tackle the question of European farming land as well. It was a highly emotive one, which he tactfully left until the main strains of the emergency were well behind him. It may seem petty at this distance of time, but in the Kenya of the 1950s every inch towards normal agricultural relations between white and black had to be laboriously travelled. It was not just that the scale of operations was so different, but a wholly different culture lay behind the two farming communities, and an entrenched legacy of mutual suspicion.

The advances in African agriculture, and in particular the decision to grant Africans freehold units, led to some pressure from Europeans for similar land security. All land in the White Highlands was still Crown land on long leases. Since 1915 most agricultural land leased by the Crown to Europeans in the White Highlands had been on a 999 year lease. Although there was no absolute bar to non-European races buying into the area, it was effectively prevented by the fact that all dispositions had to be considered by a Highland Board on which sat a permanent majority of settlers' elected representatives. Evelyn was reluctant to force through African land tenure in the area by overruling the Highlands Board in a way which would enable the settlers to say that, without any formal statement of government policy, he had by-passed the 1923 Devonshire White Paper on the settlers position, and also the 1939 order-in-Council which had given the Highlands Board its entrenched powers and its sitting majority.

The white farmers had done very well during the war, when demand for their products – cereals, wheat and dairy – had resulted in a great expansion. Their importance economically was demonstrated by the network of commodity boards which were predominantly governed by the settlers themselves. They had an important influence on the policies of the colonial government, which lead to the not unnatural conclusion by Africans and other observers, that Kenya had a white farmer's government in fact if not in name. The prosperous conditions led also to an increase in European settlement immediately after the war. Evelyn saw a chance to exploit the approach from the settler community by offering to trade their own greater security for some concessions which he hoped would lead to more flexible use of land in the White Highlands, with both Asians and Africans being free to buy into the area if they showed they were up to the required farming standards – a proposal which would have been political dynamite with the settler community only a few years previously. He tried hard to synchronise the operation, since he was determined to push ahead with the granting of African freeholds during the 1959 legislative session. His plan was to see that Europeans on farms in the Highlands were also granted freeholds. He anticipated some criticism from African quarters about this but felt that the African freehold plan gave him an adequate answer to such criticism. He warned Lennox-Boyd that he was tackling a very stormy and important issue.[3]

Over the months the positions of each side gradually took shape, with the prospect of a freehold becoming available to both races in exchange for more flexible control of the European areas. In early 1959 these positions had been mutually agreed by whites and blacks. Then came a set back. Evelyn wrote to Lennox-Boyd, 'This was a very satisfactory result and I was about to put it to the Council of Ministers. A bombshell was however now burst. Blundell's resignation has split the European elected members' organisation and a small group of European extremists are seeking a stick to beat him with. By far the best for this purpose is land.'[4] Blundell had resigned to form a new multiracial party and the effect his move had on Evelyn's delicate manoeuvring was to postpone the whole plan for several months. In the meantime Evelyn pressed ahead with his plans for African freehold, and at an emotional occasion in August, 1959, he visited a massively-attended Kikuyu meeting at Kandara, the scene of his first visit to the Kikuyu reserve in October, 1952, and there presented title-deeds to freehold land – the first ever in Kenya to black *or* white – to 20 Kikuyu farmers.

The conclusive White Paper on Evelyn's discussions did not eventually appear until after he had left the colony, and it was soon overtaken by the acceleration towards full independence which occurred between 1960 and 1963. However, before he left he had re-established a new land policy for Kenya, its first fundamental change for over thirty years, which was based on the principle of the progressive disappearance of racial land barriers. Its real objective was to provide good land in the Highlands for the outstanding African farmers who were beginning to emerge from among the Kikuyu as a result of the success of consolidation within the reserve. He wanted to avoid a situation where those farmers, denied access to a wider area, would be drawn into buying out their less enterprising neighbours in the reserve and thus depriving more Kikuyu than was necessary of a little plot they could call their own. The effect of consolidation had already been to deprive a number of Kikuyu of their strip. Though this meant that there would be employment for them working for small holders, and that they would all benefit from the twofold or even threefold increase in cultivated acreage and the ensuing profits from cash crops, it was obviously not something Evelyn wanted to be taken to extremes.

Evelyn found that land roused deeper feelings in Kenya than any other question – much deeper than constitutional change. 'It is intensely difficult and bedevilled by memories of old struggles,' he told the Colonial Office. In a closing letter in August, 1959, he described how his land reforms had developed, and explained that he believed that 'only the existence of a considerable settled European and Asian community can provide the Africans with the standard of living to which they have become accustomed. I believe that the Europeans must make up their minds to a, I hope gradual, loss of much of their political power . . . Coffee and tea is now grown by Africans though both were originally opposed by Europeans. Now Africans win all the prizes at shows.'[5]

So his contribution over these years was to take an agricultural sector dominated both politically and economically by the highly successful white settlers, accustomed to at least two generations of agricultural hegemony, and within six years to create conditions in which that hegemony has been neutralised by the rise of an equally successful African farmer class growing all the high cash crops which had hitherto been the monopoly of the European. In political terms this was less noticeable than the to-ings and fro-ings associated with constitutional reform, but it was an underlying revolution of far greater consequence. It ensured that there were economic and social conditions which could absorb the great constitutional changes thrust upon Kenya in the four years leading up to independence in 1963. There is an interesting suggestion in the Oxford History that the reason the Kenya government under Evelyn was so insensitive to the changing mood of African politics, was that it was preoccupied with the administrative problems of engineering these great social changes. The administrators wanted time to allow such very important changes to take place without 'the buffetings of political debate'.[6] Indeed, it can be argued that the changes in land, as Evelyn said in his letter, were so much more important than constitutional development that he deliberately accorded constitutional matters a lower priority, confident that if he could achieve the former, the latter would take care of itself, though probably not in his time.

There was clearly something of enlightened self-interest at work here. Although Evelyn's diplomatic qualities have often been extolled, he was not at his best when negotiating the surrender of imperial power, whereas he clearly *was* at his best as the trailblazer of an African agrarian revolution. As the *Oxford History* put it, 'The emergency gave scope to the economic and financial vision of two men – Sir Evelyn Baring and Ernest Vasey – to whom Kenya owed much of the economic stability and growth which prevailed even through the darkest days of violence and tension and which lasted up to the Lancaster House Conference of January, 1960, when independence was promised for the first time. Baring seized on the opportunity presented by a country on a war footing to foster a profound transformation of a traditional colonial administration into one that became interventionist, sponsoring change and reform, actively concerned with economic development. It was Kenya's fortune to have as a governor a man with a real interest in and understanding of economic policy.'[7] This view was very different to that held by his non-economist critics in the armed forces and the administration.

CHAPTER XXVII

Cabinet Making

Although Evelyn may have found land reform more absorbing, rewarding, and ultimately more important than constitutional questions, he was to be involved in reforming Kenya's constitution virtually from the moment he arrived. As Chief Executive Officer of a colony, he had never before had to deal at one and the same time with a combination of elective politics and colonial administration. Whereas in Rhodesia he always dealt through Huggins, and in Southern Africa through his Resident Commissioners, in Kenya there was no alternative to direct contact with the leading politicians. They came to him because there was nobody else in the colony's government who was in any sense responsible for political matters.

When Evelyn arrived in Kenya, the colony's constitution was based on the principle that, though there had to be a colonial-style government – in essence an administrative dictatorship – the settlers' economic influence was so considerable, and their taxes so predominant in the Kenyan revenue, that they were entitled to some kind of constitutional representation. Hence a white electorate voted for members of a Legislative Council (Legco), where the settlers in effect performed the role of official opposition to a government consisting of colonial office servants nominated to Legco as ministers.

The official position on Kenya's constitutional future had been laid down in December, 1950, by James Griffiths, the Colonial Secretary, when he announced plans to grant independence to the Gold Coast in West Africa. 'Our objective [in Kenya] is self-government within the commonwealth, which must include proper provision for all the main communities which have made their homes in East Africa, but in the long run their security and well being must rest on their good relations with each other.' It would be some time before Africans could be helped to reach a stage where they could play their full part in the political and economic life of the East African territories, he said, and in the meantime the British government would continue to exercise its ultimate control.

The Legislative Council which had been set up at the time of the Devonshire Declaration consisted of European and Asian elected members and a balancing number of ex-officio nominated members, including a European nominated to represent African interests. This pattern remained unchanged until 1944, when a Balliol-educated Kikuyu, Mr Eliad Mathu, was appointed to replace one of the Europeans representing African interests. He was followed by a second African in 1946. In 1948 the composition of the Legislative Council was increased by four more Africans, so that an 'unofficial' majority was created, leaving the government permanently in a minority. This was a situation which Evelyn later described as 'admirably designed to produce a timid government and an irresponsible opposition.'[1] He was determined to bring it to an end as soon as he could.

The system of ministerial responsibility had also developed slightly. First of all, in 1946, the membership system was introduced. At that stage all the members were colonial officials; but in 1950 two European elected members, Ernest Vasey and Ferdinand Cavendish-Bentinck, resigned their elected seats and accepted portfolios as members. They came from opposite poles of the political spectrum and were the first two settlers with whom Evelyn had official dealings within the Governor's Council of Ministers.

After Evelyn had been in the colony a year – admittedly a year which had been almost exclusively occupied by military matters – he wrote to Lyttelton:[2]

The Europeans of Kenya have made this country; they also make most of the trouble [an interesting thought coming from a man in the middle of coping with Mau Mau;]. If the population ratio here was the same as Southern Rhodesia there would have been a purely white government in power long ago. If the Europeans were as outnumbered as they are in Tanganyika, an ordinary colonial government could and should have continued. Kenya is between two stools. It is and will remain an exceptionally explosive country. To Africans land grievances are the most bitter of all. The European population has small farmers as the strongest political element. It is the type resented most of all by the Africans. They give a greater appearance of permanency than the larger planter who may move capital elsewhere. Therefore the African feeling is sharper than it will ever be in Uganda or Tanganyika. But the European population is sufficiently small and isolated to make its expulsion a possibility – unlike South Africa and Southern Rhodesia. In these circumstances of unique difficulty an increase of trust and an improvement in relations between different peoples of Kenya is a crying need of the country and not a remote ideal. It won't come with things as they are now.

It is conceivable that a real explanation of the oddities of Kenya Europeans lies in life at high altitude under a tropical sun; in this case white settlement is doomed. But much more probably it lies simply in the bad effect on people of British origin of being debarred from taking part in the responsibility of government, therefore the way to improve relations is the sharing of responsibility. If men of different races take executive positions in government they will be compelled to work together. My conclusion is that a chance of real improvement lies in the executive branch rather than the legislative or electoral system. Europeans must be first members of that government, first with Asians and later Africans. Glad you share this view.'

The government could now become more a mixture of civil servants and elected members who would remain in their elected seats, without having to become nominated. Non-Europeans could only at present be Asian, and he had heard – presumably through Vasey – that the Asians were happy about such a plan. So he proposed to Lyttelton that they should add six more people to the government, consisting of three elected Europeans, two Asians – a Hindu and a Muslim – and one Arab. 'I do not believe we will ever create an African moderates' party as a separate entity, but I do believe that African moderates might join a moderate party of all races.'[3] There should be no change in the racial composition of the Legco and no common roll. The development should be seen as a constitutional advance to enable unofficial members of Legco to take a bigger part in *executive* acts of government, and so start educating their electorate in the responsibilities and limits of power.

Lyttelton came out in February, 1954. It took ten days of really hard pressure before he was able to secure the agreement of all three races to the new ministerial structure, which was known therefter as the Lyttelton constitution. It worked out virtually as Evelyn had advised, with six new 'unofficial' members of the government and another five under secretaries. Lyttelton laid down that the constitution was to last until the next Kenya general election, which was to take place six months after the Governor had declared an end to the state of emergency. Its successful launch was probably due to the compressive effect of

Lyttelton's short visit, as well as his greater political clout. He had a very brutal way of doing things, in contrast to Evelyn's more ruminative and cautious political technique. Evelyn was the first to acknowledge Lyttelton's superior expertise in this field. The visit was full of the usual political rituals, with secret cabals, categorical positions defended and then yielded overnight, urgent messages coming out of meetings, late night confrontations, and all parties apparently refusing to contemplate a package which was not finally settled until the last minute before Lyttelton flew away.

One other conclusion drawn by the settler community was that Evelyn and Lyttelton got on well together. This realization slightly softened their desire for a military-style governor to replace him. They felt Evelyn was hand-picked by the Tory government, and they had been warned by Lyttelton that the next British election could easily come soon, and that an incoming Labour government would not be likely to replace a military governor with a constitution that would be at all to their liking. Evelyn and Lyttelton followed up this argument by pointing out that a future Labour Colonial Secretary would on the other hand have difficulty in making further constitutional changes which were not acceptable to a Kenya government with ministers from three races working in harmony.

The Lyttelton constitution introduced into the Kenyan polity the idea of locally elected ministers from the European and Asian communities. The next stage, after the emergency cooled off, would clearly have to be to introduce an elected *African* element into the Legislative Council, where the Africans at present were all nominated. But first the principle had to be tried without African participation because Evelyn felt that the priority at that stage was to infiltrate the settler community into the responsibilities of government. This was not in order to give them sole power but because, unless they were already accustomed to such responsibility, it would be too late to incorporate them in government once an African element was established. There would then be no chance of achieving his vision of a multi-racial government.

The successful introduction of the 1954 Lyttelton constitution concluded some strenuous political discussions at which Evelyn had been working for more than a year – virtually from the time he arrived. He was sure that it was in a sense the last chance to give the European element some continuing position in Kenya politics. Unlike many of the settlers, the effect of the emergency had not been to convince him of their right to rule the colony, and of the need to postpone, if not prevent, the arrival of a black majority. On the contrary, it had convinced him that things could never revert to what they had been before the emergency, and that he had to initiate a process which he hoped would culminate in a genuinely multi-racial polity within a self-governing colony. If the Europeans were not prepared to go along with that, then that would be their misfortune. In the end, Kenya developed in a different way. But if the outside world, and the will of the British government, had allowed a longer transition for Kenya than that which was eventually given it – independence only eleven years after the outbreak of Mau Mau – it is not inconceivable that Evelyn's hopes of a multi-racial political establishment would have been achieved.

Lyttelton's visit came at a most critical time, and must have helped to crystallise the minds of many white politicians. It was the culmination of a period of rising settler dissatisfaction with Evelyn, brought to a head by the disclosure of the first surrender offer. That had even provoked Michael Blundell, the most liberal of the settlers, into saying that everyone in the country would now be forced to believe that the Governor and his officers had themselves taken the Mau Mau oath (he repented and recanted a few hours afterwards). The offer forced the settlers to look at the future and realize that, when the emergency was over, the government was going to be paying much more attention to the Africans than hitherto, and not just the question of their administrative rehabilitation. It was clear that if the government was prepared to approach the question of Mau Mau rehabilitation and reconstruction with such seriousness then it was going to adopt a similar attitude to black questions on a much wider scale. After fifty years political monopoly, the days of the lone European voice in Kenyan affairs were effectively over. Of course this realization only percolated slowly through the small, volatile and immensely vocal settler community, and on the whole, when it did, it was not well received.

The Lyttelton ministerial structure was charged with a certain degree of mutual suspicion, both between the different communities represented there, and within them. Evelyn's chief helper in the indoctrination of the Europeans was Michael Blundell, just as his chief helper providing a bridge to the Asians, and later to the African politicians, was Ernest Vasey. They very effectively balanced each other in Evelyn's highest councils. Blundell was always under fire from the harder line Europeans. Consequently he had a tendency to exaggerate his influence within the government and even to make speeches recommending initiatives which he knew were coming anyway. He was almost immediately under attack for agreeing to the Lyttelton constitution and an anti-Blundell faction was soon formed by the settlers. They accused him of selling out to Africans and Asians in order to achieve office for himself. Vasey, a financial wizard who was an object of even greater suspicion to the settlers, cut a different figure to the emotional and rather baroque image of Blundell. He was mouse-like in demeanour, but imbued with an irrepressible taste for intrigue, for phantom resignations – and sometimes real ones – which occurred with unceasing regularity throughout Evelyn's seven years.

Vasey had come out on a holiday to Kenya in 1935, and had stayed on as a cinema proprietor, becoming Mayor of Nairobi in 1941. His origins were humble; he had no formal education, as both his parents had been on the stage, and he too had played occasional parts. His attitude to the other races in Kenya, and his advocacy of bringing Africans into responsible offices, did not endear him to the rural settlers. Vasey and Evelyn hit it off almost immediately in the complicated world of high finance which they inhabited while struggling with Kenya's economy.

Yet they were a complete contrast – on the one hand the tall, aristocratic, slow moving and deliberate Governor; on the other the mouselike, insecure Finance Minister, overcomplicating politics with the speed of his reactions and the hypersensitivity of his intrigues. Vasey was deeply unpopular with the settlers for making a series of speeches in the still dark days of September, 1953, advocating a common electoral roll to be introduced by 1959. He was only a few years out in his calculation, and took violent issue with some other European members who thought that independence would still be fifty years away. He had offered to resign many times; then he would withdraw his resignation on the grounds that 'the Africans and Asians might be upset' if a liberal minister – perhaps the only liberal minister – resigned. But he was always useful to Evelyn, because in spite of his volatility he was a convenient bridge – though not the only one – between the Governor, and, in particular, the Asian leaders. Whatever their differences, both Blundell and Vasey were united in their devotion to Evelyn. In his autobiography Blundell wrote that Evelyn was one of the most complex personalities he had ever met. 'His patience reinforced a natural tendency to postpone decisions; and I found by experience that a view must be presented constantly, almost daily, if it was to prevail over other ideas. He did not like giving orders.

'He was also a great listener; but every now and then he would slowly start to give his own views on a situation. The words would gather speed; hardly a pause would occur between sentences; any interruption would be disregarded and out would come a remarkable, far sighted, slightly disjointed, slightly repetitive analyses of the scene, with the short and long term measures to be taken.'

Blundell found that some of his colleagues who did not see Evelyn as much as he did were suspicious or antagonistic and would instruct him to speak firmly to the Governor. 'They did not realize that often this immediately made Baring conscious of his prerogative as the Governor, the chief executive in the colony to whom everyone else was advisory. Once this happened, no amount of argument would prevail; he would state his position almost bluntly, and, as far as I was concerned, the day was lost.'[4]

When Evelyn arrived back from his long sick leave in the summer of 1954 he soon found that Lyttelton would not be there to help steer their new constitution into calmer waters. Lyttelton's successor was Alan Lennox-Boyd, who had been his deputy when Evelyn had been selected for the job three years earlier, and had been a long standing, if not very close friend of Evelyn's since Oxford days. He came out to Kenya almost immediately. Evelyn found him a very different character to Lyttelton. The directness was not there. He felt the new Colonial Secretary had a dispersed mind and did not relish bouts of intense concentration of the kind which Evelyn had shared with Lyttelton. Their methods were very different; Lennox-Boyd's technique being more impressionistic, based on continuous personal contacts without much intellectual analysis. But though he may not have been quite what Evelyn wanted as a ministerial chief in an emergency, their relationship prospered over the following four years.

CHAPTER XXVIII
High Politics

In April, 1955, Evelyn sent Lennox-Boyd one of his regular progress reports on Kenyan political developments.

'The government continues to work well and the elected members find little difficulty in reaching agreement. At times there were violent flare ups, nearly always round one of the two nominated official ministers. We face two dangers: 1. cb's [Cavendish–Bentinck] continued refusals to accept the idea of the multiracial government. He makes less trouble, all the same I am convinced that he must leave the govt. [Evelyn offered him the Speakership soon afterwards] 2. The other danger is the rivalry of Blundell and Vasey. Blundell symbolises the mixed government with European leadership. Vasey, with no constituency, but a very able lobbyist, symbolises the idea of the governmental machine with the three races having equal representation. The Europeans are not used to the idea that an elected man (previously automatically the opposition) can also be a minister. Blundell himself is a success but there are few others with such knowledgeable constituencies. I hope that the government won't collapse from internal causes before 1960 [the date they then expected to change the constitution] but Vasey might resign.'

With the ending of military operations in November, 1956, however, it was clear that the Lyttelton constitution could not last another four years without some modification to accommodate rising African political aspirations. Moreover, as Evelyn had reported the year earlier, in spite of the pressures and tensions of quasi-ministerial government, the experiment had started to educate the European and Asian communities in the disciplines of more political responsibility. The time had arrived when this machinery had to be expanded to include Africans, now that the Mau Mau situation had changed from military operations to one concerned with the residual rehabilitation of the few thousand remaining detainees.

In the month that military operations ceased, a new black face started to obtrude upon the Kenya political scene. Until then Kenyans had been deprived of black leadership on account of the incarceration of most of the leading Kikuyu, and the natural reluctance of those allowed free to usurp the position of their imprisoned fellows. Tom Mboya was neither of that generation, nor a member of the Kikuyu tribe, but a Luo from the Nyanza Province. He thus had fewer such inhibitions. He returned home in October 1956 after a successful 13-month tour of America and Britain where he attracted much attention in the Labour Party and among trade union leaders. He had learnt that in the conditions prevailing in Kenya at that time his most promising route to power was through the trade union movement. He arrived in Kenya to consolidate a power base in the Kenya Federation of Labour (KFL). There, though still only a young man, with his intelligence and his incisive rhetoric he was able to exercise much more political leadership over the African population than would have been available to him within the restricted world of Legco.

Mboya actually joined Legco in March, 1957, but this did not cramp his style or his opposition. In April Evelyn wrote Molly a gloomy letter telling her that politics looked lousy and doubting whether he could hold the Asian ministers in his government much longer without conceding some of the Africans' demands. He was going to try a mixed dinner party the next night which included Mboya and some Europeans. It obviously went badly. 'The trouble is Mboya,' he wrote soon afterwards. 'He is the completely indoctrinated man. A large section of the Labour Party, larger perhaps than I originally thought, regard him as their instrument to obtain within quite a few years a pure black state in Kenya. They may differ on the speed of attainment but they all believe in this and not in the mixed state. He himself speaks very well in Legco and partly by persuasion and partly by threats holds his people together. He will not cooperate and tries to force our hand going often for advice to the fountainhead in the UK. He sees himself as the Kenya Nkrumah [then leading Ghana to independence] and is only just 27. One day he might be brought round but at present he is pretty sinister and evil. He has certainly in 6 weeks changed the whole feel of the country.'[2]

Evelyn became exasperated by Mboya's attempts to dissuade the Luo from accepting land consolidation along the lines successfully introduced with the Kikuyu. He sought permission from Lennox-Boyd to introduce restrictions on the number and scale of Mboya's public meetings. 'We won't have it. It is quite like old days,' he told Molly, after one meeting in Kisumu where Mboya had appealed to racial feelings and had derided the police and all other Africans in government service. 'World conditions after

Suez are much more against us than they were then, but our 1957
team is worth ten of the 1952 bunch.'³ He felt Mboya was trying
to bring to a halt the Kikuyu rehabilitation programme which
was something Evelyn particularly cherished, and which he regarded as essential to the next stage of Kenya's development. 'We
know that his main advice and contact is with Mrs Castle and the
Bevanites (not unfortunately with the Communists). We have also
reason to believe he is in constant touch with the executive of the
Labour Party. This is his own claim. Well we must fight him, he
is intensely arrogant, a lapsed RC with the morals of a monkey.'⁴

Throughout the summer of 1957 Evelyn was intensively engaged in the redrafting of the constitution. The key to it was his
plan to increase African elected representation in Legco and, he
hoped, in government, along lines similar to what he had achieved
for the whites and the Asians. Vasey was for it, Blundell and
some of his more moderate colleagues were for it, but both the
Africans and more entrenched Europeans were against it. Mboya
was holding to a plan for independence in 10 years, and he would
have preferred an entirely nominated Colonial Office government without the issue being confused, and therefore potentially
delayed, by the quasi-democratic trappings of elected ministers
from the different ethnic communities. However he was not finding it easy to persuade some of his African colleagues to support
this view in the face of their own desire for an increase in their
share of government then and there.

By September, 1957, after some weeks spent in London seeing
most of the Kenyan politicians he could have seen far more easily
– though less discreetly – in Nairobi, Evelyn wrote to the Colonial
Office with his thoughts on the coming constitutional talks. He
said that the background was very different to March 1954 when
the fear of civil war drove most politicians of all groups toward
an agreement.

'Events in the outside world have gone against the true Kenya
moderate who hopes for a mixed government and is in favour
of the maximum cooperation between the communities. It is
increasingly clear to those with eyes to see that Kenya may go
down one of two roads. One is that of the common approach, a
mixed government and the gradual discovery by all groups in
Kenya of how to live together in one country. The other road
is development over a fixed period towards an independent
African state, though the words used will be an undiluted
democracy. The test of conclusions for our coming talks should

be whether they assist the country to move down the first, or help to hold the country back from moving down the second road.'⁵

Their aim was to persuade a number of moderate Africans to join the government, in exchange for an increase in the number of directly elected common-roll seats, which would obviously return African members.

Lennox-Boyd had been ill, and there had been some question of his not coming out to East Africa at that time. Evelyn and Molly were hoping for a long holiday in England but they did not want to leave without reaching a new political agreement and they were relieved when Lennox-Boyd actually arrived, after a short visit to Uganda which he had set on the road to progressive self-government. The situation he found in Kenya was not very promising, in spite of the many months of exhausting and exhaustive preparatory discussions which had been held by Evelyn. All sides had committed themselves to an entrenched position in advance of the talks.

Lennox-Boyd's first task was to convince Mboya that there was no hope of Kenya going the same way as the Gold Coast/Ghana. The British government's view was that there would be a mixed constitution in Kenya for a long time ahead, and his arguments therefore were that it would be better for the brightest young African politicians to join in and help to make it work. Mboya held out for an increase in African representation, particularly through common roll seats, rather than the monoracial seats for which they had been elected hitherto. There were some intensive discussions between the African and European elected ministers, when it looked for a moment as though Blundell and one or two of his colleagues had devised a formula which would have enabled the African members to agree to a new package giving them some extra seats, though not so many as they had demanded. But, in a manner only too consistent with the hysterical nature of Kenyan politics, the plan leaked, there were European recriminations and repudiations, and Lennox-Boyd returned to London empty-handed. In fact his departure was in some sense a calculated one, since Evelyn and he were hoping that there would continue to be such an impasse in Kenya that the Secretary of State could then, under his existing powers, revoke the Lyttelton constitution on the grounds that it had become unworkable. This done, he would be able to substitute a new one of his own – having also, by then, prepared the ground with his Labour opponents at Westminster.

That is basically what happened, except that after a few more weeks of frustrating and nerve-racking discussions the European and Asian ministers resigned of their own accord. This gave Lennox-Boyd a useful excuse to bring the Lyttelton constitution to an end and usher in the Lennox-Boyd constitution, which allowed for another fifteen seats for Africans, eleven of which were for an Africans-only electorate and four on a common roll.

The new constitution was due to last out Evelyn's time in the colony; indeed it continued until a constitutional conference in January, 1960. It was clearly intended to provide enough concessions to African political demands to deter an incoming Labour government from tearing it up straight away. After Lennox-Boyd left Nairobi he spent the following few weeks securing tacit agreement from the Opposition, so that his constitution had a fair chance of lasting over an election and the change of government in Britain which both he, and Evelyn, seemed to expect as its most likely outcome. Evelyn now had a Legislative Council amounting to nearly eighty members, and political life in Kenya started to acquire a full-dress flavour with the first elections promised for March, 1958.

Evelyn's last two years of office saw him fully and constantly engaged in the business of high politics in the colony. There was always an undercurrent of instability about the 1957 constitution. It was essentially temporary – and everybody knew it to be so. Kenya had not yet come to a stable point along the journey of constitutional development which had started in 1954 – perhaps in the context of the rising African nationalism of the 1950s there could never be such stability anyway. There was clearly no turning back to the old colonial structure. Yet could there really be only one way forward – the way of the Gold Coast into Ghana, of Tanganyika and Uganda near at hand? Or was there anything to be learnt from the experiment in the Central African Federation further south, where it fleetingly appeared that the old ideas of amalgamation had at last born fruit?

At this point it may be worth analysing exactly what was the British government's long term policy for Kenya and whether it accorded with Evelyn's own private views. Evelyn had a vision for Kenya which he knew would need time to be achieved. Before his final departure, often delayed and eventually fixed for September, 1959, he hoped to create the general conditions which would be conducive to a mixed economy and a multi-racial society. In this he was largely successful – certainly in economic and social

terms – but it cannot be said that, when he left, he had successfully won over the African political leadership to an active part
in governing the country. There was still too much suspicion; and
the temporary nature of the Lennox-Boyd constitution plus the
success of African nationalism elsewhere meant that it was not
until independence had been promised at the 1960 Lancaster
House Conference that African politics in Kenya really started to
flourish. Even after that date the political atmosphere of the
colony suffered from the unfinished business of the Mau Mau –
particularly the incarceration of Jomo Kenyatta, which Evelyn
rather belatedly recognised was going to outlive his time.

These influences were not conducive to political stability, but
Evelyn persevered nonetheless with his vision of a future multi-
racial polity of Kenya. It was this vision which shaped his attitude
to the colony's evolving constitutional status, and to the restless
politicking which continued under the Lennox-Boyd constitution.

The general attitude of the British government towards Kenya's
future seemed to remain unchanged through most of 1959, until
shortly after the Conservatives won the general election in
October. The changeover was then so swift and so complete that
it is hard as an outsider to believe that Evelyn can have been
unaware of its likelihood. Was it really so unexpected? It would
certainly appear so. He toured the settler areas during May 1959
and made many speeches to reassure the European farmers that
they had no need to worry about the future: Kenya was not going
to become independent in the same time scale as were the neighbouring colonies of Uganda and Tanganyika. He told them that
the British government had completed a comprehensive review of
East African strategy, and had concluded that Kenya would be
what he called a 'fortress colony' containing a British army base
which was essential to Britain's global defence network. The
settlers absorbed these views as though from the horse's mouth –
as well they might have done.

Imagine their horror therefore when, barely eight months later,
Ian Macleod, the next Conservative Colonial Secretary, promised
Kenya's African nationalist politicians that there would be independence under black majority rule within three years. A sense of
betrayal and shock ran through the white community. It jeopardised the economic and administrative structure which Evelyn
had nursed back into life and health after the emergency. Luckily
for the future of independent Kenya, that structure withstood the

instability of 1960–1963; but who can blame the settlers for thinking then that Evelyn had deceived them?

The 'sea-change' which occurred in British colonial policy in East Africa occurred in the mind of Harold Macmillan, the Prime Minister, sometime during 1959; but it was apparently never imparted to Lennox-Boyd, who stayed on as Colonial Secretary until the general election. Evelyn never knew of it either, and, in those tours through the White Highlands he was reflecting an attitude agreed only a few months previously at a conference at Chequers, which was attended by Lennox-Boyd, his junior ministers and the Governors of Kenya, Tanganyika, Uganda and Zanzibar. The Governors agreed that the three main British interests involved in Kenya were the military bases essential for British global strategy, the need to ensure that the area remained economically friendly to the west, and the need to secure the area as a stable home for those people of Asian and European stock who over the years had been encouraged to settle there by successive British governments.

'On the assumption that there can be no question of even an independent Kenya, let alone an independent East Africa, under local European political control – an assumption which even Kenya Europeans now seem tacitly to make – it is so long as HMG retain ultimate control that these three interests can be secured for certain and it is not practical for HMG to maintain ultimate control unless that means defence, external relations and law and order,' concluded one of their working papers at Chequers.[6] But such control could not be permanently maintained even for the whole of Kenya, the Governors eventually decided. So they turned to discussing timetables for the approach to independence, and whether or not such a timetable should be made both explicit and public. They finally agreed among themselves that the timetable should be kept approximate, subject to the criterion that law and order must be preserved. On Kenya specifically they agreed that, 'During the next twelve months we may have to go further than we have so far felt able to go. We might have to state the intention of making Kenya independent but only if we were satisfied that independence would be possible without any reduction in the standard of living or any threat to Kenya's developing parliamentary democracy.'[7] At the end of the session it was decided that Tanganyika would get independence first, but not before 1970, while Kenya and Ugandan independence was pencilled in for a date about 1975, though it was clear to the Conservative ministers that neither Baring of Kenya nor Crawford of Uganda were keen for the British government to commit themselves too explicitly to such an idea. One can see how uncommitted Evelyn was by the tone he subsequently adopted in his meetings with the settlers.

This strategic plan for the future strengthened his resolve to encourage the development within Kenya of a genuine multi-racial democracy, if it was not too late already for that to be achieved. Soon after he returned from Chequers he received some help towards that objective when Michael Blundell resigned his ministry and formed the New Kenya Party. The NKP was dedicated to the idea of a multi-racial democracy and was the first Kenyan political party to be open to members of all races. It was a courageous move of Blundell's, earning him no gratitude either from many of the settlers, or from the African nationalist politicians. The latter turned their attack on him all the more strongly, much more fiercely than on the residual white politicians of the old colonial school. Blundell was dangerous to the cause of African nationalism because his vision of a mixed-race all-elected government offered a possible alternative to an early all-African government. In fact, for reasons which were entirely beyond Blundell's control – and Evelyn's for that matter – it was an initiative which came too late. The changing state of the western world and the radical forces at work in the rest of non-British Africa saw to that. However, for the closing months of Evelyn's time in Kenya the existence of the NKP certainly presented everyone, including Evelyn, with an apparently real alternative to mono-racial government, either of the colonial or of the African nationalist variety. Everybody wanted to believe in its chances, because not to do so was to see no real future for the settler in Kenyan politics, and that was something which Evelyn had been striving to avoid throughout his time in the colony.

Some years after he had left Kenya, Evelyn told Michael Blundell that he personally could not have presided over a transfer of power to the African nationalists, as his successors had to do. He left Kenya just in time to avoid this fate, and was probably still unaware of the whirlwind timetable for independence in British Africa which Harold Macmillan was about to unveil, heralded by the appointment of Ian Macleod as his new Colonial Secretary in succession to Alan Lennox-Boyd. However the new message from London cannot have been long in coming after that October election, because before the end of the month Evelyn – by then home – received an unusually gloomy letter from Sir Frederick Crawford, having spent two nights with him in Uganda only a fortnight before. 'It looks to me as though we have "had" Africa' wrote Crawford, 'and nothing remains but the dreary prospect of toning down the more outrageous claims of African nationalists. Perhaps the solution is to declare a timetable for here and Tanganyika, say 1970; do all we can to make them ready between now and then; and then leave the place to the denizens and to the human misery that will result for most of them.'

What had changed from those reasonably confident gradualist days of the Chequers conference earlier in the year, or even from the 'morning-after' euphoria of the Tory election victory of October 1959? It is difficult to get to the source of Harold Macmillan's change of view about British policy in Africa. It is not made explicit in his own autobiography and one can only piece together various influences which are said by his associates to have played their part in convincing him that the wind of change was blowing through the continent – though he did not actually use the phrase until his famous speech in South Africa in January, 1960. The summer and autumn of 1959 had contained a number of events which may have influenced him. There was the row over the atrocities at Hola Camp (which will be dealt with in the next chapter); Macmillan visited de Gaulle and heard that France would be giving up her African empire; then the final blow came in the autumn of 1959 when the Belgians announced suddenly that they were going to grant independence to the Congo in July, 1960, only ten months ahead. The Congo (now Zaire) was the lynch pin of colonial Africa, and in spite of the shambles and misery subsequently caused by the Belgians' speedy departure, the announcement of their decision had by then clinched the future of British Africa.

Evelyn got out just in time. Ironically he was doubly lucky, because, some months before, he had been asked to carry out a task which would have kept him associated for several more years with the gathering British retreat from Africa – and painfully associated too. In April, 1959, Alec Home and Alan Lennox-Boyd had asked him to chair the Commission (which was eventually chaired by Lord Monckton) to look at the future of the Central African Federation, and make recommendations. Evelyn demurred, without actually declining. He told Molly, 'I have pointed out that I am inexperienced and far from impartial. If they press the point I feel I must accept. The future of the Federation is perhaps the

most important thing in Africa, far more important than Kenya.'
Perhaps he was lucky, because a week later he was able to report,
'Alan and Alec were convinced by my arguments and think that I
am much too committed to be chairman. What a relief, I already
have the smell of a northern winter in my nostrils.' Monckton's
report actually condemned the Federation to death, but by then
the march of events in Africa and in London was accelerating too
swiftly for even Evelyn – with all his African stature and experience – to have influenced them in a way which would have
made much difference in the end.

CHAPTER XXIX

Hola

It was sad for Evelyn that he was destined to leave Kenya in September 1959 with a certain amount of unfinished business still arising from the Mau Mau emergency. The most obvious and unfortunate example of this was the atrocity at Hola Camp, where a number of long serving detainees were beaten to death by their guards. But even before then there were other symptoms of the old disease which still throbbed away under the surface calm of Evelyn's last year in the colony. He was involved in a continuous discussion about the future of Jomo Kenyatta, and the question of whether, and if so when, he should be released from detention – a possibility hotly contested by the provincial administration. There were also a number of cases involving individual members of the administration who were under threat of prosecution for misdemeanours associated with the detention camps. These were going to require another act of clemency similar to the one which Evelyn had found so troublesome to arrange at the time of the surrender offers some years before.

First of all in the summer of 1958, there was the question of Kenyatta. It was by then clear to Evelyn that the expansion of the directly elected African representation to Legco was not going to result in the eclipse of Jomo Kenyatta as the major African leader. However hard the government tried to promote the new generation of African politicians, the latter and themselves realized that – whatever their ambitions – while Kenyatta lived, in or out of detention, he was the only truly national leader in the eyes of most Africans in the colony. Of course the key question in the minds of some of Evelyn's officials was whether or not he would live to see freedom. Certainly many of them hoped that he would die in captivity and thus relieve the government of the need to consider his position. As early as 1955 Edward Windley, then Chief Native Commissioner, reported to a friend that he had visited Kenyatta and the few terrorists with him and found the former 'disgustingly well'.[1] Evelyn had also once taken the view that Kenyatta could probably never be allowed back into Kenyan life. He told one visitor in 1954 that in his view Mau Mau would be successfully conquered, but that there were probably 10, 12 or even 15 Mau Mau leaders who would have to be segregated from the rest of humanity for all time.

Towards the end of the mainly successful rehabilitation programme the question of Kenyatta began to crop up in an acute form, and would not go away. The Special Branch believed that African politics would not, indeed could not, settle down until the unknown factor of Kenyatta's continuing influence had been tested in the world outside prison. His name, and his continuing detention were asserting an influence in the reserves which was probably artificial, but could not be proved to be so until he was released. Then he would be faced by a new structure of African politics, which he might find uncongenial after six years of almost complete isolation during which a new generation of politicians had emerged. He should therefore be released. The administration, led by the Chief Secretary, Walter Coutts, were hostile to the idea; and so was Evelyn. He was coming to the end of his time; he was preoccupied with his agricultural and economic plans; he could cope, if with some difficulty and sufference, with the African politicians around him; but he was not prepared to open up a new dimension of unpredictability. Evelyn did not think that Kenyan – and particularly Kikuyu – society was ready to have Kenyatta's release inflicted on it. It would probably come later, to that he seemed to have become gradually resigned since there was no sign of Kenyatta's health deteriorating; but it would come after his time. In the meanwhile, he decided to move Kenyatta's place of detention gradually closer to the Kikuyu reserves.

But the question of Kenyatta was not the only reminder of the darker days of the emergency. On March 3, 1959, when Evelyn and his family were recovering from a highly successful but nonetheless exhausting fourteen day visit of the Queen Mother, 11 Mau Mau detainees at Hola Camp, in the coastal province, were beaten to death and another 81 injured. The prison camp at that time was divided into two, with one part containing 608 convicted prisoners, and the other a 'closed camp' containing 208 of what were known as 'hard core' Mau Mau detainees, men who had not yet responded to the programme of rehabilitation.

Evelyn first heard of trouble at Hola when the Defence Ministry informed him of a message over the prison radio network that five detainees had died, with no further explanation. He immediately decided to send three senior officers down to Hola the following morning from the Prisons, Defence and African Affairs Departments. They were to report back to him the following evening. Next morning, Evelyn was told that the death tally had risen to ten. He decided that no statement could or should be put out until more facts were known as a result of the senior officials' visit. They returned to Nairobi at midday and a meeting at Government House was hurriedly convened with the Chief Government Doctor, Cusack the Minister of Defence, Griffith-Jones the Attorney General, Johnston Minister of African Affairs, and Lewis the Commissioner of Prisons.

It is this meeting, more than any other, which provides the key to Evelyn's part in the affair. Apart from his general responsibility as Governor for the administration of Kenya prisons, once he knew about the killings he also had a particular responsibility, not for the atrocity itself, but for the way it was subsequently handled. In the subsequent enquiry into the Hola disaster it became clear that the three officials who had visited Hola carried out a rather cursory inspection of the camp, spent barely three hours there, and returned to Nairobi with a less than satisfactory account of how ten men had already died. They did not speak to any warders; they did not speak to any detainees; they did not look at any of the dead bodies or at the injured men in the hospital. They heard an account of the incident from the Hola Commandant and his deputy, and were told by the prison doctor that a quarter of those in hospital were 'putting on an act'. One of the dead men had two broken teeth, facial bruises and had died possibly of 'aspiration pneumonia' caused by inhaling regurgitated vomit. There was also the account of the prison deputy commandant who had seen a detainee collapse near a water cart from which he had been drinking. In other words, there was either deliberate concealment of a major atrocity, or else an almost unworldly readiness to believe – in default of any hard medical evidence to the contrary – that the water cart might have had something to do with the deaths and injuries.

That credulity on the part of the Hola staff was apparently shared without much scepticism by the officials during their three hour visit. They returned to Nairobi before lunch and reported to Evelyn at four o'clock that afternoon. During the meeting in Government House there was apparently a good deal of discussion as to whether violence was the cause of death. The three officials gave it as their opinion that the deaths had not been caused by violence – though there was some mention of 'scuffles'. They left Evelyn and his ministers with the strong impression that they thought a possible cause of death was the drinking of large quantities of water in the extreme heat – though it could hardly have been the quality of the water because the camp staff had drunk from the same water cart. Until then Evelyn had been reluctant to make any announcement on the grounds that there was no point in doing so until some further information was available. As a result of the meeting Evelyn authorised a statement about the deaths, which said the men had died after drinking from a water cart, and which made no mention of the fact that there had been any disturbance. Unfortunately, it also omitted any mention of the fact that a police autopsy was to be carried out. However, it soon became clear from the evidence before the official pathologist, even before the dead bodies were returned to Nairobi for extensive post mortems, that there had been considerable violence inflicted on them.

The pathologist's team had a very different and much more gruesome story to tell from that recounted by the three officials. Evelyn prepared for the political storm which was now sure to break out over his head. He warned Lennox-Boyd of the new situation and, ironically, did so just in time to prevent the Colonial Secretary going ahead with an announcement that he was proposing to retire from politics before the next election. Once the Hola affair had blown up he could not do that without it being thought that he was actually resigning on account of it, in fact if not in name. Eight days later, when the autopsies had been completed, another statement was put out saying there was evidence of violence, and that a decision whether or not to hold an enquiry would be taken after the inquest and police investigations. A week later, on March 18, the inquest opened before a senior examining magistrate in Mombasa. It unfolded a sad tale of maladministration, mismanagement, misunderstanding and ineffective control in the prison department.

At the height of the emergency there had been 78,000 Kikuyu detainees, who had gradually been rehabilitated in a complicated and extremely painstaking programme involving three types of detention camp, through which they passed on their way to ultimate release into the reserve under a type of probation supervised by the local District Officer. The basic policy of the government was to do everything to keep detainees travelling down the pipeline towards release in the reserves, but at the same time not to put any pressure on a District Officer to accept a detainee, if the D.O. was against his release. Consequently the programme had to rely on an intimate association between the Prisons Department, who mainly ran the detention centres, and the district administration, which was responsible for the eventual absorption of the detainees back into the reserves. Under their white officers, both staffs were predominantly Kikuyu.

For the 'hard core' detainees whom the authorities felt were unlikely to be reabsorbed into the community – or not for a very long time – a series of work camps were planned which would be located near areas of the bush which had been selected for reclamation and irrigation schemes. With this hard core, the emphasis was likely to be less on rehabilitation and more on hard work. And once it became Prison Department policy to insist on work, a host of difficult questions arose about the use of force on prisoners. If force was to be used, in what circumstances and to what limits?

The enquiry into the Hola atrocity revealed that the Prison Department had developed a new plan which was a modification of longstanding procedures, and which either did not work, had not been properly thought through, or else was distorted by administrative inefficiency and misunderstanding. The new plan was called the 'Cowan Plan' after the official in the Prison Department who had refined it. Departmental discussion of the plan had made it clear that not everybody was happy about it, that it would probably lead to violence, and that, before it acquired any formal authority, it should be submitted not just to the Ministers of Defence and African Affairs for their approval, but thereafter to the Governor's Ministerial Security Council for a general policy directive. However, Cusack and Johnston, the two ministers concerned, decided that this extra authority was not necessary; they authorised the implementation of the new plan at Hola involving the use of what officials described as 'compelling force'. Such force was to be applied to those hard core prisoners who, by refusing to work, had created a situation where the rehabilitation programme had made no progress for some months, and where the Commandant's authority was thus being successfully defied. Both ministers knew that there had been a risk of violence involved, yet at their meeting with Evelyn, when the water cart possibility was raised, there appears to have been no reference to the fact that the deaths occurred during the application of the plan about which their junior officials had felt so unhappy.

Could the ministers have been deliberately reticent about this background? Or could Evelyn have known about it and still decided to publicise the water cart version, if only to play for time? Although the records are still closed, and anyway may not reveal the details of this meeting, these seem to be the only two possible interpretations. Yet even if Evelyn did *not* know the background to the 'Cowan Plan', let alone that it was being applied for the first time on the very day that ten men died and dozens were injured, he did already know enough about the administration of the detention camps to have been instinctively wary of the water cart story. He knew because he was having to deal with atrocity allegations the whole time; because the detention camps, in spite of their great achievements, were beset by a series of incidents involving allegations of brutality; and many of these allegations were being upheld. So the possibility of violence at Hola was not something which could, or should, have been lightly discarded, particularly when the deaths of ten men and scores of injuries had to be accounted for.

However, if he did not know the full facts at the first meeting, he must have learnt them soon enough, because when the inquest was held the whole world started to read about the goings-on at Hola. The inquest was told that about 200 hard core Mau Mau detainees had been taken to the irrigation ditch under the supervision of 90 warders, armed with rifles and batons, whose orders were to force the prisoners to work. On two occasions the prisoners had given what was described as a 'Mau Mau howl', whereupon the riot squad had beaten them until order was restored. After they had drunk water from a water cart ten (later eleven) had died, and a number more were taken to the hospital with injuries. The police pathologist told the inquest that the men had died either from lung congestion or from shock and haemorrhage following multiple bruising and other injuries. It became clear that, though the Commandant was only legally entitled to use physical force to suppress violent resistance, the 'Cowan Plan' enjoined him to instruct the warders to 'mandhandle the detainees to the place of work and force them to carry out their tasks'. He had also told the warders to respond to any noise or movement by striking the detainees on the legs below the knee. While on their way to work they had formed themselves into a human pyramid and given the Mau Mau howl, whereupon the warders had set on them with their batons. There was much more lurid evidence of this kind, with some allegations of continuous beating while the detainees were sitting down. In his findings, the coroner made a distinction between justifiable force in answer to violence or attempts to escape, and the beating of detainees to compel them to work. The former he said was justified; the latter, of which there was far more, was 'entirely unjustified and illegal'. Nevertheless, he concluded that the commission of a specific offence had not been proved.[2]

That was too much for the British House of Commons. The MPs wanted somebody to accept responsibility; and to be punished. The coroner had explained that, after careful consideration, he did not believe that the commission of an offence had been disclosed by a known person or persons:

'At first sight it might be considered extraordinary that such opinions should be recorded in view of my findings of illegal beatings having taken place at the work site. The following factors however, in my view clearly justify such opinions. It is impossible to determine beyond reasonable doubt which injuries on the deceased were caused by justifiable and which by unjustifiable blows, and which injury or combination of injuries resulted in the shock and haemorrhage causing death. It is impossible to say on the evidence with any degree of certainty which particular person struck the blows, whether justifiable or unjustifiable. The Cowan Plan, *which apparently had government approval and backing, gave intentionally or unintentionally carte blanche in 'forcing detainees to carry out the task'.* [my italics] If criminal offences were committed which were clearly illegal, the defence of superior orders would be of no avail, but I do not consider that the orders were so clearly illegal as to justify my recommending the preferment of charges. That is however ultimately a question of policy which is a matter for the Attorney General and not for me to decide.'[3]

The coroner seems to have been implying that the Cowan Plan's instructions were illegal though not so clearly as to enable him to recommend charges. He also had some fairly dry criticisms to make of the original press-handout, though he confessed he had been unable to discover exactly how that statement had been published.

Eleven men had been beaten to death; of that there was no doubt. And were there really to be no prosecutions? It could hardly be left like that even in Kenya, let alone in the House of Commons. Eric Griffith-Jones, the Attorney General, decided that there was insufficient evidence on which to base a charge against any individual warder. However, disciplinary proceedings were started against Sullivan and Coutts, the camp Commandant

K*

and his deputy, who were suspended from duty. As part of these proceedings an official enquiry was set up, which found that Sullivan had put the detainees to work in such a way that he was unable to exercise control over them, and in a manner contrary to the Cowan instructions – though as he had never actually seen a copy of the Cowan Plan, it was unfair to order him to carry out such an operation without detailed written instructions or proper supervision from a senior officer. The enquiry ducked the question whether the Cowan Plan was itself illegal; indeed that possibility was apparently never explored within the legal department. However the enquiry found also that Sullivan had failed to supervise the warders adequately, and, worse, that he had misled the three officials who visited him the day after the affray by minimising the extent to which batons had been used. The charges against Mr Coutts, the deputy, were dismissed. In view of Sullivan's good character and past record, Evelyn recommended that he should be retired from the service without loss of gratuity. There were other departures too. The Commissioner of Prisons announced that he wanted to retire as soon as a successor could be appointed; the Minister of Defence, who was anyway due to retire, actually left before the findings were published.

In Britain the strong feelings which had been aroused by the incident continued to harass Lennox-Boyd throughout his last summer in office. Evelyn was almost continuously having to provide material with which the Colonial Secretary could defend himself in the Commons. There were two full dress debates – the first in June, on a motion of censure on the government for its failure to set up a public enquiry into the incident; the second in July, after the publication of the Kenya government's official disciplinary enquiry. In facing his critics Lennox-Boyd had been sedulously briefed by Evelyn on the great achievements of the rehabilitation programme. He told the Commons that, in its third phase, there had actually been a reduction of the expected number of hard core Mau Mau detainees from a figure of 13,000 to under 1000, of which a quarter were at Hola. He went on to say that a policy of positive rehabilitation, such as had been applied, clearly carried certain extra risks, since it meant that the authorities had to launch 'a spiritual and moral crusade'. This was bound to provoke resistance on the part of fanatics which might sometimes lead to actual physical violence by detainees; it also involved the danger that some prison officer would depart from the strict guidelines he had received. He argued that constructive

work had always been seen as an essential part of the rehabilitation process, and that unless hard core detainees could be got
working, their rehabilitation was impossible.[4]

Evelyn listened to the speech from the officials' box in the
corner of the Commons' chamber. He had returned to London
for four weeks, and had spent the whole previous weekend at
Chequers briefing Lennox-Boyd and Sir Reginald Manningham-
Buller, the Attorney General, who wound up the debate by saying that he agreed with Griffith-Jones' view that it was not possible to establish any responsibility for any injury.

However, Manningham-Buller also touched on the nub of the
matter, when he argued that to warrant a charge of 'conspiracy
to use illegal force' it would be necessary to establish a common
agreement to use it. He claimed there was no evidence of that.
But was there not? It seems to be the key point of the case; for
the Cowan Plan involved the use of force to compel detainees
to go to their work place and to work, and so was itself an illegal
plan. It was rightly found to be so by the coroner in the passage
marked earlier in italics. Why then was it that those responsible
for issuing instructions to implement the Cowan Plan were not
chargeable? And were not charged?

The Commissioner of Prisons and the two ministers took it
upon themselves to issue the instructions without seeking the
authority of the Governor's Council. One can see why after the
event Evelyn would have preferred them not to be prosecuted,
but does that fully answer the question why they were not? Certainly by 1959 Evelyn and his Attorney General had a much
closer relationship than had been possible with Whyatt, and
Griffith-Jones would not lightly have taken a decision to prosecute
ministers, knowing the bitterness this would cause in government
and administration, and knowing too that one of the ministers
was imminently to retire. After all Evelyn's efforts to foster the
loyalty and cooperation of his colonial administration, such
prosecutions would have undone all his work, and bequeathed
to his successor a sourness which might in the long run have been
more damaging than the effects of not being seen to exact judicial
revenge for the scandal of Hola. Therein, I believe, lies the key
to Evelyn's rather ambivalent reaction to Hola; to his slow response to the news of the deaths; to his apparent acceptance of the
water cart theory and his readiness to put out that ill-fated first
statement. He had thrown his whole mind into the overall objective of Kikuyu rehabilitation. Without it his strategy for the

colony, for the agrarian revolution, for the creation of an African middle class, was doomed. He wanted it to succeed; he needed it to succeed; he saw it succeeding.

Yet it was threatened by a continuous stream of complaints about brutality – even manslaughter – in the camps, undernourishment, venality and so on. Many of these allegations were well founded, though admittedly on a very small scale compared to the great overall achievement. Nonetheless they threatened to discredit the entire policy. The continuous trickle of cases involving members of the administration naturally did not come to light in the same dramatic way as did the Hola artocity. Indeed one can see how, when the Hola deaths were first reported, they were treated as something similar to the two or three other cases which were already giving trouble to Evelyn and his chiefs of administration. Shortly after the Hola exposure, Evelyn wrote home to Molly about a number of other cases. There was the Kikuyu loyalist sentenced to two years for maltreatment involving the death of a detainee; 'All the administration have got involved emotionally. He should have admitted a fault but have claimed that the stories were very exaggerated. Instead he said he had been 100% framed. The magistrate disbelieved him. I am desperately sorry for him, it will be a blow to the loyalists and coming on top of Hola it is not too good for us.' Then he reported news of another case involving an administrative officer 'who intervened in a prison and caused a man to be beaten with a kiboko in place of a regulation cane, and given above the regulation number of strokes. Unbelievably stupid.'

He had to be firm enough to stop the rot, but not so firm that he undermined the morale and enthusiasm of the hundreds of excellent administrative officers and the thousands of loyalist Kikuyu. He felt that the loyalist wing of the tribe was not yet capable of surviving any determined campaign to winkle out these malpractices. Indeed, he must have asked himself, if such a campaign was to be launched, who would carry it out, unless it was that very administration and prison service which was committing the crimes in the first place? Evelyn was acutely aware of this dilemma, and he decided that, if it came to a choice, he would have to err on the side of the administration as he had done ever since he had been in Kenya. In his closing minute on security before he left the colony he touched on this difficulty; 'Rehabilitation was to a great extent the work of the administrative officers in Central Province. Most of them are extremely hard working and prepared to take responsibility. Their weakness is that they have a slight tradition of acting on their own. This can sometimes be useful. At other times, they become emotional and do not think out the consequences of their actions, and, as a result, break the law, put the government in a difficult position, and damage the policy they are eager to put forward.'[5]

These are mild words considering the difficulties with which Evelyn wrestled. Hola was obviously the most eye-catching case of atrocity, but it was by no means the only one or the most difficult one to follow up once it had been committed. The fact that Evelyn and his administration were so used to cases of this kind probably explains why, in the initial phase, they appear to have acted with such little despatch, and such a lack of determination to treat the affair as a major atrocity.

It seems to be clear that senior government officers could, and perhaps should, have been charged with the Hola affair. However once again Evelyn turned to that useful device, the double-sided amnesty, to avoid this obligation, since there were one or two other cases where senior administrative officers had broken the law in the instructions they issued for methods to be followed in detention camps. The Solicitor General, Diarmaid Conroy, was sent home secretly to London to persuade Lennox-Boyd and Manningham-Buller that the best way to meet the clamour for prosecutions was to hasten the formal ending of the emergency, which would encompass legislation allowing an amnesty for persons guilty of crimes on both sides of the line. After some heart-searching, the plan was accepted by the two British ministers, although some months later Griffith-Jones was still aware of continuing doubts in the mind of Manningham-Buller.[6]

In fact the actual amnesty was not to be pronounced by Evelyn who had by then left the colony. It was left to his successor, Sir Patrick Renison, to introduce two bills involving an Act of Grace and the formal end of the emergency, though the government were to retain certain powers of detention. The Act of Grace was to provide an amnesty for all terrorists who surrendered before the end of the year, though they would then be detained for rehabilitation. It was made clear that the amnesty would apply to members of either side in the conflict. It sounded a simple enough formula, but behind Renison's bland announcement lay a whole series of anguished discussions in Britain and Kenya. Before he left, Evelyn had to conduct two extremely embarrassing interviews with senior officials – one of them a minister – who were threatened with prosecution. He made it clear to them that there was evidence which, if allowed to go forward, would almost certainly result in a disciplinary enquiry and their departure from the colonial service. The evidence which was held against them was that they had issued instructions, going back at least until 1957, for the 'deliberate though controlled use of force' in the detention camps. He warned them that a prosecution would lead to the collapse of the entire administration. He told them that a comprehensive Act of Grace, in the context of the end of the emergency, was in the mind of the government, and would cover their cases.[7] It was most unpleasant, and the knowledge that something of that kind was going on soured the atmosphere in his dealings with high officials within the administration during the last few months. Evelyn was warned that the administration would be up in arms if there were prosecutions. But Manningham-Buller, and more particularly Ian Macleod and Lord Hailsham, were equally reported to be extremely unhappy about the transaction, and although it eventually went through it was somehow typical that this last, most sensitive and least satisfactory aspect of the battle against Mau Mau should have dogged him from almost the beginning of his governorship until right to the end.

There remains one final question about Evelyn and Hola: should he have resigned? Historically it has come to be seen as one of the major blights on Britain's colonial reputation, yet at the time it did not cause the sense of outrage in Kenya which was being shown in the House of Commons. Officials in Kenya were anyway by then used to, if not inured to, what they regarded as unnecessary criticism and interference from British parliamentarians who failed to appreciate what had been going on in Kenya. Yet it is surprising that nobody resigned, nobody accepted responsibility.

The probable reason is that, in political terms, if one person were to resign, it might have forced a chain reaction. Harold Macmillan was determined that Alan Lennox-Boyd should not resign, although he offered to do so. Macmillan was by then planning his October general election, and would not have relished being handicapped by a major and damaging resignation in advance of the contest. If Evelyn had resigned, as the senior responsible official, Lennox-Boyd would then have come under intolerable pressure to accept ministerial responsibility as well. After it was over, Alan wrote to Evelyn, 'I was very proud to be able to show publicly my support for and unbounded confidence in you, and gratitude for all you have done. It would have been a poor return for your superlative contribution . . . had I allowed attacks on you to go unanswered or attempted to shelter behind you.'[8]

But for all that there was considerable pressure on both of them. Macleod and Hailsham, to name but two senior ministers, were out for blood – whether in the shape of resignations or prosecutions. Several acrimonious meetings were held; there was a feeling in parts of the Conservative Party – typified by a brilliant back-bench speech from Enoch Powell, the former Treasury Minister – that, even if there was no cover up going on, somebody had to be held responsible. Yet nobody was. If Evelyn had not been due to depart from Kenya within the following few months, if he had still one or two years to serve, it might have tarnished his reputation enough to have warranted a premature posting. Coming as it did at the end of a long, and by then obviously outstandingly successful governorship, it just took some of the gilt off his final days.

CHAPTER XXX

African Finale

Throughout those seven years in Nairobi, life at Evelyn's Government House had adjusted to the various changes in the political situation with all the practised ease with which Molly had come to master the task of colonial consort. It was her underlying purpose to maintain a home life for Evelyn which, in spite of the Baring's permanent residence abroad, would reproduce for him as faithfully as possible the atmosphere and the enjoyments which he would have found at Howick. It meant that, when he had moments to himself, he could indulge his appetite for birdwatching or for botany, for rockclimbing, for horses, or even just for horseplay with his children and their friends. However odd and unexpected that atmosphere may have seemed to locals and visitors, it made Government House a predictable and therefore reassuring haven for Evelyn when he emerged from his office at the end of the front hall.

Soon after the emergency began, John Gunter, the African chronicler visited Nairobi and in his *Inside Africa* captured some of the flavour of life inside that elegant white colonial palace, as it must have appeared for the first time to many visitors who had no previous experience of the Barings' *modus vivendi*:

'Sir Evelyn Baring is a tall handsome man with a deep booming laugh and a profile strikingly like that of John Barrymore; he is sensitive, high minded and just. He should have been a perfect 'white' settler governor but he was too liberal, too temperate to go all the way on their side; hence some extreme diehards practically thought of him as a traitor to his class. But he was unpopular with the Africans too, much as he had their legitimate interests at heart; any governor was bound to be unpopular during the Mau Mau crisis, because he had to take measures against almost the whole African community. Sir Evelyn is one of the most aristocratic aristocrats I have ever met, and the atmosphere of Government House of Nairobi is almost that of 18th century England, caking a little at the edges. Lady Mary Baring is the daughter of an earl, the principal private secretary is a Howard, and one of the ADCs is a Ridley. People emerged down corridors as if they had just stepped out of antique frames. They were fastidious, generous, with beautiful manners and refinement – healthy people too – but they made Government House in Kenya resemble a stately island lost in time, drowned in forces nobody could comprehend.'[1]

It was not in reality lost in time, nor were the Barings insulated from the emergency. Some of their favourite 'houseboys' were taken away for screening; terrorists were found hiding in the arboretum at the bottom of the garden; birdwatching was inhibited by the presence of armed guards posted all round the location. Yet they were able to ask 4000 people to a coronation garden party – who ate their way through 48,000 sandwiches and 16,000 cakes.

Entertaining at Government House was not lavish, but continuous and on a scale which was only possible because the Barings had a considerable private income which they were prepared to spend in this way – a viceregal style characteristic of few twentieth-century colonial governors. Their visitors were a varied lot. Apart from teeming with the world's press, Nairobi also played host to Clark Gable and Ava Gardner making a film. Ralph Richardson, the actor, arrived to open a new theatre. Father Huddleston – their friend from Johannesburg, later to become a well-known champion of the African cause – came to help fix up a chapel in the attic of Government House so that Evelyn and Molly were able to take Holy Communion upstairs every morning.

Whenever Evelyn could get away from Nairobi he did so – if not to a game park or one of the wilder provinces, then to a tribal area or some good farming country. He often used to sneak off for a Saturday sheep-shearing with Bob Wilson, a friendly Scotsman with a big farm on the Kinangcop. But more often it was the wild places which lured him. He was thrilled to get to the Northern Frontier Province for the first time, and to find himself at Wajir among Somali muslims; then on to Lake Rudolph, lost in a lunar landscape, its waters teeming with Nile perch of prodigious weight and crocodiles which looked as long as a cricket pitch. Once, when he was in the Mara River game reserve, there was a riot at Manyani detention camp – one of the worst camps at the time. The authorities sent a small aircraft to pick him up, but they could not find his camp under the trees, and the plane returned governor-less to Nairobi.

Towards the end of the military phase of the emergency there was a brief interlude in Government House routine when Princess

Margaret paid a state visit to East Africa. Evelyn had kept as far
from the preparations as he decently could, doubtless recalling
from his South African experience the enormous potential for
hysteria which a royal visit seems to create. He joked that he only
wanted to know two things about the visit: what the correct procedure was (a) if *she* yawned talking to *him* and (b) if *he* yawned
talking to *her*. They survived the visit without too much trouble,
but the relief when it was over seemed to infect all those who had
been involved. A week afterwards the Barings threw a 'thank-you'
cocktail party for 700, after which five men were carried out
drunk, two husbands rang up the next day to apologise for the
behaviour of their wives, and one man left his car outside Government House all night because he could not be sure which one it
was.

Birdwatching in Africa is intensely rewarding, though taxing
to the mind and memory; and it was thus a special stimulus to
Evelyn's passion for abstruse and detailed information. Birds of
almost unnatural brilliance abound in hundreds of different
species, as though released from a thousand different aviaries.
Evelyn's friend and birdwatching companion was John Williams,
who was by character and aspect a perfect foil for Evelyn, in a
way not dissimilar to Vasey. He was small, meticulous and
academic almost to a fault, though always a funny fault. For
hours on end, in the bush, on the hills, on the foreshore, the two
of them would stand together, binoculars clapped to their eyes.
Invariably Williams used to say 'excuse me pointing' as he
directed the Governor's eyes to some new ornithological delight.
Once somebody warned him there was a mosquito on his cheek.
'What species?' he said, without moving a muscle. He killed and
stuffed any animal or bird he could find – a habit which from
time to time used to fuss some of the tidier members of the camping party. Sometimes they would be sitting having breakfast outside their tents after an early morning prowl, with the noise of
doves cooing above them, and Williams would remark, dead pan,
'*streptopelia semitorquata australis* in an amorous condition,' to
be followed by Evelyn's laughter – itself a noise not dissimilar to
the honking of geese or a cross between a sneeze and a foghorn.

It was while at Lake Rudolf that one of his police officers discovered a more human side to a Governor who was generally
thought to be rather an aloof man, certainily by those who had no
personal contact with him. The bush lavatory had been put discreetly behind a large grove of palm trees and the inspector, while

doing his rounds one morning, found large groups of curious Turkana tribesmen huddled round the site. He chased them away, only to find Evelyn himself perched upon the throne. To his apologies Evelyn responded in high good humour, chuckling, 'I don't suppose it happens very often that these people can catch a Governor with his pants down.'

When the Chief Secretary, Walter Coutts, gave a farewell broadcast about the Barings, he put his finger on one of the factors which accounts for this contrast between Evelyn in private life, and in his official dealings. 'The real background to the Baring family life at Government House was that it was essentially a family atmosphere from which many of the good things in life are bound to flow. The happy yells of delight which one used to hear emanating from what are regarded as the venerated and almost sepuchral halls of Government House testified to the influence which, as it always should be, the mistress of the house had over the rest of the family,'[2] he said. On one occasion Evelyn's council meeting had to be discontinued until the younger members of the household had turned down their gramophone; on another his ADCs brought him fifteen minutes early to the official opening of Legco – bedecked in his plumes and orders. They discovered an empty parade ground, sans Speaker, sans Chief Justice, sans all the Queen's men. There were no reprimands; Evelyn contented himself with a short rest under a jacaranda tree in the municipal car park, and treated his offending minions to a dissertation on the intricacies of the lactation of cows. (The Speaker was furious and offered to resign for so insulting the Crown). On yet another occasion an ADC forgot to bring his glasses to church, depriving Evelyn of a text from which to read the lesson. He declaimed it from memory.

To the outside world, however, and particularly to those people who had official dealings with the Governor, Evelyn could appear to be something of a *grand seigneur*. Until one had heard that extrordinary nasal grunt/foghorn/goosehonk which signalled the arrival of mirth, or observed the boisterous tomfoolery which characterised Evelyn's family affairs, he appeared to typify the remote aristocratic proconsul, in the most superior British tradition. Yet there was humanity in him which was instantly apparent to the charmed circle who, as it were, penetrated inside the seigneurial walls. That applied to almost everybody who was with him on tour, or even some of those with whom he became intimate during the conduct of public affairs, like Mallaby, the

Secretary of the War Council, who shared with Evelyn a whole list of nicknames for their colleagues, like 'Stinker' Whyatt, 'Parsifal' Blundell, and other vestiges of the schoolboy sense of humour which had remained with Evelyn from his days at Winchester.

Perhaps for many people in Kenya, particularly Asians and Africans who had had more reason than most to assess him in strictly proconsular terms, the humanity of the man only burst on their understanding with the incident in September, 1959, only a few weeks before his departure from the colony, when Evelyn nearly died in an attempt to save two Asian girls from drowning. The family were assembled at Government House, Mombasa, while Evelyn carried out his farewell tour of the coastal province. For a few days they all went 70 miles up the coast to the holiday resort at Malindi, where the younger members of the party went surfing and Evelyn occasionally joined them snorkeling on the coral reefs. On the day he was due to depart he and Molly went alone to lunch with Colonel Archie Richie, a naturalist who had retired to a house on the shore at Casvarina Point some miles south of Malindi. It was a Sunday afternoon. The family were all away waterskiing. Evelyn and Molly were due to be collected by car in time to catch a small aircraft to Mombasa. At the airstrip, and at his hotel, officials waited in vain, with no sign of the Governor. Then shortly before dark, news reached the hotel that there had been a terrible accident – a drowning. For some time nothing more was known, then the details emerged.

After lunch Evelyn and Molly had been sitting out alone in Richie's garden when an Asian girl ran up to them and said that three of her friends were in difficulties in the sea a short distance away. They had been cut off by the incoming tide and were now struggling in the water about 150 yards out to sea. Evelyn immediately ran down to the beach and plunged into the sea, while Molly went to raise the alarm. When Evelyn reached the girls he found that one of them could swim sufficiently well to save herself and he told her to set out for the shore, which she eventually reached without harm. The other two, aged about 14 and 18, were non-swimmers, and were already very frightened. Evelyn tried to calm them down and then started to bring them back slowly to the shore, with one on his back and the older girl held up by his right hand as he paddled forward with the left.

Evelyn was a big man; but he was then nearly 56, and he was

not a strong swimmer. Yet he was now struggling in a flood tide, against a strong wind, trying to support two nearly fully grown girls to the shore. The crowd which had gathered on the beach watched helplessly: Molly was a weak swimmer; Colonel Richie was by then nearly 70 years old and suffering from a heart condition; and most of the Asian picnickers present were also non-swimmers. Yet against all the difficulties Evelyn was evidently making slow but appreciable progress, and had managed to accomplish about two-thirds of the distance. Then disaster struck.

At that point the breakers started to become severe and the girls, in panic, began to struggle. The older one on his arm became uncontrollable, slipped from his grasp and was carried away by the tide: to drown. The other girl Evelyn managed to control, though his strength and consciousness were now slipping from him and the beach was still about twenty-five yards away. He cried out 'I can't go on' and started to flounder badly. By now two other Europeans had arrived on the beach, and with Colonel Richie they plunged into the surf, rescuing Evelyn and the girl about twenty yards from the shore. So hopeless must Evelyn's condition have appeared that they concentrated on saving the girl, believing him to be already finished. Evelyn himself must have thought he was dying because, as he was hauled from the water, in a semi-conscious state, there were prayers on his lips. He was taken to hospital with pneumonia, which was soon successfully treated, but his general condition continued to worry the doctors. For two weeks he remained in an extremely exhausted state and his blood pressure made them suspect that he might have had a heart attack. An electrocardiogram showed that his heart was undamaged, though he had strained some muscles near it. He was finally allowed to return to Nairobi two weeks after the accident, though it necessarily curtailed the hectic round of farewell ceremonies which had been planned for his last three weeks in the colony.

Meanwhile there was an explosion of emotion in his favour. The shadow and the shame of Hola were forgotten; the remoteness; the seigneurial detachment; the suspicions of so many Asians that in spite of his Indian experiences and of his Urdu conversations they were too often treated as Kenya's poor relations; the sneers of the settlers that he had 'no guts'; the slights, real or imagined, which Africans might have felt from the social life he had presided over at Government House – all were submerged in that so nearly deadly tide at Casvarina Point. Messages of con-

gratulations and sympathy, of solicitude and admiration, poured
in from all over Kenya, from Bombay, Southern Rhodesia, South
Africa, Nigeria, Scotland and England. Prayers for his recovery
were said daily not just in Nairobi, but, for instance, in the
Church of St Anthony's Mission in Johannesburg where the congregation comprised Indians, coloureds, and Chinese. He had a
typically insouciant exchange with Oliver Woods, of *The Times*.
'Where were your ADCs?' asked Woods. 'Did their cavalry sabres
drag them down?' Evelyn replied, 'It was a Sunday afternoon
and if cavalry officers cannot sleep on Sunday afternoons what
indeed are we coming to?'[3] The *East African Standard* said the
rescue was a fitting climax to seven colourful and dramatic years
as Governor, during which he had selflessly served all races.[4]

Characteristically, Evelyn soon found time to test his state of
recovery in a birdwatching expedition from Nairobi. The entries
are meticulously listed in his little notebook, all with their accompanying latin names – grey-headed bush shrike, purple chested
locane, bare eyed thrush, spotted morning warbler, pied babbler,
mariqua sunbird, flappet lark, and sharef's longclaw. A modest
list perhaps compared to the 450 odd names which already appeared in the book from previous outings, but not bad for a man
in his condition. If anything was going to equip him for the next
three weeks of valediction it would be a quiet day with John
Williams. The strains of the impending departure, of the accumu-
lated emotion of seven years effort, of not slacking off before the
very end, must all have been acute. Moreover, we know from
previous chapters that he was also coping with a great deal of
unfinished business within the administration, as well as preparing valedictory memoranda for the Colonial Office and for his
successor, Sir Patrick Renison, whose appointment had only just
been announced. There were plaudits for Evelyn from all and
sundry. The *East African Standard* described him as the Governor
who led Kenya out of the shadows. On the day he left he received
a touching letter from Sir Llewellyn Woodward, his old tutor
at Oxford, who said, 'When you were an undergraduate I used
to think you would be viceroy and I hoped I would live to see it.
Well, you have had in the last 7 years far more anxious and
difficult responsibilities than most viceroys.' Julian Amery, the
junior minister in the Colonial Office, wrote, 'The full value of
your great proconsulship will only be appreciated in years to
come. But the people have a flair for the truth. The Labour smear
campaign [about Hola] only lost them votes [in the election which

the Conservatives had just won]. A reference to your name invariably got a cheer even from the purely working class audiences in my constituency and the three other Lancashire towns where I spoke.'[5]

Eventually the day came when there was the last march past; the last cheer; a farewell look-back at the white elegance of Baker's magnificent Government House; at Molly's garden; tearful goodbyes with gardeners and 'houseboys'; a last ride in the black Humber saloons which had crowns instead of number plates. It was farewell to a way of life, as well as to a place, and as the Barings boarded the Governor's train in Nairobi, which was to take them chugging up through the White Highlands on their way to Uganda, it must have seemed that they had travelled a long way since that arrival in Salisbury seventeen years before. Then they were a young couple new to the life of proconsular royalty – though not inherently ill-prepared for it. In 1942 it was still very much the way of their world; by 1959 it was a world which had gone. Evelyn was the last of a line. He had indeed been born to be a viceroy; but India was no more and Africa was soon going to show, if it had not already shown, that the imperial tradition which Evelyn embodied was never going to be given such expression again. In December, while quietly recovering from his efforts at Howick, he received two letters which recognised some of his toils. One told him he had been awarded the Queen's Commendation for Brave Conduct for the rescue from drowning. The other was from Harold Macmillan, the Prime Minister, which said, 'I have it in mind to recommend you for a peerage in the New Year Honours.' Unlike his friend, Sir Edward Twining, who chose to be Lord Twining of Tanganyika, Evelyn did not link his title with any former scene of African grandeur. He chose, instead, to be Lord Howick of Glendale – close to his beloved Cheviot Hills. It was indicative of the fact that Northumberland was now going to be the focus of his attentions, and that he had put Africa behind him. As usual it did not entirely turn out that way, and the Dark Continent was to remain very much a part of his life until the end.

CHAPTER XXXI

Commonwealth
and Conservation

When Evelyn left Kenya – two weeks after his 56th birthday – he had been living out of Britain for the best part of seventeen years. Yet he was not likely to become a typical returning colonial, out of his element in Britain and full of nostalgia for the grand imperial life, or the friendlier climates of Africa. From the end of the war and the introduction of air transport, he had been paying frequent visits both to London and to Howick. The adjustment to a settled life in Britain was almost painless, if not quite imperceptible. On the personal level there were minor things, like the fact that his diet sheet ('His Excellency does NOT eat goose, duck, beef of any kind . . .') was not sent on ahead to his hosts wherever he might be asked to stay, and his family were more on top of him at Howick, than when he had ruled a country from the spacious rooms of Government House, Nairobi. On a public level, however, the transition was made easier by the fact that even before he left Kenya he had been offered and accepted a position with the Colonial Development Corporation, first as Deputy Chairman, and then a year later, as Chairman upon the retirement of his predecessor, Sir Nutcombe Hume. He held the appointment for the next 12 years, and was able throughout that time to indulge his passion for development in the non-industrialised world of three continents, and to continue the work he had found so satisfying in Africa.

Later Evelyn was also to become Chairman of the Nature Conservancy, thus enabling him to indulge those other, more private passions for wild life, and all manner of land husbandry. There were other public duties which fell his way, yet by far the most preoccupying and satisfying task for him was to settle down at Howick and manage two or three farms, something which he had talked about to others for years, and which now became almost a charmed reality. At the Howick sheep sales, and at all the local agricultural shows along the Cheviots, he was able to poke cattle and talk about crop yields with fellow practitioners, never forgetting to jot down every tiny detail into his black notebooks which were as much part of the armoury of the new border farmer as they had been of the Governor and Commander-in-Chief.

Inevitably the calls of public life were not going to be ignored. Julian Amery had written to him about his peerage and said, 'I hope you will use the House of Lords as a platform and not as a sofa,' and in March, 1960, he found himself under pressure to speak in a big debate on Kenya – which he declined on the grounds that it was too soon. But though he did not speak in public there was a continuous unofficial involvement in the consequences of the change of policy towards Kenya – the effect on Colonial Office careers, resettlement of white farmers with no capital, Blundell's frequent correspondence, and so on.

However, Evelyn's major public contribution was to be through the Colonial Development Corporation. When he joined the CDC in 1960, he was, of course, already familiar with its workings. It had been set up in 1948 under an Act of Parliament, and one of its first ventures, after a chequered start, was the forestry scheme at Usutu in Swaziland. For the first three or four years of its life the Corporation had lost a great deal of money, until Lord Reith became Chairman in succession to Lord Trefgarne (with whom Evelyn had not got on well), and Mr William Rendell became General Manager. This combination was so successful that by the end of the next ten years the CDC had a high reputation as an efficiently organised, decentralised, prudent but imaginative combination of investment trust and management company involved in agriculture, development corporations, low cost housing, rubber plantations, and any number of other enterprises.

When Evelyn arrived the CDC was trying to persuade the Treasury to allow a change in its restrictive financial basis which involved it in annual repayments of loans to the Treasury, when so much of its capital was likely to be in equity shares which could not, and should not, be realized after such a short period of investment. But an even more important argument of policy started almost immediately after Evelyn's arrival. It was by then apparent that most of Britain's colonies were going to become independent countries in the first half of the 1960s. The original charter of the Corporation prevented it from operating in any post-colonial country. It took much lobbying in Whitehall, where Evelyn was able to bring all his seasoned political contacts into play, before the required legislation was passed. This freed the CDC from the previous inhibition and enabled it effectively to overcome that difficulty psychological and economic period of transition from a colonial environment to one involving independent countries within the Commonwealth. Evelyn had warned Conservative ministers that, if the CDC was not allowed to operate in the independent Commonwealth it would soon have to run down completely – indeed it was already losing some of its best men, he said. He insisted that the Corporation's credit-worthiness be improved so that it could provide the best supporting services for development projects in newly independent countries. It was not so much that the CDC would want to invest in unprofitable enterprises – on the contrary it always insisted that any scheme must be commercially based and show the prospect of profits. But the CDC was often able to give backing to some schemes, which, for one reason or another, had not been able to attract development capital elsewhere.

Evelyn found he was involved in new areas of the world – the Caribbean and the Far East – in addition to all of British Africa – and in new kinds of enterprises, such as secondary industries, housing, and hotels as well as the traditional agricultural fare. In fact he was not new to the world of big business and one of his less aesthetic, though most important monuments in Kenya was the £20 million oil refinery in Mombasa which he had persuaded the Shell Company to build, after years of careful courtship and some dramatic high level negotiations of the kind which one normally only associates with television serials. Evelyn's chairmanship of the CDC enabled him to lay down the grand strategy of the Corporation, while Mr (later Sir William) Rendell ran the organisation. In spite of his colonial past Evelyn seemed to have no difficulty in establishing a reputation for total independence from the British government in the decisions he made, and British ministers were happy to let him make those decisions. They really only came together in a common desire to secure more British funds for investment in the Third World, and a common frustration at the country's economic inability to do so. Evelyn found himself allied in this quest with ministers of both Labour and Conservative governments, including for a time Mrs Barbara Castle, his old critic of the Kenya days.

In the twelve years that he was Chairman, the CDC nearly tripled in size, from handling 88 projects representing an investment of £65m. to 212 representing an investment of £156m. Under his chairmanship the CDC pioneered a number of new crops – projects really dear to his heart such as oil palms and cocoa in Sabah and the Solomon Islands, and flue-cured, as opposed to fire-cured, tobacco in Malawi and Zambia. When he re-

tired in 1972 he was able to refer proudly to the statement of Mr
Robert McNamara, President of the World Bank, that the CDC
was 'a unique organisation which has shown the way to the rest
of us', in matters of development policy for the Third World.[1]
    Under the auspices of the CDC Evelyn continued to travel
widely, and for the first time visited the Caribbean and the Far
East. But it was still to Africa that his spirit took him. There was
the initial post-colonial period to be overcome when he had to be
careful not to offend the sensitivities of newly independent politicians, chary of such an obviously imperial figure as Evelyn had
been. He attended Tanganyika's independence celebration in
1961, and as long as the colonial government existed in Kenya he
found himself partially involved, not just in CDC business, but
in advising Renison on various matters, which cropped up from
time to time. When in December, 1963, Kenya achieved independence under Kenyatta, Evelyn and Alan Lennox-Boyd (by then
Lord Boyd of Merton) together decided that, as a gesture of respect for the 30,000 Kikuyu who had been killed by the Mau Mau,
they should not go to the celebration. But the story of Evelyn's
eventual reconciliation with the Kenyatta regime is a moving one.
The first time he returned on CDC business to an independent
Kenya was in October, 1965, when a senator publicly objected to
his presence. But the colossal advances in Kenya agriculture were
by then paying dividends; new irrigation projects were working;
grade cattle were breeding; and there were 40,000 new African
tea planters in a small-holding scheme supported by the World
Bank. These, and many other economic benefits such as the
refinery which could be shown to date directly from wise decisions
taken during Evelyn's governorship, perhaps influenced the
Kenyatta regime, and it eventually extended an informal hand of
friendship to him, though nothing much was said in public about
his visits.
    Finally, after a number of visits, a historic meeting was arranged
between Evelyn and Jomo Kenyatta, in the very office from where
Evelyn had despatched Kenyatta to detention nearly twenty years
before. The meeting was arranged by Charles Njonjo, Kenya's
Attorney General, and Bruce Mackenzie, the white South African-
born farmer whom Evelyn had made Minister of Agriculture, and
who became the only white minister in President Kenyatta's
cabinet. They thought that Evelyn was uncharacteristically nervous before the encounter, but after an exchange of pleasantries
he broke the ice by saying, 'By the way, I was sitting at that actual

desk when I signed your detention order twenty years ago.' Kenyatta replied, 'I know. If I had been in your shoes at the time I would have done exactly the same.' There was much relieved laughter all round and Kenyatta added, 'And I have myself signed a number of detention orders sitting right there too.' They went out and looked at the garden. 'We heard much of the "Baring trees" the Naivasha Thorns you planted,' Evelyn wrote to Molly. 'We were photographed in all sorts of poses and he walked around carrying a sort of black baton covered with bits of brass. He gave me an enormously enthusiastic send off,' and invited Evelyn to stay at Government – now renamed State – House whenever he was in Nairobi.

Shortly after his first meeting with Jomo Kenyatta Evelyn told Marjery Perham in an interview that it was possible to have three different theories about the Kenyan President.[2] The first was that he was a great villain in the early fifties and had remained so and only *appeared* to have become a responsible man – a theory which Evelyn believed was shown to be absurd by the events in Kenya since independence. The second was that Kenyatta had always been a reasonable man and that the happenings of Mau Mau were entirely due to British force, that anyway Kenyatta was not the real leader of Mau Mau and that even if he had been originally its leader it only became such a horrifying movement after his removal from the scene. To that Evelyn replied, 'I am afraid I have no doubts whatever that Kenyatta was the leader when I arrived because his was the only name that ever appeared in all the Mau Mau literature. He was the leader and he had control.' Evelyn preferred a third theory – his own – which was that Kenyatta was a double man, similar to an eighteenth century figure who 'probably led a very admirable life in Britain and was probably quite religious but who invested in the slave trade'. The trouble with that sort of double man was that the duality became acute in circumstances of civil war: 'For instance Cromwell in England and Scotland was a pretty merciful conqueror but in Ireland he was a fiend,' he said. However, one had to accept that it was the same man.

Now the old Kenyatta had gone. He had re-emerged as a first class national leader for three reasons: first, because of his decision to follow a policy of reconciliation within the Kikuyu tribe and within Kenya as a whole, after the divisions of the Mau Mau; secondly, because unlike most of his African colleagues in other ex-colonies, he had decided to preserve the provincial administration and rule through the District Commissioners; and thirdly, because he consolidated and built on the agricultural revolution initiated by Evelyn – so much so that Kenya was chosen by the World Bank as the most suitable base in Africa for its main agricultural investment. For Evelyn there could be no higher praise! With Kenyatta at its head Kenya was stable, prosperous, and as well administered as he could ever have hoped for – much better to rejoice in that fact and give Kenyatta due credit than to indulge in a fruitless post mortem on how and why it could be squared with his actual position in the Mau Mau movement.

Evelyn's last tour of Kenya was in June, 1972, shortly before he retired from the CDC. He told Molly:

'I spent two days with the Provincial Commissioner of the Central Province. The system of administration is exactly the British one down to the DCs uniform. The administrative officers are definitely in charge of the local team. They are well trained professionals, do not take bribes, despise the politicians and do all the right things e.g. encourage bench terraces and discourage excisions from the forest.

I also had a most moving personal experience at a large party. The politicians were nearly all out of Nairobi. A large number of African men and women came. One after another they opened up to me. The Chairman of the tea authority and the chief executive of Karanja said, 'We can never forget you started the tea and now look what it has become." We can never forget what you have done for us, said all the Africans. In short I got a wonderful send off from the practical men who make Kenya tick – civil servants, businessmen, those who run state owned industries. They say Africans are ungrateful but if you have really helped them where they really need help then they are full of gratitude. Though not in public.

As I looked at the acres of well kept small-holder tea, the flourishing grade cattle, the successful irrigation, the compact farms, I felt a little as Pa must have felt as he left Egypt in 1907 with the fellahin free of the three Cs – the cowerbash [whip] the corvé and corruption.'

It was the same story in Lesotho – Basutoland in Evelyn's day – where Chief Jonathan, the Prime Minister, met him and said 'you are not forgotten,' going on to prove the point in a rather negative way by saying that the soil conservation programme had been run down because he had been too insecure to enforce it. It was the same story – only more so – in Swaziland, where Evelyn was told

313

L

by a Kikuyu, who had been appointed Swazi Director of Agriculture, that the CDC settlements were the best land settlements in Africa. In this, his last tour of Africa, the memory of his father seemed to tug at him again and strongly. 'As I stood by the rough road among the sugar cotton and sweet potatoes at the foot of the long Lebombo Ridge which I had climbed the day before, I could not help thinking of the fellahin who so long ago had said to a shy, awkward, young Evelyn Baring 'you are the son of our padishah who made Egypt run with gold".'

Indeed Swaziland was in a sense Evelyn's show piece in Africa. If in Kenya the regime still felt some sensitivity about the memories of Mau Mau, in Swaziland there was only admiration for the memory of Evelyn and all his works. His name adorns public buildings, schools and bridges. King Sobhuza would go out of his way to speak warmly of their friendship and extol his 'conspicuous' contribution to Swaziland's well being. At Usutu, where the pulp mill nestles in a fold of the huge forestry scheme which would assuredly not have been planted without Evelyn's vision, there is a simple, moving plaque on the wall of the little community hall. 'In memory of the late Lord Howick, better known to all Swazi people simply as Evelyn Baring. His contributions to the forest industry of Swaziland were timely and vital. He will be remembered in this land as long as pine forests flourish on the Swazi hills.'

What he saw on his farewell tour of Africa must have warmed his heart. It was especially lucky for him that as it turned out, with less than a year to live, his departure from the CDC in 1972 had enabled him to make farewell tours of those territories into which he had poured so much of his time and his emotions. But his feelings for the Third World were not confined to the programme of work with the CDC. Towards the end of his time at the CDC Evelyn – once again in collaboration with Roger Makins (now Lord Sherfield) – became founder member of an organisation called the British North American Committee which grew out of a British Canadian Committee of many years standing. It looked as though it would start life as a group of people dedicated to the principles of free trade within the developed world, at that time potentially threatened by the emergence of trading blocks such as the European Common Market. But under Evelyn's careful if subtle helmsmanship it developed fairly soon into something much more concerned with the relationship of the developed industrialised nations to the developing world, and thus effectively preceded by about ten years the phenomenon that has now become known as the 'north south problem'.

While all this post-colonial development work was preoccupying him, it must have been with some relish, not to say amusement, that Evelyn – after all his jokes about Molly's high anglicanism, and the frequency with which he used to tease her about Lord Grey's many years as head of the House of Laity – received an invitation from the Archbishop of Canterbury to chair a new Commission of Enquiry into the appointment of bishops. At first he refused Dr Ramsay's request, on the grounds that he had just taken over the CDC and was in the middle of adapting it to a vital new role in the newly independent Commonwealth. He was worried that the terms of reference of the commission would include the question of disestablishment, and would therefore become very time-consuming. When it was explained to him that the commission would not be examining that question but would only be dealing with the need to secure some permanent procedure for church-state consultation before Crown appointments were made – in other words within the existing structure of the church's establishment – he relented and accepted the appointment in January, 1962.

The fourteen members of his commission were evenly divided between church and laity. They deliberated for many months, taking evidence from a wide number of people within the church establishment – including Lord Fisher of Lambeth, the previous Archbishop of Canterbury, with whom Evelyn had already privately clashed over Fisher's quite improper opposition to the appointment of Trevor Huddleston as Bishop of Masasi in Tanganyika. (Fisher had no right to interfere in the affairs of the East African Province and Evelyn had to tell him so.) It was work for which Evelyn, in a way, was ideally suited. He was able to advise the less wordly churchmen of what was going to be politically possible, and to contain their wilder enthusiasms. He guided the ultimate deliberations of the commission by sending them a series of questions and observations which served as a basis for the first draft of the report. He told them that Lord Attlee's evidence had shown that a Prime Minister with fixed ideas about the appointments of bishops, and still more one who was a mild crank, might over several years do considerable harm. They should consider steps necessary to protect the church against such a possibility, though he took the view that bishops clearly could not be elected. He went to see the leaders of the main political parties to canvass their views as to the likelihood of parliament accepting the commission's proposals and enacting them. Mr Macmillan told him to avoid forceful language and the recommendations would then have a good chance of being adopted, though there would always be a good deal of opposition in parliament. 'I know you will be criticised in the church assembly for not using forceful language but we will be known by our conclusions, that is by the legislation which will follow, and not by our language,' Evelyn told this to his fellow commissioners, once more showing that intensely practical political sensitivity which had always exasperated more ideological or, as they thought, more highly-principled collaborators in Africa.

The report was published in December, 1964, and received rather a moderate press. It was not a radical document; Evelyn's preference for political practicality over strong language had got the better of it. It recommended certain minor legislative changes to the existing procedure in order to give the Archibishops of Canterbury and York greater involvement in the selection of bishops and with diocesan bishops over suffragan appointments. But it came down firmly against any real alternative system, let alone one involving election. Evelyn was disappointed at the reception of the report. It was debated at the church assembly the following spring, but then became subsumed in a wider movement within the Church to suspend judgment on most of his recommendations until the fundamental nature of the church-state relationship – and the question of disestablishment – had been more fully explored. It was thus not a very significant report. Perhaps – in spite of his religious badinage at home, and his low church childhood – his mind was not really in gear for any very radical view of the structure and role of the Church of England hierarchy.

It was much more in gear for the Nature Conservancy, where he became Chairman in 1962. The choice of Evelyn for the chairmanship of the Nature Conservancy was very much the inspiration of its Director General, Max Nicholson. Nicholson had known Evelyn briefly in the war but had more recently been impressed by the great attention Evelyn had paid to the conservation of wild life and the introduction of durable game laws, while he was Governor of Kenya. In fact Nicholson had no idea that Evelyn was such a considerable naturalist himself, able to hold his own with most expert botanists, geologists or ornithologists in Africa. He chose him more because of his stature and his evident sympathy with the need to give conservation some stable basis of policy. Evelyn's first response to Nicholsons's approach was, characteristically, one of diffidence. He felt he had been too long out of the country to know enough either about the subject matter, in a British environment, or about how such an institution was to work. He was to prove himself wrong in a remarkably short time.

The Nature Conservancy had been granted a charter in 1949. Its main task was to try to reconcile a naturalist's desire to save as much as possible of Britain's natural beauty with the public need to accommodate the increasing number of people who wanted to have access to those beauties. Before Evelyn's arrival there had been no real overview of this work. On the one hand were arrayed the many splinter groups concerned with conservation and wild life; on the other were the intensive agriculturalists and industrialists – chemical and coal industries and so on – who brought weighty economic arguments to bear against the Wordsworthian attitudes of the conservationists.

In a remarkable way Evelyn managed to reconcile these often conflicting pressures by establishing a basis of trust on both sides. His emotions were known to lie with the naturalists, but he was equally recognised to be a man of affairs, a political animal and diplomatist, who perceived the basic interests of all parties to such a dispute and was able to talk as an equal to the heads of the industrial and agricultural lobbies. Under his leadership the Nature Conservancy passed through a vital transition from being the concern of a well meaning but rather insignificant naturalist lobby in the country, to the point where conservation – embodying the principles of ecology, the harnessing *and* husbanding of natural resources – had become accepted as a central issue of public affairs.

But Evelyn managed more than that; because having fulfilled the grand strategy of his chairmanship, he then surprised everybody by showing such unlimited enthusiasms for the actual field work of the Nature Conservancy. He visited every one of its 100 odd stations, poring for hours over the soil structure of Snowdonia, crawling about rare botanical corners on Rhum, demarcating between wildfowlers and birdwatchers in the Solway or at Lindisfarne, analysing vegetation in the Norfolk Broads and so on. He learnt Welsh for conversations with his Welsh wardens. He studied the effect of chemical insecticides on birds, and took a leading part in the banning of drugs like Dieldrin. He was fascinated by the work going on at the Conservancy's Monks Wood research station, and helped bring together the Conservancy's scientists with representatives from the chemical companies to find a way of farming which was as little damaging to wild life as possible. At every available opportunity he was out touring – shades of his lust for safaris – and, as always, astonished his Conservancy officers with his endurance, and mesmerised them with the ubiquitious black notebooks. Sadly for Evelyn, after what must have been ten charmed years, the last six months were clouded by having to cope, rather unsuccessfully, with the consequence of an administrative reshuffle involving the division of the Conservancy into two parts.

Apart from his work at the CDC, the Nature Conservancy, the Howick Commission, and the British North American Committee, Evelyn managed to avoid becoming sucked into many other dignified appointments. He only spoke five times in the House of Lords, probably because he felt he should observe the 'Addison Rules' which laid down that peers on the boards of state-run enterprises such as the CDC should not speak about them in the House of Lords. His rare interventions in the upper house tell their tale – a debate on the UN development decade and world trade; on the Commonwealth; on the second reading of the Swaziland independence bill; and on the second reading and committee stages of the conservation of seals' bill – one very near his heart and his home, with the seal cull being carried out annually on the Farne Islands only just up the coast from Howick. So he could hardly have been described as an active member of the House, or even active in the field of high politics behind the scenes.

In 1971 he refused one more invitation from Alec Douglas-Home – then Foreign Secretary – to explore the chances for an end to the Rhodesian rebellion. Lord Goodman was sent off instead, on a mission which culminated in the abortive Smith/Douglas-Home agreement and the decisive African veto registered with the Pearce Commission. Perhaps it was because of his lifetime of public service overseas that he had an inherent reluctance to enter any kind of domestic political area. Like his father he had a natural 'cross-bench mind,' as everybody who had to work with him soon discovered. Maybe that was why, in 1972, he had a 'secret and personal' letter from Buckingham Palace, perhaps the last such classified communication he ever received. It was from Sir Michael Adeane, the Queen's Private Secretary, who said,

'Dear Evelyn, I have it in command from the Queen to inform you that it is Her Majesty's wish to appoint you a Knight of the Most Noble Order of the Garter. I should be glad if you would let me know if this would be agreeable to you. No further steps will be taken in this matter till I hear from you.' Evelyn accepted it with pleasure.

CHAPTER XXXII
Man of Empire

By January, 1973, Evelyn had retired from the CDC, and had settled down at Howick Grange – the Barings had moved out of the big house at Howick not long after the return from Africa – farming his farms, and turning his mind to some kind of autobiography. He asked his old friend from *The Times*, Oliver Woods, himself by then in retirement, to help him organise his papers. But Woods died unexpectedly just before Christmas, 1972, and Evelyn was left wondering what to do. He had never had much of a taste for documents which might provide a meticulous and detailed historical record of his imperial stewardship. This was odd, considering his passion for detail in all those other pursuits which captured his time and his imagination. Indeed the most fascinating element of his private papers is not really the smattering of state documents which an assiduous private secretary had put aside for him here and there, but the piles of black notebooks in which Evelyn jotted down any and every piece of information which he picked up – magpie-like – throughout his life. Once noted, never forgotten. They covered such an amazing range of subject matter that I have listed them in an entirely random way, as they appear often within the same book: goldmining, railway finance, coloured manning in secondary industries, uranium production and sales, immigration flows, dam-building, sheep-rearing, hill cattle, heifers, fencing, root cultivations and stockfeeding, shipbuilding, Europe and the German question, Sierra Leone, Swahili grammar, adjectival concords, capital sins, human nature and sin, mortification, the sacraments, land colonisation by plants, cavities, dogfish biology, blood vascular system, central nervous system of earth worm, flagellates, amoeba, Tanganyika, Transkei, native names of Swazi trees and shrubs, South American bills of exchange, Roumanian debts, forward exchange transactions, options, cotton, petrol, halibut sales worldwide, whaling, tin, pepper, Sudan debts, cotton for neutrals, contrabrand control, Abyssinian lease lend, Gospel of Saint John, the miracles, Poland, US colonial ideas, post war civil aviation, flogging in Kings African Rifles, tobacco preferences, sheep dips, tropical diseases, winter wheat returns, sileage calculations, muck, grass, housing corporations, phosphates, pigs, Addis Ababa, Somalia, poaching,

defence forces. They show something of the breadth and depth of
Evelyn's mind and its basic orderliness, because, in spite of the
scrawly childlike writing, the notes were meticulously set out and
far from superficial. Throughout his official life, Evelyn's black
books held something of a mystique about them. They often induced fear in the minds of subordinates who felt they were about
to be caught out – as indeed time and again they were; and when
one has looked inside the books that comes as no surprise. Evelyn
had never fully come to terms with the fact that advancing years
precluded more and more of the reckless physical activity in
which he liked to indulge. His lifetime of riding accidents, climbing mishaps, swimming dramas, axeing injuries, all paid eloquent
testimony to his refusal to allow the weakness of the flesh to overcome an inner will which was determined to show that there was
no weakness. He once described rockclimbing as something which
brought him closer to ecstasy than anything else in life. Certainly
the ceaseless need to pit oneself against a hostile environment,
where only an extraordinary eye for detail and an endless capacity
for patience will ensure your survival, were characteristics which
epitomised Evelyn's approach to the great moments of crisis in
his life. In his last years at Howick he used to joke with Molly
that he could remember every move of every climb he had ever
made, and as they walked to church each Sunday morning he
would tell her which climb he had decided to relive that day
during the sermon.

It was on account of his passion for climbing that Evelyn was
to be denied the autobiography he was contemplating. On a
January day in 1973 he had an accident out walking at Howick
which led subsequently to his death. Most of his afternoon walks
at Howick took him along the coast, and he usually returned by
way of a steep little escarpment called Cullernose Crag down
which he used to scramble. He did not climb down using orthodox techniques – there was no need – but perhaps his descent each
time recaptured some of the thrills of his rockclimbing days.

On this particular January afternoon Evelyn had just started
his descent down Cullernose Crag, when one of his accustomed
foot holds gave way and he plunged down a kind of chimney of
shale and rock, bouncing and rolling until he came to rest among
the rocks about forty foot below. He was conscious but in great
pain; and he could not move. However, 'there is a heroine to
every story' as he later told a friend who visited him in hospital;
and in this case the heroine was a cow. She came up to him among

the rocks and expressed great bovine interest in the human figure lying crumpled there on the rough grass. It was only because the farmer came out to retrieve the cow and bring her back for milking, that Evelyn was found before nightfall, when Molly would presumably have become worried by his failure to reappear at Howick Grange. He was taken first to Alnwick Hospital, where a broken elbow was diagnosed, and then on to Ashington Hospital some thirty miles away which was more able to cope with the fracture. In spite of the optimistic early diagnosis, however, he was never to see Howick again.

When it appeared that Evelyn just needed some time to recover from the fall and allow his elbow to set, Molly went off to Washington to visit their daughter, Elizabeth, whose husband, Nicholas Gibbs, worked for the World Bank. Clare Baring, their daughter-in-law, remained at Howick to see that Evelyn's needs were being catered for. But the crashing fall down the Crag had shaken Evelyn much more than was first realised. Some days later, when all had seemed well, he collapsed with an embolism – a serious blood clot in his lungs – and, for a critical forty-eight hours, his death seemed imminent. He was put into an intensive care unit and Molly was summoned back from Washington.

Again Evelyn's indomitable spirit seemed to overcome the crisis and he pulled round, though spent of strength and physically diminished. He started to make a slow recovery, though the doctors were always worried because his lung was not clearing the way it should. Molly was able to write to a friend in mid-February saying that, though Evelyn would not be fit to go to London in the foreseeable future – he had suffered very bad internal bruising and bleeding, with clots in the lung and was still very ill – it was now getting less likely that further clots would appear, so the family were 'guardedly' optimistic. Indeed, only two weeks later Evelyn rang up his secretary at the British North American Committee and reeled off a series of instructions at high speed.

But the underlying situation – the danger of further congestion on his lung – was apparently not improving, and perhaps Evelyn in his heart knew this. With Molly, when alone together, there was a sense of peace about him as though he knew that he was going to die. Outwardly he was in good spirits, though he was still too weak to read, and some of his conversations were noticeably more discursive about himself and his life than they had used to be. After about six weeks at Ashington the doctors decided that only some movement would clear the lung congestion and avoid the risk of another dangerous clot forming. Evelyn was moved back to Alnwick Hospital where he would be much nearer for all the family to visit him. Soon after the journey, pneumonia set in, and early on Saturday, March 10, 1973, while his nurses were attending to him and chatting normally, he was suddenly gone. He was buried in Howick Churchyard a few days later, and there followed an impressive memorial service in Westminster Abbey at which Trevor Huddleston gave the address and the list of those attending made up a roll call of the splendid, rugged, compassionate, global sweep of Evelyn's life and personality.

Where does one start encapsulating such a life? Nowadays we look for greatness on an heroic scale or not at all. It is the trappings of greatness, the drama and the decibel count which have to be measured before we are sure of it. War heroes, literary giants, political maestros seem to dominate the box office. In a British world which has diminished so much, there is less room for the second eleven, whatever variety, excellence or eccentricity is to be found there. This diminution of Britain's world without empire has put a higher price on people's visible achievements, at the expense of their personalities. Perhaps there is less opportunity now, other than at the very top, to live the kind of complete life which Evelyn led, and which so amply and admirably gave reign to his varied qualities. Yet the significance of Evelyn's life lies as much in what he was as in what he did. Naturally there was, above all else, the man of empire. But the man of empire was also a man of trees, a man of flowers, of Urdu, Afrikaans and Swahili, of agriculture and of anthropology, of geology and zoology, a diplomat, a politician, an economist. How many careers now would all be so directly enhanced by such a variety of qualities?

Certainly we start with Evelyn as a man of empire, as we started with his father in the same role. I have felt irresistibly drawn to the relationship of father and son, not to compare or contrast their careers, but to combine them and then marvel at the great sweep of history encompassed by their two lives. It is truly a story of empire. Nor is it just at this superficial level that the relationship suggests a close link between them. Evelyn must have had some deeper awareness of being part of such a vivid historical tradition. It was that link which endowed him with a kind of inner certainty of purpose. He was like Sir Bartle Frere, an earlier servant of India who also went on to an imperial appointment in Africa, whose biographer could find no sign of conflict in his life, 'as though the battle had been fought and won in some previous existence.'[1] Certainly Evelyn was inspired by his father's greatness rather than oppressed by it. But Lord Cromer's life, though an exceptional one even by the spirit of late Victorian times, was very much in accordance with those times; whereas Evelyn's own life had a poignancy about it because it was actually lived on a scale – both of conception and execution – which was fast fading from the contemporary scene. He was truly the last of the proconsuls – born to be a viceroy. Imperial administrators were much in demand in Lord Cromer's generation, and Britain had needed to spawn a whole cadre of giants to play those valuable imperial roles in the second eleven of history. By Evelyn's generation, the cadre had gone; he came to be a lonely figure on the old imperial Olympus. Yet he was as Laurens van der Post once described him to me, 'an inspired instrument of empire' serving with a detachement which made him sometimes seem almost a servant of history, rather than of his own country. Certainly no person's life can embody more completely the story of British imperial policy in Africa during the two decades that Evelyn strode the African stage.

Yet this was not just a supercharged imperial machine at work. Under the plumed helmet was a man who may have had this doubt-free sense of duty, but who nonetheless suffered all the usual disappointments of this world. There may have been no inner conflict, but there were enough outward ones. It was perhaps not a particularly easy childhood as the son of old, if doting, parents; a shy ponderous young man deprived of his father, growing up at the skirts of his mother and her dotty sisters. Then there was a cautious start to his marriage followed by the long separation in the war, and only thereafter the mutual discovery of each other, creating, by the end, a complete and impregnable relationship with Molly. Then too there was this permanent semi-invalid state; the diet sheets, teetotalism, bouts of total exhaustion. When he was ill, you could see his eyes hooded, yellow and yawning. He was advised not to come down in the mornings when he looked like that.

When I started work on this biography I was troubled by the thought that Evelyn was too good a man to make an interesting life; his greatness and goodness were emphasised by so many of those who worked with him that there seemed a danger of dullness. It was soon clear that there was no dullness. Evelyn *was* good, but that goodness did not inhibit a waspish sense of humour and an unfailing eye for the socially ridiculous. His dislikes were few but when they were formed they could be savage. 'I can frighten him out of his idleness but not out of his cowardice', he said of one of his ministers in Kenya. He used to exchange salacious jokes with one or two other ministers, sometimes passing them notes across the table during cabinet meetings – often about Blundell's malapropisms which Evelyn found uproarious.

But of more point than these blemishes on Evelyn's goodness was that he was an eccentric in a pure English tradition. Funny things happened to him as they can only happen to the true eccentric. We have glimpses of him interviewing a District Commissioner in his underpants, with cocked hat and plumes on top, because he had spilt something on his trousers but had forgotten to explain the fact to the DC; we see him forgetting grace when the Archbishop came to dinner; describing Molly as an acid drop in a word game, to the consternation of fellow guests who were not *au fait* with his raucous sense of humour; playing murder with the Queen of Greece to the point of *his* exhaustion but never hers. Clothes were always his undoing – splits in his uniform, brown suede shoes at Smuts's funeral, those dreadful khaki drill shorts at all times; and he had a typical distaste for sartorial quirks which he described as bounderish, such as handkerchiefs with 'E' on them or the wearing of a flower in the buttonhole.

He was a very private person. His emotions were held on a tight rein. You do not usually get much measure of them even in his letters to Molly. There were no tears; no rages in his life; anger, when it came twice in Kenya with his ministers, was icy and aloof. It was the same with his religion. Though a lot has been made of the daily Communion service in the attic in Nairobi, Evelyn was not an outwardly religious man. He did not *have* to go to church if there were other things to be done. He preserved an outward attitude of playful scepticism and badinage to organised religion, typified by his teasing of Molly for her high anglicanism. It was almost as though it was a tacit warning to any potential questioner that as far as outward appearances were concerned, he preferred the subject to be kept at arms length. What went on in his heart and soul was a matter only for him. No trespassers.

Yet this containment of emotions did not create a cold personality. There was nothing of the recluse about Evelyn. Look at a portrait; the face is taut, amused, interested – taut for the tensions born of a first class analytical mind, and the inevitable strains of office; amused, because he was almost always amused – his amusement tempered the innate superiority of the man, and softened the rigour of his intellecutual and emotional control; interested – always – in all humanity, in its hopes, fears, weaknesses, origins, the inexhaustible interest of a 'blotting-paper mind', but an interest which generated a warmth and a compassion which made it easy to love him back. His life, like his father's, may be engraved in marble in the halls of a vanishing history. His looks, and the superior, slow way he seemed to proceed through a life almost preordained in its scale and grandeur, have the certainty and solidity of marble about them. Marble maybe, but with a softness of alabaster, when he could see that he was loved.

Source Material

The main source I have used in this biography is the Baring Papers, now in the possession of Lady Mary Howick at Howick. These contain all Evelyn Baring's letters to his mother, either in the original or copied out by his mother, and the journal he wrote of his service in the ICS in India and South Africa. They contain a large number of Evelyn's letters to his wife during the war and from his positions in Africa when she was in England. They also contain Molly Baring's letters to her mother from Rhodesia, South Africa and Kenya. In addition, the Baring Papers contain various official documents acquired by Evelyn during his governorships, either copies of letters or despatches or memoranda he had written, or the originals of letters he had received from ministers or civil servants in London.

In addition to the Baring Papers and to the sources cited in the notes and bibliography I have relied on information from a large number of colonial officials, soldiers and diplomats who served with Evelyn in India and Africa and who have either sent me memoranda, letters or with whom I have had extended personal interviews. Among these I would like to mention:

INTERVIEWS

Lord Dundee
Lord Stratheden
Lady Doris Blacker
Lord Molson
Lady Elliot of Harwood
Lady Delia Peel
Mr Mark Baring
Lady Gwyneth Cavendish
Lord Sherfield
Col Sir Guy Shaw-Stewart
Philip Mason
Sir William Christie
Mrs Marjorie Cowley
Sir Olaf Caroe (late ICS)
HRH Princess Alice,
    Countess of Athlone
Lord Cohen of Birkenhead
Sir Henry MacDowell
Capt. Alec Hampshire
Sir Robert Tredgold

Sir Hugh Beadle
Sir Frederick Crawford
Sir Roy Welensky
Sir David Scott
Sir Algernon Rumbold
Lord Gordon-Walker
Mr P. L. Steenkamp
H. E. Sir Seretse Khama
Mr R. P. Stephens
Mr V. Ellenberger
Mr David Astor
Mr Colin Legum
Mr Arthur Bottomley
Sir David Hunt
Mr Laurens van der Post
Rt Rev. Trevor Huddleston
Mr E. W. Henderson
Sir Alan Lascelles
Lady Bryan
Mrs Royds

SOURCE MATERIAL

INTERVIEWS (Contd.)

Mrs M. Sedgwick
Mr P. D. Marrian
Sir William Gorrell-Barnes
Sir George Mallaby
Lord Hale
Mrs Joy Adamson
Field Marshal Lord Carver
General Sir Gerald Lathbury
Dr Michael Wood
Mr Mervyn Cowie
Mr Henry Gathigira
Mr E. W. Mathu
Mr Bruce Mackenzie
Mr J. D. Leslie-Melville
Miss Joan Waddington
Mr Peter Colmore
Mr Humphrey Slade
Mr John Spencer
Sir Francis Loyd
Sir Anthony Swann
Lord Boyd
Mr G. J. Ellerton
Lord Dilhorne
Sir Richard Turnbull
Major General Frank Kitson
Mr J. V. Prendergast
Mr J. H. Loudon
Sir Walter Coutts
Mrs Barbara Castle
Major General Peter Gillet
Lord Head
Field Marshal Lord Harding
Mr Julian Amery
Sir Eric Griffith-Jones
Sir Arthur Hope-Jones
Mr Malcolm Macdonald
Mr Robert Wilson
Lord Ridley
Lady William Percy
Sir Richard Catling
Mr Max Nicholson
Lord Home of the Hirsel
Mr Forbes Mackenzie
Capt. Claud Lambton
Mr George Goyder
Mr Leslie Pritchard
Sir Martin Gilliatt
Sir Richard Sullivan
Lady Bowes-Lyon
Sir Francis Portal
Mr E. J. Honore
Mr Reginald Grenfell
Lord Bath
Mr Ralph Ricketts
Lord Kilmany

CORRESPONDENCE

Sir Anthony Hornby
Mr J. Johnston (late ICS)
Mr Douglas Fell (Sec. ICSA)
Sir George Schuster
Mr T. L. Ingram, Archivist,
  Hickleton Papers
Mr Hari Srivastava
Sir Sidney Ridley
Mr O. Pulla Reddi (late ICS)
Mr D. S. Barron (late ICS)
Sir Herbert Thompson (late ICS)
Mr M. C. Desai (late ICS)
Mr J. Donaldson (late ICS)
Sir Jeremy Raisman (late ICS)
Mr V. K. R. Menon (late ICS)
Lord Blake
Professor K. Kirkwood
Sir Christopher Cox
Mr C. J. Barton, CMG
Sir Eric Machtig
Dr Claire Palley
Mr Justice Greenfield
Major H. M. C. St. Quinton
Sir James Bottomley
Mr A. D. Forsyth-Thompson
Mr Robin Latimer
Mr T. J. R. Dashwood
Mr D. H. Woods (Mountain
  Club of South Africa)
Sir Alfred Beit
Mr John Wakely
Sir Morrice James
Most Rev. L. Beecher
Sir Harold Compton
Father Reginald Smith
Sir Edward Beetham
Sir Percival Liesching
Dr Anthony Clayton
Sir Diarmaid Conroy
Sir John Moreton
Mr W. A. C. Mathieson
Mr Denis Hall
Sir Melford Stevenson
Sir Kenneth O'Connor
Mr W. G. Dyson
Mr J. B. Johnston
Mr J. Megson
Lord Balfour of Inchrye
Mr James Griffiths
Major General Sir Robert Hinde
Sir Philip Rogers
Mr Robert Nimmo
Mr Ian Henderson
Major General Sir Nigel Tapp
Sir Richard Luyt

SOURCE MATERIAL

CORRESPONDENCE (Contd).

Sir Hilton Poynton
Mr H. Wongtshowski
Colin St. John Hutchinson

Sister M. Johanna
Mr F. Gerald Gough
Sir Peter Henderson

Notes

INTRODUCTION

1) Evelyn Baring: 'Ancient and Modern Imperialism.'
   Address as President, Classical Society, 1910.
2) Lytton Strachey: *Eminent Victorians*.
   In chapter on Gordon.
3) Cromer: 'Army Reform in the Nineteenth Century and After.'
   Pamphlet, 1904.

CHAPTER II

1) Cecil King: *Strictly Personal*.
   Weidenfeld & Nicolson, 1969.

CHAPTER III

1) Philip Woodruff: *The Men Who Ruled India*. Vol. I. p. 13.
2) Philip Woodruff: *The Men Who Ruled India*. Vol. I. p. 11.
3) Philip Woodruff: *The Men Who Ruled India*. Vol. II. p. 175.

CHAPTER IV

1) Philip Woodruff: *The Men Who Ruled India*. Vol. II. p. 180.
2) Baring Papers.

CHAPTER V

1) Philip Woodruff: *The Men Who Ruled India*. Vol. II. p. 213.
2) Philip Woodruff: *The Men Who Ruled India*. Vol. II. p. 218.
3) India Office. L/P&J/8/290. 20/5/29.
4) Halifax Papers: India Office. 23/5/29.

CHAPTER VI

1) Krishna Menon: 'Passive Resistance in South Africa.'
   Pamphlet. p. 32.
2) Halifax Papers: India Office. April, 1926.
3) Halifax Papers: India Office. January, 1927.
4) Halifax Papers: India Office. 31/5/27.
5) Viceroy to Secretary of State: India Office. L/E/7/1538.
   4/3/27 and 7/4/27.
6) National Archives of India: Foreign Dept. Pol. Est. 114-E/1932.
   28/5/32.

CHAPTER VII

1) Philip Woodruff: *The Men Who Ruled India*. Vol. 11. p. 291.

CHAPTER IX
1) O'Keefe to Huggins: Huggins Papers. 10/8/1942.

CHAPTER X
1) Richard Gray: The Two Nations.
1a) HMSO: Indians in Kenya. Cmd. 1922, 1923.
2) HMSO: Bledisloe Report. Cmd. 5949.
3) Palley: *Constitutional History and Law of Southern Rhodesia*.
footnote.

CHAPTER XI
1) Baring/Machtig correspondence: Public Record Office.
DO 35 1274 G 581/1/16.
2) Huggins Papers: personal correspondence. March, 1944.
3) Public Record Office: DO 35 1411/R 370/2.
4) Public Record Office: DO 35 1411/R 370/2.
5) See 1) above. 14/1/43.
6) Machtig to Evelyn and DO minute: PRO. DO 35 1390 R 208/9. 26/3/43.
7) Swinton to Cranborne: PRO. DO 35 1122 G 689/15. March, 1944.
8) Public Record Office: DO 35 1164 R 251/10. 21/5/43.
9) Public Record Office: DO 35 1409 R 342/1/4.

CHAPTER XII
1) Evelyn to Machtig: PRO. DO 35 1397 R 216/23. 10/5/43.
2) Public Record Office: DO 35 1396 R 216/14.
3) Baring Papers.
4) Baring Papers. 16/10/44.

CHAPTER XIII
1) Baring to Machtig: Public Record Office. DO 35 1168 R 342/1/5.
13/10/44.
2) Baring to Machtig: Public Record Office. DO 35 1161 R 201/4.
21/10/44.
3) Baring Papers. 20/10/44.

CHAPTER XIV
1) Public Record Office: DO 35 1122 G 673/6.
2) Public Record Office: DO 35 1288 G 715/23.
3) Public Record Office: DO 35 1864 WR 208/103. 30/7/45.
DO 35 1868 WR 208/127.
4) Evelyn to Cranborne: Baring Papers. 20/1/45.
5) Evelyn to Addison: Baring Papers. 27/8/45.
6) Public Record Office: DO 35 1214 WR 213/9/16.
7) Evelyn to Addison: Public Record Office. DO 35 1119 G 581/69.
6/11/45.
8) Public Record Office: DO 35 1777 WC 960/24.
9) Public Record Office: DO 35 1777 WC 960/24.

CHAPTER XV
1) Evelyn to Machtig: Baring Papers. 21/11/45.
2) Evelyn to Machtig: Baring Papers. 17/3/47.
3) Evelyn to Machtig: Baring Papers. 6/5/47.
4) Evelyn to Noel-Baker: Baring Papers. 31/10/47.
5) Evelyn to Noel-Baker: Baring Papers. 12/6/48.
6) Machtig to Evelyn: Baring Papers. 31/7/48.

CHAPTER XVI
1) HMSO: White Paper on Transfer of Native Territories.
   Cmd. 4948. 1935.
2) Harlech to Cranborne: Public Record Office. DO 35. 30/11/43.
3) Evelyn to Cranborne: Baring Papers. 6/4/45.
4) Evelyn to Machtig: Public Record Office. DO 35 1172/Y/706/11.
   13/9/45.
5) Cranborne to Evelyn: Baring Papers. 15/9/45.
6) Public Record Office: DO 35 1172/Y/706/2. 28/1/46.
7) Evelyn to Addison: Public Record Office. DO 35 1172/Y/706/12.
   15/4/46.
8) Evelyn to Machtig: Public Record Office. DO 35 1172/Y/706/11.
   13/3/46.
9) Public Record Office: DO 35 1172/Y/708/18. 3/8/46.
10) Dominion Office minute: Public Record Office.
    DO 35 1172/Y/708/18. 23/9/46.
11) Draft white paper on Transfer: PRO. DO 35 1172/Y/766/13.
12) Evelyn to Noel-Baker: Baring Papers. 31/10/47.
13) Chatham House Quarterly: International Affairs.
    Vol. XXVIII No. 2. April, 1952.

CHAPTER XVII
1) Mary Benson: *Tshekedi Khama.* p. 175.
2) Baring Papers: Transcript of Enquiry. Vol. IV. 7/11/49.
3) Baring Papers: Summary of developments in Seretse affair.
   1948/49.
4) Baring Papers: Summary of developments in Seretse affair.
   1948/49.

CHAPTER XVIII
1) See Chapter XVII, note 3.
2) See Chapter XVII, note 3.
3) Evelyn to Liesching: Baring Papers. ref. 16/49. 11/7/49.
4) Liesching to Evelyn: Baring Papers. 21/7/49.
5) Evelyn to Noel-Baker: Baring Papers. 20/7/49.
6) *The Times.* 6/3/50.
7) *The Times.* 14/3/50.
8) Baring Papers.

CHAPTER XIX
1) Evelyn to Cranborne: Baring Papers. 21/11/44.
2) Harlech to Cranborne: Public Record Office. DO 35. 21/12/44.
3) Evelyn to Cranborne: Baring Papers. 22/1/45.

4) Evelyn to Cranborne: Baring Papers. 22/1/45.
5) Evelyn to Cranborne: Baring Papers. 11/12/45.
6) Nicholas Monsarrat: *Life is a Four Letter Word*. Vol. II. p. 180.
7) Evelyn despatch: Baring Papers. ref: DO S. Africa No. 240. 30/6/51.

CHAPTER XX
1) Mitchell to Evelyn: Baring Papers. 16/6/52.
2) Mitchell to Evelyn: Baring Papers. March, 1952.
3) HMSO: Historical Survey of Origins and Growth of Mau Mau.
   Cmd. 1030. 1960

CHAPTER XXI
1) *East African Standard*. 30/9/52.
2) Corfield Report: see chapter XX, note 3.
3) Rhodes House Transcript: Baring Papers.
4) Evelyn to Lyttelton: Baring Papers. 9/10/52.

CHAPTER XXII
1) Evelyn to Lyttelton: Baring Papers. 24/11/52.
2) Michael Blundell: *So Rough a Wind*. page 124 *et seq*.
3) Erskine despatch: Royal United Services Institute. para. 13.
4) Erskine despatch: Royal United Services Institute. para. 38.
5) Erskine despatch: Royal United Services Institute. para. 126.

CHAPTER XXIII
1) Erskine's letters: Royal United Services Institute. 3/6/54.
2) Erskine's letters: Royal United Services Institute. 29/6/53.
3) Erskine's letters: Royal United Services Institute. 25/9/53.
4) Erskine's letters: Royal United Services Institute. 9/10/53.
5) Erskine's letters: Royal United Services Institute. 16/7/53.
6) Erskine's letters: Royal United Services Institute. 28/2/54.
7) Note of Young/Lyttelton conversation: Young Papers. May 1954.
8) Erskine letters. 16/7/53.
9) Erskine letters. 16/7/53.

CHAPTER XXIV
1) Young Papers.
2) *The Times'* Archives: Woods memo. to Editor. 19/5/54.
3) Young Papers.
4) Young Papers.
5) Young Papers.
6) Young Papers.
7) Young Papers.
8) *The Times'* Archives: confidential memo to Editor. 5/1/55.
9) Woods to Editor: Woods Papers. 4/1/55.
10) Erskine letters. 10/1/55.

CHAPTER XXV

1) Oxford University Press: *History of East Africa*. Vol. III,
   ch. VI The Managed Economy by Michael McWilliam, p. 251.
2) *Sunday Express*. June, 1954.
3) *The Times*' Nairobi Correspondent to Editor: *The Times*' Archives.
   19/2/55.
4) *The Times*' Nairobi Correspondent to Editor: *The Times*' Archives.
   2/3/55.

CHAPTER XXVI

1) Evelyn to Secretary of State: Baring Papers. 23/4/56.
2) Evelyn to Eugene Black: Baring Papers. Ref: GH 1953/23/47.
   22/10/58.
3) Evelyn to Secretary of State: Baring Papers. Ref: GH 1951/6/111.
   19/12/58.
4) Evelyn to Secretary of State: Baring Papers. Ref: GH 1951/6.
   3/4/59.
5) Evelyn to Gorrel-Barnes: Baring Papers. Ref: GH 1951/6/IV.
   17/8/59.
6) Oxford University Press: *History of East Africa*. Vol. III. p. 253.
7) Oxford University Press: *History of East Africa*. Vol. III. p. 256

CHAPTER XXVII

1) Rhodes House Transcript: Baring Papers.
2) Evelyn to Lyttelton: Baring Papers. 29/10/53.
3) Evelyn to Lyttelton: Baring Papers. 29/10/53.
4) Michael Blundell: *So Rough a Wind*. p. 99 and 100.

CHAPTER XXVIII

1) Evelyn to Secretary of State: Baring Papers. Ref: GH 1953/5/39.
   6/4/55.
2) Evelyn to Molly: Baring Papers. 27/4/57.
3) Evelyn to Molly: Baring Papers. 8/5/57.
4) Evelyn to Molly: Baring Papers. 18/5/57.
5) Evelyn to Sir John Macpherson: Baring Papers.
   Ref: GH 1950/14/V(6). Vol. II. 23/9/57.
6) Papers relating to Chequers meeting in private collection.
   Ref: EAC(59)1.
7) Papers relating to Chequers meeting in private collection.
   Ref: EAC(59)1.

CHAPTER XXIX

1) Windley to Oliver Woods: Woods Papers. 8/12/55.
2) *Keesings Contemporary Archives*. p. 17096–17098, Nov. 7–14, 1959.
3) *Keesings Contemporary Archives*. p. 17096–17098, Nov. 7–14, 1959.
4) *Hansard*, June 16, 1959.
5) Evelyn to Renison: final memo on security. Baring Papers.
   13/10/59.
6) Griffith-Jones to Evelyn: Baring Papers. 5/11/59.
7) Notes in Baring Papers.
8) Lennox-Boyd to Evelyn: Baring Papers. 3/9/59.

CHAPTER XXX
1) John Gunter: *Inside Africa.*
2) *East African Standard.* 14/10/59.
3) Woods Papers.
4) *East African Standard.* 8/9/59.
5) Baring Papers.

CHAPTER XXXI
1) C.D.C. report and Accounts: Chairman's Review, 1971.
2) Oxford Colonial Records Project Transcript: Baring Papers.

CHAPTER XXXII
1) Philip Woodruff: *The Men Who Ruled India.* Vol. II. p. 42.

Select Bibliography

BARNETT/NJANI: *Mau Mau from within*
MacGibbon/Kee, 1966
BENSON, Mary: *Tshekedi Khama*
Faber & Faber, 1960
BLUNDELL, Sir Michael: *So Rough a Wind*
Weidenfeld & Nicolson, 1964
BROWN, Jeremy Murray: *Kenyatta*
George Allen & Unwin, 1972
CAMPBELL, Alexander: *Smuts and Swastika*
Victor Gollancz, 1943
CHAUDHURI, M. C.: *Autobiography of an Unknown Indian*
Macmillan, 1951
CHANDOS, Lord: *Memoirs of Lord Chandos*
Bodley Head, 1962
CLAYTON, Anthony: *Counter Insurgency in Kenya*
Transafrica Publishers, 1976
CMD 4948: Transfer of Native Territories, HMSO, 1935
CMD 8707: High Commission Territories, HMSO, 1952
CROMER, Lord: *Modern Egypt*, 2 vols.
EAST AFRICA, History of: see McWilliam, M.D.
FERGUSON-DAVIE, Rt Rev. C. J.: *History of Indians in Natal*
SA Institute of Race Relations,
Johannesburg, 1951
GALE, W. D.: *Heritage of Rhodes*
Oxford University Press, 1950
GRAY, Richard: *The Two Nations*
Institute of Race Relations,
Oxford University Press, 1960
HANCOCK, W. K.: Smuts: *The Sanguine Years* 1870–1919
Cambridge University Press, 1962
HANCOCK, W. K.: Smuts: *The Fields of Force* 1919–1950
Cambridge University Press, 1968
KANE, Nora S.: *The World's View*
Cassell & Co., 1954
KARIUKI, Josiah: *Mau Mau Detainee*
Penguin Africa Library, 1964
Oxford University Press, 1963
KITSON, F.: *Gangs and Counter Gangs*
Barrie & Rockliff, 1960
MAJDALANY, Fred: *State of Emergency*
Longmans, 1962
MARQUARD, Leo: *People & Policies of South Africa*
Oxford University Press, 1952
MASANI, Sir Robert: *Britain in India*
1961

MBOYA, Tom: *Freedom and After*
    Andre Deutsch, 1963
McWILLIAM, M. D.: 'The Managed Economy' Vol. III, Chapter VI of
    History of East Africa
    Oxford University Press, 1976
MENON, K. N.: *Passive Resistance in South Africa*
    New Delhi, 1952
MONSARRAT, Nicholas: *Life is a Four Letter Word*. Vol. II
    Cassell, 1970
ODINGA, Oginga: *Not Yet Uhuru*
    Heinemann, 1967
PALLEY, C.: *Constitutional History and Law of Southern Rhodesia*
    Clarendon Press, Oxford, 1966
RENDELL, Sir William: *The History of the Commonwealth Development
    Corporation*
    Heinemann, 1976
ROSBERG/NOTTINGHAM: *Myth of Mau Mau: Nationalism in Kenya*
    Praeger, 1966
TREDGOLD, Sir Robert: *The Rhodesia that was my Life*
    George Allen & Unwin, 1968
WOODRUFF, Philip: *The Men Who Ruled India:*
    Vol. I—*The Founders*
    Vol. II—*The Guardians*
    Jonathan Cape 1953 (Vol. I), 1954 (Vol. II)
ZETLAND, Marquess of: *Lord Cromer*
    Hodder & Stoughton, 1932

Index

Fisher of Lambeth, Lord: 315
Forster, E. M.: 42
Fort Hare: 165
Franks, Oliver: 252

Gable, Clark: 301
Gandhi, Mahatma: 39, 42, 61–2, 67
Gardner, Ava: 301
Gathorne-Hardy, Lady Isobel: 40
George, Cape Province: 70
George VI, King: 95, 141, 151–156, 218
Germany: 22, 143
Gibbs, Humphrey: 119, 127, 136
Gilligan, A. E. R.: 40
Gladstone, W. E.: 60
Glasgow: 17, 30, 165
Goff, Tom: 97, 107–8, 128, 130
Gold Coast: 194–5
Gordon of Khartoum: 9
Gordon-Walker, Patrick: 169–170, 181, 190, 192–3, 212
Grey, Bill Anstruther (later Lord Kilmany): 28
Grey, Molly: see Baring, Lady Mary
Grey, Lord (father-in-law): 55, 81, 86, 114, 315
Grey, Lady (mother-in-law): 55, 81–2
Grey, Nisset (sister-in-law): see Dawnay, Nisset
Grey, Albert Lord: 106
Griffith-Jones, Eric: 249, 289, 293, 295, 297
Griffiths, James: 211, 216, 270
Grigg, Sir Edward: 19
Guest, Colonel: 115
Gunter, John: 300
Gwynne, Mr (Deputy Commissioner, Lucknow): 44, 47, 50–2

Hailes, Lord: see Buchan-Hepburn, Patrick
Hailey, Lord: 97, 104, 105, 116–7
Hailey Report: 116
Hailsham, Lord: 87, 298, 299
Halifax, Lord: see Irwin, Lord

Halifax, Lady: 56
Hampshire, Alec: 107
Harding, Sir John: 241, 243–4
Harlech, Lord (Billy Ormsby-Gore): 94, 106, 110–113, 115, 130, 136, 165, 197–8
Harlech, Lady: 151
Harragin, Sir Walter: 177, 187–9
Havelock, Wilfred: 245
Head, Anthony: 252
Hertzog, General: 145, 158, 163–4
Hinde, General: 236, 238
Hitler: 87, 88, 90
Hofmeyr, Jan H.: 158
Hogg, Quintin: see Hailsham
Hola Camp: 262, 288–299
Holbech, Colonel Lawrence: 106–8, 126
Home, Lord (Alec Douglas-Home): see Dunglass
Hornby, Sir Anthony: 25
Howard, Henry: 218
Howick: 81–2, 85–7, 91, 93, 125, 211, 214, 244, 300, 308, 322, 323
Howick Commission: 315–6, 318
Howick, Lord: see Baring, Sir Evelyn
Howick, Lady: see Baring, Lady Mary
Huddleston, Father Trevor: 160, 187, 315
Huggins, Sir Godfrey: 95, 96, 101, 104, 108–11, 113–118, 122, 129, 133–137
Hume, Sir Nutcombe: 308
Huntingfield, Lord: 96

India: 10, 11, 33, 38–59, 72–79, 120, 124
India Office, London: 58
Indian Government, Agent of: 61, 63–4
Indian Mutiny: 46, 54
Indian Civil Service (ICS): 33, 36–44, 50–1, 53, 78
Indian Political Service (IPS): 43, 58, 64, 71–3
Inverkip: 30, 95